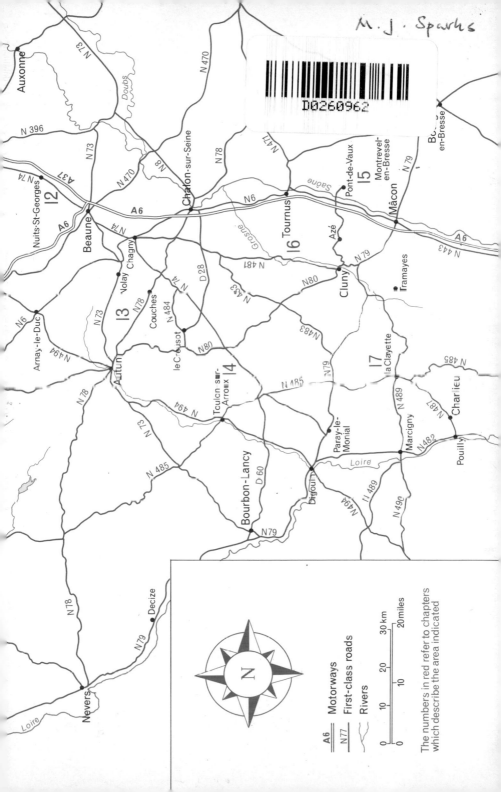

Auxonne

N 77

N 470

Doubs

N 396

N 73

A 31

N 74

Nuits-St-Georges

|2

A 6

Beaune

N 74

N 470

N 8

Chalon-sur-Seine

N 78

Saône

Grosne

N 471

Pont-de-Vaux

Montrevel-en-Bresse

Bo en-Bresse

N 79

N 6

N 9

Tournus

Mâcon

|5

A 6

N 443

A 6

Volnay

Chagny

D 28

N 481

N 483

N 80

Azé

Cluny

N 79

Tramayes

|6

Arnay-le-Duc

N 6

N 494

Autun

N 73

N 78

Couches

N 484

N 74 N

le-Creusot

N 80

Toulon-sur-Arroux

|4

N 485

N 483

N 79

|7

la Clayette

N 485 N

Charlieu

N 487

N 78

N 494

N 485

Bourbon-Lancy

D 60

Paray-le-Monial

Digoin

Loire

Marcigny

N 489

N 482

Pouilly

N 79

N 489

N 494

N 490

Nevers

N 78

N 79

Decize

Loire

**N**

| A 6 | Motorways |
| --- | --- |
| N77 | First-class roads |
| | Rivers |

| 0 | 10 | 20 | 30 km |
|---|---|---|---|
| 0 | 10 | 20 miles | |

The numbers in red refer to chapters which describe the area indicated

THE COMPANION GUIDE TO

*Burgundy*

# THE COMPANION GUIDES

GENERAL EDITOR: VINCENT CRONIN

*It is the aim of these Guides to provide a Companion,
in the person of the author, who knows intimately
the places and people of whom he writes, and is able to
communicate this knowledge and affection to his readers.
It is hoped that the text and pictures will aid them
in their preparations and in their travels, and will
help them to remember on their return.*

THE GREEK ISLANDS · SOUTHERN GREECE
PARIS · THE SOUTH OF FRANCE
ROME · VENICE · LONDON
FLORENCE · JUGOSLAVIA
THE WEST HIGHLANDS OF SCOTLAND · UMBRIA
SOUTHERN ITALY · TUSCANY · EAST ANGLIA
SOUTHERN SPAIN · IRELAND
KENT AND SUSSEX · NORTH WALES
MADRID AND CENTRAL SPAIN

*In Preparation*
MAINLAND GREECE
EDINBURGH AND THE BORDER COUNTRY
NORTHUMBRIA · SOUTH WALES · DEVON AND CORNWALL
SOUTH-WEST FRANCE · THE ILE DE FRANCE
TURKEY

The Guides to ROME, VENICE, FLORENCE, LONDON and THE
SOUTH OF FRANCE are available in the *Fontana* edition

THE COMPANION GUIDE TO

# Burgundy

❧

## ROBERT SPEAIGHT

COLLINS
ST JAMES'S PLACE, LONDON
1975

William Collins Sons & Co Ltd
London · Glasgow · Sydney · Auckland
Toronto · Johannesburg

First published 1975
© Robert Speaight 1975

ISBN 0 00 216104 4

Set in Monotype Times
Maps by Reginald Piggott
Made and printed in Great Britain by
William Collins Sons & Co Ltd Glasgow

*For Marie-Catherine and Maurice Zuber*
*who put us so hospitably on our way*

# Acknowledgements

I wish to thank a number of people whose help, and in many cases, whose hospitality, have speeded me in the writing of this book. The Marquis and Marquise de Virieu, Comte Jean de Guitaut, Colonel and Madame Darly, Professor Grivelet, M. François de Seynes-Lalenque, M. and Madame Jacques Chevignard, Mr. Kit Cope, Mr. H. W. Yoxall, and the Librarians at the Institut Français and the Senate House of London University. I am grateful to Sir John and Mr Michael Rothenstein for permission to reproduce the passage from Sir William Rothenstein's *Men and Memories* (Volume I) on pages 159 and 160.

Once again, I must thank Mrs Pat Brayne for the speed and precision with which she has typed a complicated manuscript.

*Benenden, 1975*

# Contents

# Illustrations

❧

ILLUSTRATIONS

# Maps and Plans

꙰

# Introduction

✤

Burgundy defies definition; nevertheless the reader of this book will want to know where he, or she, is going. Between the medieval duchy that extended from the Low Countries to the Loire and from Picardy to the borders of Provence, and the province of today about whose limits not even Burgundians are agreed, a line must be drawn for the purposes of travel even though it may beg a few questions of topography. In the following pages I have generally confined myself to the three Departments of the Yonne, the Côte d'Or, and the Saône-et-Loire, only trespassing into the Loire for the sake of Charlieu and into the Ain for the sake of the Eglise de Brou. Where Brittany or Normandy, Alsace or Languedoc, Périgord or Provence, evoke a fairly distinct picture for the mind acquainted with a map, Burgundy for many people is no more than a generic name for a variety of labels on a bottle. In fact it has no frontiers, and is well described as a 'bouquet of high divergent valleys leading in various directions' where the mist or the sun await you as you emerge, shortly before arrival in Dijon, from 'the famous tunnel of Blaisy'.[1] The motorist speeding down the autoroute to the midi is hardly aware at what point he has entered the province and at what point he has left it.

Distinct in some respects, Burgundy is infinitely diverse in others, from whatever angle you approach it. The eye trained to the niceties of romanesque or Gothic architecture will detect the Burgundian accent in Notre-Dame-de-Dijon or in St Philibert-de-Tournus. The rustic realism of the popular statuary is also characteristic. On the other hand you could hardly imagine two artists more opposed than Rude and Giselbertus; writers more different than Bossuet, Colette, and

1. Joseph Calmette and Henri Drouot *La Bourgogne*: 1928.

Lamartine; or landscape more various than the Puisaye and
the Bresse, the Auxois and the Mâconnais, the Morvan and
the Montagne. A country which fathered both St Bernard
and Bussy-Rabutin may claim to have reconciled within its
borders the extreme manifestations of human nature; and
even when it had lost its autonomy it seems to have taken
from its conqueror as much as it yielded to him.

This capacity for assimilation has been due to history and
geography alike. In the north – at Sens, for example – you
will expect to find the influence of the Ile-de-France or of
Champagne. In the south the Lombard towers of the Brionnais will remind you of Italy. The work of Claus Sluter on the
effigies of the great Dukes at Dijon is obviously Flemish in
character. For just as Burgundy now stands on the highroad
of pleasure to the south, so in Gallo-Roman times it stood on
the trade route from Italy, the roads from Paris, Autun and
Troyes meeting at Saulieu, and leading – as all roads then did
– to Rome. It has been said appropriately that 'Burgundy is
astride three watersheds, at the heart of eastern France. It has
its face towards Paris, towards Champagne, towards the
Franche-Comté, and towards the countries of the Rhône
valley'; and its vestigial streams find their way to the Atlantic,
the Mediterranean, and the English Channel. As Michelet
wrote, the country is *apte à réconcilier le nord et le midi*.

It is not yet expected in France that every man shall have a
motor-car, and the State acknowledges its obligation to
public transport. The Paris–Lyon–Marseilles railway has
been officially described as the *ligne de Bourgogne*. Diesel
trains serve the branch lines, and there are excellent con-
nections by bus. Nevertheless I am assuming that the traveller
wishing to explore Burgundy thoroughly will do so by car. He
will find it very comfortable going, for on the departmental
roads – which he will normally want to use – he may drive
for a long while without meeting a vehicle of any sort. He
can either approach the country from Paris, striking the
valley of the Yonne at Montereau, where the river is joined
by the Seine; or, if he is coming direct from Calais, he will
leave the autoroute at Senlis and come down through Meaux
and Provins, slightly to the north-east of Sens. He will then
have the choice of following the valley of the Yonne, radiating

as he wishes to the west and also a little to the east of it, and of proceeding in the same way down the right bank of the Saône until he reaches Mâcon. He can then return from south to north through the Bresse and the eastern part of the Côte d'Or. Or he may choose a number of radial points and travel laterally in either direction. Whichever way he prefers he will hardly avoid going back upon his tracks, but he will gain a great deal from this familiarity with the terrain. The second is the method I have chosen in composing this guide.

France is an expensive country and there is no cheap way of travelling in reasonable comfort. But you will generally get a better meal for 15 or 20 francs than you would get for the same price at a similar restaurant or country hotel in Britain; and accommodation is cheaper. At the time of writing two people, living modestly, should count on £15 a day for their total expenses, assuming that they are content with a picnic luncheon.

Prosperity has given to Burgundy a smile which warms the heart; the good temper matches the good cheer – a natural reflection, as it seems, both of the works of nature and the works of man. For this is the 'country of the great Dukes and the great abbeys, the country of the good wine and the abundant life, the country of bold and mischievous gaiety, and also the country of the great men and the great artists.'[1] The Burgundian – although it would not be hard to find exceptions – is earthy and realistic, generally balanced, physically tough, argumentative, eloquent, and slightly mischievous. They are apt to quarrel among themselves, but present a solid front to the outsider. The province has produced its quota of great preachers – St Bernard, Bossuet, and Lacordaire – but, unlike the Breton, the Burgundian is not naturally spiritual. His favourite prayer has always been, '*Que Dieu nous préserve du vin qui'a le goût du tonneau.*'[2] The same good-tempered irreverence is found in the raillery of Alexis Piron – 'pungent as the mustard of Dijon' – and in his description of a Sunday Mass at Beaune in the eighteenth century.

1. *La Bourgoyne*: Joseph Calmette and Henri Drouot.
2. God preserve us from wine that tastes of the barrel.

*Non pas qu'il y manquât de femmes,*
*Tout en était rempli, depuis la porte au choeur*
*Mais c'est qu'en vérité ces dames*
  *Aurient effrayé Jean sans Peur.*
*Mes yeux qui partout galopoient*
*N'en rencontraient qu' effroyables;*
*Et sans le bénitier, où leur mains se trempaient*
*J'aurais cru que c'étaient des diables.'*[3]

In 1974 many of the châteaux could be visited, at least from the outside, several of them for the first time. But this permission should not be taken for granted in the future, and the necessary information on the subject may be obtained from the Syndicat d'Initiative at Dijon, or from the French Tourist Agencies. Some of the out-of-the-way churches are closed, but an enquiry in the village will generally produce a key.

If you are free to take your holiday when you choose, a fine May is the best time of year for visiting the country. The days are long, the roads are uncrowded, the hotels are rarely full – although it is advisable to book ahead – and the forests bursting into leaf present a dazzling variety of green. October will give you more certain weather, and for the eye an even richer symphony of colour; but the shorter days will curtail your movement. For boating on the Yonne, or swimming in the lakes of the Morvan, the summer months are preferable; and the fisherman will know his times and seasons. It has been said that the gods have given three gifts to Burgundy: 'wine, art, and archaeology'. They have given much else besides.

The following will be indispensable for your journey:

The Pneu Michelin 1-cm to 2-km map:
  nos. 61, 65, 66, 69, 70.

3.   Not that there was any scarcity of women;
     The place was full of them from door to choir.
     But really these women
       Would have frightened Jean sans Peur;
     Everywhere I looked
       They were fearful,
       And if it hadn't been for the holy water stoup where they
         dipped their hands,
     I should have taken them for devils.

The *red* Guide Michelin to hotels and restaurants.

It tells you with unfailing accuracy what you will have to pay for a room or a meal, and lists the *spécialités de la maison*. It has maps of the principal towns, and gives the motorist all the information necessary.

The *green* Guide Michelin to Burgundy and the Morvan will be a useful supplement to the following pages.

# CHAPTER ONE

# Facts of History

❧

You will hear it said that 'happy is the country that has no history'; Burgundy is none the sadder for having had a great deal of it. Of prehistory also there are multiple traces; of the Stone Age of Solutré in the Mâconnais, and of the Bronze Age at Alésia, where the rough tracks that threaded the primeval forest were known as the 'high road of amber and tin'. In the first century BC the country was divided between several Celtic tribes: the Senons, who gave their name to Sens; the Eduens, described as 'a curious people, ambitious and not very loyal', with their capital at Bibracte, only a few miles from Autun; and the Mandubiens at Alésia. They dominated the country from the upper Loire to the Saône, to the west as far as Moulins, and to the east up to the Jura. Intelligent and shrewd, they exhibited some of the character- istics you find in the Burgundians when the power of the duchy was at its height. Their subjugation by the armies of Rome in 52 BC may be read in the terse commentaries of Caesar, and the statue of Vercingetorix now stands on the hill of Alésia where the Eduens made their last stand. They submitted easily enough to what was essentially a civilizing mission, but the quasi-divine authority of Rome was chal- lenged by the Christian missionaries. According to Caesar the conquered tribes worshipped the deities of the Roman pan- theon. But Caesar was too preoccupied to observe the indigenous character of the local cults. These testified to the rural preoccupations which the urbanizing innovations of the colonizers had done little to disturb. The gods, embracing their barrels of wine and often standing on a sphere, seemed to enlarge the boundaries of the province to cosmic dimen- sions. Epona, the goddess of war, astride a horse, and the mother-goddesses with their cornucopias of plenty, invited the prayers and propitiation of those who lived close to the soil and depended upon it – as so many Burgundians still do. In default of any recorded mythology among the Gallic tribes, it is safe to conclude that this was both vigorous and varied, with its roots deep in Celtic antiquity.

The decline of the empire exposed Roman Gaul to invasion, and gave Burgundy its name. 'Burgundia' first appears in a letter of Théodoric the Ostrogoth in 506. The Burgondes were vandals from Germany, with blond hair, dyed and greased with rancid butter, white skin, and clear eyes. They were also exceptionally tall, and for that reason known as 'Septipedes'. Their occupation of the country was peaceful, and they fused easily enough with the more civilized but less warlike Eduens. Thus, in AD 407 Gondicaire became the first king of Burgundy and reigned for 40 years. He repelled Attila, who had ravaged Autun, Mâcon, and Chalon-sur-Saône, and he annexed the Langrois, the Nivernais, and the Lyonnais. Chilpéric, the son of Gondicaire, inherited the crown but was killed by his brother Gondebaud, whose hair was compared to a 'lion's mane'. He had other leonine propensities, notably a passion for the chase. He was also responsible for the admirable *loi Gombette*, which imposed a fine of three *écus* on anyone who refused hospitality to a stranger – a piece of legislation which may have earned him a flattering comparison with Solon. He assassinated Chilpéric's widow and children, with the exception of Clothilde, whom he brought up and married to Clovis, king of the Franks. The alliance was to recoil on his own head, since Clovis was quick to avenge his murdered father-in-law. The Burgundians were defeated near Dijon, and the duchy became tributary to the kings of France.

The Burgondes were converted to Christianity soon after their establishment in Gaul, and were seduced by Arianism – the heresy that maintained that the Son of God was inferior to the Father, not only in dignity but in essence. Clovis was baptized by St Rémy at Reims with the words: 'Bow your head. Adore what you have burnt, and burn what you have adored.' With the conversion of Clovis the Burgondes abjured their heresy and Gondebaud, repenting of his crimes, built the monastery of St Symphorien at Autun. Clothilde died in AD 545, and was immediately canonized.

The second Burgundian dynasty, inaugurated by Gontran, was bedevilled by the rivalry of his two sisters-in-law, Frédégonde and Brunéhaut. On the death of Gontran, a pacific and sensible ruler, Brunéhaut imposed her son Childebert on the throne, and her grandson Thierry succeeded him. Meanwhile Clotaire, the son of Frédégonde, pursued Brunéhaut after his mother's death, and had her tied by her white hair to the tail of a mare not yet broken in to polite behaviour – after which she died, herself broken in several pieces. It was belated compensation that her ashes should not be scattered, but preserved in the abbey of St Martin at Autun. In Burgundy, as elsewhere, these ages were dark indeed. Even the 'bon roi Dagobert' – known as 'King of Burgundy and France' – was not, it seems, particularly good, since he had his brother, Burnulle, assassinated.

There were exceptions. Girard de Roussillon ruled over the districts of Avallon and Tonnerre. His government was said to exude 'a perfume of honesty and justice'. On his father's death in 841 his brothers, Louis, Lothair, and Charles the Bald divided the Carolingian empire between them. Lothair ruled over Burgundy, Lorraine and Provence – all this territory thus acquiring the name of Lotharingia. It extended from Friesland in the north to a point south of Rome, and was known as 'the median Kingdom' or 'little Mesopotamia'. In 869 Lothair died without an heir, and immediately Charles took the offensive, besieging Girard's wife, Berthe, at Vienne. The town surrendered, and Girard retired with his wife to live peacefully in the château of Mont Lassois. From here they founded the abbeys of Pothières and Vézelay, to which the Pope sent the relics of St Mary Magdalen. Eva, their daughter, took the veil at Vézelay, and they themselves were buried at Pothières, where Girard's effigy showed a falcon on his wrist – for he preferred the chase to the battlefield if the choice were open to him. He and Berthe were the subjects of a medieval epic:

> Girard and Berthe prayed with all their heart,
> For two days and nights they neither ate nor drank.

While their son, Thierry, was still a child Girard foretold that he would one day fight more bravely than his father, and in consequence of this prediction Thierry was killed by a baron who feared the resumption of war. Girard forgave him and founded Vézelay as a visible sign of magnanimity.

On the death of Robert le Pieux in 1032 Henri I gave the duchy to his brother, Robert sans Terre, and thus established the Capetian dynasty. For three centuries the Capetian dukes successfully combated the fissiparous tendencies of feudalism. The pyramid of hierarchies was solidly constructed; French feeling grew weaker; and a strong Burgundian personality asserted itself. But the dukes were generally found allied with the French kings, even after the accession of the Valois. They suffered in 1359 and 1360 from the ravaging of Burgundy by Edward III, when Flavigny and Saulieu were sacked. Philippe de Rouvres was the last descendant of Robert sans Terre, and upon his death on 21 November 1361 the new dynasty of the Valois was inaugurated by Jean le Bon, who gave the duchy to his youngest son, Philip. The great dukes now enter upon the stage, and for more than a hundred years they hold the centre of it. Entitled, or entitling themselves, as the *'grands ducs de l'Occident'*, they justified the description of their House as a *'maison de plus en plus princière et envahissante'*, and of their reign – in the words of a Dutch historian – as 'a memorable story of fine diplomacy, high-handed enterprise, and good luck.' Their little empire comprised eventually Belgium and Holland, Picardy and Artois, Luxembourg, the 'counties' of Thionville and Rethel, ducal Burgundy, lower Lorraine and upper Alsace, Franche-Comté, and the 'counties' of Charolais and Nevers.

Philippe le Hardi (Philip the Bold) was born in Paris in 1332. In 1369 he married Marguerite of Flanders – described as *'laide et creuse'*,[1] who brought him not only the Flemish territories, but Artois and Nevers, as her dowry. By 1409 the two Burgundies extended as far as Montbéliard and Belfort to the east, and to Château-Chinon on the west, to the duchies of Lorraine to the north, of Savoy to the south, and of Bourbon to the west. Philip had transferred his headquarters to Ghent, while Marguerite was installed at Dijon with his four unmarried sisters 'to enjoy better air and nourishment, which they would not have had in Flanders, and to allow our son to get to know the nobles of Burgundy.'

1. Ugly and insipid.

Philip ruled for forty years – as assiduous in the library as he was intrepid in the field. Christine de Pisan, the historian and poet, and daughter of his astrologer, was a favourite *protégée*. He remained on good terms with the King of France, and arranged the marriage between Charles VI and Isabeau de Bavière when Charles was only eighteen years old. Having arranged his own marriage to such advantage, he was good at arranging other people's. On 7 February 1390 he met Charles at Châtillon-sur-Seine, and escorted him to Dijon, where, we are told, *'le duc y fit éclater sa magnificence'*. The walls and garden of a monastery were summarily cleared to make room for their fraternal jousting. He built the Chartreuse of Champmol, on the outskirts of Dijon, to house his tomb – the masterpiece by Claus Sluter and Claude de Werve, which may now be seen in the Dijon museum. He died in the Stag Inn at Mal, near Brussels, on 24 April 1404.

His son, Jean sans Peur, was born at Dijon in 1371. Pope Gregory VII was his godfather. In 1396 he fought in the Crusade against the redoubtable Bajazet, was taken prisoner and ransomed. In 1404 he inherited the duchy from his father, attended the Conseil du Roi in Paris, quarrelled with Louis of Orléans, and in 1407 had him assassinated. As from 27 January of that year Jean retained Flanders, Artois and the two Burgundies, while of his brothers Antoine kept the duchies of Brabant and Limbourg, and Philip became Count of Nevers and Rethel. The Dauphiné was placed under his protection, but he was defeated by the English at Agincourt. This was the Duke of Burgundy who speaks to us with such eloquence in Shakespeare's *Henry V*. A Carthusian monk from Champmol exhibited his skull to François I with the following comment: 'Sire, this is the hole through which the English entered into France.' In 1419 he was murdered by the partisans of the Dauphin, in alliance with the turbulent nobility of the Armagnacs, on the bridge of Montereau, and in the presence of the Dauphin, who was then only sixteen years old.

Philippe le Bon – born in Dijon in 1396 – also came to be known as the '*Duc Soleil*', for he was not to be outshone by the brilliance of Jean sans Peur. His father's murder threw him into the arms of the English, with whom he must share the responsibility for the burning of Jeanne d'Arc. They had met – uneasily, no doubt – when the maid was captured at Compiègne, but he was subsequently reconciled with Charles VII by the Treaty of Arras in 1435. He reigned for 47 years; died at Bruges in 1467; and was succeeded by his son, Charles le Téméraire, the last and the least successful of the great dukes. He lost his head, and in consequence lost his duchy. Indeed he was not much interested in his duchy, describing it as 'a dagger of lead' in contrast to his 'comté', which was a 'sword of honour'. With these sentiments it is hardly surprising that he did not get on well with his immediate subjects. In 1465, at the age of 32, he joined the Ligue du Bien Public against Louis XI, was defeated at Monthéry, and forced to yield several towns in Picardy to the French crown. Philippe had been wiser, presenting Louis with the finest gold vessel in his treasury for his coronation, and Louis – while still the Dauphin – had agreed to be godfather to Charles's daughter, Marie de Bourgoyne. Immediately upon his accession Charles excited the revolt of Liège, and Louis was taken prisoner at Péronne. Only the wise counsel of Philip de Commines prevented Charles from dethroning him or contriving his death. Louis was freed, but this did not deter Charles from his extravagant ambitions. He was defeated at Beauvais, and disowned by the Emperor of Germany and the Duke of Lorraine. Louis seized his opportunity; broke the nine years' truce he had signed with Charles; and sent help to the Duke of Lorraine, whom Charles was besieging at Nancy. The Burgundians were defeated, betrayed by an Italian condottiere, Campobasso, and Charles's body was found two days later embedded in the ice.

At the beginning of the fifteenth century up to half the revenue of the dukes came from royal sources, but they all had recourse to taxation. Philippe's credit stood high, but Charles's extravagance was ruinous. The duchy and *comté* of Burgundy provided only five per cent of his ordinary revenue; three quarters of the extraordinary revenue for both came from the Low Countries. These amounted to 110,000 ducats a year, almost equal to the revenues of Venice, four times those of Florence, and twice those of the Vatican. The Dukes were also aided by bankers from northern Italy. One of them

– Giovanni Arnolfini – comes to us in a famous portrait by van Eyck. The State was not without representative institutions. Bourgeois careerists found the way to nobility open to them. The grand assembly in Dijon in 1314 – long before the inauguration of the third dynasty – was attended by 110 nobles, the representatives of eighteen abbeys and eleven chapters, and deputies from the commonalty of eleven Burgundian towns. The Three Estates could always be summoned if required, and when they met in Beaune at the end of the fourteenth century the nobility equalled in numbers the clergy and the third estate put together. In Burgundy, at least, there was little sign that the sun was to go down on feudalism, even when the Lotharingian dream of Philippe le Bon had been shattered before the walls of Nancy.

Louis XI was only waiting for the ripe plum to fall into his lap, but the marriage of Marie de Bourgogne to Maximilian of Austria in 1477 delayed the inevitable. In contrast to her father's, hers had been a singularly happy childhood; her marriage was not less so. She taught her husband Flemish and French; he taught her German. The first book to be printed in English – Caxton's translation of the *History of Troy* – was dedicated to Marie de Bourgogne, and one of the few surviving copies has a copper engraving showing him presenting it to her. She and Maximilian shared the same tastes for music, skating and falconry, and were both fond of birds. Marie nursed her own children, ordered her own menus, and dined out with the merchants of Dijon. She was a keen gardener; loved her dogs and horses; and cherished the monkeys and parrots from Africa which were a gift from her grandmother. Maximilian declared to the States-General: 'There is nothing in the world I desire more than to be in her company, to see her and to please her.' Few dynastic marriages were so happy, but the happiness was short-lived. In 1482 Marie died after falling from her horse at Bruges; and by the Treaty of Arras between France and the Low Countries it was arranged for her daughter, Marguerite d'Autriche, to marry the Dauphin – Charles – and for Burgundy to be attached to the French crown.

Matters did not work out so neatly. Marguerite was duly brought to France, but Louis had now changed his mind and married the Dauphin instead to Anne de Bretagne. Marguerite was sent back to her father; the Dauphin died; and the widowed Anne espoused the future Louis XII in his place. His father did not shrink from *force majeure* to subdue the proud duchy. 'The time has now come' he declared to the Sieur de Craon 'to use all the five senses that nature has given you to put the duchy of Burgundy in my hands.' There was resistance in the Charolais and around Dijon, where Jean Jouard, president of the ducal council, who had thrown in his lot with Louis, paid for his treachery with his life. But the resistance failed, since there was no longer a duke to sustain it. Simon de Quingey, one of its more ardent adherents, was taken to Tours and imprisoned in a cage.

'The *palais des ducs*' now became the '*logis du roi*', and Louis XI built a château at the gates of Dijon to remove any misunderstanding as to whom the city belonged; but he recognized the Franche-Comté on the left bank of the Saône as Spanish or imperial territory. Parliament issued decrees and heard appeals; the Estates voted the taxes. The province was under the immediate authority of a Governor; Louis de la Trémouille, Philippe de Chalon, and the Guises were prominent among them. But Marguerite did not give up so easily. In 1513 she encouraged the Swiss to invade Burgundy. The governor of Dijon, La Trémouille, disposed of barely 7,000 men to face an army of 30,000 Germans, Swiss and Franc-Comtois. He tried to negotiate, but the Swiss opened fire and had already breached the walls when La Trémouille resorted to a ruse worthy of Ulysses and Agamemnon. He sent fresh envoys to the besieging army, leading a procession of carts laden with barrels of wine; the invaders drank their fill; and the siege was raised. La Trémouille agreed to pay an indemnity of 400,000 *écus*, and promised that the French would evacuate Milan. But Louis XII, not having concluded the treaty, refused to ratify it. In the following year Marguerite persuaded Maximilian to join the Pope and Ferdinand of Spain in a league against Louis. He signed a truce with the Pope and Ferdinand, but Marguerite dissuaded her father from adhering to it. A single idea possessed her: 'the counties of the Maconnais, the Auxerrois, and Bar-sur-Seine,' she declared, 'have been usurped by the King of France.' After the defeat and capture of François I at Pavia in 1525, Charles V laid claim to Burgundy. In this case resistance was successful. François declared that the 'first oath he had made to God was to preserve the rights of the throne and to alienate no land belonging to it'; and that 'to detach the Burgundians from France would do them as great a wrong and as great a violence as to cut off an arm from a human body.'

Marguerite d'Autriche was the last, and not the least remarkable, offshoot of the great Burgundian dynasty. She was married, first, to Don John of Spain, and then to Philibert de Savoie. She was a patron of the arts, and herself wrote poems and stories. She also wrote letters '*malgracieuses*' to her father, whose chimerical plans were an affront to her realism. He did not reply in kind, but sent her jewels in the hope of keeping her quiet. She lived in the *comté* at Bourg-en-Bresse, and employed Flemish and Burgundian artists to build and decorate the great church where she is buried. But after the death of her brother, Philippe le Beau, in Spain she retired to a private house in Malines, where she quietly brought up her nephews. She was known as '*la bonne tante*'.

The history of Burgundy is henceforward inseparable from the history of France, and we shall meet it at every stage of our journey. During the wars of religion Henri IV received his baptism of fire at Arnay-le-Duc – some years before he decided that Paris was worth a Mass. The Catholics celebrated their victory over the Protestant '*maladie*' at Dijon, but Burgundy had no part in the disgrace of St Bartholomew. In 1574 the government of the province passed to the duc de Mayenne, brother of Henri, duc de Guise. He became head of the Ligue after de Guise had been assassinated. The Parliament of the Ligue met at Dijon, and that of the King at Semur. On 5 June 1595 Henri IV entered Dijon and won the battle of Fontaine-Française in the *comté*. The 'great Condé' led the revolt of the Fronde, and being then Governor of the province involved it to that extent in what was essentially a protest against the power and influence of Mazarin. The wings of the nobility had been too severely clipped by Richelieu for them not to wish to take it out on his successor. Louis XIV bore the province no grudge, and restored it to something of its former shape, though to nothing of its former power, by acquiring the *comté*, which had remained first in Austrian, and then in Spanish hands. It did not escape, however, the centralizing policy of the *Roi Soleil*. While scrupulously respecting its institutions, he assimilated it by degrees to the other provinces of France. Effective power rested with the intendants – professional administrators like Boucher, Trudaine, and Joly de Fleuret. When President Brulart resisted this encroachment he was exiled to Perpignan. But the memory of greatness and of grandeur remained. In 1581 Pierre de St Julien was writing: 'I am a Burgundian, but I am not ashamed of the name. Once upon a time it caused the standards to tremble and forced the Romans themselves to pay a tribute to which they were not accustomed.'

Burgundy avoided politics after the failure of the Fronde. Dijon became instead a brilliant centre of society and intellectual life. Its Académie was founded in 1723, and the Université de Bourgoyne, subsidized by the city of Dijon and the Three Estates, in 1750. There were Parliamentary crises under Louis XV and Louis XVI, and the ferment of ideas in the capital was such that the Revolution was generally welcomed, although it was less bloody in Burgundy than elsewhere. Delegates to the Committee of Public Safety like Carnot and Berlier, whose republican sympathies were not in doubt, prided themselves on the exercise of a *'sage liberté'* when they proffered their advice. But the shreds of provincial autonomy were lost, and the ancient duchy was divided between the new and artificial departments of the Yonne, the Côte d'Or, the Saône-et-Loire, and parts of the Aube, the Haute-Marne, the Nièvre, and the Ain. It says much for the strength of Burgundian personality that it has resisted this dismemberment. The rare talents and rich characters it produced will be noted as we come upon their traces.

Of Napoleon's generals Junot came from Bussy-le-Grand, and Marmont from Châtillon-sur-Seine. It was at Châtillon that the Allies met with Napoleon between 7 February and 11 March 1814. The Austrians invaded the province after Waterloo; the Emperor Francis installed himself at Dijon; and the occupation was harsh under von Bartenstein. On 5 October 1815 the Emperors of Austria and Russia, the King of Prussia, and Wellington reviewed their troops on the plain of Arc-sur-Tille. The territory was freed from Allied control on Christmas Day of the same year.

During the Franco-Prussian War Burgundy did something to redeem the French conduct of the campaign. The Croix de la Légion d'Honneur incorporated thereafter in the city's arms commemorates the defence of Dijon. Cremer, who commanded the army of the Loire, was threatening von Moltke's communications, and Werder was ordered to make a strong and rapid offensive. At the Battle of Nuits, on 18 December 1870, the French won the day, and gained a second victory under the walls of Dijon, between 21 and 23 January 1871, capturing a German standard and forcing the evacuation of the city. This did not, of course, affect the outcome of the war, and the final German occupation lasted until 12 October of that year.

The First World War left Burgundy unscathed, and it suffered less than other parts of France from the second. The line of demarcation between the occupied and unoccupied zones ran through Chalon-sur-Saône; and although the province contributed its quota of resistants, the country was too open and accessible to lend itself easily to the organization of a maquis, like the Vercors to the east or the mountains of the Massif Central.

# CHAPTER TWO

# Sens and the Senonais

❧

1

First impressions are important, and whether you are coming to Burgundy from Paris, or more directly from the north by way of Provins, I should advise you to make your first head-quarters at **Villeneuve-sur-Yonne.** In the former case you can reach it very quickly – an easy hour and a half's driving – by the autoroute, turning off at Courtenay and following the D.15; otherwise, you will come down the N.376 from Provins to Pont-sur-Yonne, and then take the N.6 – the old highway to the south – until you reach Villeneuve, 13 kilometres beyond Sens. Do not allow the superb profile of Sens cathedral to distract you, for you will be coming back to it very soon.

Villeneuve is not only a charming little town in itself, comfortably removed from the main road, but it also contains a hotel, the **Dauphin,** in which anyone's dream of the French provinces is perfectly distilled. This stands in the wide central street, close to the church, and whichever way you look you see the two magnificent stone gateways – the **Porte de Sens** and the **Porte de Joigny,** with its four pepper-pot towers and high central gable – which at either end seem to imprison the town in its medieval past. You enter the courtyard of the hotel between the fluted pillars of a Renaissance archway; and if a local failure of electricity compels you to dine by candle-light, as it did on my last visit, you will make no complaint. The cuisine is excellent, the prices are reasonable, and the service is everything you could wish.

The **Church of Notre-Dame,** though its foundation stone was laid by Pope Alexander III in 1163, drapes its façade in elegant, classical ornamentation, for the perpendicular style, which in England had met the reaction against decorated Gothic, had never caught on in France. But the vast proportions of the nave are a reminder that the architects of Cham-

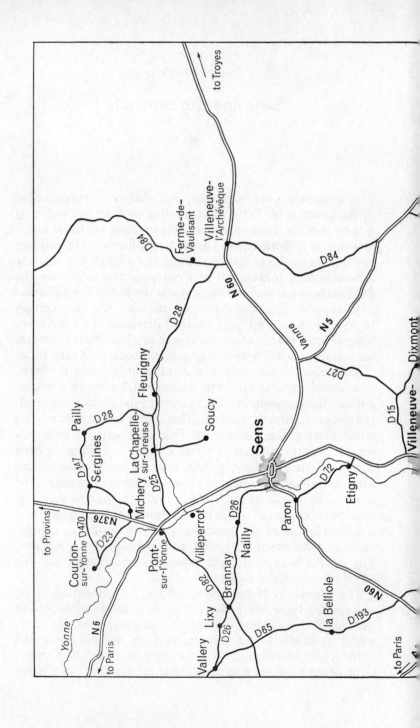

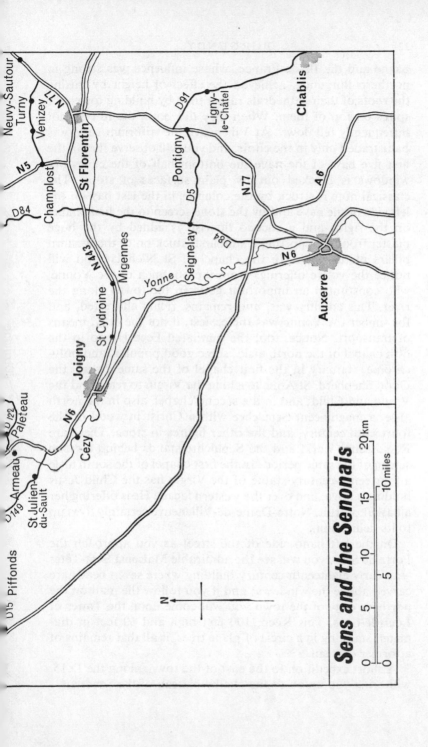

Sens and the Senonais

0 5 10 15 20km
0 5 10 miles

N

pagne and the Ile-de-France, whose influence was strong in
northern Burgundy, achieved the effect of height by raising
the roofs of their cathedrals rather than by building towers or
spires on top of them. When they did both, the towers not
infrequently fell down. At Villeneuve the triforium gallery is
balustraded only in the choir, and you will observe that in the
first five bays of the nave the bottom half of the clerestory
windows is blocked out by plain surfaces of stone. The
classical note is struck by the columns in the last bay on the
left side of the nave and by the stone screen to the first chapel
on the right; and a rococo flourish is added by the huge
plaster fronds supporting a sunburst, stuck on to the western
pillars of the choir. In the chapel of St Nicholas you will
notice the votive offerings from the boatmen of the Yonne,
who constituted an important guild in the towns along the
river. This country was, and remains, richly afforested, and
for timber the Yonne was the easiest, if not the only, means
of transport. Notice, too, the mutilated Ecce Homo in the
fifth chapel of the north aisle; some good popular, and polychrome, statuary in the first chapel of the same aisle – the
Good Shepherd, St Anne teaching the Virgin to read, and the
Virgin and Child; and in the second chapel, also in the north
aisle, a magnificent **Sepulchre** with a Christ in wood of the
fourteenth century, and the other figures in stone. These are
Renaissance work, and the Sepulchre stands behind a stone
screen of the same period. In the first chapel of the south aisle
a fourteenth-century statue of the Virgin has the Child Jesus
holding a dove; and over the western façade He is offering her
a basket of fruit. Notre-Dame-de-Villeneuve certainly lives up
to its dedication.

On the left hand side of the street as you approach the
Porte de Sens, you will see the admirable **Maison à Sept-Têtes**
– an early eighteenth-century building where seven heads are
carved above the windows; and if you follow the mall on the
northern edge of the town you will come upon the **Tower of
Louis-le-Gros.** This Keep, 100 feet high and 60 feet in diameter, standing in a circle of plane trees, is all that remains of
a former château.

A short expedition to the east of the town, along the D.15,
will bring you up on to the chalky plâteau of the Senonais –

strewn elsewhere with megaliths, dolmens, and menhirs – and after ten kilometres to the exceptionally interesting church of **Dixmont**. Notice, outside, the *polissoir* for sharpening Gallic axes and flint heads, and the mill-stone for crushing fruit and corn. This stands on a triangle of grass under a young oak beyond the east end of the church. On the left of the entrance there is the statue in stone of a man being martyred with a pair of executioners pressing him to death, and on the tower a very coquettish angel is announcing the Incarnation. The interior is packed with detail. A polychrome Virgin with Child in the south aisle, her hands very full with a palm, a book, and a bunch of grapes; the traces of colour on another Virgin and Child set on a high stone pedestal; the carved woodwork on the choir stalls and sedilia; and the painting at the west end of the south aisle remarkable for nothing except that it was the gift of Napoleon III. You may prefer to recall that St Louis and Blanche de Castille were the former *seigneurs châtelains* of Dixmont.

The D.122, south-west of Dixmont, brings you past the eighteenth-century château of **Paleteau**. This is not open to the public, but you may get a rewarding glimpse of it from the end of a triple avenue of chestnuts. It stands behind a moat and a walled demesne. A turning to the left out of the village will bring you down to the N.6 at Armeau, where you should bear left again and cross the river a little farther on to **St Julien-du-Sault**. The place takes its name from the legendary jump of St Julian's horse to escape his enemies. A stone from the Bastille is embedded in the ramparts with the following magniloquent inscription: '*Le patriotisme l'a consacré à un meilleur usage en l'élevant ici pour donner à cette place le doux nom de la Liberté.*'[1] Standing on a hill to the east is the Château de Patteau, reputed to have sheltered the 'Iron Mask' on its way to the Bastille. The thirteenth-century collegial church has some admirable stained glass of the same period and later.

A short drive on the D.3. now takes you to **Joigny**, a picturesque little town perched high above the Yonne. Renard de Sens built a fortress here at the end of the seventh century;

1. Patriotism has dedicated it to a better use in raising it here to give this place the sweet name of Liberty.

C.G.B.—C

the cloth market was attracting its trade by 1224; and of the thirteenth-century ramparts the Porte du Bois, opening on to the Forêt d'Othe, is still standing. In 1530 the town was almost totally destroyed by fire, but it was quickly rebuilt, and a Renaissance château took its place among the monuments which now deserve attention. In the **Church of St Jean,** at the north end of the rue Dans-le-Château, you should notice the thirteenth-century tomb of Adelais, Comtesse de Joigny; the coloured statues over the pillars of the nave, with its border of salamanders and mythical beasts; a **still life** by Pieter van Slingelandt (1640–91); and particularly the fifteenth-century Sepulchre of white marble in the right side aisle. One of the figures holds a jar and sponge; the other has the crown of thorns and the nails. There is a statue of the Visitation on the corner opposite the church, and you will observe the wooden pillars supporting a number of houses in the square.

**St-Thibault,** off the rue d'Etape, and quite close by, is a mixture of late Gothic and early Renaissance. It is worth a visit for its paintings and sculptures, of which you will find a plan beside the pulpit in the left side aisle. A Nativity on wood and a Crucifixion, both of the early Dutch school; a stone Crucifixion; the statues of Etienne Porcher, and St Yves – the patron saint of lawyers; and the lovely fourteenth-century **Vierge au sourire,** against the fourth pillar on the right of the nave, opposite the pulpit. On a wooden sixteenth-century house in the place du Pilon, close to St Thibault, you will notice the sculptured figure of St Martin. This was made by a hunchback mason of that name, who had been cured by a relic of St Thibault brought from Rome by pilgrims in 1080. On the outbreak of war in 1939 a local poet composed the following verses:

> *O vous qui d'un bossu naguère*
> *Fites un Martin svelte et beau*
> *Au seuil de cette étrange guerre*
> *Priez pour nous, grand saint Thibault.*[1]

In **St André,** on the outskirts of the town, with its Renaissance doorway and romanesque arches on the south side of

1. You who once made a slim and handsome Martin out of a hunchback, pray for us, great St Thibault, on the threshold of this strange war.

the nave, you will find the ladder by which the English attempted to storm the ramparts on 12 May 1429, and from which they were repelled by the inhabitants. The statue of the Virgin holding out a parchment to a kneeling figure with a skull evidently represents Our Lady of Mercy receiving a petition for the redemption of prisoners.

The bridge over the Yonne at Joigny has kept six of its eighteenth-century arches, and as you cross it you have a charming view of the river, the quays, and the shaded tow-paths.

It will be worth your while going 6.5 kilometres along the N.445 to **St Cydroine,** where eight men recently worked for eight months to restore the transept crossing of the church. You will observe two elephants among the capitals. Then rejoin the N.6 at Joigny, and head north for Villeneuve. If you stop off at **Cézy,** you will find a moving inscription on the Arvers tomb in the churchyard. '*Mon âme a son secret, et ma vie son mystère.*'[1]

2

A second excursion will occupy the best part of a long day. Follow the D.15 in the opposite direction from Villeneuve until it joins the D.193 at Piffonds, and then strike north to **Vallery** – a total distance of 36 kilometres through the wooded uplands of the Gatinais. The château of the Condé can be visited only from the outside (every day, except Tuesday and Wednesday, from 10 to 12h, and 14 to 19h), but Condé is so great a name in Burgundy that historical pietas demand that you shall visit their mausoleum in the adjoining church. Its gloomy splendour sheds a sad commentary on those who behaved like kings even if they only wore a prince's coronet. All that remains of the original château is a gateway and two round towers of the thirteenth or early fourteenth century; the rest was partially destroyed by Warwick the Kingmaker. The new building was begun by the maréchal de Saint-André, the friend of Henri II, but it was never finished. At his death it passed to his widow, who gave it to Louis de Bourbon, Prince de Condé, in the hope that she would marry him. She

1. My soul has its secret, and my life its mystery.

passed from Catholicism to Protestantism at the same time.
Louis accepted the château, but disappointed the hope which
accompanied it. He was killed at the Battle of Jarnac (1569),
and his son – the 'grand Condé' – was brought up at Vallery.
The château is impressively situated on the side of a wooded
hill, and protected by a moat. It has been well restored by its
present owner, the chief inspector of historical monuments,
and is a good example of Renaissance feudal architecture.

Now turn east along the D.26 through Lixy and Brannay –
where both churches have fine romanesque towers – and
follow the D.26 to **Nailly,** which also has a good romanesque
church. Observe the statue of a silversmith making a crown
on the south side of the choir. Then take the D.358 till you
come to the river; and turn left up the D.58 until it crosses
the Yonne just north of Villeperot and joins the N.6; you are
then only a few kilometres from **Pont-sur-Yonne.** Here the
name is disappointing because only three arches of the original
bridge remain, and the view of these is spoilt or obscured by
the strident green paint on the iron construction which has
replaced it. But look upstream from the open air café, built
over the first arch of the old bridge, and the charm of this
lovely river between its wooded banks will not fail to captivate
you. The barges pass up and down, and the old men just
below you are patiently fishing. If you have ever seen the
junction of the Seine and the Yonne at Montereau, you will
have noticed that the Yonne is much wider than the river to
which, thenceforward, it is obliged to surrender its identity. I
am wholeheartedly with those who regard the Seine as a
usurper.

The church at Pont-sur-Yonne, with its one big and five
mini spires, is a good example of early Burgundian Gothic
(1185–1245), and there is much to be seen in the neighbourhood. Cross the river to the right bank; follow the N.376 till
you are clear of the town; and then take the little side road on
your right to the ruined abbey of **Notre-Dame.** The flamboyant façade (1532) with its engraved motto – *'Probet
dilectionis exhibio operis'* – is now part of a farm building.
Cattle troughs lie up against it. You can enter the ruins from
the other side, where you will notice the blind rose window
above the chevet, and a pair of blocked-in medallions, and

also wonder how the rose comes to be *above* the level of the interior roof. The eight ribs of ogival vaulting spring from halfway up the lancets. An engaging colony of white rabbits give life to a place 'where prayer has been valid'.

The church at **Michery,** a little farther up the same road, hovers between the late romanesque and the early Gothic, and is remarkable for its exceptionally tall clock tower. This presents a perfectly plain surface from the belfry to the arch of the single-bayed narthex. The vaulting is sexpartite in the nave and quadripartite in the side aisles. You should turn left in Michery and crossing the N.376 proceed along the D.23 to **Courlon-sur-Yonne.** The first church to be built on this site, which stood on the old Roman road, was erected by the early Christians to replace a temple to Mercury. Courlon had stood for the Ligue during the wars of religion, and the church was burnt by the Huguenots under Condé. It was subsequently rebuilt on orders from Richelieu in 1631, and the tower was heightened. Notice the carving of St Loup with his horse on its southern face; the church is dedicated to St Loup, who repelled the Huns in the seventh century. Fifteen steps lead up to the west door, and you will observe in the interior the coloured statues of various saints – St Edmé, St Nicholas, St Sebastian, St Roch, and St Blaise – who look down on you from the pillars in the nave and choir. The eighteenth century strikes a discordant note with the fluted columns and baroque drapery of the baldachino.

If you come to the Senonais in September you will notice the maize stacked in narrow wire cages, and the fields ablaze with sunflowers; and here, on this high chalky soil, you will come upon an occasional patch of vines. From Courlon you should take the D.470 to Sergines, continue along the D.147 to Pailly, and turn right down the D.28 to **Fleurigny.** The château of Fleurigny has been described as 'the pearl of the Senonais'. You walk up the drive among the beeches, planes, and poplars, until you find yourself in front of it. The moat is fresh with water from the Oreuse, and animated by parading swans. Four circular, pepper-pot towers flank the Renaissance building of patterned stone and brick. You cross a three-arched stone bridge to the gateway, elaborately carved with armorial bearings upheld by a pair of female figures, and pass under three mullioned windows into the *cour d'honneur*. This was formerly rectangular, but one side has been pulled down to give an attractive opening on to the park. On your left is the lower chapel with a window by **Jean Cousin** (1490–1560), a larger version of which may be seen in Sens Cathedral. The frieze above the door – angels and Cupids and garlands of flowers – is also the work of Cousin or his school. Birds, fruits, and flowers, exquisitely carved, adorn the forty compartments of the roof inside, and bear the same signature. So do the sculptures in the loggia.

Jean Cousin was orphaned in early childhood and earned his living by keeping pigs until a villager, struck by his designs, took him under his care to study. He became an engraver, sculptor, writer, and geometrician, setting out his ideas in the *Traité des Perspectives*; went to Paris in 1547 and was employed by Henri II.

He designed the monumental mantelpiece, five metres high, in the guard room at Fleurigny, which is generally considered not inferior to a similar mantelpiece in the château of Blois. Here, as at Blois and Fontainebleau, your attention will be drawn to the papered ceiling; and unique is a Polish sledge for children in the shape of a hen brooding on its nest! Boars' heads and other trophies of the chase are much in evidence, for 1200 acres of woodland lie around Fleurigny, where the game is various and plentiful. You will also be shown the upper chapel with its carved wooden ceiling; the picture gallery with its mythological paintings; and the small round oratory where the walls are 6 feet 5 inches thick. It is worth taking a look at the old forge outside the château, and the dovecote with its mobile ladder, of which we shall find a more perfect specimen at Epoisses. The château is open from Easter to All Saints, between 14.30 and 18h. It is closed on Monday.

You should now follow the river valley along the D.25 as far as **La Chapelle-sur-Oreuse.** This is a charming village with a château too modest to find its way on to the visiting list, and more attractive than many that do. It stands with its round tower on the river bank, and beyond it, close to the church, is a weir, and a garden profusely in flower. The high ground to the north is strewn with outcroppings of rock; some of these, no doubt, are the vestiges of prehistoric habitations, but it needs a more expert eye than mine to decide when a rock is a dolmen! Turning left out of the village you come to **Soucy,** which was the birthplace of Jean Cousin. His stained-glass work may be seen in the church – if you have the luck to find it open – and a portrait of his brother-in-law in the sacristy. You are now only six kilometres from Sens, which will demand a day to itself, but I cannot decently discourage you from dining at the Hotel de Paris if your appetite and purse feel up to it. The courtyard open to the street, and the clientèle bent over their apéritifs, will undoubtedly tempt you as you drive through. The hotel has two stars in Michelin, and for 40 francs and upward you will eat and drink as well as anywhere in France, and no doubt sleep as comfortably. Alternatively, it is only a short drive back to Villeneuve-sur-Yonne.

Whether you stay in Sens or return to it the next day, you may easily park your car in the Boulevard Garibaldi, just north of the cathedral. The city takes its name from the Senons, who were for many years the most powerful of the Gallic tribes. In 390 BC they invaded Italy under Brennus, and captured Rome; the Romans had their revenge under Caesar, although the city held out for a little when Drapes came to its assistance after the fall of Alésia. It was subsequently made the capital of a Roman province. If you are puzzled by the motto of the cathedral – 'Campont' – this stands for the bishoprics of which Sens was the metropolitan church until 1627: Chartres, Auxerre, Meaux, Paris, Orléans, Nevers, and Troyes. When Paris was created an archbishopric, Sens lost Meaux, Chartres, and Orléans at the same time. It was from here that its first archbishop, St Savinian, evangelized the country to the north-east, and was martyred; here, in 615, that St Loup rang the great bell of the cathedral and put to flight the rough soldiery of Clotaire II; here, in 732, that another archbishop, St Ebbon, repelled the Saracen invaders; here, in 1140, that a Council, spurred on by the polemical zeal of St Bernard, for the second time condemned Abelard for setting no limits to the discoveries of human reason. It is pleasant to record that another great Cistercian, Peter the Venerable, absolved him on his death-bed. This was only one episode in the dialogue, which was so often a dispute, between

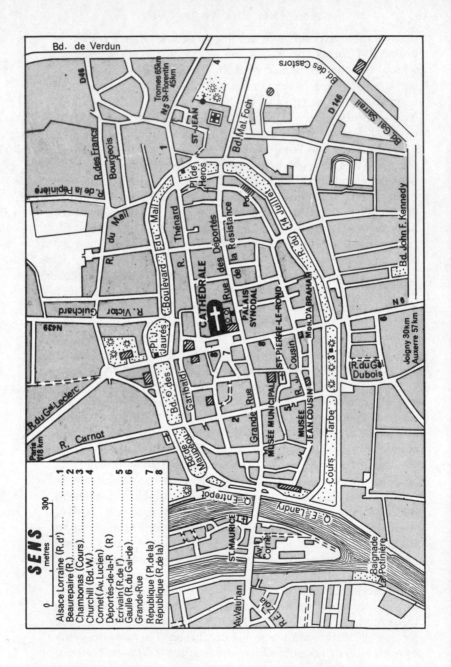

Cluny and Cîteaux; and just as here, and at Pontigny, we meet St Bernard at the outset of our journey, so we shall meet Peter the Venerable at the end of it. For the international story of the Cistercians is set in a Burgundian context. It was here, in 1164, that Alexander III, beset with his own troubles, confirmed the primacy to Becket, and here that they met during Becket's exile. There was a good deal of *va-et-vient* between Sens and Pontigny for the unyielding archbishop; and it was in the cathedral at Sens that St Louis was married to Blanche of Castille in 1234. The place has seen a great deal of history, including the '*grand* Condé' riding naked through the streets – just to show, one imagines, how little he cared for any opinion except his own.

Before attempting to describe the cathedral and register its magnificence, we should try to understand it. Founded, it seems, shortly after 1130 by Archbishop Sanglier – quite naturally known as the 'Boar' – it obeyed the same Cistercian principles as Pontigny, different as they are in style. Among all the French prelates of the time, Archbishop Henry was the most thoroughgoing exponent of the Bernardian reform. His early career had been worldly, but after incurring the reproach of St Bernard – and this could never be described as temperate – he submitted in 1126 to the austere dictates of the most eloquent voice in Christendom; with this difference, however, that St Bernard himself realized that a church designed for the laity should not be the same as a church designed for monks. St Bernard was a purist, but he was not a philistine. He shared with Augustine, and also with Plato, both a distrust of images and a belief in the metaphysical significance of mathematical relationships, which Augustine had applied to music. The consonance of the octave – the musical equivalent of the ratio 1 : 2 – was an echo of theological truth, and our ears had been created to respond to it. Beauty resided in figures; figures depended on proportion; and proportion on number. The relevance of these principles to architecture was clear. Gothic art owes its very existence to the Platonic cosmology of Chartres and the spirituality of Cîteaux. Thus the equality of the Three Persons of the Trinity was symbolized by the triangle, and the relationship of the Father to the Son by the square. The cathedral was a model of the order created out of

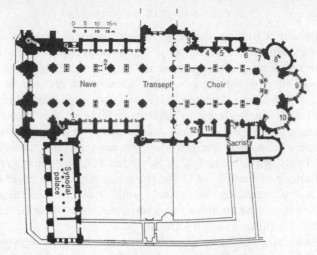

SENS CATHEDRAL

1 Window by Jean Cousin (1530)
2 Fragments of a monument erected by Archbishop Salazar in memory of his parents
3 Chapel of St John, and 13th century Calvary
4 Becket window
5 Window: story of St Eustace
6 Window: parable of the Prodigal son
7 Window: parable of the Good Samaritan
8 Tomb of the Dauphin, father of Louis XVI
9 Windows of the 13th century
10 Window attributed to Jean Cousin
11 Renaissance reredos
12 Virgin of the 14th century above the altar

chaos by the Divine Mind, and an image of the Heavenly City apprehended by reason and faith. A Renaissance architect, Philibert Delorme, regretted that he had not observed those excellent proportions which the 'great architect of the Universe had revealed to Noah for the ark, to Moses for the Tabernacle, and to Solomon for the Temple'. A simple glance at the first Book of Kings will tell us how precisely they had been laid down.

Now St Bernard was deeply sensitive to music and Augustine was his master. Instead of dismissing him as an iconoclast, we should see him as one who propagated the terms of a new aesthetic, so that 'the main aesthetic and technical features that characterize Cistercian architecture, the unadorned perfection of workmanship, the attention to proportion [are] equally present in the cathedrals of the Ile-de-France. Cistercian and early Gothic architecture may thus be described as two branches growing from the soil, and realizing

the same religious and aesthetic postulates . . .'[1] And just as –
by a process inevitable, as it seems, in the evolution of any
art – the severity of romanesque gave way to the exaggerations
of Cluniac architecture and iconography, so the simplicities of
early Gothic were complicated by the *flamboyant*. That, however, is another story; what interests us here is the Bernardian
influence on Archbishop Henry, and his successor; and the
masterpiece that resulted from their submission to it.

**St Etienne de Sens** was the first of the Gothic cathedrals.
It does not stun you with its height, like Amiens and Beauvais;
nor, like Chartres, does it distract you from the contemplation
of form by the splendours of sculpture and stained glass,
though it has much of both. Rather, it satisfies you with the
measure of due proportion. Whereas at Chartres the famous
west portal is flanked by two towers, disconcertingly dis-
similar, the façade of Sens describes a square of fairly regular
design with a small rose window in the middle and two rows
of arcading on either side, and high up, one of them occupied
by statues. The towers were obviously meant to harmonize
with each other, but only the southern one was completed.
This was crowned in 1576 by a Renaissance campanile for the
big clock with its inscription:

> *Les borgois de Sens m'ont fait faire*
> *L'an M cing cens soixante seize.*[2]

Although the clock may strike the hours, the campanile
strikes a discordant note on the façade of a Gothic building.
The tower below it had collapsed on the Thursday in Holy
Week 1267, and was shortly afterwards rebuilt.

The Gothic cathedral was not built in a day, nor even in a
decade. Taste would change and technique develop, so that
the personality of the building was not always the same when
it was finished as when it was begun. Very often, on the other
hand, we simply have the impression of organic growth.
Apart from the excrescent campanile, this is the case at Sens.
Once the 'Boar' had decided to pull down the previous
Carolingian basilica, work proceeded quickly. On the accession
of Hugh de Toucy in 1142 the yards were in full activity, and

1. *The Gothic Cathedral*: Otto von Simson: 1956.
2. The burghers of Sens had me made in the year 1576.

when he died in 1168 the cathedral was virtually complete except for the façade, which has an obviously later look, and for certain ornamental details. Already, in 1163, it was big enough to accommodate the ceremonies entailed by the visit of Pope Alexander III, and the identity of style and continuity of structure between the nave and choir prove that they were built at the same time. William of Sens, who rebuilt the choir at Canterbury, certainly had a hand in the later stages of his own cathedral, although he cannot have been its original architect.

In 1184 a fire broke out in the city, causing considerable damage to a number of arches in the vaulting of the cathedral. Instead of rebuilding them in their previous spherical shape, it was decided to heighten them, and in this way to enlarge the windows. So we are brought to the second principle of the Gothic aesthetic; after proportion, light. In the literature of the time the beauty of the object seen was constantly described as 'luminous'. For a philosopher like Grosseteste light was an 'embodied spirit', and for Dante it was *'la luce divina e penetrante per l'universo'*. These ideas gave the builders and glaziers of Sens their opportunity. The clerestory windows had originally sprung from the point of the triforium, and were very much smaller than those you see today. So the groins, with their corresponding arches, were now raised to leave room for an opening in the wall above. The oldest glass, however, dating from the end of the twelfth century shortly after the fire, can be seen in the apse; the history of St Thomas of Canterbury, the legend of St Eustace, the parable of the Prodigal Son, and the parable of the Good Samaritan. The **Becket Window** is of particular interest to the English visitor. It takes up the story from the point where Louis VII of France brings Henry and Becket together in an insincere and inconclusive peace; and shows Becket returning to England by sea, welcomed by the people of Canterbury, preaching and otherwise ministering to them, and finally murdered by the four knights. Notice here how the story is illustrated by the history of the Redemption alongside. One begins to understand St Bernard's distinction between a church designed for contemplatives and a church designed for people who could read in pictures what they were unable to read in manuscript.

The Bible was open in one way long before the Reformers opened it in another.

The higher windows in the apse trace the life of the Blessed Virgin, the scenes of the Passion, and the martyrdom of St Stephen; and in the second chapel of the apse you can read the history of St Paul. Two other windows deserve particular attention, for they are both attributed to Jean Cousin. One of them, in the south transept crossing, is strangely Pre-Raphaelite in feeling, showing the Sibyl of Timur pointing out to the Emperor Augustus the Virgin who is to give a Saviour to the world; it was pierced by a German bullet in 1814, and has been considerably restored. The other describes the legend of St Eutropus, and has now been placed in a wall of the south aisle. It dates back to 1536. Jean Cousin also painted the high altar at Sens and designed the copes of the clergy. His **Last Judgement** hangs in the Louvre.

The most recent glass in the cathedral is the work of Antoine de Soulignac, a master painter from Paris. It dates from 1646; is set in the north transept; and depicts the saintly protectors of Sens.

So much for light and colour – and it is much. Nevertheless, as you enter the church, what will strike you are its infallible proportions. There is no striving after effect; the serene harmony of mass and line is undisturbed. The eye takes in the whole before giving its attention to the separate parts. In all the French cathedrals built during the second half of the twelfth century a gallery and triforium were placed between the clerestory and the arches of the nave. But the architect of Sens was content with a 'false' triforium – openings, not a passageway, over the side aisles. This was a Burgundian innovation, of which we shall later find an example at Autun. It had the twofold effect of greatly reducing the space between the windows and the arcades, thus laying an added stress on the supports at the expense of the walls between them; and of consequently reducing the height of the building. But St Bernard, and the architects he inspired, were not primarily interested in height; they were concerned with due proportion; they were not romantic, even when they were still romanesque, and they were no more so when they developed the Gothic style. A classical precision and restraint governed all their building. At Sens the square bays of the nave have twice the width of the bays of the side aisles, and you find the same proportions in the height of both. Moreover, the raising of the nave to the point of juncture with the vaulting is sub-divided into two equal parts at the level of the arcade imposts. These mathematical calculations are very characteristic of Cistercian architecture in Burgundy. The cathedral of Sens is as easy to measure as it is to admire.

Structurally, its plan is very simple: three double bays in the nave, and two in the choir, each divided by twin round pillars, from which a thin column ascends to support the sexpartite vaulting – except in the apse, where eight ogival ribs meet in a keystone above the altar. The pillars rest on a square base, and the **Capitals** are generally decorated with conventional floral or vegetable designs. A few suggest, however, that the artists of the time took whatever opportunities they were allowed. On the last bay on the north side of the ambulatory two figures are shown digging the ground, and a man is pruning a vine while a woman picks up the branches. Above the entrance to the vestry a man on horseback is hunting a bird; possibly both these illustrate the calendar, since March is the month for pruning, and May for hunting. Above the small column of the first twin bay in the triforium at the north entrance to the choir three sides of the capital are sculpted. In front the Virgin presents the Child Jesus to Simeon, while on one side St Joseph carries the doves of the ritual offering, and on the other the angels are warning the Magi not to return to Herod. In the second bay of the north aisle we catch a head emerging from the foliage, and elsewhere the creatures, mythical or real, of the medieval bestiary – griffins and lions, winged lizards and grimacing monsters, doves reposing on an ear of maize, sparrows pecking at the corn. The best are on the joists of the ambulatory on the north side, where two lions each have their claws into a goat, and winged dragons with serpents' tails are devouring a small figure whose hair bristles under the ordeal.

The **High Altar**, designed by Servandoni, was erected in 1742; but the jasper table belonged to an altar of the four-teenth century. Against the third pillar on the north side of the nave stands the **Salazar Altar** in alabaster and black marble

(1500–15) dedicated to the memory of his parents by Archbishop Tristan de Salazar. It is all that remains of an imposing
shrine. In 1897 a statue of St Thomas of Canterbury was
discovered in the wall of a house near the cathedral, where,
according to tradition, St Thomas had stayed when he came
to Sens. It now stands under his window in the north ambulatory. In the chapel of St Colombe, at the north end of the
apse you will see the monument erected by Louis XV to the
Dauphin and his wife Marie-Josephe of Saxony. It is the work
of Guillaume Coustou the younger, and originally stood over
the tomb of the prince and his princess in the centre of the
choir; but it was saved at the Revolution, and reconstituted
in 1814. The figure of conjugal love depicts the twelve-year-old
duc de Berri, later Louis XVI. In the same chapel four alabaster bas-reliefs and a much mutilated recumbent figure have
survived the destruction of Cardinal Duprat's mausoleum.
Duprat was the minister of François I, and the bas-reliefs
represent his entry into Paris as Papal legate, his enthronement,
and his presidence over the Council of the Province of Sens
in 1532. The martyrdom of St Savinian is illustrated by a
stucco group in the chapel dedicated to him at the centre of
the apse. You should note the reredos of the Passion in the
chapel of St Martial, and particularly the statue of the Virgin
and Child over the altar in the chapel of the south transept.
Formerly gilded and coloured, this was presented to the
cathedral in 1334. The Virgin is seated on a throne, with
reliefs of the Annunciation, Visitation, and Nativity carved
on its base. Her expression is wonderfully serene, as she
contemplates the mystery of the Incarnation, abstracted in
some way from the Child whom she supports. There is no
hint of the realism so often found in popular Burgundian
treatments of the same theme.

You should on no account omit a visit to the **Treasury**.
Here are the two magnificent tapestries presented by Louis de
Bourbon, Cardinal Archbishop of Sens in 1556. The Adora-
tion of the Magi, woven in silk and gold, is evidently Flemish
in design. The donor, who stands with St Joseph on the left,
is probably Cardinal Charles de Bourbon, Archbishop of
Lyon and nephew of Philippe le Bon. The Coronation of the
Virgin shows a French influence; it has lost its border, but is

equally fine. A large hanging of Judith and Holofernes was part of the furniture with which Wolsey decorated Hampton Court, but how it came to Sens is anybody's guess. Did someone purloin it from the Field of Cloth of Gold? Was it given as a present to François I? An early fifteenth-century altar-cloth representing the Virgin and St Stephen is thought to have completed the series of tapestries – now disappeared – designed for the choir stalls in 1505, and illustrating the life of St Stephen. Sacred and secular themes mingle in the silk and linen cloths, some of great antiquity – the story of Joseph, from some Coptic studio; personages crowned with the Sassanid tiara from Iran; St Edmé's stole, and the Eucharistic vestments of St Thomas of Canterbury. There are also a number of priceless incunabula and ivories, and the Byzantine **Holy Shrine** – a miniature house with twelve panels illustrating the story of Joseph, which is continued on the roof. This was doubtless brought over from the east at the time of the Crusades. Of the gold and silver ware a silver gilt pyx of the twelfth century, which formerly hung over the high altar, is the principal relic of a collection long since dispersed.

The exterior of the church has lost something of its sobriety by the addition of side chapels – some of the nineteenth century – and the flying buttresses linking them to the main structure. The flamboyant balustrade above the Lady chapel and the elaborate northern façade – known as the **Portal of Abraham** – take us a long way from St Bernard. The door, divided by a pillar, is surmounted by seven niches – now despoiled of their statues. At the second coving of the pointed arch which frames them seven headless figures represent the tribes of Israel; and at the third are fourteen seated statues of prophets and sibyls. A highly decorated balustrade runs along the top of the arch, and across it rises a pointed gable to the level of the rose window above, crowned by a modern statue of Abraham.

The **Portal of the Western Façade** was savagely mutilated by the iconoclasts of the Revolution, but for some reason they left intact the lovely statue of St Stephen on the pier dividing the central door. The supple drapery of the dalmatic, the hair falling in cylindrical curls, the nobility of the expression, and the feet resting on an inclined plane, stamp this as a perfect

Sens Cathedral: The Choir. 'It satisfies you with the measure of due proportion.'

Pontigny: The Choir Stalls.

example of the way Gothic sculpture was beginning to emancipate itself from Byzantine formalism. In the little arcades at the right foot of the door you can recognize the Wise and Foolish Virgins, and in the spandrel above scenes from the life of St Stephen. The sculpture on the vaulting of St John's portal, giving entrance to the northern tower, dates from the end of the twelfth century and describes the history of St John the Baptist and the search for his relics. It is remarkable for its dramatic vigour and technical accomplishment. The **Portal of Notre-Dame** was carved a century later. On the base of the spandrel the Virgin's death, burial, assumption, and coronation are easily made out. The **Moses Portal** to the south transept is the most recent (1490–1500), and it lacks the flamboyance of its pair. Certain scenes from the life of the Virgin can be followed, beginning from the bottom on the right: the Annunciation, Visitation, Nativity, message to the Shepherds, Adoration of the Magi, Circumcision, and Flight into Egypt. A modern statue of Moses stands above the gable.

A word should be said about the cathedral bells. Two of them, of enormous weight and dimensions, were cast by Mongin Viard, a master foundryman of Auxerre, in 1560. Three others, cast in 1376 and 1377, still serve as chimes. You may not have the luck to hear them, but it is more than likely that organ music, live or recorded, will be playing in the cathedral when you visit it.

Next door to the cathedral, and extending its western portal, is the **Synodal Palace,** built in the second quarter of the thirteenth century. The collapse of the adjacent tower in 1268 severely damaged it, but in 1861 Viollet-le-Duc directed its restoration at the Government's expense. On the ground floor a vaulted passage leads to the palace court; four galleries occupy what used to serve as a prison, where you may still read scratched up on the walls the pathetic graffiti of those who were once interned there; a large vaulted hall with two aisles separated by pillars, which houses a museum of sculptured fragments from the cathedral; and a lower room which serves as an annexe to it. The upper floor is occupied by an immense nave of six bays, lit by lancets on the eastern side, and by much bigger windows on the west. The western façade is divided by six buttresses with statues framed in the pinnacles above them. These are modern copies. At the northern end you will notice the kneeling figure of the founding archbishop, Gautier Cornut; at the southern St Louis is shown prostrate. The original of this can be seen in the museum. The Palace is open to visitors from 10 to 12h, and 14 to 18h (or 16h in winter) every day, except Tuesday, for one hour. But you may have trouble in getting an answer to the bell.

Behind the Synodal Palace is a wide courtyard enclosed by the cathedral to the north and by the archbishop's palace to the south and east. The building which adjoins the Synodal Palace dates from 1683, but its extension was erected by Archbishop Stephen Poncher under Louis XII. Only the ground floor is original. The gateway from the rue des Déportés into the courtyard has a remarkable frieze where the executioners of St Stephen are dressed as early Renaissance knights, but where the martyr is an absentee.

Immediately opposite the cathedral are the **Halles** – a splendid example of nineteenth-century commercial architecture. Iron girders with brick infill support the two storeys of glass walls, and the interior, which has the shape of an interrupted triangle, is divided into twenty-four bays. A pair of elegant double staircases at each corner of the west side give access to the upper storey. There is nothing incongruous in the juxtaposition of cathedral and market-place, of medievalism and (relative) modernity, for each building is perfectly adapted to its purpose. But I fear for the future of the Halles if the town planners follow where London and Paris have shown the way.

The first street to your left, as you go down the Grande Rue west from the cathedral, will bring you to the **Musée Municipal.** This has a remarkable collection of Gallo-Roman antiquities. A captive Gaul with his hands tied behind his back; the torso of a recumbent woman; funerary monuments illustrating the trades of those they commemorate – the draper with his cloth, the tanner with his feet in a vat, the blacksmith's pincers, and the woodman's axe; a frieze describing the *vendange*; the figures of a mother with her two children, and of two men with a child; a young woman crucified in agony; wrestlers and disc-throwers; and, in the courtyard, the reconstruction from original materials of a mill and a Roman arch. A room is set aside for Napoleonic souvenirs; the tunic he wore on St Helena, and the hat he wore at Waterloo. Elsewhere there are curiosities – a lamb with two bodies, a lamb with two heads, and a calf with three humps on its back. The museum is open from 9 to 12h, and 14 to 18h (or 17h in winter) except on Tuesday.

Next door to the Musée is the church of **St Pierre-le-Rond.** This was recently closed for restoration, but it may well be open by the time these lines are in print. The nave and choir date from the early thirteenth century, and the Lady Chapel on the north side was built in the first years of the sixteenth century by Jean Laisne and his wife – members, no doubt, of a rising middle class. They both appear in the sculptured group of the Descent from the Cross above the altar. The side aisle, which prolongs the chapel, was built about the same time, and the five flamboyant windows that light it have beautiful glass of the period. The church has some fine sculptures; a seated Virgin in wood, and a St Anne of the fourteenth century, notable among them.

The **Musée Jean Cousin,** in a pretty Renaissance house close by, was temporarily closed when I was last in Sens. It contains souvenirs of the artist, and documents relating to the history of the city.

At the corner of the rue de la République and the rue Jean Cousin, only three minutes' walk from the Musée Municipal, is the **Maison d'Abraham** with its intricate wooden carving of the Tree of Jesse facing the angle of the two streets.

At this point you may profitably return to your car, and drive out to the suburb of **St Savinian,** where the church that bears his name is the oldest sanctuary in the city. It was rebuilt over his tomb in the eleventh century, and saved from the revolutionaries in 1793 by Simon Blanchet, who bought it and then gave it up for public worship. On a corbel of the north arcade which joins two side chapels to the transept you can read the following inscription: *Vir clarus Baldvinus et Petronilla uxor eius hanc . . .* These are the names of the founders who rebuilt the church. The crypt, also marked with inscriptions of the same period, occupies the site of the *martyrium* in the primitive basilica, and contains a stone altar stained with what is piously believed to be the martyr's blood.

Returning to the outer boulevards of the city, you should follow them to the point where they are crossed by the N.5, to Troyes and St Florentin. Turn left and almost immediately to your left again, you will find the chapel of **St John's Hospital,** which is all that remains of the abbey church built in the first half of the thirteenth century by the Canons Regular of St Augustine. Only the choir and an apsidal chapel of great elegance survive of the original building. The wall of the ambulatory is decorated with semi-circular arcading supported by little columns with foliated capitals. The triplet windows are traversed by a stone gallery – further evidence of the influence of Champagne on the Gothic architecture of northern Burgundy.

To vary your route back to Villeneuve, you can follow the N.5 for a few hundred yards until it crosses the inner ring of boulevards, turn left, and drive round the city until you reach the bridge over the island in the middle of the Yonne. Cross the river and immediately to your right you will see the church of **St Maurice,** conspicuous for its slender steeple.

Although it dates from the second half of the twelfth century, damage and restoration have considerably altered its character. It contains, however, several classified works of art; an admirable equestrian statue of St Maurice in polychrome wood (sixteenth century), and an unusual bas-relief in polychrome stone (1567), representing St Magdalen in the desert.

Now cross the second bridge and take the N.60 as far as **Paron.** Here you will find traces of the chapel of St Bond, whom legend reports to have lost his wife in the crowd at Sens and to have returned to his parents' home without her. Waking up in the middle of the night, he mistook his mother and father for his wife in bed with a lover, and promptly killed them. He subsequently took a half-burnt stick and vowed to water it until it flowered again, dipping it in the Yonne several times a day until, after seven years, it obeyed his instructions. How these performances qualified him for canonization is rather difficult to determine.

From Paron the D.72 will take you to **Etigny,** where

Catherine de Medici in 1571 treated with the rebellious
Calvinists, and persuaded them to expel their unruly mer-
cenaries from the kingdom once they had been paid. Etigny
was described as the place where '*la bique a pris le loup*'.[1] The
church stands on a high slope above the river which you can
here cross, and rejoin the N.6 only a few kilometres to the
north of Villeneuve.

## 3

The moment will now have come for you to pay your bill at
the Hotel du Dauphin and explore the eastern area of the
Senonais. The D.15, the D.27, and the N.60 will bring you to
**Villeneuve-l'Archevêque** in the valley of the Vanne – a distance
of 31 kilometres. This was founded in the twelfth century by
the Archbishop of Sens – hence no doubt its name – and it was
here that St Louis and Blanche of Castille received from the
Venetians the Crown of Thorns, for which they built the
Sainte Chapelle. The church dates from the thirteenth and
sixteenth centuries. A fine group of statues – the Virgin and
six saints – stands above the west door, and the north porch
is especially notable. Here the Coronation of the Virgin is
shown, still bearing traces of its original colour, with angels,
Apostles, and the Kings of Judah – David with his harp distinguishable among them. The interior is chiefly remarkable
for the **Sepulchre**, saved from the abbey of Vauluisant – one
of the finest of many to be seen in the province. You will find
it in the south-west corner of the church. Behind the tomb
stand the Virgin, St John, and St Mary Magdalen with a
bowl and holding a veil as if she had been wiping her eyes.
St Joseph of Arimathea and another man are realistically
dressed, with pouches at the waist, and two more figures with
graveclothes and oil jars for embalming stand by. The Crown
of Thorns lies on the ground. On the north transept wall you
should notice a Renaissance bas-relief of the mocking of
Christ, and other scenes of the Passion.

Three kilometres to the north of Villeneuve, on the D.84,

1. 'The nanny-goat has captured the wolf'. *Bique* also has the meaning
of 'hag', and the allusion may be to Catherine's unprepossessing
appearance.

you will find the **Ferme de Vaul-uisant** – in fact the remains of a former abbey – on the right hand side of the road. The abbey was destroyed at the Revolution, but the cloister is still partly intact, although its shrine is empty. The property was bought by a Polish Jew, Javalovski, and by an ironic twist of fate his descendant perished at Auschwitz. The present owner has restored the vaulting in the eighteenth-century stables, and the magnificent barn with its stone buttresses, wooden vaulting, and three lancet windows. You will admire the octagonal tower, standing apart from the other buildings; the dovecote; and the line of poplars and weeping-willows beside the stream. The château as it stands today was built in the eighteenth century, but you still enter the grounds through the original stone gateway. I found the bailiff and his young wife both informative and hospitable, and envied them their comfortable quarters.

Returning to Villeneuve – a well planned town with a straight broad road leading to the church – you may follow the D.84 and the N.5 south-east to St Florentin, a distance of 37 kilometres across the Forêt d'Othe. I picnicked here among the young beech, the birches, the tall oaks and occasional firs and heard only a single passing car during an hour's halt, while the brimstone yellow butterflies were fluttering around. At the village of Champlost, shortly before you reach St Florentin, you can turn left to Venizy and **Turny,** where a curious inscription on a pillar of the church is worth inspection.

> *Ce pilier ci pour vérité*
> *Au mois de Mars ne fault douter*
> *Fut comancé par Bôno Guise*
> *El la première pierre assise*
> *Par Edmon Girard fut dosée*
> *Et de vin tres bien arrosée*
> *En l'an de grace Jésus Xt*
> *1518*[1]

1. This pillar was truly
   Begun by Bôno Guise
   In the month of March,
   And the first stone laid down

A carving of three men may be observed at the corner of the south buttress at the west end beyond the flamboyant porch. The church is normally closed, but an enquiry at the Post Office will tell you from whom to ask the key. At **Neuvy-Sautour,** near by, the fifteenth-century church has a nave and side aisles of equal height, and windows 14 metres high in the sanctuary. Notice the very tall and heavily buttressed tower; the staircase turret, square at the bottom and cylindrical half-way up; and a pair of curved dragons on the north porch.

From here a run of 7 kilometres on the N.77 will take you to **St Florentin.** This is the Roman Castrodonum, perched on a hill above the confluence of the Armance and the Armançon; and is a favourite resort for fishermen. Two excellent cheeses are made in the locality; St Florentin and Soumaintrain. The church, begun in 1376 and finished in 1614, stands on high ground and is a good example of how the late Gothic and the Renaissance mix in northern Burgundy. Legend records that a countess of the place brought the humerus of St Florentin's right arm from the site of his martyrdom, and built a church to guard the relic. Its rebuilding in the early sixteenth century took a hundred years, and its style certainly confirms the title given it by Emile Montégut: '*Maison de plaisance de Dieu*'. It is without a steeple, and the uncompleted nave has only two bays. An attractive stone balustrade with delicate columns surrounds the choir, and there are two rood screens (1600) – one of them in the organ loft has two storeys, with the smaller pipes below. The stained glass, of the Champenois school from Troyes, describing the creation of the world, is particularly fine – some of it in grisaille, and some in brilliant colour. Notice in the Lady Chapel a statue of the Virgin and Child, where the latter is holding a bird pecking at His right hand. A tower said to have been raised by Queen Brunéhaut remains of the city's fortifications. On 1 July a bull-fight is held in the arena at St Florentin, but the killing of the bull is forbidden in these northern latitudes.

By Edmond Girard was measured
And well and truly sprinkled with wine
In the year of grace, of Jesus Christ,
1518

Now take the N.443 and turn off on the D.84 to **Seignelay** –
one of the many places in Burgundy to boast that Joan of Arc
passed through it. The détour is worth while for the sake of
the **Halles,** which are remarkable for so small a village. Then
follow the D.5 to **Pontigny** – and the heart of Cistercian
romanesque; worlds away from the flirtatious *flamboyant* of
St Florentin. Pontigny is a place with many English associa-
tions. In 1113 the land was offered to Stephen Harding, abbot
of Cîteaux, and a year later twelve monks, with Abbot Hugues
de Macon at their head, were sent to establish a foundation
on the banks of the Serein, where the soil was fallow and
suitable for cultivation. The new abbey was the second
daughter of Cîteaux. It stood at the cross-roads of three
bishoprics – Auxerre, Sens, and Langres – and of three
provinces – Auxerre, Tonnerre, and Champagne – so that it
used to be said that the abbot, three bishops, and three counts
could dine on the bridge at Pontigny without leaving their
own territories. In 1150 Thibault, count of Champagne, gave
the money for the building of a church big enough for the
growing community, and for a wall, 4 metres high, to enclose
the monastic dependencies. Several traces of this remain.
Three archbishops of Canterbury found refuge at Pontigny.
Thomas Becket, at the height of his quarrel with Henry II,
retired here in 1164, and the fasts and vigils did nothing to
modify his intransigence. He remained, a troublesome guest,
for six years. Stephen Langton, at loggerheads with King
John, stayed from 1208 till 1213; and Edmund Rich spent the
last two years of his life – 1240–42 – at Pontigny, liberally
endowed the monastery, and was buried behind the high altar.
He was afterwards canonized as St Edmé and his relics were
for a long time the object of great popular veneration – by
Cardinal Wiseman among others in more recent times.

Forty-five monasteries were founded from the abbey, but it
declined very rapidly under François I, and at the time of the
Reformation only twenty-five monks were left. These were
expelled, and the abbey was twice invaded and pillaged by
the Huguenots. The church was restored, and inappropriately
embellished, by Abbot Charles de Boucherat early in the
seventeenth century. At the Revolution the conventual
buildings were put up for sale, and the cloister demolished.

The Société Populaire de St Florentin demanded that the candelabra and the wrought iron gates before the sanctuary should be melted down for cannon; the gates were preserved, and the candelabra disappeared. The furnishings were appropriated by other churches in Burgundy and Champagne, and it was not until 1843 that Prosper Mérimée secured the preservation of the church by the State.

At this point, as we approach it down a noble avenue of limes, we encounter again the formidable spirit of St Bernard. Two schools of Burgundian romanesque must be carefully distinguished. One is the Cluniac, derived from Lombardy and well established by 1100. The other is the Cistercian, taking its name from Cîteaux, and developing its style in protest against the Cluniac elaboration. We shall discuss the characteristics of Cluniac romanesque when we meet it towards the end of our journey; meanwhile listen to St Bernard's outraged rebuke to his Cluniac brethren:

'The faithful are more engaged in admiring the beauty of the statues than in honouring the virtues of the saints. And then, instead of crowns, what you put in the church are jewelled wheels; you surround them with lamps, but they shine with the fire of their precious stones. For candelabra one sees a kind of decorated tree, heavy with metal and wrought with an extraordinary art . . . The church sparkles on every side, but the poor go hungry. The walls of the church are covered with gold, but its children go naked.

'And in the cloisters, what are these monsters doing – these horrible beauties and beautiful horrors, these disgusting apes, ferocious lions and monstrous centaurs? . . . There you have a head on several bodies, and there a body with several heads; there a quadruped with the tail of a snake, and there another that finishes up as a fish; here a beast that begins like a horse and ends up as a goat; and here a horned animal with a horse's rump. In God's name, if you are not ashamed of these idiocies, why at least are you not sorry to put yourselves to such expense?'

There was not much left of the medieval imagination by the time St Bernard had done with it; nevertheless, his eloquent diatribe gives us a clue to the austere majesty of Pontigny.

The original tower fell down in 1793 and was not replaced. The church measures 100 metres in length and 58 in width, including the transepts – nearly as broad as Notre-Dame-de Paris. There are two bays in the narthex and seven in the nave, which was the first Cistercian nave to have ogival vaulting. The roof of the aisles with their ribbed vaulting is much lower. Two rose windows give light to the transepts, and the choir, rebuilt at the beginning of the thirteenth century, has eleven chapels radiating in an elegant hexagonal from the ambulatory. It has been compared to 'a squatting mother hen with her wings outstretched to protect her brood of chickens'. The capitals are plain and spherical in the nave, and lightly sculptured in the choir. The elaborate stalls, grilles, and woodwork – all of the seventeenth century – and the organ buffet of the eighteenth alone contradict the Bernardian ideal that a church should be 'a workshop of prayer'. The cluster of chapels in the transept is particularly Cistercian; and you will notice how the wall rib, strengthening the joint of wall and vault, and the pilaster behind the colonnette of the pier, are apparent in the nave. In 1155 the rectangular pilaster was replaced by colonnettes in the western bay, the ogive altering the form of the pier. Pontigny is the only Cistercian structure in Burgundy that dates from the latter part of the twelfth century. It is still evidently a 'workshop', but one cannot help wishing that the workmen were not on strike – for it is a long time since the church was put to monastic use.

In the nineteenth century what remained of the abbey became the headquarters of a new Congregation – the Société des Pères de St Edmé. The débris had been saved by the Archbishop of Sens; the entrance porch, two pavilions, and a long hall with a loft above. One side of the cloister, adjoining the church, was restored, and the washing basin which had once stood in the middle of it became a fountain in the garden. In 1901, however, the Pères de St Edmé were dispersed by the anti-clerical legislation, and the property was acquired by the philosopher, Paul Desjardins. Every summer until 1939 he lent his prestige to the *décades* for which Pontigny became famous. It was transformed, for a few weeks, into a lay monastery of secular contemplatives where André

Gide, equivocal and charming; Charles du Bos, solemn and sympathetic; François Mauriac with his hoarse voice, and features over which every shade of thought or feeling passed like a scudding cloud; Enid Starkie flashing, as Sir Maurice Bowra put it, in 'all the colours of the Rimbaud'; Ernst Robert Curtius, Thomas Mann, and many others, were all engaged in passionate discussion. They read aloud their poetry and plays; walked and talked in the gardens, or browsed in the great library, trying to sustain a dialogue of European minds *avant le déluge*. After the war, and the death of Desjardins, the Perès de St Edmé returned to found a Franco-American college in the restored and modernized buildings, which in turn became the Seminary of the Mission de France. This was the last echo of Pontigny's supernatural vocation. The place is now under secular, though useful, auspices; and there is not even a curé in the village.

Four kilometres from Pontigny on the D.91 is **Ligny-le-Châtel**, where the two parts of the church are quite separate. It has a romanesque porch and nave, and a late fifteenth-century choir. The chapels to the north of the altar, and in the northern ambulatory, are even later. An inscription reads that to one of them '*Claude Rouget, homme devost, le premier posa la pierre sans rien débattre*'[1] in 1554. Notice the sun and moon as keystones to the vault above the high altar; and the coloured statues of the Virgin and St John.

A short drive, due south, will bring you on the same road to Chablis and the Auxerrois along the wide valley of the Serein. This is rolling country, well afforested on the upper slopes, and already on the exposed ground below them and in neat formation, what you have come to Burgundy to see and taste – the vines.

1. Claude Rouget, a devout man, was the first to lay a stone here – and there was no argument about it.

CHAPTER THREE

# The Tonnerrois and Auxerre

1

For exploring the country to the south of the Senonais the traveller cannot do better than make his headquarters at the Hotel de l'Etoile at **Chablis.** This has been in the Bergerand family since 1848, and has a deserved reputation for cuisine and hospitality. A distinguished clientèle have written their names in its *livre d'or*: Briand, who always had an *andouillette grillée* and a *petit chablis* for breakfast, and his secretary, who redressed the balance with a cup of chocolate; Herriot, who wrote that the hotel might have been in Lyon, and that he could give it no higher praise; President Doumergue, for whom 'Dieu was *bon* because he had created Berger*and*'; Millerand, Tardieu, and King Alfonso XIII of Spain. Jacques Copeau testified that he had come to dine with someone he did not know, and that they ended up by exchanging kisses. Reynaldo Hahn, the composer and friend of Proust, defined imagination, *esprit*, and above all technique, as the qualities required for the complete artist, finding them all exemplified in the cuisine of the Etoile. And Jean Cocteau, on receipt of an importunate telegram, wrote on the back of it that he had written *La Voix Humaine* in a single night while in occupation of room no. 3. Let not the visitor be deterred by these testimonials into thinking he will be fleeced. He will not need to look higher up the wine list than a *petit chablis en carafe*, and he will not get better value for his money in Burgundy.

Chablis announces from a distance of a hundred miles the glories of the Côte d'Or: the *grand crus* of a good year hold up their heads against Mersault and Montrachet. Its vineyards are the northernmost in France, with the exception of Champagne, and the smallest area producing wine of the finest quality anywhere in the world. The plateau on which they stand lies 1350 feet above sea level, and is thus exposed to frost, and even to hail, in the early spring when the grapes are ripening. For this reason the grapes are planted close to the soil to get whatever benefit they can from the moisture of the ground. The soil is quickly exhausted so that the fields have to lie fallow for certain periods, though fertilization has made these shorter than they used to be. The vines are trailed on wires that follow the contour of the slopes, and among them you will notice various heating devices to compensate for the weakness and uncertainty of the sun. But the total area of the vineyards does not exceed 1700 acres, and of these only 400 produce a wine of the first quality. With an output so restricted and vulnerable, even a good year for the Côte d'Or may be bad for Chablis; and there is no wine on the market about whose label and provenance you must be more careful.

In 1759 the Chanoine Gaudon was writing to Madame d'Espinay: 'My Chablis this year has a fine rich aroma; after it has been drunk it perfumes and charms the throat and leaves behind it a soft mushroom fragrance.' Others have compared the taste of the wine to gun-flint, and even described it as 'brutal'. Its qualities certainly derive from a bituminous flinty soil only to be found elsewhere above Kimmeridge Bay in Dorset. In a sense Chablis may claim to be a daughter rather than a distant cousin of the Côte d'Or, for it was the Cistercians of Pontigny who acquired an extensive vineyard on the terrain and cultivated it with all the experience they had brought from their mother house at Cîteaux. The vineyards are now divided into 25 communes, of which those immediately surrounding Chablis produce the best wine, all from the chardonnay grape – known here as the *beaunois*. It is classified as follows: the *grands crus*, producing not more than 1877 bottles per acre, with an alcoholic content of 11° or over; the *premier crus*, producing not more than 2170 bottles per acre, with an alcoholic content of 10.5°; simple *chablis* with a similar output, but a slightly lower alcoholic content; and *petit chablis*, where the alcoholic content need only reach 9°. The output is not restricted, and any grapes can be used so long as they come from ungrafted briars. Most chablis requires discreet sugaring, but not enough unduly to soften its dryness – or even its 'brutality'. The vineyards are co-operatively owned and worked by their proprietors.

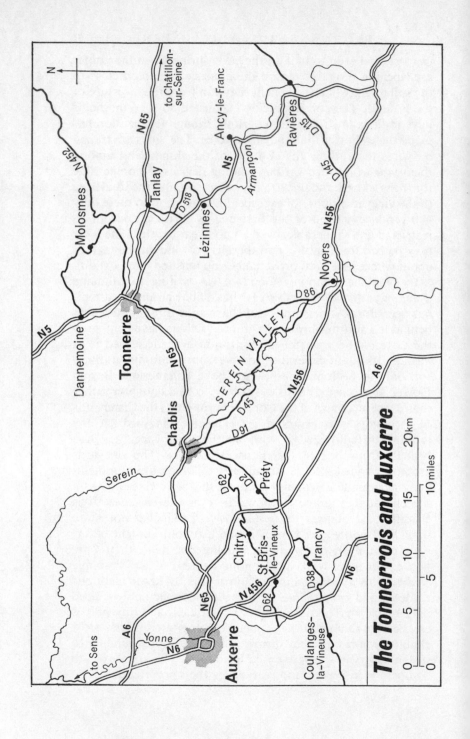

# The Tonnerrois and Auxerre

Chablis is a pleasant town entered from the road to Auxerre between two circular pepper-pot towers. The collegial **Church of St Martin** probably derived its dedication from the Abbot of St Martin's at Tours, to whom Charles the Bald, in the ninth century, made over his rights in what was then a royal vineyard. The church, begun in 1160, is one of the earliest examples of Gothic architecture in France; a replica on a reduced scale of the Cathedral at Sens. The nave has six bays, with clerestory and two side aisles; and the ambulatory recalls that of Pontigny. The horse-shoes fixed to the southern, and romanesque, porch are peculiar to churches dedicated to St Martin. They were probably ex-voto offerings in thanksgiving, or prayer, for the cure of disease to a horse, naturally addressed to St Martin, who was the patron saint of cavaliers. A large bas-relief over the west door shows him in the familiar gesture of dividing his cloak. The legend ran that Joan of Arc nailed up one of the horse-shoes as she rode through Chablis on her way to Chinon in 1429; but here it is reasonable to suppose that the wish was father to the thought. On the summit of the flying buttresses which support the apse you will notice a number of sculptured motifs; the heads of a king and a bishop, and a dragon waiting to devour the child to which a woman is about to give birth.

**Tonnerre** – the Roman Tornodorum and the chief town of a Gallic *pagus* – is reached after 16 kilometres along the N.65. Here you will notice the houses covered with *laves* – thin plaques of stone – characteristic of the Tonnerrois. The stone of the country was particularly favourable for sculpture; Claus Sluter's *Puits de Moïse* at Dijon, and the ducal tombs may well have been quarried from it. The outstanding monument of Tonnerre is the **Hôpital Notre-Dame des Fontenilles,** founded in 1293 by Marguerite de Bourgoyne, countess of Tonnerre, and sister-in-law of St Louis. The great hall, 80 metres long and 18.50 wide, is remarkable for the oak carving on the roof, and the altars at the east end indicate that this was not only an infirmary but a church. It was here, in 1542, that François I received the envoy of Charles V and the Emperor's declaration of war. Later it served as a burial ground; you will see many tombstones let into the floor, and also the ingenious gnomon, or meridian line, constructed in

1545 by the Benedictine monk and astronomer Lalande. The time of day is indicated by the sun striking the point of intersection between two thin iron bars set in the paving. Marguerite's tomb stands in the middle of the choir. In her private oratory on the right a sepulchre remarkable for its dramatic intensity was the gift of a wealthy merchant of the town, and the work of two 'ymageurs', Jehan Michiel and Georges de la Sennecte. In the side chapel to the left François Michel Le Tellier, Marquis de Louvois, the minister of Louis XIV, who acquired the *comté* of Tonnerre, is appropriately interred. A beautiful Virgin and Child in the apse, with Moses and the burning bush, should not be overlooked. The hospital was turned into a shop during the Revolution, and was the scene of a 'patriotic' banquet in 1793.

The principal **Parish Church of Notre-Dame** has an impressive tower, 40 metres high, and a stone balustrade formed out of the letters 'Jesus Maria'. The large, and smaller, west doorways were built respectively in 1536 and 1545, and the tower in 1620–2. Notice the coloured statue of St Eloi at his forge, making a chalice. The interior was badly damaged by bombardment in May 1944; and the delicate bas-reliefs of the life of the Virgin over the entrance to the church are much defaced. In the collegial **Church of St Pierre,** standing above the town, the romanesque doorway and capitals, apse of the late thirteenth century, Renaissance south front, grisaille windows of the sixteenth century, organ buffet and lectern of the seventeenth, and Jean Nicole's pulpit of the eighteenth, show a happy disregard for precedent.

There is no such mixture of style in the **Hotel d'Uzès,** now the savings bank and formerly the birthplace of the eccentric and sexually ambiguous Chevalier d'Eon (1728–1810). The façade, with its three-sided courtyard, is a gem of Renaissance architecture. Charles Geneviève Louis Auguste César Andrée Timothée Déon de Beaumont studied in Paris and was sent to Russia as a secret agent in feminine disguise to which his physique, and certain of his numerous Christian names, plausibly lent themselves. His mission to the Empress Elizabeth was so successful that on his return he was appointed secretary to the Embassy in London with the altogether simpler name of the Chevalier d'Eon and the clear declaration

View of Auxerre, with the Cathedral, and the Pont Bert over the Yonne.

Château de Tanlay: 'the most celebrated château in Burgundy and one of the most beautiful.'

Château de Tanlay: ceiling of the Tour de la Ligue.

that he was a man. Like many another diplomat he demanded more money for his expenses, and when this was refused he resigned from the service, remained in England, and announced that he had now become a woman. He was commonly supposed to be a hermaphrodite, although Versailles remembered him as a keen horseman with beard and moustache. He did, however, make a short visit to France, and confirmed his change of sex. Marie Antoinette gaily dubbed him *chevalier* with her fan, and gave him the name of her corset-maker; but the King, hearing of his intention to resume his military uniform, imprisoned him for a month at Dijon. This decided him to return to England, and disenchanted him with the *ancien régime*. He was an assiduous reader of Mirabeau and Machiavelli, and a letter offering his services to Carnot was read before the Convention, which not unnaturally regarded him as a sexual risk. He remained in England, lodging with an octogenarian friend, Mary Cole, near Westminster Bridge, and at 65 was amusing the public by fencing with an old companion in the London squares. Beaumarchais was in town when he announced his change of sex, and there seems to have been some kind of affair between them; but Charles prudently declined an offer of marriage. Eventually he returned to France, restored his property on the outskirts of Tonnerre, and – now a bent old maid – practised musketry with the neighbours. His appetite was enormous. He was known to have consumed at a single meal an entire chicken, *haricots verts*, *tarte frangipane*, fresh cream, apples, all washed down by the wine of Epineuil. He loved the *bons crus* of the Tonnerrois – '*souple et chaud*' – and boasted to have given the whole diplomatic corps a taste for them. When he died at the ripe age of 82, the doctor declared that he had 'the perfectly formed body of a man'. The Chevalier d'Eon was not a typical Burgundian, but Burgundy can claim him.

An interesting curiosity of Tonnerre is the **Fosse Dionne** (a corruption of Fosse Divine), situated on the plateau above the city. The pool, 15 metres in diameter, encloses a spring which was the only source of water supply in Gallo-Roman times. The bluish green water comes from a hollow under the rock, flows at the rate of 100 litres a second, and joins an arm of the Armançon – known as 'a bad river with good fish' – in the valley below. A trough was built around the pool in the eighteenth century.

If you call upon M. Gerard, a Knight of Malta and respected chemist of the town, he will show you something of his private excavations which date from pre-Gallo-Roman times.

Just to the north of Tonnerre, on the N.5, there is an interesting church at **Dannemoine,** with a late thirteenth-century statue of St Roch, a saint so popular in Burgundy that his legend is worth recalling. Born in Montpellier about 1356, he gave all his money to the poor and went on a pilgrimage to Rome, where he stayed for three years. He was then only seventeen. Finding the town of Acquapendente, in the Apennines, ravaged by plague, he comforted the sick and cured many of them by making the sign of the Cross over their diseased limbs. At Piacenza he was warned by an angel that he, too, would soon be stricken; and when this happened he withdrew to the solitude of a forest. An angel applied balm to the ulcer on his groin, a spring was provided to quench his thirst, and each day a dog belonging to a local lord brought him a loaf from its master's table. Roch was eventually cured, but disfigured beyond recognition, and was thrown into prison as a spy. Here, at the age of 27, he was found dead by his jailer, radiating a supernatural light. It was only in the fifteenth century, when the Council of Florence was threatened by an outbreak of plague, that his cult became widespread, although it subsided when the danger was over. Roch was canonized by Urban VIII in the seventeenth century, and two hundred years later the Burgundians invoked him once again against the phylloxera. You can recognize him in his statues by the pilgrim's cape, staff, gourd, and scrip, and by the ulcer – decorously placed, not in his groin, but on his thigh. He is sometimes shown in company with the angel who dressed his sores, and the dog who brought him bread. At **Molosmes,** five kilometres to the east of Dannemoine, the twelfth- and thirteenth-century church has been restored. St Nicholas rivalled St Roch in popularity, and here – as so often – the statue shows him with the three children.

Following the N.5 for fifteen kilometres to the south-east of Tonnerre, you come upon **Tanlay,** the most celebrated château in Burgundy and one of the most beautiful. It can be visited from Palm Sunday to All Saints Day between 9.30 and 11.30h, and 14 and 17h. In 1547 Louise de Montmorency – mother of Admiral Gaspard de Coligny, the Protestant leader assassinated in 1572 – bought the property for her fourth son, François d'Andelot, who undertook extensive work upon the *Grand Château* and started to build the *Petit Château*, which he did not live to finish. The place was a favourite rendezvous for the leaders of the Protestant faction during the wars of religion. In 1574 Anne de Coligny, daughter of François d'Andelot, married Jacques Chabot, Lieutenant-Governor of Burgundy, who built the upper part of the *Petit Château*, embellished a number of other rooms, and also built the new stables. In 1642 Tanlay was bought by Michel Particelli, superintendent of the royal exchequer and himself immensely rich. With the architect Pierre le Muet he completed the *Grand Château*. In 1704 Tanlay was sold to Jehan Thévenin and has remained in the same family ever since.

You approach it through a double avenue of elms, a mile long. The *Petit Château* is an elegant building with huge vermiculated reliefs, and its few windows deeply recessed. Those on the upper storey are framed by Corinthian pilasters surmounted by a frieze and delicate sky-light in the roof. To the right you see the quadrilateral **Stables,** which must have delighted the heart of Le Muet, for whom symmetry was the alpha and omega of architecture. You then enter the 'Cour Verte' – so called for its well-tended grass; cross the bridge over the moat, which is always full of water, between a pair of sentry-boxes crowned with obelisks; and find yourself in front of the *Grand Château*. The *cour d'honneur*, 42 metres by 32, is another imposing quadrilateral, with the arcaded wings joined to the central part by two domed turrets. Circular towers stand at each angle of the 'Cour', two of them capped by hemispherical domes. The one on the right, as you enter, contains the chapel with a *Descent from the Cross* by Perugino.

We pass inside and note the vestibule '*des Césars*', with an admirable wrought-iron grille of the sixteenth century from the abbey of Quincy; the bust of Coligny in the salon de Compagnie, and the eighteenth-century panelling; the portrait of Arnauld of Port Royal by Philippe de Champagne in the dining room, and the Pannini over the mantelpiece, a cunning exercise in perspective; the statuette of Pascal, the Jansenist crucifix, and the pair of rosewood chiffoniers in one of the bedrooms; portraits by Vigée Lebrun in the blue room; the *trompe d'œil* in the great gallery. Very evocative is the Tour de la Ligue, where the Huguenot leaders used to lay their plans. The ceiling by a Burgundian artist shows Henri II in armour with Diane de Poitiers; Catherine de Medici in the guise of Juno, and the Cardinal of Lorraine as Mercury; Admiral de Coligny as Neptune and François d'Andelot as Hercules; and the King of France as a two-faced Janus, smiling indifferently on Protestants and Catholics alike. The north façade of the *Grand Château* is generally considered le Muet's masterpiece, luxuriantly framed by the trees overhanging the moat.

A few kilometres along the D.518 bring you to Lézinnes, where you join the N.5, and it is only another ten minutes' drive to **Ancy-le-Franc**. The château is open to visitors from 1 March to 30 November, at 10h, 11h, 15h, 16h, 17h and 18h. It was built by Antoine, duc de Clermont-Tonnerre, brother-in-law of Diane de Poitiers, in 1546. The architect was an Italian, Sebastian Serlio, who had been summoned to the court of François I. Primaticcio and his pupils were responsible for much of the interior decoration. In 1683 the domain was bought by Louvois and remained in his family until the middle of the nineteenth century, when it reverted to the Clermont-Tonnerre. It is still in the possession of their descendants, who are prominent in local and public affairs. Henry IV and Louis XIII both resided here, and Louis XIV was a visitor with Louvois and Vauban. Mme de Sévigné wrote a number of her letters from a room on the first floor.

You enter the *cour d'honneur* from a noble avenue of limes. The château is a four-sided building, with pavilions and stone staircase at each angle. A stone balcony, supported by fluted columns, was built over the central doorway in 1684. The sober symmetry of the courtyard is echoed by the interior court, but here, to the north and south, arcades open on to two long galleries. Between the pilasters at ground level the proud motto of the Clermont-Tonnerre is engraved on black marble: '*Si omnes ego non*'. This borrowing from St Peter is an allusion to Comte Sibaud II de Clermont's loyalty to Pope Calixtus II during the quarrel over Investitures in the twelfth century. The interior is notable for the work of Primaticcio and his school on the floors and ceilings. You will admire particularly the hall of the Roman Emperors with its curious acoustic; the gallery of Sacrifice on the first floor, where the sacrifices of antiquity are represented *en grisaille* on the panels; the pastoral paintings by Nicolo dell 'Abbate in the cabinet of Pastor Fido; the salon in blue and gold which housed the slumbers of the *Roi Soleil*, with Louvois's motto: '*Melius frangi quam flecti*';[1] the Sèvres dinner service, presented by Charles X, in the dining room; the portrait of Henri III in the guard room, and the death-mask of Henry IV; the eight beatitudes surrounding God the Father in Meguassier's bizarre decoration for the chapel; the portrait of Louis XIII in the gallery of Pharsala, and the painted wood panelling in the *Chambre des fleurs*; the canopied bed where Louis XIII slept in the *chambre des arts*. The setting of Ancy-le-Franc has not quite the charm of Tanlay, but the bloodshot intrigues of the wars of religion haunt it hardly at all. What it revives is not the Reformation, but the Renaissance.

Continuing along the N.5 you will notice the torso of a man playing on the side of the church tower at **Fulvy**, and a little farther on the carved double doors of the church at **Ravières**. An inscription of 5 February 1701 informs you that 'a solemn service with Benediction and Exposition of the most Holy Sacrament is to be held on each of the three evenings preceding Ash Wednesday as reparation for the Carnival debauch.' At Ravières you should turn right along the D.115 to **Noyers** (14½ kilometres), where you join the valley of the Serein. The little town has a quite unusual charm with its Place de la Petite Etape aux Vins, arcades, and steeply gabled houses. The Three Estates of Burgundy used occasionally to meet here before they found a permanent home at Dijon. The church is a massive, strongly buttressed building of the early fifteenth century. Observe the much disfigured *gisant* against the wall to the right of the south door. From Noyers it is a pleasant

1. Better to be broken than to bend.

drive of 25 kilometres on the D.45, following the course of
the Serein, to Chablis between low wooded hills.

2

Auxerre is easily reached along the N.65, but you will more
pleasantly and profitably approach it by a devious route
slightly to the south. The D.62 brings you to **Préty,** a late
thirteenth-century church standing by itself in the fields with
good, though mutilated frescoes; and then, close by, to
**Chitry,** where the church, also of the thirteenth century,
adjoins the keep of the same, or an earlier, period. It contains
a superb Calvary and a number of coloured statues typical of
the popular Burgundian school. A separate tower stands on
the south side; and the situation of the church is impressive
when you see it from above with a forest of pines to your left,
and the cowslips and wild orchids in the hedgerows.

Only 4½ kilometres farther along the same road **St Bris-le-
Vineux** stands among its cherry orchards. St Bris is, in fact,
a corruption of St Prix, who was martyred in the Puisaye in
the third century. St Cot, a fellow Christian, survived the
massacre, and buried St Prix's head in an adjoining village,
where St Germain of Auxerre found it beside the body of
St Cot, and built a church at St Bris dedicated to them both.
The affix 'le-Vineux' was earned by the local vineyards. In the
church at St Bris, begun in the thirteenth century and finished
in the middle of the fifteenth, you should notice the two-
storeyed elevation with solid clerestory; the Tree of Jesse (early
sixteenth century) in the Renaissance choir, of which a copy
may be seen in Paris at the Musée des Monuments français in
the Palais de Chaillot; the tomb of St Cot, with an old
inscription above; a painted triptych of the German school;
the octagonal stone font; the statues of St Roch and the
Blessed Virgin, the second of these uncoloured and of an
impressive gravity; the elaborate wooden carving on the
doors; and especially the sixteenth-century pulpit. This has
seven facets, each with two panels, on which birds, grapes,
snails, ears of corn, a fence, a stream, a wild boar, a dog
catching a rabbit, and a man with antlers for legs, are
attractively represented. The windows are all of the sixteenth

century; St Philibert, St Reine, and St Hubert in the south aisle, St Roch, St Bond, and St Denis in the Lady Chapel. On the exterior observe the sixteenth-century stonework on the south side; the romanesque west door; and the arched flying buttresses, false chimneys, and Renaissance windows. Observe, too, the Renaissance archway to the school; and ask permission from the proprietor of the Maison Roucheron to visit his remarkable cellar with its double nave. This dates from the twelfth century.

Just south of St Bris **Irancy** is exceptional in the district for its red wine. You will rarely find this on a list outside the vicinity, but it repays attention if you happen upon a good bottle of a good year. Irancy also has a fine thirteenth-century church, of which the nave has recently been restored. This is normally closed, except in summer when a Belgian *colonie de vacances* look after it, but the key hangs on a nail by the window of the house at the corner. Irancy was the birthplace of Soufflot, the architect. **Coulanges-la-Vineuse,** a few kilometres to the east, also produces a red wine of quality, and its white is particularly rich. In the nineteenth century a local vigneron was accused of fortifying it with alcohol when he tried to sell it in Paris, and was only believed when he added to it a third quantity of water. He returned with an order for two barrels.

At St Bris-le-Vineux you join the N.456, which very quickly takes you to **Auxerre** (9 kilometres) – the Roman Autricum and capital of *basse Bourgoyne*, oddly so called since it is the northern part of the province. It had temples to Apollo and a sanctuary to the goddess Icaunia – the 'influence of the river' – naturally venerated here since the city was built on a steep hill beside the Yonne. It was a bishopric from the late third century, and by 561 had seven chapels or churches. Of those who occupied the see St Germanus (Germain) was the most celebrated, for it was he who evangelized the countryside, defeated the Saxon invaders, and ruled the diocese for eighteen years. As Pierre Grognet wrote in the sixteenth century:

*Tu as bon vin, bonne eau, bon blé, bon pain*
*Aussi tu as le corps de St Germain.*

Auxerre became a *comté* under Charlemagne, and quickly grew in importance. The twelfth-century *enceinte* of fortifications was destroyed in the eighteenth and nineteenth centuries, and replaced by boulevards; and today there is much industry on the right bank of the river where the terrain lends itself to development. Under the *ancien régime* the Corporation des Mariniers had their headquarters at Auxerre, and a statue of St Nicholas stands in a niche at the foot of the hill, overlooking the river whose traffic he was petitioned to protect.

The city has witnessed some bizarre ceremonies. In 1793 Robespierre commanded that the Fête de la Raison should be celebrated in the cathedral. The statues of St Etienne and other saints were removed, and the Fathers of the Church over the doorways decapitated. The goddess of Liberty – a certain Marie-Marguerite Duthé – was enthroned and led into the Jardins de l'Arquebuse, where three mannequins, representing Despotism, Fanaticism and Federalism, were propelled upon her and set fire to her clothes. She repelled them and pushed them into a brazier – an easy task since they were made of willow – while the cannon proclaimed her triumph. Mlle Duthé subsequently married and became the concierge of the local prison.

Alexandre Dumas describes the *Retraites Illuminées* held during the Congrès Scientifique in 1858, with an elephant in the procession:

'I then saw something extraordinary, magical, and strange. First of all, a dozen Chinese drummers, with their pointed bonnets, their drums, and their robes all illuminated. How, you may well ask? But that is something I can't explain to you. I can only tell you what I saw – transparent bonnets, transparent robes, and transparent drums. All that in motion, marching, and beating the drums amid the deepest obscurity – and the cries and bravos of 50,000 people. And observe that through it all one did not see a single candle. All the lights were invisible, and the various colours of the transparencies were marvellous. Then came the Emperor of China's chariot, a veritable pagoda rolling along with its roof lit up, and the columns and even the wheels illuminated.'

It was at Auxerre, on 17 March 1814, that Bonaparte was welcomed by the Préfet and joined by Marshal Ney. The Emperor was prepared to let bygones be bygones:

'Kiss me, my dear Marshal, I'm happy to see you and I have no need of explanations or excuses.'

Nevertheless, Ney dilated a little on the reason for his fluctuating loyalties:

'I am devoted to you, Sire, but what matters is the country – the country beyond everything else. Your Majesty may be sure that we shall support you, for one can do anything one wants with the French so long as you treat them fairly. But the time is gone by for dreaming of conquests, we must think only of France and what will make for her happiness.'

Bonaparte replied that it was for the sake of the country, and for that alone, that he had returned from Elba, and he called Ney 'the bravest of the brave'. Ney returned to Dijon with orders to lead his troops to Paris by way of Joigny and Melun. Once again, as so often through the centuries, Burgundy had become a *pays de transition*.

The sanctuary built on the site of the present **Cathedral** about 400 by St Amâtre and embellished during the following centuries was entirely destroyed in 1023. Hughes of Chalon then undertook the construction of a romanesque church, of which only the crypt remains. In 1215 Bishop Guillaume de Seignelay, captured by the Gothic fashion, started to rebuild the cathedral from top to bottom. We read in the *Gesta Pontificum* of Auxerre that 'the piety of the people far and wide waxed hot for the construction of churches'. Guillaume gave nearly 1000 livres of his private money for the work he had inspired, and his successor, Henri de Villeneuve, left an equal sum and donated the glass for the windows. Contemporaries described the church as *structuram clariorem*, in contrast to other buildings of the time. In 1217 the south tower collapsed on the Sunday before Advent in spite of warnings from a mason's apprentice, and was never rebuilt. By 1234 the apse was completed, although parts of it had to be rebuilt or restored at the end of the century. By 1400 the choir, nave, aisles and side chapels were finished, and by 1520 the cathedral stood as it does today.

Over the **Central Doorway** of the flamboyant west façade

Christ is enthroned between the Virgin and St John, and on either side of the door the wise and foolish virgins are shown, respectively, with their lamps held upright or upside down. In the niches below you may read the life of St Joseph and the parable of the Prodigal Son. The tympanum of the left doorway shows the coronation of the Virgin, and the medallions below illustrate various scenes from the book of Genesis. The doorway on the right is all of the thirteenth century, and the sculptures represent the childhood of Christ and the life of St John the Baptist. On the upper level of the base the story of David and Bathsheba is told in six scenes, and the eight statues between the gables of the trilobate arches symbolize Philosophy and the seven Liberal Arts. To the right of the doorway the judgement of Solomon is depicted in high relief. The sculpture of this façade lacks the originality of Autun, and it has been badly mutilated, but it is admirable within the conventions of medieval iconography.

The influence of Chartres and the Gothic of the Ile-de-France is still marked at Auxerre, particularly in the column flanked by four shafts, the rosette over two short lancet windows in the clerestory, and in the struts between the upper and lower courses of the flying buttresses. Structure, space, and sculptural effect are closely united. The cathedral is the work not only of believers but also of visionaries. This has rightly been described as 'diaphanous' architecture. The relationship of the support to the part supported is clearly visible, but the true function of the support is not always the same as it appears. The side aisle of the apse is an example of this illusion, where the single columns in front of the chapel each support four ribs of the vaulting, and the vaulting only *seems* to depart from the impost. Similarly, the triforium is reinforced on the rear side by heavy longitudinal arches, and the real functions of the structure are cleverly and purposely concealed. The triforium at Auxerre seems larger than at Chartres because the supports are slenderer, the arcading lighter, and the full depth of the passage is visible. The rounded, instead of square, pilaster to back the colonnettes is a Burgundian acquisition, and you may see it at Vézelay and St Seine l'Abbaye. It was developed from Soissons, where the masons of Auxerre may well have worked.

The cathedral, designed in the form of a Latin cross, measures 100 metres in length and 30 in height. The nave, built in the fourteenth century, with five lofty bays, is both shorter and higher than the nave of Sens. There are two shallow transepts; five chapels round the apse; and four on each side of the choir. The great rose window over the west door is of the sixteenth century, but the stained glass above the triforium dates from the thirteenth, although it has been considerably restored. The prevailing reds and blues of the medallions around the ambulatory, all of the thirteenth century, have a jewelled brilliance that you meet nowhere else in Burgundy except at Sens. Some are difficult to decipher, but you can pick out various scenes from Genesis, the stories of David and Joseph and the Prodigal Son, and legends of the saints. The stoning of St Stephen is described in a wood painting by Felix Chrestien, a canon of the cathedral (1543) on the left wall of the ambulatory. An inscription in the first chapel of the north aisle reads like a page out of Froissart:

> *Ici reposent les nobles et puissants*
> *Seigneurs, Claude de Beauvoir, Sire de*
> *Chastellux, Vicomte d'Avallon, Chevalier*
> *Banneret, Conseiller et Chambellan du Duc*
> *de Bourgoyne, Gouverneur du Nivernais,*
> *Lieutenant-Général du duché de Normandie,*
> *Maréchal de France, premier chanoine*
> *héréditaire de cette église, mort en 1453,*
> *et Monseigneur Guy de Beauvoir de Chastellux,*
> *Amiral de France, son frère.*

Another inscription tells us that the Maréchal acquired the right

> 'for himself and his descendants to assist at all the Offices in surplice and hood, booted, spurred, with a sword at his side and a bird on his wrist, for having generously restored to the chapter of the said church the town of Cravant, after withstanding the siege for six weeks at his own expense and having won what is called the battle of Cravant, where he took prisoner with his own hand the Constable of Scotland, general of the besieging army.'

A Renaissance sculpture in the cathedral records this

Anglo-Burgundian victory over the Franco-Scottish forces in 1423.

If you are impatient for the severity of the romanesque, the **Crypt** of Auxerre will satisfy all your longings. There is nothing finer of its kind in the province. Built between 1023 and 1030, with a nave, side aisles, and two rows of square pillars, it contains two striking frescoes, supposedly of the twelfth and thirteenth centuries. One, on the vaulting, shows Christ on a white horse escorted by four equestrian angels, and is said to be unique in the history of art. The other, in the small apse, shows Christ in majesty with seven stars, seven candelabra, and the symbols of the four evangelists. Notice the four-tiered capital on the pillar at the opening to the apsidal chapel. Bishop Humbaud (1087–1114) had the entire cathedral and crypt covered with frescoes. In the **Treasury** you may see the tunic of St Germain, a MS of Duns Scotus' *Commentaries* – here known as Jean Scott; a Bible, crucifix, and reliquaries of the thirteenth century; the first and second books of the *Sentences* of Peter Lombard – a particularly rare possession – and some fifteenth-century chasubles. Before leaving the cathedral remember that Joan of Arc prayed here on 27 February 1429 when she was on her way to meet the Dauphin at Chinon.

In the sixth century Queen Clothilde, the wife of Clovis, founded a basilica to contain the body of St Germain, and later an **Abbey** was built to protect his tomb. It is easily reached along the rue Cochois to the north of the cathedral. The choir, porch, and crypt dated from the ninth century. In the time of Charlemagne there were nearly 600 monks and more than 2000 students. It was at once a fortress and a centre of learning. The upper, and Gothic, church was raised between the thirteenth and fifteenth centuries, but a part of this collapsed during the last century with the result that the fine romanesque tower, 51 metres in height, now stands isolated from the rest of the building. Nothing remains of the abbey, which was rebuilt after the Norman invasion of 1270, but the interior of the church is beautifully proportioned, and the **Crypt** is well worth a prolonged visit under an exceptionally informative guide. Both can be visited from April to

October between 9 and 12h, and 14 and 18h (16h during the rest of the year). Closed on Tuesday.

The crypt was begun by Charles le Chauve (Charles the Bald) in 858. The capitals, Roman and Greek – and some with Egyptian and Merovingian motifs – were taken from the temple at Arles. From 860 date the two frescoes – one of St Alande (472), the other of St Sensurius (502) – which are the oldest in France, and similar to those in similar catacombs outside Rome. You can also see the Byzantine cross offered by St Clothilde, who celebrated her betrothal to Clovis in the neighbourhood of Auxerre; a Carolingian mosaic, similar to that in St Germigny-des-Près, near St Benôit-sur-Loire; and the sarcophagus of Pope Urban V, who was an abbot of St Germain. The upper church is now a museum of Burgundian art. Especially notable are statues of St Roch (1530), St Martin (late sixteenth century), a *Christ de Pitié* (sixteenth), St Antoine (early sixteenth), an early St Anne teaching the Virgin to read, the Virgin and St John from a late sixteenth-century Calvary, and a Pietà of the same period; and a twelfth-century woman holding some fruit. A painted wooden retable (Flemish) illustrates the life of the Virgin.

Important work has been carried out on the monastic buildings. The romanesque hall has been admirably restored, and fine romanesque arches leading into the chapter house from the seventeenth-century cloister were recently discovered.

The church of **St Eusèbe** is all that remains of a former priory. It has a fine romanesque tower, thirteenth-century nave with high triforium, choir of the fourteenth century, clerestory of the fifteenth, and windows of the sixteenth. Notice the large wooden crucifix in the north aisle, and in the chapel opening from the fourth bay of the south aisle a sumptuous piece of Byzantine woven material is preserved – known, apocryphally no doubt, as 'the shroud of St Germain'. The figures of St Eusèbe and St Lawrence are carved on the west doors of the church.

The abbey of **St Pierre-en-Vallée** was built during the reign of Charles IX (1560–74); an uneasy imposition of Renaissance classicism on flamboyant Gothic. The motifs on the very fine porch through which you approach the church have been much disfigured.

The **Musée Leblanc-Duvernoy**, 9 bis rue d'Egleny, contains an interesting collection of regional earthenware, some good furniture, and magnificent Beauvais tapestries of the seventeenth century. In the **Municipal Museum**, Place du Maréchal Leclerc, you may see the products of local excavations, and some paintings and sculpture. On the first floor Napoleonic souvenirs have been gathered together in the **Musée Eckmühl**. Marshal Davout, prince d'Eckmühl, was born in the Yonne.

The **Tour de l'Horloge** once formed part of the city's fortifications. It dates from the fourteenth century, and is sometimes referred to as the Tour Gaillarde after the name of the gate which it defended, and which was the principal entrance to the Gallo-Roman city. The belfry, with its seventeenth-century clock, symbolized the communal liberties granted to Auxerre by the Dukes of Burgundy. The clock has two faces, registering on one side the position of the sun and moon during the day, and the hours on the face opposite.

The Tour received an unwelcome addition when, in 1763, a young man from the Jura arrived on foot in Auxerre, became sheriff to the bailiff, and built a loggia to his house. Part of this adjoined the Tour, with a gallery and three windows and highly decorated façade. But in spite of local protests it was municipally recognized as an *'objet de l'utilité'*. 'Cadet Roussel' (1743–1807) – for as such the young man came to be known – won a certain notoriety when he substituted his own name for 'Gaspard' in an old Burgundian song. 'Gaspard' had three houses, three suits, and three locks of hair,

> *Et quand il va voir sa maitresse*
> *Il les met tous les trois en tresse.*[1]

The song spread through the armies of the Revolution from the battalion of Auxerre, and it was compared to 'a great outburst of laughter in a tragic century'. While Robespierre was addressing the Convention Danton embroidered on the theme:

---

1. And when he goes to see his mistress,
   He makes a pigtail of all three

*Cadet Roussel fait des discours*
*Qui ne sont pas longs quand ils sont courts*[1]

The point would have been well taken by an audience wearied by the *pure et dure* eloquence of Robespierre. Cadet married a Morvandelle sixteen years older than himself, and then her niece, who was twenty-three years younger. These disparities may have been responsible for an orgy, after which he was arrested, imprisoned, and subsequently released on the gounds that his 'misdemeanour might have been worse'. He died at Auxerre.

Should your tastes lie elsewhere than in architecture and antiquity, Auxerre is an excellent starting point for a short holiday on the rivers and canals of Burgundy, and its adjacent provinces. For particulars you should apply to Bases Nautour, at Auxerre (Yonne). In comfortable motor-boats of various sizes you may go down the Yonne to Paris and beyond; or up it to its junction with the Cure, and then cross the Morvan by canal, to join the Seine just below the point where the Yonne flows into it. From here you may follow the Seine upstream for as far as it is navigable. All you require is a Navigation permit, to be acquired by passing a simple test at one of the Nautour bases.

If you come to Auxerre by the N.65, or by the route that I have indicated, you will be obliged to cross the Yonne by the Pont Paul Bert, named after a citizen of the town, one of its municipal councillors after 1870, a deputy, and minister of Instruction Publique. Paul Bert (1833–86) was Professor of Zoology at the University of Bordeaux and the Sorbonne. He made a study of viruses and the effects of opium, and debated hotly with Victor Hugo on the subject of vivisection. When Hugo, who was president of the anti-vivisectionist league, called him a scoundrel, Bert replied, 'If I am a scoundrel, it is because I am too good. How would you have discovered a cure for whooping cough, if you had not practised vivisection?' He later promoted the law for primary education, compulsory and free, and for the secondary education of girls. He was opposed to capital punishment; was often regarded as a 'bear';

1. Cadet Roussel makes speeches
   Which are short when they are not long

and like Colbert gave short shrift to unexpected visitors. His family had long been established in Burgundy. Towards the end of his life he went to Indo-China on a paçifying mission and died at Hanoi.

Known to a more limited public than Bert, but not less appreciated, was the poet Marie Noel (1883–1969), also a native of Auxerre. It was she who wrote of the Yonne, as she might have written of many other rivers:

> *La rivière qui n'est jamais finie,*
> *Qui passe et ne reviendra jamais.*

# CHAPTER FOUR

# The Puisaye
# and the Châtillonais

❦

## 1

Striking westward from Auxerre you soon notice a change in the landscape. The fields are larger; the hedges have disappeared; and pasture has given place to grain. You are now on the plateau of La Puisaye, which extends to the boundary of the Nièvre. The word, probably of Celtic origin, is a corruption of *poel* (lake, swamp, or pool) and *say* (forest). It is indeed a country of vast woods and rivers – the Loing, Vrin, Ouanne, Branlin, Orcière, Agriou, and Bourdon – though none has the importance or charm of the Yonne. Colette described Puisaye as a poor district 'principally exploited by the charcoal-burners, expert at constructing the fine ricks where a vertical thread of blue smoke went up from each dome, secretly lit, in the damp mornings'. She also wrote of the 'sandpits and the red pearls of heather and juniper trees springing out of them'. In general the soil is flinty, and you will notice the isolated farms, and the number of small ponds. You must also beware of the creeping adders.

Old superstitions still linger here. By St Mary's Fountain at Mézilles, much frequented by those who hoped to obtain a cure for their animals, the pilgrims would break off pieces from the pedestal of the cross and place them in the fields to drive away the vermin. Elsewhere the parings of a sick person's nails would be stuck in the hollow of an oak; or a slice of mutton be thrown to the four corners of a patch of earth to charm away the wolves; or the peasants would walk on tracks where the grass had never grown to avoid misfortune. Colette's mother was followed in her 'victoria' for five hours by a large, grey, and evidently hungry wolf.

Take the N.65 to Auxerre and the D.89 to Aillant-sur-Tholon; then, crossing the N.455, follow the D.145 to **Villers-sur-Tholon** just beyond. The church has a *flamboyant*

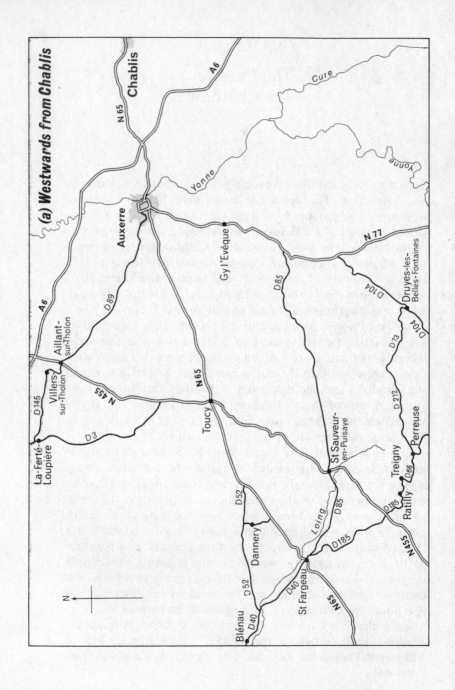

(a) Westwards from Chablis

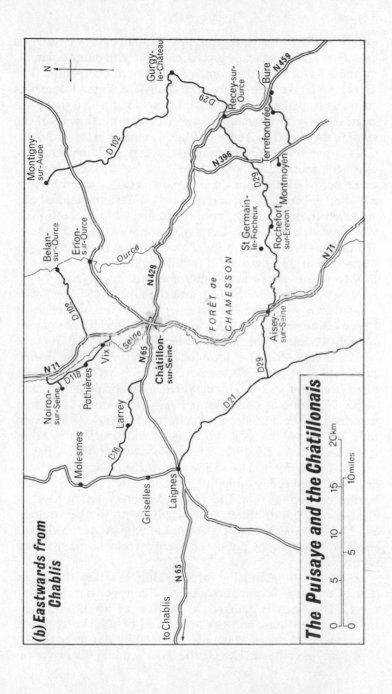

**(b) Eastwards from Chablis**

*The Puisaye and the Châtillonais*

south façade with a turret and low arcaded gallery and fluted pilasters. The west façade is classical, also with fluted columns. In the interior there are some good modern choir-stalls. The D.145 will take you to **la-Ferté-Loupière,** eight kilometres farther on, which is the excuse for so long a detour to the north-west – for the *danse macabre* on the north wall of the nave in the church is, so far as I know, unique in the province. This is a fifteenth-century fantasy, where children, citizens, cavaliers, musicians, clerks, labourers, bootmakers, a pope, an emperor, a king, a cardinal, a papal legate, an archbishop, a bishop, a hermit, a constable, a lady of fashion, and a baby snatched from its cradle, are all marshalled in procession to whatever awaits them in eternity by the walking skeletons of the dead. There is also a good wooden statue of the Virgin and Child in the south aisle, and fifteenth-century murals of St George and the Dragon, and of a saint in prayer.

Now turn south on the D.3, and then the N.455, for **Toucy** – a distance of sixteen kilometres. This was the birthplace of Pierre Larousse (1817–1875), to whom any serious student of French is bound to be indebted. He became the first director of the Ecole Primaire founded by Guizot in the town; published in 1849 his *Grammaire, Cours de Style*, and *Traité d'Analyse*; and in 1852 inaugurated a classical library, and began his famous *Dictionnaire Universel*, which has been described as 'the providence of people in a hurry'. At the same time he started to edit his educational journal: *L'Ecole Normale*. Larousse worked fifteen or sixteen hours a day – 'my brain and my heart swelling with Burgundian sap'; and if he was advised to lay off a little he replied that eternity would be time enough for that. In Paris, as a young man, he lived in a garret on a pot of butter, sent weekly by his mother, onions and bread. Sometimes in collaboration with Augustin Boyer, also a Burgundian, he published twenty works in the space of twenty years.

Toucy has an interesting fortified church, where the lower part of the nave is romanesque and the upper part Renaissance. The apse is flanked by a pair of twelfth-century crenellated bastions, and the north wall of the church is all that remains of the *enceinte*, built in 1170 by Baron Narjot II to protect his château. The Grosse Tour – much the bigger of the two – is 12.30 metres in diametre and 3 metres thick; and the Tour St Michel has a cupola on top of it. The church was burnt by the Anglo-Burgundians in 1423, which explains the rebuilding of the nave between 1536 and 1550. Here you will notice that the stone of the upper part is lighter in colour; and you will be equally struck by the forbidding darkness of the exterior walls.

You should now follow the N.455 that will bring you to **St Sauveur-en-Puisaye** (sixteen kilometres). Here you will find the birthplace of Colette (1873–1954). Let her describe it for you.

'a dark, double-fronted house, with large windows and small grace, the middle-class house of an old village, but the steep slope of the street jostled its gravity a little, and the steps up to the door went limping four on one side, six on the other. A big, serious, peevish house, where you rang the bell, as you would to an orphanage, and where the thick bolts on the door reminded you of a gaol; a house that smiled on only one side of its face.'

Since the house is now occupied by a dentist, the smile has not noticeably extended its radius. Readers of *La Maison de Claudine* will recognize the upper and lower garden, although they may regret that a swimming pool has replaced the vegetables for which Colette had so robust an appetite. Mauriac compared her to a 'fat bee', and her shade still buzzes about her birthplace. 'I should like the taste of the springs of my native country,' she wrote, 'to fill my mouth at the moment when everything comes to an end.' She was not the less Burgundian for dying in the Palais Royal, for just as Chambertin and Clos Vougeot had strengthened her health as a child, so on her eightieth birthday 100 bottles of Mersault arrived to celebrate the occasion. Before leaving St Sauveur notice the twelfth-century Saracen tower looming above the roofs of the sleepy little town which cradled so wide-awake an observer of her sex.

A short distance of eleven kilometres along the D.85 will bring you to **St Fargeau** and the château of the *Grande Mademoiselle*. Anne-Marie-Louise de Montpensier (1627–93) was the stormy, strong-minded, and somewhat masculine daughter of Gaston d'Orléans, brother to Louis XIII, and therefore a cousin of Louis XIV, whom she would have liked to marry, in default of the King of Spain, the Emperor of Austria, or Charles II of England. She joined Condé during the Fronde, and fired the cannon from the Bastille to save him – which provoked Mazarin's comment: '*Mademoiselle vient de perdre son mari.*' She presided over the Council of War at Bléneau, and rode into Orléans at the head of Condé's troops; but when he and the King were reconciled in 1652, she retired by royal command to her abandoned château at St Fargeau. It is at this point, therefore, that she crosses our itinerary. Arriving at 2 a.m., with her lady-in-waiting, *maître d'hôtel*, and six servants, she found the bridge broken down and was forced to scramble, knee deep, through the grass. Faced with the six massive circular towers, she could see only 'an old house with neither doors nor windows which filled me with dismay. They led me into a dreadful room, with an upright beam in the middle of it. Fear, horror, and grief so took possession of me that I began to cry. I considered myself most unhappy, exiled from the Court as I was, having no better residence, and realizing that *this* was the finest of all my châteaux.' Accordingly she rode off to Dannery, nine kilometres away, and returned to St Fargeau only two days later. Discontented with her room, she commandeered the bed of her steward, who must have surrendered it with reluctance since he was a newly-married man; and brought in an architect from Paris, François Le Vaux, brother of Louis Le Vaux, who had worked at Versailles and Vaux-le-Vicomte. When the place had been altered to her liking she set up a hand-press and wrote her Memoirs. 'St Fargeau,' she wrote, 'was a wild place when I came there, one could not find a herb to put in the pot.' But she planted a mall, cut away the brambles, and brought in fresh soil. From the terrace she could see the woods where she loved to ride, or to walk with her two greyhounds, La Reine and Madame Souris; there was good hunting with a pack of harriers brought from England, and she delighted in a team of cream-coloured ponies with black manes from Germany; she played battledore and shuttlecock for two hours every morning, and again after luncheon; there were picnics to the accompaniment of violins; and in the evening a troupe of actors from Lyon –

known as the '*comédiens de Mademoiselle*' – played in the private theatre. An Italian boy called Lulli came to teach her Italian, and they read Tasso together. But Lulli asked for his dismissal; he had other ideas in his head, and many years later she recognized him as a mime in the royal ballet.

The *Grande Mademoiselle* spent four years at St Fargeau, but a fire in 1752 destroyed with much else the rooms where she had received the Grand Condé, Turenne, and Mme de Sévigné. The château with its five-sided courtyard and twenty semi-circular steps leading up to the main entrance is not, however, without a certain grandeur. The twin towers – de Toucy and de Bar – were so named after the first proprietors. The original château was founded by Hérébert, Bishop of Auxerre and the natural son of Hugues Capet, elective King of France. The moat is now covered with grass and threaded by a winding path; two huge fir trees stand in the middle of it. You will notice the low box hedge starred with roses; the delicate pink colour of the brickwork, and the parc à l'anglaise, with an island in the middle of the lake, laid out by Lepeletier de Mortefontaine in 1809; the plantations of pines, oaks, and beeches; and the ivy in the form of arches trained over the long side wall. The Tour Jacques Cœur recalls that St Fargeau was bought in 1450 by Jacques Coeur with the money left over from financing Charles VII against the English. After his disgrace the property passed to Antoine de Chabannes, the former companion in arms of Joan of Arc, and subsequently to the *Grande Mademoiselle*.

St Fargeau has now passed out of private ownership, and there is not a great deal to be seen inside; but there are portraits of the *Grande Mademoiselle* and Louise de la Vallière by Mignard in the dining room, and David's *Assassination of Louis-Michel Lepeletier* is said to be walled up somewhere in the building. An engraving of this, however, has escaped destruction and can be examined in the print room. The château can be visited from 9 to 11.30h, and 14 to 18h (17h from 1 November to 31 March). It is closed on Tuesday.

The clock tower of St Fargeau in brick and stone was part of a fortified gateway (fifteenth century); and the thirteenth-century **Church** with its Gothic façade is worth a visit. Notice the very beautiful coloured Pietà, where the Virgin's ample

drapery is spattered with the fleurs-de-lys; another rather
dumpy Virgin with Child over the principal altar; the high
vaulting and low arches; and a curious holy water stoup. But
most remarkable is the late fifteenth-century wooden reredos
where the itinerary of the Passion is described with extraordinary realism, and a plastic rhythm that proclaims a
master's hand. The large central panel is occupied by the
Crucifixion. Here the luminous and contemplative face of
St John in the left hand corner stands out against the turbulent drama of the scene. The eye is led up from it to the
white neck and mane of the horse on which a bearded
officer is astride, and so along the whole length of the lance
that pierces the pale body of the Saviour to the angels who
catch His blood. It is as if the executioners of Calvary were
unconsciously pointing its significance. The lances of the
soldiery are also seen in the background coming round the
slope of the hill as, in the panels on the left, they are seen
crowding behind the kiss of Judas, and below – slanted in the
opposite direction – above the heads of the mob outside the
praetorium. In the panels on the right the lance is echoed by
the long staff with which Christ releases the souls from limbo
and, again in a different posture to balance the composition,
rises from the dead. Of all the works of art to be admired in
the churches of the Yonne this is the most elaborately
executed and conceived.

Now follow the N.65 for a short distance, and turn off on
a side road to what remains of the château of **Dannery**, where,
as we have seen, the *Grande Mademoiselle* took temporary
shelter when she found the aspect of St Fargeau too dis-
couraging. Only two of its seven towers are now standing,
but in the medieval hall you may read her motto engraved
over the fireplace: '*Ne Fay ce que tu blasme en Aultruy*' ('Don't
do yourself what you blame other people for doing') – a
counsel of perfection which few of us live up to.

From Dannery you can join the D.52 and follow it through
St Privé to **Blénau.** It was here that Turenne defeated Condé
in 1652 and saved the young Louis XIV, who escaped to the
Loire at Gien. The town has a late-twelfth-century church,
and pilgrimages to the spring of St Fort brought the lame, the
blind, the humped-back, and under-developed children.

We have not quite done with the *Grande Mademoiselle*. Follow the D.185 out of St Fargeau and thirteen kilometres will bring you to the château of **Ratilly,** where she once spent a week. This ranks high among the splendours of Burgundy. It was built in the thirteenth century of massive red stone with a deep moat, and two round pepper-pot towers, beautiful and forbidding, guard the entrance. Two others, slightly lower, stand at each corner of the quadrangle. But the interior of the château smilingly contradicts its exterior frown. The place belongs to M. and Mme Pierlot, who have turned it into a pottery with two ovens, one of wood and the other of charcoal. Pupils study here for periods of three weeks during July and August, and it is open to the public from 15 July to 14 September. There are few châteaux in Burgundy where the sense of a family, as distinct from a remote proprietor, in possession is felt so strongly. M. Pierlot was an actor of distinction before he learnt pottery from his wife. Ratilly is not easily accessible if you are without a car, but there is direct communication from Paris by bus once a week.

The church in the adjoining village of **Treigny** has been called 'the cathedral of La Puisaye'. *Flamboyant* Gothic of the fifteenth and sixteenth centuries gives an added *élan* to its immense proportions. It contains a particularly fine wooden chest, presumably for liturgical vestments, of which the side that faces you is composed of five sculptured panels, the central one of Christ crucified is a little lower than the others to make room for the lock. Joining the D.66 you come to **Perreuse,** with a number of splendid medieval houses. Notice two inscriptions: *'Rendre nous fault le compte du nos ans'*, and *'A bien faire rien craindre'*.[1] Moralizing was here evidently the fashion. A sequence of quiet roads – D.66, D.212 and D.73 – will now bring you to the impressive ruins of **Druyes-les-Belles-Fontaines.** The château – or what remains of it – dates from the twelfth century. It was the fortress home of the Courtenay, counts of Auxerre and Nevers. Here, in 1216, Pierre de Courtenay received the emissaries who had come to offer him the imperial crown of Constantinople; here, in

1. We have to account for our years.
   If one does good one has nothing to fear.

1188, he had signed the charter to enfranchise the inhabitants of Auxerre. You pass under a fortified gate of the fourteenth century, heavily machicolated, with only a single slit for window, and wearing thick tufts of greenery on the roof. The keep stands in the centre of the outer walls. On the west side nine semi-circular bays of the romanesque gallery look out over the valley, and the north-west tower, eroded with ivy, presides over the village and fortified church below.

From Druyes-les-Belles-Fontaines the D.104 will take you to its junction with the N.77, and from there it is an easy drive of 23 kilometres to Auxerre. You will pass, regretfully, the ruined church of **Gy-l'Evêque.** When this fell down in 1924 it smothered and mutilated a magnificent wooden Crucifix, with traces of blue and yellow polychrome, which was afterwards recovered and is now in private hands. A photograph in the second volume of *Trésors d'Art des Eglises de l'Yonne* shows a head of striking grandeur and gravity, and a very masculine torso beneath. One is not surprised that this Christ should have risen from the dead.

## 2

If your headquarters are still at Chablis, you may now turn east and crossing over into the Côte d'Or make for the northern part of the Châtillonais. It is 47 kilometres along the N.65 to Laignes, by way of Tonnerre – an uneventful drive, mostly through woods. **Laignes** has earned the encomium of '*beau clocher, belles filles, belles fontaines*'. The church has three romanesque naves, double transept, and sixteenth-century choir. A semi-circular tower stands flush with the gable on the north side of the irregular façade. Notice the large pool ('*belles fontaines*') in the village, and the elegant swan that animates it. At **Griselles,** three to five kilometres to the north on the N.453, the church, standing on high ground outside the village, has a pair of simple romanesque doorways (restored) and shelters the sarcophagus of St Valentine, with an inscription, in the crypt. A very old stone cross of unusual shape may be noticed in the village street. On the high ground above Vertault – the Roman Vertillum – the cellars and walls of a Celtic oppidum are well preserved; and if you enquire the way to it from a farm below, you will see more tame rabbits than you ever saw in your life.

**Molesmes,** ten kilometres farther along the same road, was an important abbey, and its dependencies, destroyed at the Revolution, are being restored. A broken arch, with a fragment of Renaissance décor, gives entrance to the space before the church, where a tall stone crucifix – very typical of the country – stands between two limes. The church is late thirteenth-century romanesque with ribbed vaulting, and lofty transept crossing and choir. It contains a fine pietà of the popular Burgundian school, and interesting statues of St Catherine and her broken wheel; a monk with bell, book, and (broken) candle, and an inexplicable pig below; a bearded and anxious St Roch, with angel and dog; a young bishop with book and crozier; and a Virgin and St Humbert on the left pillar of the transept crossing. On the right hand side of the road, as you approach Molesmes, observe the symmetrical farm buildings of Bachineul on a small rise. You will see nothing more handsome of its kind in the province.

The D.16, leading east off the N.453, will take you through **Larrey,** where the church and the château face each other on opposite hills, to the N.65 and thence to **Châtillon-sur-Seine.** This stands at the confluence of the Seine and the Douix and only ten kilometres from the boundary of the Aube. The most southerly vineyards of Champagne at Les Riceys are within easy reach. In 1186 Châtillon was besieged by Philippe Auguste and captured from Hugues III, Duke of Burgundy. Guillaume le Breton, Philippe's chaplain, celebrated the victory in an epic – *la Philippide.* This was the town:

> *Quem fluvius medium renitenti perluit unda*
> *Sequana nobilium pater instructorque virorum.*[1]

There was also a lake, or large pond, at Châtillon into which, according to legend, St Bernard plunged 'to extinguish the fire kindled in his veins by one of those faces which it is impossible to hate'. Of the fortress of the Dukes, with their war cry of 'Châtillon au noble duc', only the tour de Gissey now stands. The town had a college which the inhabitants of

1. Through the middle of which the river flows with gleaming waters – the Seine, father and teacher of noble men.

the neighbouring suburb, Chaumont, declined to support on the grounds that, although they were ignorant and unlettered, there was a writer in their street capable of teaching them all they needed to know. So much for compulsory education at Châtillon!

In February 1814 the representatives of the Allied Powers met here with the emissaries of Bonaparte, who rejected the harsh terms they offered him. Almost exactly a hundred years later, in September 1914, Joffre had his headquarters at Châtillon-sur-Seine, and it was from here that he issued his famous order before the Battle of the Marne: '*Au moment où s'engage une bataille dont dépend le salut du pays, il importe de rappeler à tous que le moment n'est plus de regarder en arrière.*' And it was near Châtillon in 1944 that the army of de Lattre de Tassigny and the Division Leclerc joined forces, with the aid of the local maquis, to expel the Germans from France. The Monument de la Forêt, fourteen kilometres south-west of the town, commemorates the 37 *résistants* who were taken prisoner here and shot after a violent skirmish on 10 September.

The **Maison Philandrier**, now a Museum, has the best collection of Gallo-Roman antiquities anywhere in Burgundy; notably the Vase de Vix. It is open from 9 to 12h, and 14 to 19h (17h in winter). The village of Vix, a few kilometres to the north-west of Châtillon, standing on a low hill, is known alternatively as Mont Saint-Michel, Mont Roussillon, or Mont Lassois. It was inhabited even in neolithic times, as you can tell from the arrow-heads, knives, and polished axes subsequently found there. But it was during the end of the first Iron Age, the sixth century BC, that it became a rich and important centre of tribal commerce. Amber from the Baltic and Adriatic, coral from the Mediterranean, Attic pottery with black figures on a red background, arms, jewels, and clasps are all to be seen in the Châtillon museum, with miscellaneous objects of daily, domestic use. In 1953 the remains of the burial tumulus were discovered, 40 metres in diameter and probably 5 or 6 metres high at its summit. Certain stones, not normally found in the vicinity, put the archaeologists on the scent, but they hardly suspected that the funeral chamber itself with its furnishings would have survived 3 metres below the ground. A wooden roof had been built above it, and upon this the tumulus had been erected. When it collapsed the objects beneath had not, of course, escaped undamaged; but at the same time the water thus allowed to penetrate had proved a factor in their preservation.

The tomb was about 3 metres square, and in the north-west corner of it stood an immense bronze vase – the **Vase di Vix** – the largest yet known from antiquity. It is 1·64 metres in height, and weighs nearly 208 kilograms. The two voluted handles enclose a Gorgon's head, and the monster's hands rest upon two serpents, themselves a prolongation of its body. A pair of smaller snakes are seen emerging from underneath the arms. The neck of the vase is adorned by a frieze where eight chariots, each followed by an armed hoplite, with helmet and breastplate, are drawn by four horses. The horses are grouped in various attitudes, and driven by a charioteer, in helmet and tunic, who must originally have held thin reins of metal, since traces of these were found. The wonderful vessel was made in a single piece, and could have held 1100 litres. It was covered by a hollow lid, still in place when it was found. The base of this was pierced with holes, like the petals of a daisy; and an umbilical cone in the centre of it supported the statuette of a woman, 19 centimetres in height, whose hieratic forms suggest the stylized simplicity of modern sculpture, and whose smile would have brought an envious frown to the Mona Lisa. The work can almost certainly be attributed to some artist in bronze from one of the Greek colonies in Southern Italy.

A silver cup was found resting on the lid, and another in ceramic with a wide black band circling the rim and the painting of warriors below. At the foot of the vase stood a bronze Etruscan wine jar. Two bronze basins with upright handles were lying along the west wall of the chamber, and a bronze basin similar to that depicted on the frieze of the Auguri tomb at Tarquinium. In the middle of the chamber was the metal framework of a funeral chariot from which the wood had perished, but a reconstructed model may be seen in the museum. It was a kind of litter on wheels, 1.40 metres long and 0.60 wide, the sides decorated with plaques of perforated bronze. Four cylindrical wooden feet allowed the coffin to be placed on the ground, and the wheels of the chariot had been dismantled when the body was interred, and ranged vertically along the east wall. The chariot was evidently drawn by hand. A skeleton was found inside, with the skull of a woman aged about thirty. The length of the skull suggested a Celtic origin. The young woman was lying on her back, and adorned with all her jewels – anklets of bronze, a bronze necklace on the abdomen, three bracelets on each wrist, and a necklace of eleven pearls – amber or polished stone – on the breast. A heavy diadem of gold, with a lion's paw at each extremity and a little winged horse attached to them, had tilted back the skull it encircled.

Such then is *La Tombe Princière de Vix*. The date of burial can be fixed with some certainty in the second half of the sixth century BC. M. René Joffroy, to whom we owe these details and conjectures, explains as follows the presence of these valuable objects, clearly of Mediterranean craftsmanship, so far north as the borders of Burgundy and Champagne.

'It seems that there existed at Vix a kind of emporium . . . where merchandise brought from far afield was traded against Greco-Italian products. One cannot help thinking of a tin market, where the raw material had made its way from the distant Cassitorites or from Cornwall. The Celtic princes, strongly established on Mont Lassois, must have levied a heavy tribute, and perhaps this enormous vase, this heavy jewel, represented an ancient duty which the Etruscan merchants were obliged to pay, when they had crossed the passes of the Julian Alps and after their passage through Switzerland had emerged on to the plateau of Langres.'[1]

Only fifteen funeral chambers of the early Iron Age have been found in France, five of them in Burgundy, and three at the foot of Mont Lassois. Also to be seen in the museum are an infant Bacchus and helmeted Minerva from Vertillum. This was in the territory of the Lingons, who occupied it between AD 100 and 300. The city was destroyed at the end of the third century, rebuilt, and finally ruined at the end of the fifth. Among the more curious objects brought away from it

1. *La Tombe Princière de Vix:* Ed de la Société Archéologique et Historique du Châtillonais: 1968.

is a plucked chicken in lead. You may linger for hours examining the objects of domestic use collected from Vix and Vertillum; pins and needles, knives and forks, candle-holders, ophthalmic instruments, the heads of snipe, and the teeth of wild boars. The latter were as familiar in Burgundy as grouse in Scotland – but what traveller had brought tales of a porpoise, and who had imaged it in bronze?

Rather improbably a portrait of the duc de Reichstadt presides over these antiquities – the gift of Marshal Marmont, duc de Raguse, who was a native of the town and is buried in the cemetery. The duc de Reichstadt is seated in an armchair contemplating the bust of the Emperor, with the following inscription from *Phèdre* below in the Marshal's handwriting:

> *Arrivé près de moi par un zèle sincère*
> *Tu me contais alors l'histoire de mon père*
> *Tu sais combien mon âme, attentive à ta voix*
> *S'echauffait au récit de ses nobles exploits.*

We shall meet other examples of Bonapartist piety before we have come to the end of our journey.

The most important church in Châtillon is **St Vorles,** a fine example of Lombard romanesque, with its square tower and very few windows, built by Bruno de Roucy, Bishop of Langres, about 980. The small apses have been lost, and the vaulting was restored in the seventeenth century, thus spoiling the proportions. Work was still going on at St Vorles when I last visited the place, and its principal treasure – an astonishing **Sepulchre** of the sixteenth century with the characters in contemporary dress – had been temporarily housed in the museum. The Virgin, St John, and St Mary Magdalen stand behind the body of Christ; figures with a headcloth and a jar of ointment stand to left and right; a man and a woman kneel a little farther away, and two soldiers are posted beyond them. One of them has his head averted, and two witnesses look on from the far background. It was at St Vorles, in an underground chapel, that St Bernard prayed before a statue of the Blessed Virgin which is said to have moved and revealed to him the mystery of the Incarnation; and here that he composed the *Salve Regina* and the *Ave Maris Stella*.

Of the once famous **Abbey of Notre-Dame** only the romanesque nave is standing, amputated of two bays and turned into a hospice. But enough is known of its history to divert the visitor. Here the licentious abbess, Rose Le Bourgeois, resisted all attempts at reformation. She kept a whipped and branded prostitute as her personal maid; lovers were admitted through a trap-door; and balls were held in the convent. At other times the community were left to starve. Equally colourful and recalcitrant was François de Bois-Robert, canon of Rouen, and Prior of La Ferté. As abbot of Notre-Dame he was conspicuous for his absence, and for activities hardly relevant to his office. He was in England for the marriage of Charles I and Henrietta Maria, and complained of the '*climat barbare*'; travelled in Italy and was given a small Breton priory by the Pope; won the favour of Richelieu, inspired the foundation of the Académie française, became one of its first members, and was appointed one of the five poets commissioned to write tragedies. Richelieu maintained him as a kind of clown; his parody of *Le Cid* was acted by lackeys and scullery boys in the presence of the cardinal. He was also a remarkable mimic. Generous in his help to other poets, he was described as a '*solliciteur des muses affligées*'. On the rare occasions when he said Mass it was claimed that his chasuble was woven out of one of Ninon d'Enclos' dresses. He seldom resided in the abbey; gambled and lost its revenues; and resigned his benefice two years before he died. But he always remained on good terms with the town. Exiled to Champagne for some peccadillo, he still could write of his '*joli Chastillon*':

> *J'y suis aimé, j'y passe pour habile,*
> *J'y suis enfin le premier de la ville.*[1]

Worth visiting is the **Church of St Jean** with an Ecce Homo of the late sixteenth century; and the **Chapel of St Thibault** (twelfth century), which belonged to the Knights Templar. Châtillon-sur-Seine has been described as a '*ville dans un parc*'. A walk along the banks of the Douix, where morsels of bread used to be thrown into the river at Candlemas, or a pause from sight-seeing in the gardens of the Hôtel de Ville

1. I'm loved there, they think I'm clever, in fact I'm the most important person in the town.

(notice the menhir preserved there), do much to confirm the description.

You would do well to spend the night at Châtillon, where they will make you comfortable at the **Sylvia**, though it has no restaurant. You can eat superlatively at the **Côte d'Or**. There is much to be seen and to enjoy in the district. North of the town the church of St Marcel at **Vix** has a double nave of the twelfth century, a choir of the fifteenth, and an attractive Virgin and Child of the fourteenth. At **Pothières,** founded in 863 by Girard de Roussillon, governor of Burgundy under Charles le Chauve, only the remains of the Abbot's house (1761) are standing. At **Noiron-sur-Seine** the batons of the Confrèries again St Nicholas on his boat – recall the activity of river commerce. Turning east along the D.102 you will come upon the flamboyant Gothic of Champagne at **Belan-sur-Ource,** and south for a mile or two on the D.13 you will find a similar style at **Brion** on the same river. At **Montigny-sur-Aube,** thirteen kilometres farther east, the church has a Renaissance façade, and a diamond-shaped chapel in the park.

To the south the **Forêt de Châtillon** opens out before you. This was cultivated in Roman times, and for long formed one of the principal centres of metallurgy in France until it was destroyed by English competition and the discovery of minerals in Lorraine. Wide glades radiate in all directions which echo in winter to the music of the chase, as the equipage of the 'Piqu'Avant-Bourgoyne', in their pale blue and scarlet, gallop in pursuit of the stag, and the hounds give cry. A straight road (D.16) crosses the forest from Châtillon in a south-easterly direction, and this is much the pleasantest route to take if you are making for Dijon. A slight deviation to your left will bring you to the ruins of the **Abbey du Val des Choux.** This was founded in 1193 by Eudes III, Duke of Burgundy, and was for a time the mother house of the Cistercian Order before its affiliation to Cîteaux. The abbey was reformed at the beginning of the seventeenth century, and both Louis XIII and Louis XIV stayed there to make retreats under the direction of the monks. Neglected now in its wild valley, it evokes a comparison with Eliot's *Little Gidding.* Two stone basins, where the pilgrims used to wash their feet, stand to right and left of the entrance.

From here you may quickly join the D.29 for **Recey-sur-Ource,** the birthplace of Henri Lacordaire (1802–61). The story of Lacordaire belongs more properly to Dijon and Flavigny, but he was baptized in the romanesque church at Recey – much altered over the centuries. The high altar and paintings came from the Chartreuse at Lugny, three kilometres to the north, founded in the twelfth century and later turned into a tile factory. Continuing south along the N.459 you come upon a cradle of the Knights Templars at **Büre,** with its thirteenth-century church. This has a double nave – something of a rarity in the Côte d'Or. You will find it in a church of the same period at **Gurgy-le-Château,** 5.5 kilometres north-east of Recey. From Büre you may turn west to the adjoining village of **Terrefondrée,** where the church has a fine porch with crenellated arcades, and thence regain the forest a little way beyond Montmoyen.

You should now turn west to **Rochefort-sur-Brevon,** with its sixteenth-century château, and **St Germain-le-Rocheux,** where traces of Roman temples and villas have been discovered. In the cemetery of the romanesque church you will notice the *pierre dépositaire* – a stone on which the coffins were laid before being carried into the church. This is the oldest and finest example of its kind in Burgundy. At **Bremur-en-Vaurois** you pass the château de Rocheprise, and then join the N.71, which is the main road to Dijon. This, as we have seen, is Templar country; the ruins of one of their chapels, and those of a ducal château, can be seen at **Aisey-sur-Seine.** The road through the Forêt de Chamesson follows the river closely and brings you back to Châtillon after fifteen kilometres.

# CHAPTER FIVE

# From Châtillon to Vézelay

✧

1

To reach the vague limits of the Auxerrois and the Avallonais there is no need to return to Chablis. Take the N.80 southward out of Châtillon as far as Puits, and then turn right along the D.101Γ to Savolsy, where there are a couple of fifteenth- and sixteenth-century churches. Continue along the D.101, D.29, D.15 and D.5D, to Asnières-en-Montagne. Here, in the farmyard of M. Abriet, you will find a fascinating agricultural museum; hoes and axes, plough and yoke; instruments for cutting potatoes, binding sheaves, slicing bark, and baking bread; spades for collecting ash from the wood fires; scythes for cutting and holding grass. The display covers one whole side of a large stone barn; and M. Abriet, if you are lucky enough to find him at home, will explain to you its mysteries. The thirteenth-century church, though unpromising from outside, has much of interest within. A St Roch, younger than usual, with the crossed keys on his hat to signify that he is on pilgrimage to Rome; a Notre-Dame de Miséricorde extending her compassion to various high ecclesiastics who, to judge from their extremely disagreeable faces, were badly in need of it; and a St Sebastian, with holes in his body and a squirrel peeping out of the tree to which he is bound.

From Asnières you cross back at once into the Yonne by the D.119, and from Nuits-des-Ravières you follow the road you have already taken in your exploration of the Tonnerrois; leaving it at Noyers for Nitry; and crossing the autoroute – which has as little to do with its immediate surroundings as a railway line – to arrive a few kilometres farther on at **Sacy**. Here is an interesting twelfth-century church and the birthplace of Nicolas Restif de la Bretonne (1734–1806). The author of 50 novels – *Le Poids de Fauchette*, *Le Paysan Perverti*, etc. – friend of Beaumarchais and Mme de Stael, he was a

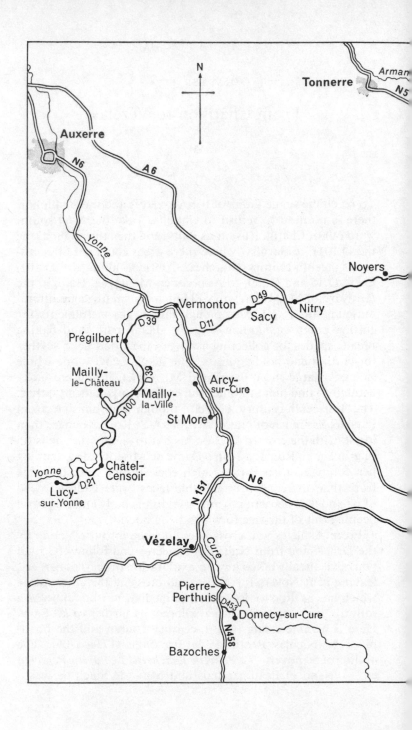

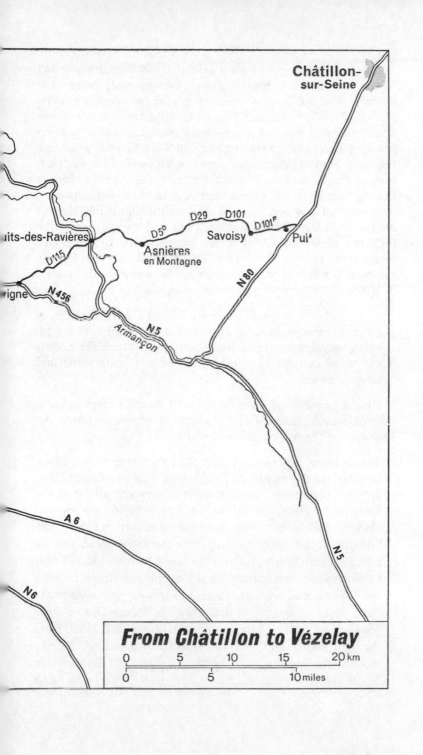

Châtillon-
sur-Seine

D29   D101
D5ᴰ        Savoisy   D101ꜰ
uits-des-Ravières              Pui⁴
Asnières
en Montagne
D115
N80
igne   N456
N5
Armançon

A6

N5

N6

N5

## From Châtillon to Vézelay

0      5      10      15      20 km
0              5              10 miles

notorious libertine who kept a calendar of his mistresses, 365 in all. One of them, Jeanette, two or three years older than himself, was the only woman of whom he admitted to be afraid. '*Tu m'agrandissais l'âme*,' he told her – for in these affairs the soul was not his primary preoccupation. Meeting her long afterwards at the cobbler's in Sacy, he nearly fainted. His matrimonial adventures were not successful. He married, first, an Englishwoman who left him, and then Agnès Lebèque, from whom he quickly separated. Insatiable in his appetites, he nourished, however, certain ideas on the higher life. He was interested in the education of children and dreamt, under the influence of Rousseau, of a new organization of society to revive the golden age. This dream was not necessarily Utopian, for he had only to remember Sacy as he had known it as a boy.

'I was born in a village where life was never worried by a master, where hunting was free for any man with a gun, where wood was common property, and where the people met to elect their syndics, tax collectors, shepherds, and schoolmasters.'

Only a single large room remains of Restif's farm at Sacy, but his recollections of the place were not rosy-tinted. An historian of the Yonne describes how:

'it was there they supped with Restif's father seated like a patriarch in the middle of 22 guests. Children, plough-boys, drovers, shepherds, and a couple of servants all sat at the same table. The father of the house was beside the fire and his wife close to him. She alone busied herself in the kitchen and served the meal. Everyone ate the same bread, for the odious distinction between white and brown – Restif tells us – was unknown in the house. The children drank nothing but water; that was the rule; and it was only when they were past the age of 40 that even the women had a little wine mixed with it. After supper the father read aloud from the Scriptures, and was respectfully listened to. During Advent he liked to sing the Noels – the old Burgundian Noels merrily sung at the corner of the fire, with their familiar, happy naiveté, and their Jesus a Jesus that simple, decent folk could recognize.'[1]

The key to the church at Sacy will be found in the village, and you should have no difficulty in tracing it. The nave of four bays has simple twelfth-century capitals, and simple transversal vaulting. The choir is later (thirteenth-century) and there is a good statue of St John the Baptist. The annual fair in May at Sacy is an occasion of much festivity, with temporary trees in the village street and coloured paper decorations.

The D.11 will bring you very quickly to the N.6, which used to take most of the traffic to the midi, and thence after two kilometres to **Vermonton.** The church was begun in 1170, and here you may detect the northern influence by the ribbed vaulting which originally covered only the nave. It is supported by alternating compound piers and twin columns. Each compartment is flanked by two arcades with a single clerestory unit above. The capitals at the east end are similar to those you will find at Sens and at St-Loup-de-Naud near Provins. The church is the only example in Burgundy of an *église-halle* – three naves of equal height.

You may now cross over to the charming valley of the Yonne and follow it to **Prégilbert,** with its isolated church, on your right as you leave the village, where the statue of St Mary Magdalen shows her carrying prisoners' chains; and on to **Mailly-le-Château,** which stands high above the river. In the thirteenth-century church with arcaded triforium you can read the story of St Adrian in rather good modern stained glass. The Stations of the Cross are also a respectable example of contemporary sculpture. The previous curé of Mailly was more adventurous in these respects than most of his colleagues in Burgundy, and perhaps more fortunate in the means at his disposal. You will do well to make the acquaintance of the present curé, Abbé Camus, who has converted a former school into a presbytery, with several furnished apartments to let. From his garden there is a magnificent view over the valley. On the west façade of the church four allegorical statues stand at the foot of the columns; they depict the Comtesse de Courtenay, a châtelaine of the district, giving freedom to the serfs. When you come down on to the river level do not pass

1. R. Vallery-Radot: *Un Coin de Bourgoyne.*

the garden of M. Max Levant without giving visible signs of your admiration. You may be invited inside and shown how a bare, precipitous slope can be transformed into a paradise of colour.

The fine romanesque basilica of **Châtel-Censoir,** a little farther on, has ribbed vaulting and transversal fan tracery. It contains a coloured statue of St Anne teaching the Virgin to read – a favourite Burgundian theme – and a Last Supper in stone, very touching in its naive realism; loaves, jugs, Paschal lamb, and the Apostles' feet under the tablecloth. In the collegiate church of St Potentien there is an admirable Flemish Crucifixion on wood, from the Antwerp school (early sixteenth century). The background is reminiscent of a Lombard or Tuscan landscape.

The romanesque church of **Lucy-sur-Yonne** close by, with its very wide tower, is rather dilapidated, but its doorway is worth attention; and just to the south of the village you will see the château of **Faulin** on the slope of a wooded hill. With its courtyard flanked by towers, this was built at the end of the fifteenth and at the beginning of the sixteenth centuries, and over the gateway you may read the inscription '*Deo conscientiae et honori 1577*'. This noble motto suggests a title of nobility, but in fact that château is now a farm. Its occupants, however, will make you welcome and show you the fine stone mullioned windows, the spiral staircase, the mantelpieces, and the gilded ribs that support the vaulting in what remains of the chapel. Faulin is on no list of advertised châteaux, but it is more lively and hospitable than many that are.

You should now retrace your steps to Mailly-la-Ville and strike east to the grottos of **Arcy-sur-Cure.** For these you will have been prepared by the cliffs of Le Saussois, towering above the Yonne, which you pass on your way to Mailly. There is here a school of *alpinisme*, as you can see for yourself from the hair-raising rehearsals on the rocks. The grottos of Arcy might have been carved by a surrealist stage designer for a production of *The Tempest*; Prospero's cave could not give a clearer intimation of magic. Discovered in 1666, but remaining closed to the public until 1903, they extend for 876 metres in a succession of halls and galleries, with a lake of

Vézelay: Eglise de la Madeleine. 'The basilica of the Madeleine at Vézelay is like an illuminated manuscript of the medieval imagination, once you have got the key to it.'

*overleaf.* Vézelay: Eglise de la Madeleine: The Tympanum: 'the grandest, the most accomplished and the most moving statuary of its time to be seen in Burgundy, or perhaps anywhere in France.'

Vase de Vix.

View of the Morvan. 'Fossils have been found in the crystalline rock, and stone tools in large quantities are proof of human occupation and industry from the end of the neolithic age.'

vivid emerald green. They were frequented for twenty years
by a singular priest, Père Lebeu, who had discovered an
auxiliary vocation in the hunting of snakes, and they were
known to Buffon in the eighteenth century. He noted 'the
representation of various kinds of animals, fruits, plants,
furniture, and implements; parts of buildings, and draperies'.
There is no trace of previous habitation. Here are what look
like the pipes of an organ, a hanging noose, a devil's mouth,
and a sheep's head. You will be shown the Hall of a Thousand
Columns, and the Hall of Waves; the wash-house of the
Fairies; drawings of mammoths; and the salle du Cheval,
where a horse seems to have been sculpted out of the rock.
The stalactites are elongated by one centimetre every hundred
years. It will take you three quarters of an hour to explore the
grotto from end to end, and to note its fantastic formations,
by the skilful and unobtrusive light of electricity. It is open
from 9 to 12h, and 14 to 18h: closed from October to Easter.
Near at hand are the grotto and fountain of St More, a
favourite quarry for sarcophagi in the high middle ages; and
the Gallo-Roman camp of Cora.

Rejoining the N.6, you leave it a little farther on and follow
the valley of the Cure until 'Vézelay rises from its luminous
hill-top, solid and authoritarian, like the country's act of
faith.'[1] The apse of the basilica has also been compared to the
prow of a great ship sailing towards the Ile de-France, and
the winds that sweep its esplanade recall 'the winds of change'
that have scarred its history. The sanctuary of St Mary
Magdalen is more than a monument or a shrine; it stands
sentinel and miiltant over the sweeping forests of the Morvan.

A monastery for women was founded here by Girard de
Roussillon – whose exploits are recorded in the *chansons de
geste* – between 855 and 859 in the valley where now stands
the village of St Père. At the same time he founded an abbey
for men at Pothières. In 863 a Bull of Pope Nicholas I placed
both houses under the protection of the Holy See. Fifteen
years later the monks had replaced the nuns at St Père, and in
887 the Normans sacked and burnt the monastery. The monks
took refuge on the top of the hill, where there were already
the remains of a Celtic oppidum, and early in the tenth century

1. Gaston Roupnel.

they began to build a monastery, dedicated to St Mary Magdalen in 1050. The rumour quickly got around that it sheltered her body, and credence was given to this by the popularity of her cult in Burgundy. Pilgrims crowded to Vézelay, but in 1279 Pope Boniface VIII declared that St Maximin in Provence possessed her mortal remains, and in Vézelay both trade and piety were the sufferers. Here St Bernard had preached the second crusade; from here the third crusade was also preached. St Thomas of Canterbury had prayed here during his seven years' exile; the roads to Jerusalem and Compostella crossed at Vézelay, and both Philippe Auguste and Richard Cœur de Lion had assembled their armies here before embarking for the Holy Land; and here, three years before his death, St Louis came for the last time to implore the intercession of St Mary Magdalen. But these memories grew dim, and Vézelay passed into eclipse. It was fruitless for Pius II to complain, in 1458, that the pilgrims were so few and the collections so small. In 1537 secular canons replaced the monks, and in 1569 Vézelay was the scene of a revolting massacre by the Huguenots. In the seventeenth century the abbey came under the authority of the Bishop of Autun, and in 1796 the monastic buildings were sold as national property and completely destroyed. Only the church remained standing. Gradually it fell into decay until, on 22 October 1819, a thunderbolt struck the west tower. When Viollet-le-Duc saw it in 1840 the great basilica was no more than a rotting corpse, and that it stands today in the radiance of its resurrection is due to him, and to him alone. Some critics will declare that he spoilt it; it should not be forgotten that he saved it.

It is built on simple lines; a nave of ten bays with perfectly rounded arches, in contrast to the slightly pointed arch characteristic of Burgundian romanesque; a very shallow south transept and narthex built a little later (1132–8); an early Gothic choir and apse (late twelfth century) supported by flying buttresses; and a Gothic pediment with windows added to the façade at the same time as the Tour de St Michel, adjoining the southern transept, was completed at the end of the twelfth century. Except for the ogival vaulting in the transept, the barrel vaulting is supported by strong ribbed

## VÉZELAY CATHEDRAL

*Capitals in the right aisle*

1 A duel. 2 Lust and despair. 3 Legend of St Hubert. 4 Sign of the Zodiac: the scales. 5 The mystic mill: (Moses and St Paul). 6 The death of Lazarus and the wicked rich man (Dives) 7 Lamech kills Cain, hidden in a bush. 8 The four winds. 9 David astride a lion. 10 St Martin brushes aside a tree that threatens to fall on him. 11 Daniel unhurt by the lions. 12 Jacob wrestles with angel. 13 Isaac blessed by Jacob.

*Capitals in the left aisle*

14 St Peter freed from prison. 15 Adam and Eve. 16 Two of the capitals illustrate the legend of St Anthony. The third represents some animals. 17 The execution of Agag. 18 Legend of St Eugénie. Thanks to a disguise, she has become the abbot of a monastery, and is afterwards accused of assaulting a woman. She opens her dress to prove her innocence. 19 Death of St Paul the Hermit. Two lions dig his grave, and St Anthony prays for him. 20 Moses and the golden calf. 21 The death of Absalom, caught by the hair in the branches of a tree, and then beheaded. 22 Two incidents in the fight between David and Goliath. 23 Moses kills the Egyptian. 24 Judith and Holofernes. 25 Slander and avarice. 26 Entry to the crypt.

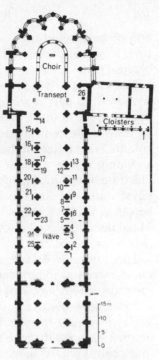

arches of alternating black and white stone. Proust, writing to a correspondent, described the church as 'a delightful Christian mosque', and thought it 'resembled a Turkish bath as much as it resembled Notre-Dame'. The arches certainly reinforce the unambiguous romanesque impression of the church, which the Gothic choir lightens but does not disturb; and they suggest that Vézelay was modelled on the Brionnais romanesque of Anzy-le-Duc rather than on Cluny. For it was an abbot from the Brionnais, Renaud de Semur, who reproduced and enlarged at Vézelay a style with which he was already familiar. The first tier of the building, that of the side aisles, is divided into bays and supported by buttresses; the second, of the nave, is strengthened by flying buttresses springing from them. The walls both of the nave and the side aisles are relieved only by windows and the cornices of the roof. Standing at the east end of the exterior you may regret that Viollet-le-Duc saw fit to build a low wall with round holes and pediments between the high lancet windows of the choir and the roof of the apsidal chapels. This robs the east end of height and breaks an organic continuity of line. The total length of the church is 393 feet, only 33 feet shorter than Notre-Dame de Paris.

The external façade is disappointing because the central spandrel is a pale reproduction of the tympanum that awaits you over the door of the narthex inside, and the stones used to restore the central and left hand portals are too light in colour. The capitals of the columns and pillars are all modern, and only faintly suggest the originals in the church which illustrate the same themes. The gable is pierced with high bays; statues of the apostles and St John the Baptist are set between them. Christ, the Blessed Virgin and St Mary Magdalen are placed above the windows in the centre with a pair of angels below.

There is some dispute about the purpose of the **Narthex.** Did it merely accommodate the pilgrims when the church was too crowded inside? Was it reserved for catechumens, or just a convenient place for liturgical processions to assemble? Today it serves the spectators of *Son et Lumière*,[1] as they start on their progress through the basilica. With its three bays and four central pillars, flanked with columns, and its three doorways leading into the church proper, the narthex at Vézelay derives a certain significance, perhaps unconscious, from the statue of St John the Baptist over the central opening. Just as he announces the advent of one greater than himself, so do the capitals on the pillars announce the greater sculpture inside, although a number of these are of considerable beauty. Notice especially St Benedict raising an infant from the dead, the hermits St Anthony and St Paul sharing a frugal meal, Joseph and Potiphar's wife, the beheading of St John the Baptist, and King David contemplating the wages of sin with the prophet Nathan.

Once inside the narthex you are transfixed by the prodigious **Tympanum** over the central doorway of the church – the grandest, the most accomplished, and the most moving statuary of its time to be seen in Burgundy, or perhaps anywhere in France. The immense elongated figure of Christ seems almost to sway upon His throne, for the multiple folds of drapery are an expression of movement as well as of

1. Every night from Pentecost to 30 September.

majesty. He is sending out His apostles on either side with a gesture of His outstretched hands; and they, too, are infinitely mobile, and maybe a little bewildered, as they clutch their scriptures and turn one to another as if in doubt how best to set about their task. Below is the fabulous world of which Othello spoke to Desdemona – cynocephalous Indians, pig-snouted Ethiopians, giants and pygmies, and Panotians with enormous ears – all derived, of course, from Herodotus. Around the central figure are the signs of the Zodiac and the labours of the months, and young men dancing in the Maytime. Beyond all this animation the eyes of Christ look out with a kind of tragic prescience on the human drama which His coming has unloosed upon mankind. They comprehend the mystery of salvation, and seem to warn us that it will not be easy.

Two smaller doorways give entrance to the church; on the right and left, under rich covings, we can follow the scenes of the Nativity and the episodes that follow the Resurrection. After taking in the graceful and grandiose proportions of the interior, you will naturally turn to the **Capitals** on the pillars of the nave. They comprise a hundred in all, evidently the work of many different hands, various in quality, illogical in sequence, and happily capricious in subject. Here in the south aisle is the education of Achilles; here on the south side of the nave is the rape of Ganymede. These recall the rediscovery of classical antiquity in the last years of the eleventh century, and remind us that Peter the Venerable, whose writings allude to it, was regent of studies at Vézelay. Of the many Biblical themes – the fall of Adam, the death of Cain, Daniel in the lions' den, David and Goliath, Judith and Holofernes – none are immediately related to the life of Christ, and none to the life of St Mary Magdalen. It was felt, apparently, that a more direct reference might detract from the tremendous figure of the tympanum, and that since the church housed the relics, if not the body, of the Magdalen these should satisfy the piety of the faithful.

One capital merits special attention; it has been called **Le Moulin Mystique**,[1] and you will find it in the south aisle. From the depth of its symbolism and its perfect workmanship it has been attributed to the sculptor of the tympanum. A

1. The Mystic Mill.

man is pouring grain into a mill while another collects the flour in his hands. The wheel, which is marked with a cross, may be taken to represent Christ, who grinds the grain of the Mosaic law into the nourishing flour of the Gospel. The first man can be identified with Moses and the second perhaps with St Paul. The intense and loving concentration of these two figures is a masterpiece of delicate imagination and sure technique. Elsewhere you will admire the four rivers of Paradise, symbolized by nude figures wearing crowns; the building of Noah's ark, with Mrs Noah looking out of the window and wondering a little, as it seems, on how seaworthy a craft she is expected to keep house and home; and the deaths of Lazarus and Dives (also in the south aisle). On the left the soul of Lazarus is borne aloft by angels; and on the right he is welcomed by Abraham under the trees of Paradise. In the centre Dives, surrounded by prostitutes, has his riches devoured by serpents and his soul wrenched out of him by demons armed with pincers – presumably red-hot. The contrast between the peace of one death and the violence of the other is naively and strikingly dramatized.

Two staircases from the transepts lead down into the large **Crypt,** divided into three aisles by two rows of thin columns. In a small 'confessional', enclosed by a grating, are preserved the relics of St Mary Magdalen. This probably dates from as early as the ninth century. A painting in the centre bay shows a seated Christ, surrounded by four coats of arms, possibly those of Blanche de Castille. The wooden figure above the altar is a much later work. The flexible floral design of the capitals has a certain similarity to those of Fontenay and Pontigny; a Gothic grace which is confirmed by the ogival vaulting of the choir, built in three storeys with a gallery between the windows and the arcades. This has double bays with a colonnette dividing them. A group of three colonnettes rests on the abacus of each base at the ground level, and ascends, their flight broken by three rings, to receive the weight of the ogives above. Here at Vézelay, as rarely elsewhere, one can say that Gothic and romanesque have met and kissed each other.

The symbolism, so marked in the *Moulin Mystique*, is stated triumphantly in the apse. The altar stands for Christ and the

eleven columns surrounding it for the eleven apostles, Judas
no longer being among them for the breaking of the bread.
On the upper storey twelve columns are grouped around the
central pillar of the triforium – Judas here represented by a
square column, the second on the right. The square was the
symbol of imperfection. The 24 aged persons whom the
Apocalypse describes as prostrated in adoration before the
throne of God are translated in eight groups of three pillars
that rise from the columns around the altar; and the 144
pillars that decorate the chapels of the choir may be compared to the multitude of the saints – twelve times the number
of the tribes of Israel. The basilica of the Madeleine at
Vézelay is like an illuminated manuscript of the medieval
imagination, once you have got the key to it; and the *Son et
Lumière* which delights the visitor (and disturbs the town) all
through the summer, with an excellent commentary by
Maurice Druon of the Académie française, will do much to
open the door for you.

Both Théodore de Bèze (1519–1605), who was born in
Vézelay, and Romain Rolland (1866–1944), who died there,
resisted the appeal of the Madeleine, though in different
ways. Bèze was converted to Protestantism and, after a short
attachment to the Lutheran reform, joined Calvin in Geneva
as professor of theology. He paid several visits to Germany,
and tried – understandably without success – to convert the
Emperor Charles V. But Catherine de Medici was prepared to
listen to him, and treated him with flattering familiarity. In
1561 he attended the Council of Poissy with twelve ministers,
and made a favourable impression on the Catholic courtiers
and clerics. An amicable discussion on the Eucharist drew
from him the declaration that 'the secret of the faith is incom-
prehensible to the senses', and from the Cardinal of Lorraine
the admission that 'I am very glad indeed to have heard you –
you will find that I am not as black as I am painted.' Bèze
signed an ambiguous document on the Eucharist, which was
disapproved of by Condé but led the King of Navarre a tiny
step farther towards the conclusion that Paris might, after all,
be worth a Mass. With his translation of the New Testament
and his history of the Reformed Churches, Bèze exercised an
emollient influence on the Reformation in France, although

it was said that without the ice-cold logic of Calvin, he would have been 'nothing better than a little seventh-rate Catullus'. Certainly the ecumenical dialogue at Poissy rings a contemporary bell, and it is not easy to imagine Calvin signing an 'ambiguous document' on any subject whatsoever. Bèze has been described as a 'Protestant Fénelon', and his mind as *'élégant et souple, subtil et passioné'*. The elders of Geneva elected him as Calvin's successor, but unlike Calvin he was not a man to be afraid of. He was buried at Vézelay; you can see the house where he was born; and a street bears his name.

Romain Rolland was born at Clamécy, only 23 kilometres away, and he belongs to Burgundy far more intimately than Bèze, for Geneva and Vézelay stand at the antipodes of Christian belief, facing each other like irreducible antagonists across the plateau of Langres. Although it was Rolland's lifelong principle that 'there is something greater than the fatherland, and that is the conscience of humanity' – a principle that cost him dear in the esteem of many of his countrymen – he remained a Burgundian to the marrow of his bones. No one, he claimed, had 'more faithfully and tenaciously sucked the teats of the same mother and nurse, the fat sweet earth of Burgundy *nivernaise*, entwined as it is in the tresses of the Beuvron and the Yonne,' – where 'at the age of 88 my father gaily watered his garden.'

'I spent my childhood in a lovable and harmonious countryside, and I still today know of none that satisfies all my senses so completely . . . the perfect harmony of its supple contours: hills and rivers, woods and meadows, the pink and white earth and its pure reflection in the water, like a beautiful naked torso under its scarf of flowering bushes; my grandfather's property at Montboulon where we used to go in summer, with the bees flying over our heads, and the organ pipes of the pines; the taste and smell of the resin, of the honey and the acacias and the warm earth. They have entered into my flesh and bones for ever.'

In 1914 Rolland declared his conviction that 'the present war is a European suicide – a crime against civilization'. He worked for the Red Cross in Switzerland, and in 1916 was awarded the Nobel Prize for the ten volumes of *Jean-Christophe*. This may have been a tribute to neutrality as well as to literature. He returned to Switzerland after the war to write his pacifist works, and in 1937 settled in Vézelay. He had found his friends among those who felt as he did – Gandhi and Tagore – and with one who did not. Yet his biography of Charles Péguy is a masterpiece of dispassionate sympathy and understanding. Towards the end of his life, he entered into a copious correspondence with Paul Claudel; and his *Voyage Intérieur* (1942) shows that Péguy and Claudel had brought him at least to the narthex of the Madeleine.

Rolland is buried in the cemetery at Vézelay, and close to him, in an obscure grave, lies one whose story will live in literature, and whose destiny was dramatically linked with that of Paul Claudel. For here rests the original of Ysé in *Partage de Midi*, buried, as it fitted her, against a flaming sky.

You will find it agreeable to wander about the streets of Vézelay, where the houses cling to the steep slopes. One of them – the fifteenth-century arcaded 'Maison des Colombes' – will attract your notice, with an inscription that may stand for many others for whom anonymity was the sign of decent living:

> *Comme Colombe humble et simple seray*
> *A mon nom mes mœurs conformeray.*[1]

2

Among the last and more striking impressions of *Son et Lumière* at Vézelay is the church of **St-Père-sous-Vézelay**, picked out by the flood-lighting in the valley. A greater contrast with the Madeleine could not be imagined. The tower, façade, first five bays of the nave, side aisles, and chapels, and upper parts of the choir, were all built in the thirteenth century; most of the narthex belongs to the fourteenth, but its pinnacles, balustrade, and terrace were added later. The lower part of the choir, apse, and adjacent chapels, although they include certain traces of an earlier period, were rebuilt in the fifteenth century. Only the short spire is modern. In the niches formed by the arcading of the west front the statue of Christ,

---

1. I shall be as humble and simple as a dove
   And my conduct shall conform to my name.

crowned by two angels, is framed by the Blessed Virgin, St
Mary Magdalen, and other saints. You will notice that Christ
has gathered the souls of the faithful in a sheet. The narthex,
completely restored by Viollet-le-Duc, has a haloed crucifix
from which the figure has disappeared, three openings into
the church, and shelters the thirteenth-century tomb of the
donors. Notice the inscription over the porch:

> *Rente n'a ne seigneurie*
> *Ne terre ne possession*
> *Car gran nomble y a de pardons*
> *D'un page et de vingt-un cardinaux*
> *Donnés aux vertueux et bons*
> *Et a tous bienfaiteurs loyaux.*[1]

At each angle of the tower an angel sounds his trumpet to the
four corners of the countryside.

The interior, with a gallery unprotected by a balustrade at
the level of the high windows, is remarkable for its purity of
style. It also contains some lively sculpture; the head of a
Negro in the nave, and in the choir the head of a miser, two
monsters devouring a pair of ears which are deaf to the
supplications of the poor, and a bag of money hanging from
the neck of a condemned man – possibly Judas Iscariot.
There is an impressive *gisant* in the north aisle, where the
patron of the knight presents the soul of his protégé to Christ
in the shape of a little child; a Carolingian font; and holy
water stoups of the fourteenth century.

Adjoining the church is the **Musée archéologique,** but
before inspecting its exhibits you will do well to examine the
site of their provenance which lies hardly more than a mile
along the road to Pierre-Perthuis at **Les Fontaines Salées.**
Mention in the local archives of a place called 'Vau Bouton'
between Pierre-Perthuis and Vézelay clearly indicated that
here was the 'Vaubeton' of the *chanson de geste* recounting
the exploits of Girard de Roussillon, and 'Valle Betun' of the

1. He has neither rents nor overlordship,
   Neither lands nor possessions.
   For a great number of pardons are given
   By a Pope and twenty-one cardinals
   To good and virtuous people,
   And to all faithful benefactors.

*Vita Gerardi Comitis*, both written in the twelfth century. Why had the medieval poet chosen this place rather than another for the site of his imaginary battle? Another name on the map, on the same road, was significant. Matrat – in old French Martray – designated a Christian cemetery, and here a number of sarcophagi had been brought to light. Had these contained the bodies of those slain in the battle? Moreover, a neighbouring field was known as *La Gotte Sang* – in other words 'the stream of blood'; and an old saying had come down through the centuries: *'En la Vau le sang a coulé'*. A thick block of sandstone was then discovered; might not this have been the 'block of marble from the steps of an ancient temple' beside which the poet had imagined Girard planting his standard? In 1934 these clues were followed up, and instead of the ruins of a château the archaeologists discovered a thermal establishment of the second century AD. The circular baths had been mistaken for the towers of a medieval fortress, and subsequent exploration took one back deep into the night of time.

Traces of a mesolithic (10,000–3000 BC) camp were found, and a necropolis from the period known as the 'Civilization of the Fields of Urns' (1200–800 BC). The latter refers to the practice of incineration and urn burial, which persisted up to the first iron age. In the second it gave way to inhumation, and was revived under the Roman occupation until the spread of Christianity finally put an end to it. Examples of funerary urns may be seen in the museum. For centuries before the Roman conquest salt water had been extracted from this terrain, and nineteen wooden vessels – reckoned to be 3000 years old – have been discovered. These were made in a single piece out of the trunk of an oak, scooped out by fire; and measured nearly four metres in height and rather more than one in diameter. They were placed in the sand where the salt water was likely to emerge, and where it was pumped out. Planks of oak, covered with stones, clay, and moss, composed more or less water-tight channels through which the liquid was drained towards the different well-heads. These springs were quickly invested with a sacred character. The Gauls believed that the divinities inhabiting them had curative powers, and in the first century BC they built a circular, open

air sanctuary in their honour – 14·50 metres in width and
93·68 metres in circumference. The essential element of a
Celtic sanctuary was not the temple but the wall enclosing the
sacred space, and separating it from unhallowed ground. In
the centre of this area was a square pool, 1·40 metre on each
side and 1·50 metre in depth, into which the water sprang
perpetually. A dyke, set 5 metres away, protected it from
impurities. The pool was originally roofed with four pillars in
support, and the whole sanctuary was shaped like a huge
wheel. It was probably dedicated to the sun god Taranis
himself.

The temple was destroyed in the second century AD, and
upon its remains the Romans built their thermal station. A
certain divinity clung to it, however, since as many as 500
coins of the fourth century had been showered into it by
pious hands.

A second sanctuary in the form of a reversed T, and like
the first of Celtic origin, measured 52 metres from north to
south and 21 metres from east to west. An oblong vestibule,
built in the second century, was added to the façade, and a
portico gave access to the sacred enclosure, which was set at a
slightly lower level. In its hollow was the pool, 13 metres
square, where the druids officiated and the sick came to be
cured. Many ex-voto offerings in the shape of limbs and
members were found there. The whole ensemble was destroyed
during the German invasions of the third century, and the
pool became nothing more than a patch of marshy ground
where the local inhabitants still came for their supplies of
salt water.

It was to Petronius Arbiter that we owe the cynical couplet:

> *Balnea, vina, Venus corrumpunt corpora nostra*
> *Et vitam faciunt, balnea, vina, Venus.*[1]

Martial has told us that with the Romans bathing was 'the
occupation of every hour and every moment'. They bathed in
the morning, the afternoon, and often at night. Already in the
first century AD a thermal station was built close to the Celtic

1. Baths, wine, and love corrupt our bodies
   And baths, wine, and love make life worth living.

temples, and very soon the druidical enclosures were put to secular and luxurious use. You may still see the outline of the circular cloak-room; the *frigidarium* for cold baths; the *tepidarium* for warm baths; the *calefactorium* for hot baths; and the *laconicum* for steam baths. The women's pool was discovered intact with seventy-two piles of bricks to support the floor; and here were found a number of objects serving hygienic or decorative purposes – brooches, needles, combs and hairpins, the keys to beauty cases, and particularly a bronze-enamelled clasp representing a wild duck. Examples of all these are shown in the Musée archéologique; they suggest how inventively the Roman lady of fashion could waste her time.

In the garden of the museum the fragment of a pillar dedicated to four divinities stands under the staircase; and in the vestibule a Gallo-Roman flour-mill – not remotely '*mystique*'. Elsewhere a marble head of Aphrodite (first century BC); an Etruscan statuette in bronze of a naked man (seventh century BC), his virility strongly emphasized; a bronze with the head of a panther from the circular temple at Fontaines-Salées; coins, ceramics, intaglios, funeral urns, and Carolingian vases; a dog with a bone between his paws serving as the handle to a knife; pottery of the first and second centuries with the mark of the makers – Germanus, Januarius, Vitalis; mosaics and a ram's head in stone from Quarré-les-Tombes; triangular ex-voto amulets, schematizing the female sex; a Christ in majesty and a Saint James of Compostella, both of the thirteenth century, from St-Père; the clasp in enamelled bronze of a sea horse, and a pair of others in the same material representing a tortoise (third century AD) from Fontaines-Salées; and a stone statue of St Peter, seated and wearing the tiara (sixteenth century) are among the exhibits which should not be overlooked. A model of the excavations illustrates more clearly than a visit the chequered history of a site which is not at all times open to inspection. The distance from Vézelay to Fontaines-Salées is short in one way, long in another; the pagan and the Christian centuries lie between them.

The museum is open from 9 to 12h and 14 to 19h. It is closed from 20 December to 20 February, and on Thursday from 1 September to 31 March. The same ticket is valid for the excavations.

3

A few kilometres along the road from Pierre-Perthuis on the D.453 brings us to the picturesque, but now dilapidated, fifteenth-century *manoir* of **Domecy-sur-Cure.** Its desolation is contradicted by the prosperous farm adjoining, but a little of its former elegance may be deduced from the round pointed towers at each angle of the building. Rejoining the N.458 we find outselves at the gates of Vauban's château at **Bazoches.** Sébastian le Prestre, known to posterity as the Marquis de Vauban (1633–1707), has a unique place in the history of military science. Orphaned when he was still a boy, and a child of the *petite noblesse*, he was born a little farther to the east at a village, St Léger-de-Foucheret, which now bears his name. Meeting Condé, who was passing through the district, he enrolled at seventeen in the army of the Fronde; was taken prisoner; and then entered the service of Louis XIV. He changed his name to Vauban after some land belonging to his family, and in 1675 acquired, and reconstructed, the château of Bazoches. Three years later he was appointed *Commissaire Général des Fortifications*, and as a military architect he had no rival, covering the frontiers with a chain of fortresses from Lille in the north to Montlouis in the south. Such leisure as he found from these defensive measures he devoted to civic works. He built the canal at St Omer, improved the harbours at Dunkirk and Antibes, constructed the aqueduct at Maintenon and the jetty at Harfleur, and laid plans for joining the Saône and the Loire. In 1703 he was created a Marshal of France.

A Catholic who made no secret of his beliefs, Vauban was still revolted by the Revocation of the Edict of Nantes – for he held that religion was a personal affair and that every man's conscience was his own – and he was alarmed by the passing of so many military secrets with the Protestants who had fled abroad. He was the friend of Fénelon and openly supported him against Bossuet. But here, at Bazoches, where he spent so much of his time with his wife, sister, and two daughters, and where enough remains of the thirteenth-century château to remind us that this was a soldier's home, we meet him in the landscape of the country that he knew so well. Experience had taught him that the pastures of the Morvan were better for sheep than for cattle; that donkeys went better than horses on the rocky paths; that birds were useful to the farmer, even if they preyed upon the grapes and cherries; that rivers were the best means of transporting timber; and that chestnuts should not be left lying on the ground. He could always recognize a burgundy, although he never drank it beyond 'honourable measure'; and it was another great Burgundian soldier, Carnot, who sang his praises before the Académie de Dijon:

'Vauban's principal care was always the preservation of his men. This kindness of heart, so characteristic of him, impregnated all his maxims and ideas. He could not bear buildings to be destroyed, or the house of a besieged town to be fired upon. He liked to speak of the fortresses he designed because they helped, more than anything else, to spare his troops in concealing them from the view of the enemy.'

Saint-Simon, whose pen usually preferred vinegar to honey, describes him as a man 'of medium height, a little squat, looking like a soldier, but at the same time rough and coarse in appearance, not to say brutal and fierce. In fact, he was nothing of the kind. No man was ever more gentle, compassionate, obliging, and respectful. There was no limit to his courtesy, and no one treated the lives of his men with a stricter economy, bravely on occasion taking every risk upon himself and giving every credit to other people.'

The château may be visited from the outside on Monday and Friday from 15 to 18h, throughout July and August and until 15 September. It stands behind a moat and is built round an irregular court. Vauban's study was in the square tower, and all along the south front are the windows of the offices where he had his assistants at work. Horsemen stood ready at the gate to take his plans to the four corners of the kingdom. The old Roman road runs along the north of the château under an avenue of trees; and a pretty rectangular lake, bordered with stone ornaments, occupies the centre of the outer court. A bust of Vauban is set outside the church in the village, and he is buried in the transept chapel under the simple inscription: '*Ici repose le Maréchal de Vauban*'. In 1805 Napoleon had his heart transferred to the chapel of the Invalides, where his monument faces that of Turenne.

Having now set foot in the Morvan, just across the border of the Nièvre, you will be in no hurry to leave it. But further exploration must wait a little, and you will do better to return to Vézelay, where the Lion d'Or will give you all the hospitality you require at a fairly reasonable cost.

CHAPTER SIX

# The Avallonais and the Morvan

## 1

Avallon does not belie the beauty of its name, but to explore the town and the surrounding district you will do better to stay a little outside. Here you have the choice of two delightful hotels in the wooded valley of the Cousin: the Moulin des Ruats and the Moulin des Templiers. The former is renowned and expensive; the latter more modest, and not less charming. It stands among its trees, and there is little question that the trout have been caught near by. If you come here in April the valley will look very much as Stephen Gwynn described it, whether you enter it from Pontaubert or from Avallon itself.

> 'Up the valley, where the road got finally clear of houses, the gorge turned, and steep above me ran a great cliff of mingled wooding, lit with the flames of spring; and through the green and silver-grey and olive were many cherry-trees in blossom, shell-white and diaphanous, most aerial of all flowering things. Broom was bright too on the slopes, and I walked along in a maze of beauty and strangeness; for the gorge narrowed still closer, crags of granite stood out fantastically from the trees, giant rocks were tumbled in heaps: a Salvator Rosa country in the very heart of France.'[1]

You will find **Pontaubert** about ten kilometres along the road from Vézelay (N.457). It was so called after the first bridge built by Aubert, brother of Robert le Fort, Count of Avallon. A cross with the Virgin and Child on one side and a crucified figure on the other stands between pleached limes in front of the church, built by the Knights of Malta in 1160 and contemporaneous with the choir at Vézelay. The lower part of the tower is romanesque, the upper thirteenth century;

1. *In Praise of France*, 1927, p. 7.

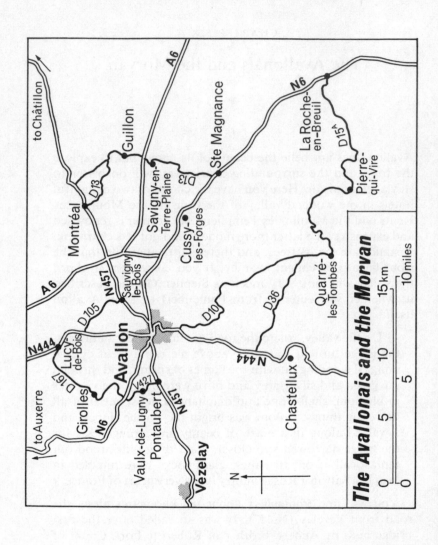

## The Avallonais and the Morvan

to Châtillon

A6

N6

Guillon

La Roche-en-Breuil

D15ᴬ

Montréal

D13

Savigny-en-Terre-Plaine

Ste Magnance

D13

Pierre-qui-Vire

A6

N457

Savigny-le-Bois

Cussy-les-Forges

D105

Avallon

D10

Quarré-les-Tombes

D36

N444

N444

Lucy-de-Bois

D167

V427

N444

Chastellux

to Auxerre

Girolles

N6

Vaulx-de-Lugny

Pontaubert

N451

Vézelay

N

0        5        10miles

0      5      10      15km

and the Virgin sits crowned between angels and Magi on the tympanum. The interior has a nave with five bays and side aisles, lancet windows, and barrel vaulting. Notice the polychrome statue in stone of St Barbe (late fifteenth century), a slightly less perfect version of the St Barbe at Autun, and its typically Burgundian drapery; the painted wooden crucifix with the figures of the Virgin and St John, and their gently expressive faces; and the stone seated statue of Notre-Dame-du-Saulce-d'Island on the north side of the sanctuary.

At Avallon, as at Vézelay, you are on the very edge of the Morvan, much of which lies outside the three departments to which I have decided to confine this survey, although we shall be skirting it continually as we go south and west. To reach the **Château de Chastellux** – ten kilometres along the N.444 directly south of Avallon – it is not necessary to leave the Yonne. Pause for a moment on the bridge which crosses the upper, and now turbulent, waters of the Cure, and there on a peak of granitic rock you will see the west façade of the château standing up before you. With its walled terrace for pedestal and its roofs and towers in dramatic profile against the sky, it appears almost exactly as a horseman riding over that bridge might have seen it in the fifteenth century. The oldest of the four towers (Saint-Jean) dates from the end of the eleventh century, 41 metres in diameter with walls 11 metres thick. It is connected with the rest of the building by a courtyard. The square crenellated clock-tower on your right is of the fifteenth century, and the round Tour d'Amboise on your left was built in 1592. To the south you see the pointed roofs of the Tour de l'Hermitage and the Tour des Archives, both of the fifteenth century. This was the feudal home of the Maréchal de Chastellux, whose tomb we visited in Auxerre. It now belongs to the duc de Duras, and it is not open to the public; but a view, no matter how distant, of the exterior is not to be missed.

The family of de Chastellux have not ceased to deserve well of Church as well as State. In 1850 they gave to Père Muard the property on which now stands the Benedictine abbey of **Pierre-qui-Vire.** This takes its name from a huge block of granite on a spur of rock overlooking the steep wooded banks of the Trinquelin, about 25 kilometres to the east of Chastellux. The rock does actually turn at a comparatively light touch without falling on the inquisitive tourist or into the river below. The abbey is best approached on the D.36 by way of **Quarré-les-Tombes** – where more than 100 sarcophagi of disputed origin surround the fifteenth-century church – and then by the V.15 leading out of St Léger-Vauban. The buildings of Pierre-qui-Vire, which is a school as well as a monastery, are all modern and have no great interest in themselves; but the place is an important cultural centre. Its illustrated studies of romanesque architecture in France are essential for a serious study of the subject, and whatever other reading matter you may bring to Burgundy, *Bourgoyne Romane* should never be far from your hand. It is the monks from Pierre-qui-Vire who have re-animated the church of St Bênoit-sur-Loire.

There is a certain contrast between their sophisticated erudition and the ancient superstitions which still linger in the Morvan. On Shrove Tuesday bouillon is sprinkled on the houses to charm away the snakes, and the adage runs:

> *Sarpant, sarpant, vai-t-en*
> *Vouéchi le bouillon de Carmentran.*[1]

Here, as you look out from Pierre-qui-Vire, is *'l'horizon qui toujours finit et recommence'* and it extends deep into the Saône-et-Loire. The greater part of the Morvan is a regional *'parc'*, and this protects its wild and varied beauty. For those whose energies decline the stiffer challenges of mountaineering it is ideal walking country, for the hills never exceed a height of 3000 feet. Hostels, strategically placed, give adequate and cheap accommodation. The rivers are suitable for canoeing, and the lakes for sailing. The Lac de St Agnan (190 hectares) just south of Pierre-qui-Vire, receives the upper waters of the Cousin, and the Lac du Crescent (138 hectares) stretches immediately below Chastellux. The Morvan is a land of granite, swept by the north wind – the *vent de galarne* – and the pasturing is poor. The sheep are sent to the Auxois for fattening, and the cattle to the Charolais. The children are often dependent on public assistance, and Morvandelle

1. Serpent, serpent, be off with you now
Here comes the bouillon of Carmentran.

'nannies' were as much sought after in Paris as Scots 'nannies' in London. The villages and farms reveal something of the local poverty, which a discreet tourism is doing something to relieve; but popular as the country may be in the holiday months, it keeps its secrets.

Some of them are open. You will not go far without falling for *jambon de Morvan*, *soupe à choux*, and *canard à châtaignes*; and the trout are abundant. The geologist will easily satisfy his curiosity. Fossils have been found in the crystalline rock, and stone tools in large quantities are proof of human occupation and industry from the end of the Neolithic age. The high level of the waters during the Iron Age covered the Morvan with forest and brushwood, and for this reason the Celtic tribes, coming from the distant corners of Europe, were obliged to place their camps on high ground where there was, nonetheless, no lack of material under the luxuriant verdure for such building and implements as they required. At Bibracte or Fou de Verdun you can deduce the evolution of architecture from the palaeolithic huts to the luxury of Gallo-Roman villas. Amethyst, malachite, azurite, and chalcopyrite are among the minerals which have been discovered; the iron at Prabis was exploited by the Eduens; and in our own day manganese has been found near St Prix, and coal in the *gorges de la Canche*. The forests which cover nearly half of the Morvan are notable for beech and oak, and they now revive a former prosperity in the paper-mill at Sougy-sur-Loire. Christmas trees find a ready market at Saulieu, and the most casually observant visitor will delight in the broom and bracken, the bilberries, pink heather, purple digitalis, and wild orchids.

Leaving Pierre-qui-Vire by the twisting road through Le Bon Ru and L'Itâte, you may join the D.226 at Romanu and follow it to **La Roche-en-Breuil** on the N.6. This was originally surrounded by cyclopean walls, of which a few traces remain. The medieval château was once the home of Montalembert, the historian and friend of Lacordaire. A short distance farther north on the N.6 brings us to **Ste Magnance.** Magnance was a Roman girl who, with four others, found St Germain dying at Ravenna. They brought his body back to Auxerre for burial, but Magnance died in

this village on her way home. Some years later a knight
passing through dreamt that a snake was putting its head
into his mouth and that Magnance, with one of her friends,
was warning him. Waking up, he found the snake doing
exactly as it had done in his dream, and he afterwards discovered the head of Magnance buried in the village which
came to bear her name. She is now interred in a tomb, where
sculptures show the knight asleep with the head of his horse
for a pillow, the apparition of the two women, and the snake
clearly visible. Relics of the saint are preserved alongside.

You can now either follow the N.6 to **Cussy-les-Forges,**
where a *gisant* corpse crawling with worms presents a certain
morbid interest, or take the D.13 to **Savigny-en-Terre-Plaine**
– so called from the flattish open country that lies between
the Morvan and the first hills of the Auxois. Here the church
is exceptional in the perfection of its appointments and upkeep. The motif on the modern wrought iron altar rails is
repeated on the font. A tiled and beamed porch with stone
pillars gives entrance to a very simple romanesque door. At
**Guillon,** barely a kilometre farther on, you will find a painted
crucifix over the altar; a short nave with curving gallery, and
two slender pillars in support; and the frescoes of a pair of
more than life-size figures kneeling in prayer. Again the west
door is romanesque. Another four kilometres along the same
road brings you to Montréal.

**Montréal** – the Latin Mons Regalis or Mons Regis – owes
its title to the stay of Queen Brunéhaut and her grandson
Thierry in the sixth century. The Revolution, which attempted
to change everything, made a vain effort to change its name
to Mont Serein; but royalty persisted here if nowhere else. In
the ninth century the place was so pillaged by the Normans
that the following invocation was added to the Litany. 'From
the fury of the Normans, O Lord deliver us.' The feudal
dynasty of Anséric built the present church, and in 1255 a
decree of St Louis incorporated Montréal in the duchy of
Burgundy. Henri IV raised the barony to a marquisate. Of
the original château only the upper and lower gateways, the
snail-shaped watch-tower, and a few stretches of wall – some
enclosing private property – now remain. But the strength
and signature of the past are plainly written upon them; few

towns in Burgundy could have so confidently defied a siege. François I twice honoured it with a visit, and expressed his gratitude by allowing the salamander to figure in its armorial bearings.

On your left, before entering the principal street through the lower gateway, you will find the **Priory of St Bernard,** where Vauban received his first lesson in mathematics. This is now a home for aged or retarded adults, but the romanesque chapel is open and Mass is celebrated here every morning. The mystical significance of God the Father in the east window will not escape you, and there are some excellent painted statues of the popular Burgundian school. Notice also the Devil's head on the wall outside. Passing a number of old houses with sculptured doorways, you climb the steep hill to the **Collegial Church,** founded in 1068, which stands on the same level as the original château with a commanding view of the countryside in all directions. Viollet-le-Duc admired it and was active in its restoration. One of the rose windows reminded him of the rose that blossoms over the façade of Notre-Dame de Paris. All three rose windows that adorn the sanctuary, apse, and west door are purely romanesque, and as a late transitional example of this style in Burgundy the church belongs to the same family, though lacking the same perfections, as Paray-le-Monial, Vézelay, and Autun. The modern abbey church of Pierre qui-Vire was partly modelled upon it.

The interior is packed with interest. The floor is partly paved with tombstones. One of these, commemorating two women, is especially beautiful, and another – anonymous – depicts the implements of a butcher's trade. Notice a stone cross with the sun and moon symbolizing the universal jurisdiction of Christ; the hexagonal wooden pulpit of fine craftsmanship, and the poignant wooden Christ that hangs opposite; the lectern of the same period as the pulpit; and a wooden fifteenth-century triptych, where Christ has the Virgin and Child on one side, and St Peter in contemplation of the heavens on the other. But these are all secondary to the principal treasures of the church – the alabaster reredos of the Nottingham school, and the wooden carvings on the choir stalls. The reredos was designed for ten bas-reliefs, but three

of them were stolen. Of the seven that remain four describe
the life of the Virgin, with the two deacons, St Lawrence and
St Stephen, at either end. The centre panel illustrates the
Mass of St Gregory the Great. On the stalls there are 26
carvings, several of remarkable vigour and finesse. You will
easily pick out Adam and Eve in the earthly Paradise; the
Visitation against a background of mountain, windmill and
château; the annunciation of the Nativity to the shepherds;
the baptism of Jesus, where both He and St John have their
legs amputated; David at grips with a lion; the Presentation
in the temple; the meeting with the woman of Samaria by
Jacob's well; and the homage of the Magi. Most striking of
all is the scene in Joseph's workshop. Here two men – presumably the sculptors, the brothers Rigolley – are seated at a
table and pouring out wine from a jug. Are we in Nazareth,
or in Nuits-sous-Ravières where they were born?

If you come to Burgundy in spring you will notice the
bundles of long branches leaning up against certain doors.
These are known as the *mais*, and they are put up by the boys
of the village whenever a girl living there is thought ripe for
marriage. On 14 January Montréal used to celebrate the Fête
des Buffenis, when the inhabitants walked through the town
threatening the naughty children.

Taking the road to Avallon, N.457, you should pause at
**Sauvigny-le-Bois,** where the absence of a west door to the late
twelfth-century church, and the chapel of the Grandmontains
are worth attention. A short détour by way of **Lucy-le-Bois**
(D.105) with its fine Renaissance fonts, and **Girolles** (D.167),
where a two-headed ox is carved on the stem of one of the
arches, will bring you back to the N.6, and thence – almost
immediately – to **Vaulx-de-Lugny** on the D.427. Here the
large church, otherwise without character, is remarkable for
an immense fifteenth-century fresco – 66 metres in length –
describing the episodes of the Passion. From Vaulx-de-Lugny
it is only a step to Pontaubert and the valley of the Cousin.


2

You may now turn to **Avallon** itself, perched on its granite
promontory between two ravines, and accessible in a few

minutes from the valley of the Cousin. In the Middle Ages the town was one of the keys to Burgundy, and strongly fortified. When its military importance declined, Louis XIV sold the ramparts to the municipality, which preserved them as a promenade. Now that so much heavy traffic has been diverted to the autoroute, the place is quieter than it used to be.

In the fourth century a **Church** was built here, of which only the crypt remains under the present choir. In the year 1000 Henri le Grand, Duke of Burgundy, presented the church with a relic of St Lazarus supposed to protect the population from leprosy, and by the end of the eleventh century the pilgrims were flocking to the church in such numbers that it was decided, after consultation with the architects of Cluny, to enlarge the building to include the apse and choir as you see them today. The new church was consecrated by Pope Pascal II in 1106, but even then it quickly proved too small, and a further 20 metres were added to the nave.

The façade will strike you by its oblique stance in relation to the rest of the church. Originally it had two towers and three doorways, but the north tower collapsed in 1633, destroying the left-hand doorway. The existing tower was raised shortly afterwards to replace it. The central doorway is sculpted with the signs of the Zodiac and the labours of the months; you will observe that, as at Vézelay, six of the latter have been added to the calendar year. The smaller doorway is a good example of 'flowery' romanesque, with the adoration of the Magi and the Presentation in the Temple on the tympanum; and underneath a man showing a bear, another with a stick helping a dog to get the better of a wild boar, a horseman in pursuit of a beast, and a centaur drawing his bow against a hunter.

Six steps lead down into the nave with its six bays and foliated capitals from which a devil's head may here and there be seen peeping out. There is an elaborate stone crucifix (sixteenth century) over the south-west door, and in the baptismal chapel on the right as you come in an attractive group of the Virgin and St Anne. The choir is three metres lower than the threshold of the church, following the sharp fall in the ground.

C.G.B.—I

A tour of the ramparts will take you back to a time when they served a purpose practical rather than picturesque. Starting from the Bastion de la Petite Porte at the southern extremity of the town, you will pass St Lazare immediately on your left, and the Tour de l'Escarguet a little farther on. Turn left at the Tour Beurdelaine and then left again at the Bastion de la Porte Auxerroise, and return to where you started from past the Tour des Valois, the Bastion de la Côte Gally, the Tour du Chapitre, and the Tour Gaillard opposite the Bastion de la Petite Porte. In the middle of the town, on your way to St Lazare, you will pass under the magnificent Tour de l'Horloge, built in the fifteenth century, with its turret and campanile.

Avallon has an interesting little **Museum** devoted to pre-historic discoveries in the neighbourhood, local religious cults, engravings and paintings by Jacques Callot, Forain, Rouault, and Toulouse-Lautrec. It is open, with no charge, on the first Sunday of the month from 11 October to 14 June between 14 and 17h; from 15 June to 10 September on Sunday and Wednesday between 14 and 18h. It is closed between 11 September and 10 October. For a general view of the town you should look at it from the Parc des Chaumes on the eastern side. The terraced gardens, the apse of St Lazare, the ramparts, and the Tour de l'Horloge compose an impressive ensemble. If you wish to stay in Avallon the Hotel de la Poste justifies its high reputation for comfort and cuisine.

The French are proud of the places through which Joan of Arc had passed, very much as the English are proud of the beds in which Queen Elizabeth had slept. The Maid passed through Avallon on her way to Chinon, and again on the return journey to Reims. On 16 March 1815 Napoleon found a recalcitrant and royalist municipal council, but an enthusiastic populace.

# CHAPTER SEVEN

# From Avallon to Fontenay

✤

## 1

Before leaving the valley of the Cousin turn left on the D.53 at Pontaubert for a glance at the château of Island, hidden and rather melancholy among its trees. The elegant sixteenth-century façade is flanked by a pair of towers and looks out on the park. A deserted avenue leads to a fine gateway which must originally have been the principal entrance. The château is not among those that open their doors to visitors, but you may well be tempted to invent its history for yourself.

Your route now lies eastward into the Auxois, and there are several châteaux on the way that invite, if they do not positively demand, inspection. Retracing your steps on the N.457 to a point just beyond Montréal, turn up the D.133 to Thizy. Not very much remains of the formidable thirteenth-century château beside the church, but a fine fifteenth-century tower dominates the valley, and underneath it the cellars, divided into four bays with pointed arches, seem to clamour for their absent contents. Equally abandoned is Santigny, a few kilometres farther east; a small manor of the sixteenth century with round towers. The windows are shuttered and cattle browse in the adjacent meadows. At Pisy, very close by, the château begun in 1235 and entirely rebuilt about 1480, is solidly rooted in the hillside, the façade supported by huge buttresses. You can trace the original fortifications, and the four towers. In the courtyard a fine octagonal tower stands out from the main edifice with a kind of tattered elegance, for what was once a fortress is now a farm; and although it will be polite to visitors, it does not solicit them.

You should now turn left and rejoining the N.457 at Vassy, follow it to Bierry-les-Belles-Fontaines and the château of Anstrude. This was built in 1710 by André François Anstruther, whose name owed much, no doubt, to the 'auld

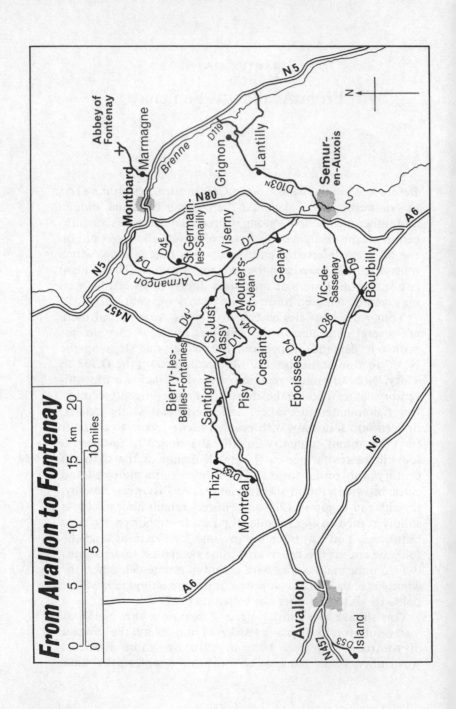

# From Avallon to Fontenay

N

alliance'. But Louis XV, in 1737, decided that what M. Anstruther was in nature he should also be in name – unambiguously a Frenchman. His portrait hangs over the mantelpiece in the salon. You approach the château down an avenue, cross the bridge and moat, and enter the spacious courtyard by an imposing wrought iron gate. The main building of three storeys, flanked by a pair of attractive round towers, has an extension of two wings in the same style but with a lower roof. The château is enclosed by a handsome stone balustrade, where the ivy does more or less as it pleases. Although, in 1973, it was on the list of those properties open to the public, more detailed information left its accessibility in doubt. The exterior, at any rate, is worth attention.

From Rierry-les-Belles-Fontaines you cross immediately into the Côte d'Or and strike south through St Just – where there is a fine romanesque chapel – to **Moutiers-St-Jean.** This was the oldest monastery in Burgundy, founded at the end of the fifth century, rebuilt in the twelfth and thirteenth, and destroyed at the Revolution. A door of the church may be seen in the Cloisters museum at New York. The monastic buildings were rebuilt in the seventeenth and eighteenth centuries, and a hospital founded with the encouragement of St Vincent de Paul. There are some good statues in the church. At **Corsaint,** a little farther on, you will find a thirteenth-century choir and fifteenth-century nave, and a St Anthony armed with a sickle – not as an instrument of death, but as a guarantee that he will keep the Reaper at bay for you.

A short distance on the D.44 brings us to **Epoisses,** and one of the most important châteaux in Burgundy. It may be visited from Easter till 3 September at 10h, 11h, 14h, 15h, 16h, 17h, and 18h. If you were tracing the footsteps of St Columba you would hardly expect to find them here; nevertheless tradition ascribes to him a role of some importance in the history of Epoisses. Queen Brunéhaut, anxious to get her grandson Thierry out of the way during the last years of his minority, surrounded him in the château with dissolute women calculated to distract him from an importunate concern with affairs of State. Columba, who was then evangelizing Gaul, arrived at Epoisses intending to reproach the young king for his scandalous behaviour. He was unwilling, however, to enter the château, baptize the King's illegitimate children, or to attend a banquet in his own honour. The chronicles relate that when he repaid the royal hospitality with curses the plates broke in tune with them. One cannot escape the conclusion that the saint's zeal outran his discretion, and that a son of St Ignatius Loyola would have set about his business differently.

Epoisses became a ducal residence until in 1189 Hugues III exchanged it for Montbard. From the Counts of Montbard it passed through various hands to Jacques de Savoie, duc de Nemours, a fervent Catholic and as successful in love as he was in war. The good or evil that he did lived after him, and a century later Madame de Lafayette took him as the hero of *La Princesse de Clèves*. His extravagance was such, however, that in 1561 he was obliged to sell the castle to the Maréchal de Bourdillon. This was the only occasion on which Epoisses has been bought and sold. Bourdillon gave his name to one of the towers, and the château was left to his niece Françoise, the wife of Louis d'Anssienville, baron de Revillon.

From 1589 to 1593 it was occupied by the forces of the Ligue, who pillaged it from floor to ceiling. In 1602 the *élus* – or representatives – of Burgundy, fearing the return of civil war, asked for royal permission to demolish it, but Henry IV decided that it should be spared. In 1613 Louis XIII raised the barony of Epoisses to a marquisate as a reward for Louis d'Anssienville's services to the Crown. Louis, however, had only a single daughter and when she married Achille de la Grange d'Arquien the title died out. In 1661 their daughter Madeleine married Guillaume de Pechpeyrou, Comminges de Guitaut, and this is how the château came into the possession of the family which has held it ever since. A neighbour of the Guitaut was Mme de Sévigné; and Bourbilly, where she had spent so much of her childhood with her grandmother, St Jeanne de Chantal, was a fief of Epoisses. She loved the country and the air – 'which you only have to breathe to get fat' – and she depended a good deal on her overlords to collect her rents, and dispose of her wealth to the best advantage. She was a frequent guest at Epoisses, and teased her hosts when at last, after seven years' arduous efforts, they produced a son. 'Look after him well, because you don't produce sons whenever you want to.'

At the Revolution the family papers were saved by the devotion of the servants and villagers; for relations were easy between the château and the *bourg*, and the latter were allowed to store their wine and grain in the feudal cellars. But in 1793 more than half of the adjacent property, with much furniture, was sold by order of the Committee of Public Safety on the grounds that Charles de Guitaut's sister had emigrated. It was then decided that the château should be destroyed, but M. de Guitaut was allowed to keep whichever half of it he preferred. He chose to retain the more habitable part, including the apartments restored by his ancestor, who had supported the *Grand Condé* during the Fronde. Even the towers of this section were ordered to be razed to the level of the living quarters, but fortunately the money ran out to pay the workmen who were to execute these barbarous instructions. Nevertheless when the Comte and Comtesse de Guitaut were released from prison after the fall of Robespierre, they found the courtyard and moats of the château piled deep with the ruins of the towers, and their living quarters half destroyed. They set about to restore them and throughout the nineteenth century the château gave its hospitality to many illustrious visitors – the philosopher Joubert, Louis Veuillot, the champion of Papal Infallibility, Marmont, who began to write his Memoirs at Epoisses, Chateaubriand and his wife, who stayed there.

If you looked down at the château from an aeroplane, you would see a double *enceinte* of fortifications with the space between them filled in with plantations designed by Le Nôtre; the château itself in the shape of an extended horse-shoe with its four square towers rising to a point, two storeys of windows and a mansarde; in front an oval lawn bisected by a path, and a fairly wide space encircling it. The short spire of the collegial church rises beyond the trees. Nothing suggests the turbulent history of what is now a quiet family domain; only the thickness of the outer walls reminds you of a time when Epoisses was subject to assault. The Renaissance well-head in the courtyard with its wrought iron-work dates from the sixteenth century, and the façade was considerably refashioned under Louis XIII and the *Roi Soleil*.

In the vestibule the walls are covered with the portraits of eminent personalities. The spelling of their names suggests that somebody was having their little joke, for we find among others '*François Rables*', '*Theodore de Baize*', '*La Rene de Cose*', and '*Jasne la Pusselle*'. In the adjoining room hang the Comte and Comtesse de Guitaut, who defended Epoisses during the Revolution. Some attractive hunting scenes by Snyders decorate the staircase, and in the room where Henri IV had slept – the '*chambre du Roi*' – the portraits of the '*grande Condé* – the full bottomed wig falling over the black armour, framing the dark eyes, long nose, and receding chin – and of François de Guitaut by Philippe de Champagne are of particular interest. The latter was an experienced diplomat, never more successful than when he brought about a reconciliation between Louis XIII and Anne of Austria. Seizing the excuse of a rainy evening he persuaded the King to take shelter with his wife in the Louvre, and nine months later Louis XIV was born. François de Guitaut had much to answer for, whichever way you look at it.

The room which Mme de Sévigné is said to have inhabited when she stayed at Epoisses bespeaks her personality, resilient and gay. 'The beauty and grandeur of this house are astonishing' she wrote to her daughter in 1673. But a melancholy (and curiously spelt) quatrain inscribed on one of the small beams casts a tiny cloud on the Arcadian sunshine of the tapestries.

> *Nos plaisirs ne sont caparence*
> *Et souvent se cachent nos pleurs*
> *Sous lesclat de ces belles fleurs*
> *Qui ne sont que vainne éperance*[1]

Her portrait hangs beside the elegant four-poster bed.

Certain works of art in the **Collegial Church** have survived the savagery of the Revolution; a large Christ above the choir;

---

1. Our pleasures are illusory
   And often our tears are hidden
   Beneath the brilliance of these lovely flowers
   Which are no more than an empty hope.

and a fifteenth-century Pietà in the chapel of St Anne. A pair of tombstones from the funeral vault of Louis d'Anssienville and his wife are let into the wall of the chapel on your right below the armorial bearings of Montbard and Bourdillon. But no other memorial remains of the families that formerly ruled over Epoisses.

You should not leave the grounds of the château without inspecting the immense dovecote, where a wooden ladder, pivoting on a central beam, gives access to no less than 3000 pigeon holes. Epoisses was once a prosperous market town with four trade fairs in the year, and a dozen principal streets. It has now considerably declined in importance and population; and you will look in vain for *eight* butchers' shops. But the cheese is not to be despised.

2

A glimpse of Mme de Sévigné's handwriting will probably send you back to her letters, and naturally direct you along the D.36 to **Bourbilly**, standing below you among its pines and beeches at the end of a long drive. The recent plantation of Douglas fir is peculiarly appropriate, for Bourbilly can reasonably be described as the Burgundian Abbotsford. When Mme de Sévigné wrote: 'I have just arrived in the old château of my forebears . . . here are my beautiful meadows, my little river and my magnificent woods, and my lovely windmill, just where I had left them,' she little guessed how romantically Bourbilly would be brought up to the century of Sir Walter Scott; and for Lamartine it was the 'château of the Sleeping Beauty'. It contains many souvenirs of St Jeanne de Chantal (1572–1641). Born at Dijon, the daughter of a councillor at the *cour de consignes*, she first met St François de Sales, Bishop of Geneva, when he was preaching a course of Lenten sermons in the city. Deeply impressed, she moved her seat in the church to see and hear him better, and they soon became close friends. He was then 36 years old, and she considerably younger. She subsequently married the Baron de Chantal, by whom she had several children – one of them was the father of Mme de Sévigné – and they lived in great happiness at Bourbilly until, after eight years, her husband was killed in a hunting accident. For a long time she was unable to forgive

the man who had been the involuntary cause of his death, and
François de Sales understood her feelings. 'I know how the
blood boils in your veins; nevertheless you must forgive.' In
1607 they founded the Order of the Visitation at Annecy,
where they are buried side by side. Their last meeting was at
Lyon. '*Je m'en irai*,' said François, '*sans trompettes.*' The
relics of St Jeanne are preserved in the chapel, where every
year, on her feast day, 21 August, Mass is celebrated by the
Abbot of Pierre-qui-Vire. A fine fresco of the Visitation by
one of the monks decorates the wall facing the altar.

A short stretch now takes you across the 'world elsewhere'
of the autoroute to **Vic-de-Sassenay,** with a closed-in porch to
the church, and square romanesque tower spoilt by plaster;
and on very quickly to **Semur-an-Auxois.** This is the *pagus
alisiensis* of Gallo-Roman times; a country of deep valleys,
rich pasturing for sheep, and hedges – '*bouchures*' – limiting
the fields. The '*Sinémurien*', or bluish stone veined with am-
monite, gave its name to Semur. No other part of Burgundy
has so many châteaux tenaciously occupied and kept up by
their proprietors; and of all its towns none is more striking
than Semur as you approach it, as we are doing, from the west
over a deep ravine. The Armançon and the Soussiotte wind
like a snake around the walls, and the four circular fourteenth-
century towers with their pointed, red tiled roofs, stand up on
a cliff of pink granite with the spire of Notre-Dame in the
background. A triple enceinte of fortifications originally
protected the town, and you may still enter it through the
Porte Sauvigny, which gave access to the enceinte du Bourg
Notre-Dame. The ramparts are conveniently adapted for a
walk in the shade of the chestnuts and the limes; or below
under the shadow of the rock. The legend runs that Semur was
founded by Hercules – an attribution not altogether un-
deserved.

It has been said that in **Notre-Dame de Semur,** built
between 1220 and 1225, it is 'almost as if the Semur master had
written down for us a list of the places where he had been'.
The triplet window in the ambulatory is typical of Picardy
and Flanders, the jutting corbels of Normandy, the windows
in the choir and transept of Chartres. The clerestory with its
interior passage is unique – almost equal in height to the

arcades and triforium combined; and in the choir the triforium and windows are three times the height of the arcading
below. The narrowness of the nave emphasizes the height of
the vaulting, and in the transepts the wall space above the
triforium is of virtually the same dimensions as the windows
above. Ten pillars define the ambulatory. Notice the remnants
of colour on the foliated capitals and on another a very small
girl reading a psalm; a Sepulchre of the late fifteenth century
in the second chapel of the left aisle has been described
among many others of its kind as 'the most French in its
restrained emotion'. In the third a fine window (sixteenth
century) illustrates the legend of St Barbe; in the last two
chapels of the same aisle are windows offered by the confrèries of butchers and drapers; and just before you reach
the transept notice a remarkable bell-shaped ciborium of the
fifteenth century. The lady chapel has three very beautiful
thirteenth-century windows restored by Viollet-le-Duc, and
over the door leading into the north transept – the Porte des
Bleds – the legend of St Thomas may be read on the tympanum, while the pair of snails sculpted on one of its columns
– with scenes of harvest and the threshing of corn – throw
out a sly hint of gastronomic pleasure. Notre-Dame de Semur
is the most elegant Gothic church in Burgundy, and also the
most eclectic. Where Vézelay reconciles the Gothic and the
romanesque, Semur reconciles the Gothic with itself.

The Course de la Bague is the oldest horse race in France.
It is run annually on May 31. The first prize is a gold ring engraved with the arms of the town; the second a white scarf
with a gold fringe; and the third a pair of gloves. Today a
gift of money is added to them. The race is run over a course
of two and a half kilometres, and an important horse and
cattle fair is organized at the same time.

A small local **Museum** and **Library** are installed in the
former Jacobin convent. The museum has an interesting
collection of minerals and fossils; and the library a number
of precious tenth-century illuminated MSS, and the oldest
incunabulum to come from the presses of Gutenberg. Both
museum and library are open on Tuesday and Friday from
9 to 11h, and 14 to 16h. The museum is closed from 16
September to 30 June; the library from 14 July to 30 August.

You can stay pleasantly enough in Semur, for the ambiance of the town should be imbibed in slow draughts; but for quiet, reasonable prices, and exceptional cuisine I recommend the Hotel du Lac de Pont three kilometres to the south. This has everything you require, except atmosphere – and of this you will find plenty elsewhere. From here you can explore in various directions and conveniently return to base.

Take the N.80 going north out of Semur in the direction of Montbard; and turn off to the left on the D.1 for **Genay,** where there is a very fine bridge over the Armançon, and a stone Calvary set on a small triumphal cross at the southern exit to the village. This evidently illustrates St John's 'I am the gate, and whoever enters through me will be saved.' Another five kilometres brings you to **Viserny,** where the vine, which you will not have seen since Chablis, makes a welcome re-appearance, and the *vignerons* honour an obscure Alsatian saint, St Vernies. This does not make their wine any less Burgundian. Notice also the covered steps to the houses that you will find later on in the Maconnais. Then proceed along the same road to **St Germain-les-Senailly.** Here there is a notable reredos in the church, with a dramatic Magdalen at the foot of the cross, and the thieves vividly characterized. Neither drama nor theft have been wanting to St Germain. Some years ago a statue of Christ was discovered here by the curé, broken and discarded on the road, and a service in expiation of the sacrilege was held on 10 January 1910. On the following day the head of an angel was found on the same road, and placed with the desecrated Christ in a reliquary. There are some good coloured statues, including one of the Virgin with a bunch of grapes as well as the Infant Jesus.

From here it is a short step to **Montbard.** If you have made the sensible rule to eat only a picnic luncheon, M. Belin's Hotel de Gare is the place to break it at – if possible with a *saupiquet montbardois.*[1] But note that the restaurant here, and also at the Lac de Pont, is closed on Mondays; you will, however, do very well at the Ecu. Of the **Ducal Château** at Montbard nothing remains but the crenellated Tour de l'Aubepin, excellently preserved, and the Tour St Louis, where the souvenirs of Georges-Louis Leclerc, Comte de

1. Sharply flavoured sauce.

Buffon (1707–88) have been collected. Buffon was born, lived, worked, and was buried at Montbard; and the Dukes – great or little – are simply not in the picture. In 1739 he became Intendant of the Royal Garden, which included stones from the King of Denmark and the King of Sweden, as well as plants from the King of Prussia. The Emperor of Austria treated him as an equal – 'as one power to another, for here I am on your imperial territory'. He was on easy terms with his own royal master. When Louis XV requested a roebuck from Montbard, Buffon sent him half a one. The King replied by sending Buffon half a pâté. The great naturalist spent four months of the year in Paris, though he described the city as an '*enfer*', and was always glad to get back to the study which he had built on the site of one of the ducal towers, having destroyed most of the château when he bought it in 1744. Here he was perfectly content with Dauché, his gardener, Mlle Blesseau, his housekeeper, and Père Ignace, a veteran soldier turned Capucin, whom Buffon called '*mon enfant*'. Buffon remained a bachelor for many years, for he held that a grand passion took four or five years out of a man's life: 'two months to consummate it, four months to enjoy it, two years to be deceived, and a year to lose weight, travel, and pull oneself together'. He confined himself to brief adventures which 'occupied only the two minutes when the angels, as they say, hide their faces with their wings so as not to be jealous of our pleasures'. When he married at the age of 43, he was faithful to his wife, whom he had met in the parlour of an Ursuline convent, and they had five children; when she died he sought the company of Mme Necker and other intelligent women in society. Mme Necker, recalling that Buffon had been called 'the man of the century', described him as 'the man of all the centuries' – and Buffon would not have deprecated the compliment. He had a pretty turn of humour, congratulating his son on the cut of his breeches because they 'had a face'; and ordering the workmen who were building his funeral vault to 'make it solid, as I shall be there longer than anywhere else.'

In 1752 Buffon delivered his famous oration on style to the Académie française. If '*le style est l'homme même*' Buffon certainly practised what he preached. A writer from Dijon,

Estaunié, standing before his bust by Houdon in the Louvre, noted 'the voluptuous mouth and the wrinkles in the cheeks, so eloquent of bonhomie and the love of well-being. Look particularly at the profile, where the habit of pleasure and a sly mockery are written unforgettably on the features. There you have a key to the man; if you didn't know it already, this bust would have revealed it to you. M. de Buffon is a Burgundian.' As a thinker he was closer to Locke than to Descartes, believing that 'the only true science is the knowledge of facts'; that its object was 'the how of things, not the why'; and that no preconceived system should influence its observation. He maintained that 'nature was in continual flux', but that evolution was possible only within the species; and, in contrast to Rousseau, that social life was the mark of man's ascendancy.

Here then – where it was said that 'modern thought began to meditate on the world' – we can imagine Buffon walking about the park, which he had laid out, in his red coat, short skirt, silk stockings, and buckled shoes. A visitor in 1785 described the 'twelve terraces, as irregular as the house . . . plantations of quincunx and pines, plane-trees, sycamores, hornbeams, and everywhere flowers among the trees.' And there were also the pair of factories – for Buffon was as interested in metals as he was in forestry and flowers. The park is now a public promenade, the hornbeam arbours have disappeared, and there are no flowers. But you may admire the wide vistas and the massive trees. Buffon had built a comfortable house – No. 1 of the Place that now bears his name – and a bridge connected this with his study. He is buried in the vault of a little chapel adjoining the church of St Urse, outside the park.

The park, the Tour d'Aubepin, the Tour St Louis, and Buffon's study can be visited from 9 to 11h, and 15 to 18h. They are closed on Wednesday. For the Tour St Louis apply to the caretaker, 3 rue Daubenton.

A number of old customs in Montbard long survived the spirit of scientific enquiry that presided there. At Candlemas boys and girls eager to marry used to throw their *mariottes* – anthropomorphic cakes – to the fairies who were supposed to

haunt the springs of the Douix; and on the first Sunday in
Lent fireworks were sent up before the houses of tradesmen
and young couples recently settled in the town.


3


Take the N.5 out of Montbard to **Marmagne,** where there is a
small but very fine romanesque church with a single nave;
and then turn up the D.32 to the **Abbey of Fontenay.** The
road leads through a narrow, wooded valley, and on the left
as you approach the entrance is a large pool which nourishes
no less than 10,000 trout. These were formerly reserved for
the Kings of France and the Dukes of Burgundy, although
Buffon enjoyed them. Fontenay is the oldest Cistercian abbey
in France, and none demonstrates more clearly the Cistercian
genius for a site. It was the second foundation of St Bernard,
who arrived here with Hugues de Macon and ten abbots at the
end of 1118. They planned it as follows: 'The monastery will
be built, as far as possible, to include within its enclosure
everything essential – water, a mill, a garden, workshops for
various uses – so that the monks shall have no need to go
outside.' By the sixteenth century the abbey comprised more
than three hundred monks and lay brothers, but then the
decadence set in with abbots appointed by royal favour. The
wars of religion hastened its decline, and at the Revolution it
was sold and turned into a paper mill. But in 1906 the new
proprietors carefully restored it, and the present owner,
M. Aynard, maintains its monastic integrity – as far as this is
possible in a monastery without monks. The guide is perfectly
familiar with its history, and admirably explains it.

The gate of the **Porter's Lodge** is surmounted with the
armorial bearings of the abbey, and as you pass under the
vault you will notice a small niche below the staircase. This
permitted a watch dog to keep an eye on the entrance, and
also on the eighteenth-century guest house to your right. The
**Church** stands back away to your left, built between 1130
and 1147 through the generosity of Ebrard, Bishop of
Norwich, who took refuge from persecution at Fontenay, and
is appropriately buried there. It was consecrated by Pope
Eugenius III. Many have considered it the best surviving

example of early Cistercian architecture; and planned as it may well have been by St Bernard himself, and illustrating his fidelity to the aesthetics – which were really the mathematics – of St Augustine's Christian Platonism. When the medieval architect spoke of something being determined 'according to true measure', what he had in mind was the square or cube – the geometrical expression of the Godhead. Thus at Fontenay the bays of the side aisles are of equal length and width, and the façade describes a square, if one includes the buttresses and upper stringcourse. The 'perfect consonances', so dear to the Christian Platonists, are maintained in the 1 : 1 ratio of the transept crossing; 'the 2 : 3 ratio which regulates the width of the crossing to its length, including the choir, and the relation between the width of the crossing and the total width of nave with side aisles; the 3 : 4 ratio which determines the relation between the total width of nave plus side aisles and the length of the transept including chapels'.[1] If truth lies in proportion, Fontenay illustrates as well as any other sacred building of its time the identity of beauty and truth.

The façade is void of ornament, with two buttresses and seven semi-circular arches to symbolize the seven sacraments of the Church. The leaves and paintings of the door exactly reproduce the originals. The nave, 66 metres in length, and the transepts, 30 metres wide, follow the usual Cistercian plan. Exceptionally, however, there are four chapels round the sanctuary; a first sign, perhaps, of the reaction against St Bernard's severity which, according to Viollet-le-Duc, began after his death. The Constitutions had laid down that 'sculpture and painting shall have no place in the church, and the windows shall be of uncoloured glass, without cross or ornament. No tower of an excessive height, whether of wood or stone, should be raised to contradict the Order's simplicity.' Nevertheless, as A. Hallaye, a French authority on the subject, has pointed out, 'there was something that carried more weight than the word of a great apostle, and that was the irresistible instinct of the Burgundian stone-carver, incapable of cutting a block without stamping it with his taste, and unresigned to doing so.' The effect at Fontenay is of mingled sobriety and grandeur; and one only regrets that

1. *The Gothic Cathedral*: Otto von Simson: 1956.

Semur-en-Auxois: view of the town from the west.

'A Farm in Burgundy' painted by William Rothenstein 1906.

Abbaye de Fontenay: the monks' dormitory.

in restoring the church the floor, though lowered to its original level, has not been paved. The nave of eight bays is barrel-vaulted, and supported by rib-vaulted side aisles. The choir is lighted by a double row of triplet windows, to represent the Trinity, just as the seven in the façade symbolize the seven virtues, the seven sacraments, and the seven notes of music – a 'symbolisme linéaire', as M. Hallaye has called it. There is no apse. Notice a late twelfth-century statue of the Virgin; an early fourteenth-century reredos of the Nativity, where St Joseph seems very tired, and the animals are preoccupied with the Child, an ox preventing with his teeth the cradle from imminent collapse; and three impressive tombs. The first of Chevalier Mello, a cousin of St Bernard, who was killed in the second crusade, and of his wife, who had accompanied him; the second of Jeanne de Riego 'duchesse d'Athènes, comtesse d'Eu, dame de Château-Chinon, d'Fpoisses, de Sombernon', escorted by the pleurants – or mourners – which are a feature of Burgundian sculpture; the third of Bishop Ebrard, who had paid for the church.

You pass from the south transept by a stone staircase into the **Monks' Dormitory** – a superb room, 53 metres long and 12 wide, and notable for its chestnut timber-work which no insect has been able to erode. A window into the church allowed the aged monks to assist at the offices, although they were not normally long lived and many of them died at thirty. You reach the **Cloister** by a door to the right of the dormitory staircase. This is the oldest part of the monastic buildings, with 200 double columns to support the arches; almost a perfect square – 38 by 36 metres – with eight openings on each side; but a mechanical regularity is avoided by the slightly differing shapes of the pillars, and by placing two entrances on one side and only one on the other, not directly opposite. Only in the cloister were the walls of the abbey painted, although any trace of this has disappeared. From the middle of the garth you have an excellent view of the campanile, which rises, not from the church but from the roof of the dormitory.

You enter the **Chapter House** from the Cloister. It lies underneath the dormitory and has two small annexes. A passage leads into the **Scriptorium**, which adjoins the **Chauffoir** or heated rest-room – for only here and in the kitchen was a fire allowed to be lit. It was important that the books, the MSS, and the aged or ailing monks should be kept reasonably warm, even if their younger and healthier brethren shivered elsewhere. Leaving the Chauffoir you find yourself outside, and opposite a two-storeyed building of which the upper part was the library and the lower the monastic prison. Here a sombre text accompanied solitary confinement. 'The sun shall not shine on you by day, nor the moon by night.' The infirmary stood at a safe distance from the other buildings on the farther side of a medicinal garden, for there was a natural fear of infection at a time when the plague was always ready to claim its victims.

The forge, 53 metres in length, depended on the minerals from the adjacent hill. A single stream turned one big water mill, which operated two smaller ones. These crushed the wood and gave the power to work the bellows for the furnaces, and the hammers for beating the iron. The only important part of the abbey totally destroyed was the refectory; it stood opposite the forge and perpendicular to the cloister from which you entered it. It had taken 150 years to build the abbey of Fontenay, and nowhere else can you more easily reconstruct the Cistercian way of life. You can visit it officially every day from 8 to 18h, but on my last visit the hour of *déjeuner* claimed its usual rights.

You should not miss the opportunity of a walk among the tall beeches and pines of the forest, which stretches northward from Fontenay until it merges into the Forêt de Châtillon; and do not be surprised if you startle a deer or a roebuck in your path.

Two châteaux lie conveniently on your way back to Semur. Rejoin the N.5, and branch off to your right along the D.119 to **Grignon**. This feudal fortress, built in the eleventh and twelfth centuries, was entirely restored in the fourteenth, and then from the beginning of the eighteenth century allowed to go to ruin. It has since been progressively restored again, and important work is still in progress. Of the original château the tower, ramparts, moat, and double-arched entrance gateway remain. Parts of the interior can be visited, from 1 April to 30 June; in September on Saturday, Sunday, and public holidays; in July and August every day from 10 to 12h, and 14 to 18h.

You will admire the large rooms with their monumental fireplaces and wooden ceilings – one of them with carved beams of the twelfth century – and people the spiral staircases with the figures of a medieval past, and indeed of a past even more remote. For here are traces of the cell where St Reine was imprisoned in the third century. After accepting baptism from her nurse, she was turned out of the house and lived as a shepherdess. Later she was beheaded under the walls of Alésia for refusing to marry Olibrius, Prefect of Gaul, and buried at Flavigny. A statue of her by the Burgundian sculptor, Jean Dampt, may be seen at Grignon. The château deserved its restoration, for this was one of the few villages where the inhabitants were given the right to shoot and fish. The church is notable for the sixteenth-century chapel of the Twelve Apostles, and for a number of attractive statues.

Turn to your left out of the village at Grignon and proceed to **Lantilly,** where the 'Château of a Hundred Windows' – I counted them and the addition is as correct as makes no matter – stands with a formal modesty and elegance in its grounds just off the road. The public are invited by the Marquis de Virieu to admire the exterior; you will notice a magnificent cedar and catalpa tree, and a double box hedge, planted quite low. But the inside is not shown. It will be appreciated that when the proprietors are in Paris for most of the week, and there is no guide to show people round, more intimate access to these places is not to be expected. Lantilly is situated on a high plateau, and it is quite a steep drive along the D.103N back to Semur, and beyond to the Lac de Pont.

# CHAPTER EIGHT

# From Alésia to Saulieu

⋟

## 1

Take the N.454 out of Semur; turn to the right along the D.9 to Pouillenay; then to the left for a short distance on the N.5, and branch off on the D.103N to **Alise-Ste-Reine.** The village takes the first part of its name from the Celtic *oppidum*, Alésia; the second from the shepherdess saint whose prison we visited at Grignon. Here she was martyred, and still attracts her pilgrims. The romanesque and Carolingian church was restored in 1965, and must now be reckoned among the treasures of the Auxois. A special Mass for tourists is celebrated here at 7 p.m. on Sunday during the summer months and, whatever your beliefs, attendance at it would enrich your visit with an impression of the faith that went to the building of the church and to its restoration. The stained glass is all from the Taizé workshops, and among other details you should notice a Christ of the seventeenth century caught, as it seems, in the moment of the outcry: 'My God, my God, why hast thou forsaken me?'. An eleventh-century carving of St Anthony the Hermit on the west wall, and on the right the head of a Celtic divinity with a Latin cross inscribed on the forehead; the holy water stoup – probably Carolingian – and a Latin cross disguised as a swastika; a paten of the fourth century inscribed with a fish and the word *Regina*; a fifteenth-century Pietà in stone; the ambo with a Roman statue; the twelfth- or thirteenth-century blazon of Agnes, duchess of Burgundy and daughter of St Louis; a fifteenth-century Virgin and Child in stone, where the Virgin has a slight smile and is holding some grapes and an apple, and the Child has its hand on her cheek; and the tomb (1740) of a curé who died here while celebrating Mass. You will observe that the steps of the stone staircase at the west end are made out of single blocks; and there is evidence of a cemetery underneath the church. If the lady who looks after the building happens to be there when you visit it, you could not wish for a more willing or informative guide.

As you walk up the hill to the summit of Mount Auxois you will pass on your right the Théâtre des Roches, where the *Mystère de Ste-Reine* is annually performed. This holds 5000 spectators, and is used for other productions in the summer months.

The whole of this area is called **Alésia.** It may be described as the tomb of Celtic Gaul and the cradle of what we know as France. This is where the old civilization died and where the new was born. This is where France first came to an awareness of itself, and where the *pagus* realized, however obscurely, that it was on the way to becoming a *patrie*. Rome and Christianity, in enmity and afterwards in alliance, were the agents of its rebirth.

Just as Mont Auxois dominates the countryside, so that you are aware of it long before you undertake this expedition, in the same way Millet's colossal statue of Vercingetorix dominates the hill. In the spring of 52 BC Caesar had been defeated near Clermont-Ferrand in the Massif Central. He then retreated northward to join his principal lieutenant, Labienus, in the neighbourhood of Sens, and together they marched south. He was met, however, by Vercingetorix and his forces near Alésia, and defeated them. Vercingetorix gathered his routed troops into the *oppidum* of Mont Auxois, and the siege began. It lasted for six weeks.

Caesar disposed of 40,000 legionaries, who surrounded the place with a double line of field works – trenches, walls, palisades, and towers. The first line, facing the hill, was intended to seal the exit of the Gauls; the second to block the way of a relieving army. When this arrived, 200,000 strong, it was unable to penetrate the Roman defences; but the battle – like another Waterloo – was a 'damned near thing'. Let Caesar describe it for us:

'A day passed during which the Gauls contrived a number of hurdles, ladders, and cramp-irons. In the middle of the night they came silently out of the camp and approached our lines in the plain. Suddenly a shout went up,

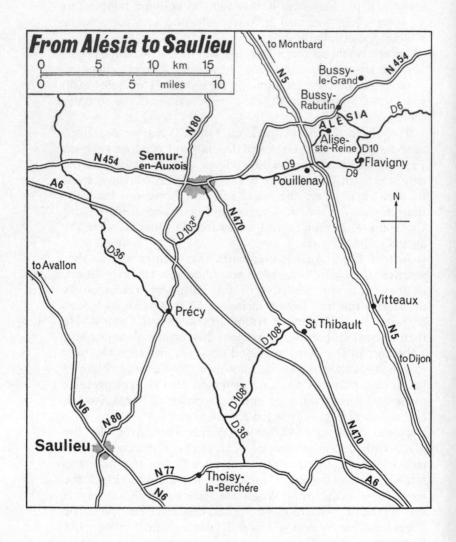

the signal to warn the besieged of their approach. With slings, arrows, and stones they chased us from the parapet, and everything was ready for the assault. At the same moment Vercingetorix, warned by the noise, sounded the call to rally and led his troops out of the place. Our own men stayed in the positions assigned to them during the preceding days, and held the lines. The man-traps and stakes, disposed about the entrenchments, and the leaden balls terrified the Gauls. In the dark there were a great number of wounded here and there. The machines launched a hail of darts, and when the legates, Marcus Antonius and C. Trebonius, who were in command of this sector, felt that our men were wavering, they brought in for their support reinforcements from the rear.'

On the Gallic side Camulgenus, with a sword studded with coral nails and silver motifs on his shield, had given the signal for the fatal sortie from a trumpet shaped like a dragon's head. He fell fighting; and Vercingetorix surrendered to save his people from massacre. Caesar paraded him in triumph through the streets of Rome; kept him in prison at Tullianum for six years; and then had him strangled to death. Any lingering hopes of an independent Gaul died with him.

Certain historians of the nineteenth century maintained that the battle had taken place at Alaise, a village in the Jura, and Napoleon III, to settle the matter, initiated the excavations at Alésia in 1862. The traces of various military works, with the bones of men and horses, coins, and the debris of weapons, and miscellaneous objects abandoned during the siege, though conclusive for most people, did not silence the controversy. But the existence of an important *oppidum* on Mont Auxois was not in doubt. Here were uncovered – and may now be seen – the remains of Gallic living quarters, wells and cellars, Roman baths, a Roman theatre, temples, a Forum, and the basilica dedicated to St Reine. You will need a good half-hour to visit them, with the help of a documentary guide that explains them clearly. (Open from Easter to 11 November, 9 to 19h. Ticket valid for the Musée Alésia.) If you continue along the side of the hill beyond the path leading up to the statue of Vercingetorix, and then turn down to your left, you will find the two museums. The **Musée Alésia** contains all the objects discovered during the excavations undertaken by the Société des Sciences of Semur – pottery, statuettes, and sarcophagi – since 1906. Among these, on the ground floor, is the admirable **Vase Argenté,** with carvings in relief of Bacchus, Pan with his goat's feet blowing a horn, a faun with grapes and a basket of fruit, and a faun blowing on a double flute. On the right you will see the large mutilated statue of a goddess, with her basket – here the drapery shows skilful workmanship – and elsewhere there is Epona on her horse; a bronze vase dedicated to the Celtic divinities, Ucuetis and Bergusta; evidence of the near-eastern cult of Mithras, Cybele, and Attis; a lamp in the shape of a leaping lion; fetters that shackled the slaves who were up for sale; sandals for the sore feet of horses; and most particularly the **Chalice of St Reine,** with the Christian sign engraved on it. The museum is open from 10 to 12h and 15 to 18h. Ticket valid for the excavations.

The **Musée Municipal** was inaugurated at the same time as the first excavations ordered by Napoleon III. It also houses a variety of Gallic, Gallo-Roman, and Roman exhibits, and an important collection of weapons and coins. Open from 9 to 12h and 14 to 19h. If you find it shut apply to the Syndicat d'Initiative at the town hall.

The **Hospice Ste-Reine** was founded by St Vincent de Paul in 1660 for the sick who had come to the shrine on pilgrimage. A number of paintings illustrating the life and martyrdom of St Reine were presented to the chapel by Anne of Austria, and in the pharmacy there is some good earthenware and eighteenth-century woodwork.

If you feel like a drink after much arduous observation, a notice in a neighbouring café will inform you that credit is given to no one under 99 years old.

You should now turn out of the village on to the N.454 and bearing right you will presently see the **Château of Bussy-Rabutin** standing out on the steep slope of a wooded hill. This is not only perhaps the most famous château in Burgundy, but exceptional in belonging to the State since 1929. For this reason or another you will get much less information about it on the spot than you have the right to expect. A rather hustled visit, therefore, should be well prepared beforehand.

Roger de Bussy-Rabutin (1618–93), a cousin of Mme de Sévigné, was born at Epiry and died at Autun. He rallied to Condé during the Fronde, and then changed sides, fighting in Flanders under Turenne – with the result that Condé and Turenne equally detested him. His sensational and scandalous *Histoire amoureuse des Gaules* – where the gallantries of the Court were plain to read under the pseudonyms of their principal actors – was written to amuse his mistress, Madame de Montglat. But it gave great offence to Louis XIV, who consigned the author to the Bastille in 1665. By the grace of the Queen Mother he was allowed to see his confessor, Père Nouet, S.J., who visited him every day and brought him ink and paper, and also to receive visits from his wife. The King at last sent him to a health clinic, and in 1666 ordered him to return to his château in Burgundy with the clear intimation that he would be *persona non grata* at court. Bussy was then 46 years old. When in 1683 he put in an appearance at Versailles, the King cut him dead. Here St Evremond's dry comment is evidently to the point:

'One exposes oneself to contempt when one comes back into high society after a certain age . . . with the reputation of a mordant and bitter disposition that everyone distrusts and fears; not to mention the fact that one's manners can hardly fail to be out of fashion, and this makes a man disagreeable, troublesome, and frequently ridiculous.'

Nevertheless, life had been tolerable enough at Bussy-Rabutin, where Bussy wrote his memoirs and embellished his château.

'I get along very nicely here . . . I live very well, I have neither master nor mistress, because I am without ambition and am not in love. I experience what I should have thought impossible two years ago – that one can live without these two passions.'

He did not always feel like this. Mme de Montglat, who had betrayed him while he was imprisoned in the Bastille, continued to obsess him, and he even invited Mme de Sévigné to become his mistress. One could not, he told her, 'be an *honnête homme* unless one were permanently in love'; besides what better way than this to avenge her husband's infidelities? But the sensible woman was not to be tempted. 'Let us be content, my dear cousin,' she wrote, 'to enjoy the good blood that circulates so gently and pleasantly in our veins.' Bussy did not persist. 'Let us laugh and make good cheer,' he replied. Marriage was incidental to his pleasures, although in fact he was twice married, having kidnapped Mme de Miramion in the Bois de Boulogne. His latter years were marked by a certain piety, though he had a sacred horror of Jansenism. 'Let us win our salvation with our good relative St François de Sales. He leads people to Paradise by more ways than the gentlemen of Port-Royal.' In the year before his death Bussy made a translation of the Easter hymn, '*O filii et filiae*', to expiate the scandalous 'Alleluias' which had once brought obloquy upon his name.

We must now inspect the château, for not many places are so firmly stamped with the character of their most famous occupant. You will observe the immense lime tree outside the gate, and two others on the east side of the building as you approach it; the barn with its wooden pillars; the elegant cordon of apple trees; the Renaissance lanterns on the terrace; the moat; and the broad flights of stone steps. The château, freely adapted from an earlier building, dates from 1649, and the *mansardes* were added in the reign of Louis XIV. It has four large towers, and arcaded wings frame the *cour d'honneur*. Viewed from the exterior it resembles many other châteaux of the *grand siècle* – several of these you may see reproduced on the walls of the *salle des devises*, for Bussy was nothing if not competitive. In the hall of warriors hang the portraits – mostly imaginary – of 65 famous soldiers, among whom Bussy did not hesitate to include himself as the '*maître-de-camp général* of the light cavalry in France'. Bayard and du Guesclin rub lifeless features with Buckingham and Cromwell, 'whom great talents and the greatest of crimes have condemned to an eternal fame' – for here, as elsewhere, each portrait has its inscription. On the wainscot panelling Fortune is depicted with the features of Mme de Montglat, accompanied by two mottoes: '*Leves ambo, ambo ingratae*'[1] and '*Levior aere*'[2] – the second over a pair of scales of which one side displays the same unforgiven and unforgotten features, and the other is blank. In the *chambre du Comte* we meet the *Grande Mademoiselle*, and two likenesses of Mme de Maintenon – one in advanced age; and in the *Tour Dorée* the portraits of those women who had interested Bussy in one way or another. Many of these, too, we shall have met before, if we have glanced through *L'Histoire Amoureuse des Gaules.*

Here notably is 'Isabelle-Cecile Huraut de Cheverny, Marquise de Montglat, whose inconstancy has done honour to the matron of Ephesus' – although in the *Histoire* Bussy gives her better marks than this.

'Belise is a good friend and takes, even brutally, the part of those she loves when people speak badly of them in front of her, and at need would give them all she possesses. She keeps their secrets as a sacred trust, and she gets on well with everybody. She doesn't win hearts as soon as others who are more insinuating; but once you realize her strength of character, you are all the more firmly attached to her.'

Then there are a pair of sisters – 'beautiful and well-intentioned, but their conduct has benefited from the care of a clever husband'; Mme de Gouville – 'beautiful, lovable, and lively, and as able as any woman in society to make a man happy, if she chose to love him; no one ever had a better friend'; the duchesse de Châtillon, 'to whom one could refuse neither one's purse nor one's heart, but who wasn't interested in lesser things'; the comtesse de Fisque – 'a woman to be admired for her appearance, and for the heart of a queen'; the duchesse de Choiseul – 'pretty, lively, and very well informed, particularly about the faults of other people. Strictly economical in her friendship, but economical in nothing for those to whom she gives it'; the marquise de la Baume – 'she would have been the prettiest and most lovable mistress in the land, if she had not been the most unfaithful'; the marquise d'Humières – 'a woman whose virtue, though it was neither

1. Both loose, and neither pleasing to look at.
2. Lighter than air.

rustic nor austere, would have satisfied the most fastidious'. Bussy did not, after all, want for company at Bussy-Rabutin.

The adjoining room is devoted to Mme de Sévigné; she hangs in a triptych with Mme de Grignan and Louise de Rouville, Bussy's second wife – fat, meaningless, majestic, and resigned. Elsewhere there is Bussy at the age of twenty in Roman costume – 'the beardless face of the vicious and insolent youngster'; and Bussy's verses underneath the mythological painting of Pygmalion:

> *Tout le monde en amour est tous les jours dupé,*
> *Les femmes nous en font accroire*
> *Si vous voulez aimer et n'être point trompé,*
> *Aimez une femme d'ivoire.*[1]

and of the Rape of Europa:

> *Les femmes font mille façons*
> *Pour duper les pauvres garçons*
> *Les garçons feignent mille flammes*
> *Pour attraper les pauvres femmes.*[2]

Most families have written their own history on the walls of their châteaux; Bussy-Rabutin has written his autobiography.

On the high ground opposite the village is **Bussy-le-Grand,** the birthplace of Andoche Junot (1771–1813), one of the most famous of Napoleon's generals – popularly known as '*La Tempête*'. They met at Toulon when Junot was only a sergeant. Napoleon appointed him as ambassador in Portugal, and then summoned him to Austerlitz. It was a December night; a sudden noise was heard outside the crumbling cottage where Bonaparte had set up his headquarters; and the huge silhouette of Junot appeared in the doorway. '*Me voilà, Sire.*' He returned to conquer Portugal; was created duc

---

1. Every man in love is every day deceived,
   The women make us love them all the more for it.
   If you want to love and not to be deceived,
   Love a woman made of ivory.

2. Women have a thousand ways
   Of deceiving the hapless young fellows
   The young fellows pretend to burn with a thousand flames
   To catch the hapless women.

d'Abrantès; and was badly wounded in the Russian campaign. After the great retreat he governed the Illyrian provinces for a time, fell ill in Italy, and returned to Montbard, where he committed suicide by throwing himself out of a window. He was spared the humiliation of Waterloo but he remains, nevertheless, among the more pathetic casualties of the Grande Armée.

There is nothing to detain you at Bussy-le-Grand, and you should retrace your steps for a kilometre along the N.454, turn left on the D.6, right on the D.10, and you will see **Flavigny-sur-Ozerain** perched on the other side of the valley – a total distance of about five kilometres. The view inspired Chateaubriand to an exalted comparison.

'I shall be indebted to the valley of Flavigny for one of my most vivid and moving memories. It looks like the valley of Jerusalem. There is the Cedron bathing the feet of the Holy City; and those ancient fortifications remind you of the ruined ramparts of the Temple. And surely those clumps of trees, in vigorous leaf – are the austere shades of the Mount of Olives?'

You enter the town through the machicolated Porte du Bourg (fifteenth century) and go straight on to the **Church of St Genest** – a thirteenth-century building considerably refashioned in the fifteenth. In the last chapel to the right of the nave there is a very beautiful Angel of the Annunciation – a masterpiece of the popular Burgundian school as this had developed by the end of the fifteenth century. Notice the carvings on the choir stalls of a cross-legged devil, a man holding his nose over an open book – what, one wonders, was he reading? – a man playing a bagpipe, another getting a stone out of his shoe, and a beggar clasping his leg; the stone screen to the gallery dividing the nave from the choir; and at the east end the cross erected 'à l'honneur de Dieu par Isaac Menassier 1627'. You will also observe, if you go up to the gallery, that the pews are graded – a very unusual feature.

The **Abbey Church of St Pierre** – or what remains of it – stands at the extreme south-west corner of the town. This was founded in the eighth century, and the upper parts were rebuilt in the eleventh and thirteenth. In 1956 a hexagonal chapel of the eighth century was discovered by a young American. This is known as the 'crypt of St Reine', who was buried there. The Gallo-Roman pillars, probably taken from the temple of Ucuetis at Alésia, and the early capitals, confirm its antiquity. You are obliged to find your way about the abbey by the aid of a gramophone record which leaves your questions unanswered – and you will probably have a good many of them, for the story of St Pierre is not easy to follow. No worse form of guidance could be devised. The former chapter house contains a number of sculptured fragments of no especial interest. The abbey and crypt can be visited from 9 to 12h and 14 to 18h.

Flavigny has very much taken St Reine to itself. A '*montreur de Ste Reine*' was a wooden, ogival reliquary, and when it was opened the saint – a doll-like figure – appeared in a purple cloak. She had a fervent clientèle among the vignerons, and gave her name to a particular kind of sideboard. Servants or children were told to '*ranger les assiettes dans la saintereine*'; young people danced in front of the *sainte-reine*; and the faithful chanted the praises of the

> *Vierge illustre dont la gloire*
> *Rejaillit sur Flavigny.*

Another '*gloire*', less popular than St Reine, but more relevant to Christianity in a century of unbelief, was Henri Lacordaire (1802–61), whose birthplace we have already noted at Recey-sur-Ource. He was the son of a doctor in Dijon; studied at the Lycée there; and lost his faith under the influence of an agnostic headmaster. He then practised at the bar for a couple of years; was converted by Chateaubriand's *Génie du Christianisme*; joined the seminary at Issy; was ordained in 1827; and became chaplain to the Lycée Henry IV in Paris. He had developed an early penchant for preaching, for which his forensic triumphs in the law courts were a temporary compensation, as they had been an occasional trial to his companions at home and at school. 'Sit down, Colette; this will be a long sermon.' 'I've had quite enough of it; you upset me. You get too excited.' 'No, no, Colette – there is too much sin in the world; it doesn't matter if it tires me, I always want to go on preaching' – such exchanges before he had lost his faith suggested what might happen when he regained it. In 1837 he felt a vocation to the Order of Preachers (the Dominicans), while he was staying at the Benedictine Abbey of Solesmes – where preaching enjoyed a very low priority. What he looked like in his Dominican habit – ardent and a little melancholy – is wonderfully conveyed by Chassériau's portrait in the Louvre.

The friend of Lamennais and Montalembert, and a Liberal deputy in the National Assembly, Lacordaire was among the fathers of liberal Catholicism. He contributed to Lamennais's journal *L'Avenir*, with its motto of *'Dieu et Liberté'*, but unlike Lamennais he submitted when this was condemned by the Roman authorities. He lacked the prophetic gifts of Lamennais and the erudition of Montalembert, but he was the greatest orator ever to occupy the pulpit of Notre-Dame. In 1848 he returned to Dijon – with unconcealed delight – but did not remain there for long. With seven novices he occupied the former *petit séminaire* at Flavigny, and furnished it with a few beds, two or three tables, and seven chairs – one for each novice, which they transported from one room to another. The Bishop of Dijon was reproached for allowing Lacordaire to leave his diocese; but he could not resist the great Dominican's appeal. 'The letter he wrote me was so simple, and not always correct in its spelling, that I took him for the biggest fool in my diocese.' You may still visit the **Maison Lacordaire,** which overlooks the twin round towers and double archway of the Porte du Val on the northern edge of the town. It is now a retreat house for women.

Flavigny is delightful and evocative to stroll in. You will admire the many stone roofs, and Renaissance houses. If you have left your car in the Esplanade des Fossés, you can very agreeably walk round the ramparts from here to the Porte du Val. Burgundy has not tempted the modern artist like Normandy and Provence, but Flavigny was a favourite centre for Augustus John and William Rothenstein in the early days of the New English Art Club. Rothenstein describes in *Men and Memories* a visit to the abbey of St Pierre, where he was lucky to find a monk in a monastery.

'I was so touched by the beauty of the interior and the

sense of peace and security it induced, that the monk who was with me hoped that perhaps I was on the verge of conversion. He led me at last to his plain, whitewashed room, where he bade me sit down, and then and there he tried to prevail on me to remain. All without was vanity, he said; only with them, and with others like them, could there be peace. I was moved, but a little uncomfortable. I was a painter, I explained, and to me the world was appealingly beautiful: in any case, I needed time for reflection. The Benedictine sighed, and conducted me to the door of the monastery where, with her bright gold hair, Miss Kingsley was waiting.'

Nobody looking at Rothenstein's portraits of Alice Kingsley, whom he was shortly afterwards to marry, would be surprised that she was not waiting there in vain.

The Porte du Bourg (or Porte de Semur) leads you straight on to the D.9J. Facing the junction of this road with the N.5 you will notice an unpretentious but attractive château of considerable antiquity. **Villiers** belongs to an Englishman, Mr Arnold Fawcus, director of the Trianon Press in Paris. Burgundy already owes him much for the magnificent illustrated book on Giselbertus's sculptures at Autun, and will be further indebted to him for the patient restoration of Villiers. When this has been completed, visitors may hope to be allowed to see the interior at appropriate times. Having enjoyed this privilege myself, I can testify to Mr Fawcus's aesthetic discretion; you will get here something of the family, as distinct from the feudal, impression that you got at Ratilly. In both cases craftsmen are evidently at work. Mr Fawcus is also a leading expert on delphiniums, and has some choice specimens in his garden. From Villiers it is an easy drive back to Semur on the D.9.

2

Another excursion – this time farther afield – should be undertaken from the Lac de Pont. Follow the D.103F to its junction with the N.80; turn left and drive the twenty kilometres to **Saulieu.** This was the Roman Sidolocus; it stood on

Château de Bussy-Rabutin: Paintings in the Hall of Warriors.

Château de Bussy-Rabutin: The garden front.

Saulieu: Eglise de Saint Andoche. 'Balaam on his ass, hammer in hand and feet firmly in stirrups, rides against a rich background of foliage, and you can read his vision in his eyes.'

the main trade route to the south; and three Christian
missionaries from Autun were martyred here. St Andoche
was a priest from Greece, St Thyrsus a deacon, and St Felix
a merchant of the town. Once again we find ourselves in the
high windswept corridor between the Auxois and the Morvan.
Saulieu was once a prosperous centre of commerce with
twelve annual fairs; and in the nineteenth century a factory
was set up where a hundred workmen produced 200,000
*sabots* a year for the peasants of the Morvan, who had been
used to making them for themselves. Gradually, however, the
mechanization of the industry and its wide dispersion reduced
the importance of Saulieu, and the local factory had difficulty
in maintaining itself. No such decline has affected the gastro
nomic reputation of the town. It was a natural halt for
luncheon if you had made an early start from Paris, and is
now only a few kilometres from the autoroute. Rabelais
praised its cuisine, and Mme de Sévigné, stopping here on
her way to Vichy, confessed that for the first time in her life
she had been the worse for drink.

In our own times a succession of famous chefs – Victor
Burtin and Alexandre Dumaine – have placed the **Côte d'Or**
among the first restaurants in France. M. Dumaine described
himself as 'simply an artisan with a deep love of my profession,
and to exercise it is my *raison d'être*'. He served his apprentice-
ship under Raymond Baudoin, nicknamed '*le mal nécessaire*',
for he was not the easiest of masters any more than his pupil
was the most tolerant of chefs. When Léon Daudet, having
ordered a *daube de bœuf*, poured over it the contents of a pot
of mustard, Dumaine went alternately pale and red with
anger, and took the plate back to the kitchen. When General
de Lattre de Tassigny gave orders that he should be served
without a moment's delay, it required all Madame Dumaine's
diplomacy to prevent his immediate expulsion. King Alfonso
XIII was a faithful client of the Côte d'Or, with a preference
for cold saddle of hare and red currant jelly; and when
Salvador Dali, who had not rallied to the Republic of Neo-
Encyclopaedists, arrived at the restaurant, he observed simply,
'*Je veux manger comme mon roi*'. The 21 August 1944 was
a sad day for M. Dumaine, whatever may have been his
political sympathies. Marshal Pétain, under German escort,

stopped in Saulieu on his way to Sigmaringen, never again to enter France as a free man. The menu befitted the occasion: potage, omelette, potatoes, salad, fromage à la crème, and fruit. M. Dumaine had 450 different wines in his cellar, but it would then have been an insult to misfortune to serve anything but a *vin courant*. Like many other great chefs, he set his face against *plats flambés*: '*Pas de pyrotechnie*' he told you '*mais de la cuisine vraie*'. But his *poularde de Bresse Belle Aurore*, his peewits' eggs, his *lièvre à la royale*, and his duckling with turnips from Jarnois, grown on a narrow strip of ground at Alligny in the Morvan, were classics of the table; and the sleek, expensive limousines that stand in front of the door are a provocation to slender purses. If you are already feeling poor, they will make you feel poorer still.

Good food and romanesque architecture are among the chief pleasures of travel in France, and at Saulieu you will be wise to give priority to the second. In other words you should visit the **Church of St Andoche** before you visit the restaurant of M. Dumaine, for here you will need all your wits about you. In the fifth century a tomb was raised over the bodies of the martyred missionaries, and a monastic community established which drew many pilgrims to Saulieu. Among them were King Clovis and Queen Clothilde, the 'good King Bontran', Queen Brunéhaut, St Columba and St Germain, and Charlemagne himself. In 706 the abbot Waré, who had founded St Pierre at Flavigny, left all his money to the basilica, which was rebuilt by Charlemagne after it had been ruined by the Saracen invasions. The crypt, now unfortunately buried, probably dates from this time; we know that, like many others built at about the same date, it contained a rotunda. The church was consecrated on 21 December 1119 by Pope Calixtus II, and it showed certain influences from Cluny. The bones of the saints were then transferred from the crypt into the choir.

In the twelfth century St Andoche was taken over by secular canons, but it was not spared by the English during the Hundred Years War. Indulgences freely bestowed helped to restore the sanctuary, and in the fifteenth century the Bishop of Autun (who also had the title of Abbot of Saulieu) built chapels to the nave, which had survived the previous desecration. During the wars of religion a strong Protestant faction was dominant at Saulieu, causing much trouble to the chapter; and the church slumbered on through the seventeenth and eighteenth centuries. One of its deans, André Frémyot, brother of St Jeanne de Chantal, became Archbishop of Bourges. In the eighteenth century the choir was rebuilt, and the steeple, which had twice fallen down, was placed on the north tower of the façade, and crowned with a pretty Italian dome.

The façade itself is quite unimpressive, and all your attention will be fixed on the six bays of the nave, which imperceptibly widens as you go from west to east. The side aisles are closed at their eastern end. The choir is visibly wider than the nave, with two bays and polygonal apse. It is generally agreed that the nave was inspired by the third, and largest, of the churches built at Cluny, freely interpreted by the Saulieu architect. The fluted pilaster has given way to the traditional half-column, so that one has the impression of a transition between Vézelay and the churches of the Brionnais that we shall be visiting later on. The nave is constructed in three storeys; a slightly pointed arch, a 'blind' triforium of circular, quadruple arcades, and a single lancet window above. The door opening from the second bay of the south aisle, which originally gave access to the cloister, with its row of diamond-pointed keystones and very simple tympanum, is a magnificent example of the purified Cistercian style.

The fifty-nine Capitals which adorn the pillars of the nave add incomparably to its lustre, and one need not ask whether St Bernard would have approved of them. St Bernard disapproved of many things that we should admire, and approved of certain others – notably the Crusades – that we should probably condemn. Most of the capitals are rhythmic variations on floral themes, and in one of them you may see the solemn countenance of an owl staring through the foliage. Elsewhere two cocks are furiously fighting; a pair of wild boars not less savagely come to grips; and a couple of monsters, by contrast, exchange the kiss of peace. But these excursions into the world of creatures are rare, except when they illustrate, incidentally, a Biblical subject. Here we have five masterpieces of romanesque sculpture; Balaam on his ass with the angel, the Flight into Egypt, the Temptation of Christ, the meeting with Mary Magdalen after the Resurrection, and the suicide of Judas. They merit a particular attention.

Two things will strike you. First the alliance of imagination and technique; the sculptor knows exactly what he wants to say, and how to say it in the limited, and rather awkward, space at his disposal – a space that presents no problems to acanthus leaves, but lends itself less easily to human and divine drama. Each of these capitals is a miracle of dramatic and emotional concentration. Secondly, you will notice that there is no apparent connection between them, except their Biblical source. The artist chose the subject that appealed to him, and placed it where he pleased. (There may have been more than one sculptor at work, but the stamp of the same workshop is evident.) Balaam on his ass, hammer in hand and feet firmly in stirrups, rides against a rich background of foliage, and you can read his vision in his eyes. The angel, from the left of the ass's head, grasps a branch of the tree, and is thus integrated in the total design. Similarly, an angel supports Christ in the Temptation, and Christ holds the trunk of a tree in His right hand, while the Devil offers Him a loaf of bread. The maniac ferocity of the one is contrasted with the slightly inquisitive expression of the other, as if Christ were looking beyond the Devil and the proffered loaf, and seeking to penetrate the deeper significance of His trial.

Even more profound in religious feeling is the apparition to Mary Magdalen, where the '*Noli me tangere*' is translated by the hieratic and stylized folds in the robe of the Risen Christ, and by His uplifted, outspread hands – like the priest's '*Dominus Vobiscum*' in the Mass. But this is counterpoised by the anxious compassion in the face, and by the much freer treatment of the Magdalen, who holds the jar of spikenard in her left hand and gathers up her dress with her right. This extends to the two other women at the empty tomb, shown with the grave-clothes hanging out through a pair of low romanesque arches, and an angel seated above, thus completing the story on the adjoining face of the capital. In the *Flight into Egypt* a rather plain Virgin, with pointed nose and receding chin, rides in profile side-saddle, clasping a worried infant in swaddling clothes, among oak-trees that dangle their heavy acorns. In the *Suicide of Judas*, implacable in its symbolic realism, the tree has an obviously functional purpose, and the weight that tightens the noose is a bag of money held by a devil grinning, as it seems, more in anguish and anger than in mirth. What fascinates, and sometimes perplexes, the observer of these astonishing works of art is to decide how far the intensity of feeling is correlated with the perfection of form; and to see how certain motifs – the fall of a drapery or the interlacing of a branch – are common to all of them, and are repeated in other capitals which have no human or divine content.

Do not miss the superb marble **Sarcophagus of St Andoche** in the north transept, unsigned and undated, with a Maltese cross, an Alpha and Omega, and the formal images of grapes and cattle. There are good coloured statues of St Roch, without his angel; and of Notre-Dame de Miséricorde enfolding her clientèle in a wide cloak.

Next door to the church is a particularly interesting **Museum,** with Gallo-Roman steles from a neighbouring burial ground; the figures of dead people clasping the tools of their trades dating from the third century, and more Etruscan than Roman in style; a St Jacques that formerly stood by a miraculous spring and was the object of a popular cult until the middle of the nineteenth century; Charlemagne's 'Gospel' bound in wood, silver, and ivory; Marie Antoinette's handkerchief; a complete Morvan kitchen with its utensils, showing how the peasantry ate and cooked up to 1914; and examples of the local tanning industry. The museum is open from 15 June to 30 September between 10 and 12h, and 14 and 18h.

The sculpture of François Pompon (1855–1933), a native of Saulieu, deserves a place in any museum. He was apprenticed to a marble-cutter in Paris, and frequented the Jardin des Plantes to get ideas for his studies of animals in motion. 'I used to carry a miniature carpenter's bench round my neck, held by a piece of string, and I worked as I walked along, looking at nothing but the animal and the shapes it took.' But Pompon was more than a mere copyist; he knew, supremely, how to simplify – as you can see from his mole,

smooth black pigeon, and jumping pig in the Saulieu museum.
Dunoyer de Segonzac was a warm admirer of his, which is
more than can be said for the municipality of his native town.
They refused his design for a war memorial – a peasant of the
Morvan leaning on a cow with upraised arm – and substituted
what Pompon described as a 'wart on the promenade'. Much
of his work is reminiscent of Gaudier-Brezska, and we shall
meet it again at Dijon.

On leaving Saulieu follow the N.6 for four and a half
kilometres, and turn left on the N.77 *bis* for the château of
**Thoisy-la-Berchère.** This dominates the Auxois from a steep
buttress of what is still the Morvan, as you emerge from the
Forêt de Thoisy. The present building was raised between
1430 and 1483 by Cardinal Rolin, Bishop of Autun, and son
of a famous chancellor of the Dukes. It passed through several
different hands until it was bought by the Marquise de
Choiseul in 1740. It is now owned by the Comtesse de Durfort,
to whom it has come down through the female line. The
twelfth-century keep of the former château was restored in
the nineteenth century, and other restorations were undertaken at the same time. It looks down to a lake below a sloping
lawn, and faces a grove of trees on the rising ground beyond.
You may notice a large sequoia, reputed to be 300 years old.
The chapel, restored in the sixteenth century, contains relics
of St Victor and St Boniface; and elsewhere there is a portrait
of Mme de Montespan by a pupil of Mignard, and in the
long gallery with its painted wood carvings illustrating the
siege of Nancy and the Sieur de Thoisy leaving for the
Crusade, you can read the following motto above the fireplace: '*Ayez l'amour de la Magdelaine*'.

Follow the N.77 *bis* out of Thoisy, and then strike north for
**St Thibault** by way of Mont St Jean, Thore, Charny, and
Verchlay (D.36, D.117, D.108B). The late Gothic church at
St Thibault is of remarkable elegance. Statues of the Blessed
Trinity stand over the west door in a lively composition with
Chaucerian ladies to right and left. A *columbarium* hangs over
the principal altar for the exposition or reservation of the
Blessed Sacrament, manipulated by a system of pulleys and
chains. Notice the impressive reredos illustrating the life of
St Thibault, with a Crucifixion in the centre panel, and the

agonized expression of the soldier who is drawing or sheathing his sword. The founder of the church is shown in full armour on his tomb; monks are reading at two of the corners, and a third swings a censer; and a bas-relief of the funeral is set behind, while at its foot a lion is gnawing at a bone. Wood panelling with carved medallions surrounds the short nave, and there are no side aisles. Observe the very tall and narrow four-storeyed window behind the altar, divided by two galleries; here is the virtuosity of Gothic aspiration and transparency which over-reached itself at Beauvais, but which in Burgundy is generally controlled. The choir at St Thibault is so much higher than the west end of the church that you get the effect of a complete separation. There are two very beautiful coloured statues of the Virgin and Child (fourteenth century), and a monumental Calvary.

From St Thibault you have a straight run back to the Lac de Pont by the N.470.

# CHAPTER NINE

# From Semur to Dijon

It is an easy day's drive, even with the detours I shall suggest. Take the D.10C to **St Colombe,** where there is a fine statue of St Michel (sixteenth century) in the church, and on to **Marcilly-les-Vitteaux.** Here you will see a particularly impressive monumental crucifix on the *parvis*, with St Sebastian and St Roch, and another saint below. The fourth is missing. Turn left on the 117D for **Vitteaux,** which should detain you for more than a moment. As the old rhyme went:

> *Dieu nous gard' du feu, de l'eau*
> *Et du baron de Vitteau*

So you will expect to find the traces – the towers, in fact – of the fortress from which Guillaume Du Prat terrified the countryside. In the fourteenth-century church notice the flamboyant tribune to the organ loft, the painted vault in the chapel to the right of the choir; the fifteenth-century stalls; Van Hoey's triptych; and the funeral vault of the Languet, with its cruciform sarcophagi, and black flames, skulls and crossbones on the walls – a macabre invention of 1640. Among the members of the family buried here are Hubert Languet (1518–81), minister to the Prince of Orange, and J. J. Languet, Archbishop of Sens. Another native of Vitteaux was the intrepid Colonel de Chambure whose troop of a hundred men at the siege of Danzig in 1813 was known as the '*compagnie infernale*'. Notice, too, the old well on the esplanade; Maison Belime, with its thirteenth-century façade; and on other houses the corbels, pillars, and dovecotes.

A turning to the right on the D.117 will bring you to **Lignières,** with its open air oven and market-hall; **Beurizot,** where the sixteenth-century statues of no less than fifteen saints adorn the church; and **Soussey-sur-Brionne,** with a twelfth-century chapel that deserves a glance. Turning right in the village you will quickly join the N.470 which runs parallel with the railway line and brings you after seven kilometres to Pouilly-en-Auxois, at the foot of Mont de Pouilly (561 metres) and at the mouth of the **Tunnel** where the Canal de Bourgoyne passes from the basin of the Rhône to the basin of the Seine. The tunnel was built under Napoleon with a number of ventilation chimneys and is three kilometres long; you can just see one end from the other. By craning forward at the left entrance to it, holding on to the wire, and raising your voice, you can produce a remarkable echo. The canal emerges between wooded banks and a high stone cutting; 56 steps lead down to it from the street, just off the D.16 to your right as you leave the village. Topographically speaking, Pouilly-en-Auxois is a strategic point; a more heavily wooded and spectacular landscape lies before you to the east.

**Pouilly-en-Auxois** was the chief town of a Gallo-Roman *pagus* up to the eighth century, and you must stop here to visit the little church with the charming name of Notre-Dame-Trouvée. The *trouvaille* was a statue of the Virgin in painted wood said to have been miraculously discovered. The church is late Gothic (fourteenth and fifteenth century), standing half-way up the slope of a hill in the middle of a cemetery, outside the town on your right, as you follow the N.484 in the direction of Arnay-le-Duc. It has a double nave, and an over-dramatized sixteenth-century Sepulchre. Nine characters compose the *mise-en-scène*; the women grouped in the centre, as you find them in the Sepulchres of Champagne, but with recognizably Burgundian draperies, while the sleeping soldiers and the angels carrying the instruments of the Passion betray an influence Italian rather than French. There is a small and very serene Christ in wood, from the Château de Fretois in the Aisne, on the left wall of the principal nave. If you climb the sloping passageway at the end of the church, you will admire the timber work above the quadripartite vaulting – but do not be surprised if you startle an owl in doing so. Notice also, close to one of the entrances to the cemetery, a curious grouping in stone of a pulpit, altar, and Calvary – all of the sixteenth century. The church is normally

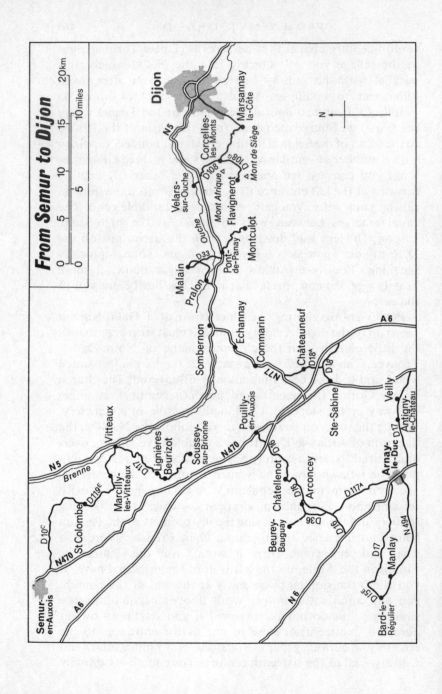

From Semur to Dijon

shut, but the key is readily obtainable from a house close by. St Peter's Day in Pouilly used to be celebrated with a good deal of fun by the lords of the district. They built a fort which was attacked and defended with competitive zeal, and the victors were escorted home with a fanfare.

From Pouilly, turning to your right in the middle of the town, you can follow the D.16 and D.16B to **Châtellenot.** Here there are the remains of a windmill and a feudal château, and a Cluniac apse in the church. The village stands among marshy meadows and has been called 'the roof of France', since their waters eventually find their way to the Atlantic, the Mediterranean, and the Channel; for this reason Gabriel Hanotaux described all this country as a 'French St Gothard'. (Note that the French do not give the Channel its English prefix; it has meant less to them than to us.) At Châtellenot ceremonial fires are lit at Christmas; and this is rare in the Côte d'Or. You may then proceed by way of Arconcey to **Beurey-Bauguay,** where you should notice the fountain in the churchyard with its Gallo-Roman cupola and tombs. People with a high temperature used to walk three times round one of these, lie down beside it, and drink some water. The D.36 and D.117A will take you from here to Arnay-le-Duc – a distance of about twelve kilometres.

**Arnay-le-Duc** has earned the title of 'the heart of France', although it does in fact stand some way from the centre of the country. It was here that the Huguenots gained a decisive victory against enormous odds in the spring of 1570, and the young Henri of Navarre – a lad of sixteen – won his spurs. Coligny, whose fortunes seemed at their lowest, had marched south with Condé and Navarre in what was afterwards called '*Le Voyage des Princes*'. Another journey through Arnay-le-Duc, two hundred years later, might well have been called '*Le Voyage des Princesses*', for the two aunts of Louis XVI – Adelaide and Victoire – were arrested here on their way to Italy. They were held in the presbytery by the 'constitutional' priest, and went to bed immediately after tea, having been obliged to wash their single set of underwear, and hang it out to dry till the morning. The little town gave its name to the motto that stood over the Renaissance château bought as a hunting seat by the 'grand Condé', Governor of Burgundy, in 1634: '*Arneti laeta juventus*'. The classical style of the church, with its domed vestibule of the eighteenth century, will lessen your surprise at the nude statues within; and perhaps something in the *genius loci* had inspired Bonaventure Des Periers, a native of Arnay, to the verses of his *Cymbalum Mundi*. This *valet de chambre* to Marguerite of Navarre was described as 'a little Voltaire of the day before yesterday, who must have known Rabelais'; Rabelais certainly inspired him. Behind the apse of the church a thick fifteenth-century tower, with machicolated gallery, is all that remains of the feudal château which changed hands several times during the wars of religion, and was finally destroyed by the Catholics.

Arnay is a sizeable and attractive town, and do not let a star in Michelin deter you from eating (or staying) at the Hôtel Terminus, on your right as you follow the N.6 in the direction of Chalon. You will get excellent value at moderate expense. At the corner of the rue President Carnot there is an admirable Renaissance house in stone with pepper pot turret and watch tower.

If time permits you should strike off to the west from Arnay, by the D.17 and the D.15E, to visit the priory of **Bard-le-Régulier.** The choir, single transept and central nave with semi-circular arches remain of what was once a flourishing foundation. The inscription on a *gisant* of 1305 reminds you that '*tu seras ce que je suis*'. The woodwork on the late fourteenth-century stalls is extremely rich with their carvings of animals, a woman acrobat, and scenes from the life of the Virgin and St John. Returning by the massive fortified church of **Manlay,** just to the south of Bard, you should take the road to Chalon out of Arnay-le-Duc, and turn off almost immediately on the D.17 for **Antigny-le-Château.** The château is not open to visitors, but you can admire its single, round, machicolated tower with pepper pot roof at one corner of the quadrangle. The place stands in agreeably domestic contrast to the ruins of a feudal keep beyond.

Turn left again at the next village, **Veilly,** where a fine *Vierge de Miséricorde* in the church is worth attention; join the N.470 and follow it north to **Ste-Sabine,** which has an impressive church tower and porch; then turn right on the D.18, and left on the D.18A, which will take you across the

autoroute to **Châteauneuf**. Here the twelfth-century fortress
was enlarged and refashioned at the end of the fifteenth
century by Philippe Pot, seneschal of Burgundy under
Philippe le Bon. His magnificent tomb by Claus Sluter is now
in the Louvre. The château was presented to the State by
Comte Georges de Vogüé, who had done not a little to restore
it. With its moat, drawbridge, and five massive towers, it is a
striking example of military architecture, and imperiously
commands the plain. You can visit it at all times throughout
the year; in summer from 10 to 12h and 13.30 to 18.30h, in
winter from 10 to 12h and 13.30 to 16h. You will admire the
delicate pale blue dining room, which is pure Louis XV; the
various baldaquin beds, one of them Polish in design, others
in the style favoured by Louis XI or Louis XIV; the Aubusson
tapestries in the guard room; and even the stone W.C. From
one of the bedrooms a window gives on to the chapel; so that
it was easy to attend Mass in one's dressing-gown. The church
has a good pulpit with early wooden bas-reliefs; and the old
houses in the village – dating from the fourteenth to the
seventeenth century – formerly occupied by rich Burgundian
merchants, are remarkably well preserved. Châteauneuf was
not too far from Dijon for a man who could afford 'a place
in the country'.

A turning to the left out of the village brings you very
quickly on to the N.77 *bis* and, striking north for three
kilometres, to **Commarin**. The château now belongs to the
Comte Louis de Vogüé, although the motto above the archway
(which originally stood nearer to the house) '*Tout bien à
Vienne*' reminds you that the place was once the property of
the Comte de Vienne, '*premier chevalier de la Toison d'Or*', in
1430, whose portrait in the costume of 1600, and commissioned by his grandson, you may see inside. The château has
a wide moat, and was built on piles under Louis XIV. It has
four towers, two square and two round; one of them, higher
than the others, with a campanile, encloses a charming
romanesque chapel. Notice the miniature Sepulchre, and the
painted heads supporting the window arch. The former
occupants of the château evidently had a mind for entertain-
ment, for you will observe the pulleys over the stage in the
great salon. The tapestried chairs are particularly fine, and

Talleyrand's mother (in default of Henri IV or the *Roi Soleil*) slept in one of the bedrooms. There is a curious carving of an antelope laying his paw on the archway at the foot of the staircase. You look out on to a *parc à l'Anglaise*, which has replaced the former terraces. The château is open to visitors every day, except Tuesday, from 14 to 18h between 15 April and 30 September.

Do not leave Commarin without visiting the **Church**. A superb early-sixteenth-century reredos is set behind the altar in the chapel on the right of the choir.

The N.77 *bis* will take you to **Echannay,** where another reredos of the same period merits a momentary halt, and thence to the N.5 at Sombernon. Turn right for a few kilometres, and then left to **Pralon,** which is just off the main road. An abbey of Cistercian nuns was founded here in 1135. St Bernard was their spiritual director, and you may see the stone where he is said to have sat, and the spring which is reputed to have answered with alacrity to the touch of his stick. There is a stone crib (sixteenth century) in the church. Just north of Pralon you will come to **Malain** – the Roman Mediolanum. The remains of a palaeo-Christian basilica underwrite the claims of the village itself to canonization, for St Seine and St Baudry were born here, St Eustace lived here, and St Antège died here.

You can return quickly to the N.5 by the D.33, cross it at Pont de Pany, and follow the D.35 to **Montculot,** a steep ascent from the valley of the Ouche. You are now in the heart of the **Montagne,** where the hills, divided by narrow wooded valleys, or *combes*, rise to over 600 metres, until they fall away abruptly to the Côte. The contrast is equally striking with the fertile pastures of the Auxois, which you have left behind, and the 'slopes of gold', very differently fertile, that beckon you to the east. Burgundy, in the restricted connotation of the word, is now on the tip of your expectation.

In the meanwhile the château of **Montculot,** isolated on its hill-top at a bend in the road, will easily induce you to a Lamartinian '*méditation*', for Lamartine inherited the domain from his uncle, the abbé de Lamartine, and wrote many of his poems here during the first thirty years of the nineteenth century. One of them was inspired by a stream –

the source du Foyard – that runs through the park. The château is an elegant eighteenth-century building, its formality only enhanced by its sombre romantic setting and the romanticism of the poet who so often stayed here. Montculot is not normally open to the public. It was shuttered and secret when I last saw it; but its situation and its loneliness make it different from any other château in Burgundy, and it whispers a discreet introduction to the poet who will claim our closer attention on his native ground at Milly and Saint-Point. 'This château,' he wrote, 'was built by the stars, for only they can see it.' For another observer, Jacques Chenedolent, 'A delicate scent of the past still clings to it. You seem to recover something of the life of its late inhabitants; the trace of their elbows on the balconies, their footsteps on the sand, and under the lime trees of the adjoining park; and the faint echo of the romances sung in the great salon, with the windows open to a summer evening, some time about 1830.'

You should now retrace your steps to the N.5, and turn right for **Velars.** Here, on the hill opposite the village, is the shrine of Notre-Dame d'Etang – a statue of the Virgin said to have been discovered by an ox; a ruined château below; and mural paintings of the thirteenth century in the chapel of Notre-Dame la Noire. The D.108 will take you up, once again, from the valley of the Ource to Corcelles-les-Monts, and then by D.108G to the village of **Flavignerot,** beyond which you can go no farther. Immediately to the north is the crater – a narrow platform two kilometres long – of Mont Afrique; to the south is Mont de Siège; and another mountain, just as high, faces you to the west. Away to the east, you can see the blue ridges of the Jura and even, on a fine day, Mont Blanc. If you have arrived here in the early evening, you should follow the footpath – a distance of five and a half kilometres or an hour's walk – which encircles the crest of Mont Afrique. This will give you incomparable views on every side. The Romans built a camp at the south-eastern end of the crater, and a number of tombs have been discovered there.

Now prepare yourself for as dramatic a contrast as any that I know in landscape. Continuing along the road from Corcelles-les-Monts, you will come out on to what seems a broad plateau, where the trees have given way to thin pasture and brushwood, and then – here and there – a tentative patch of vines. At last, in a matter of seconds, you are at the summit of a *combe*: there, below you, is the village of Marsannay-la-Côte, whose delicious *rosé* you will presently be drinking; beyond, uninteresting and indistinct, is the Pays-Bas; and everywhere, to your right and left and almost under your feet, the vines, in the words of Belloc's *Heroic Poem*, 'swell the rich slope or load the empurpled plain.'

As I shall indicate in the next chapter, there are other ways of approaching Dijon – but none so rewarding as this. A ten minutes' drive from Marsannay-la-Côte will bring you into the heart of the city.

CHAPTER TEN

# Dijon

❧

## 1

Dijon has been called 'the cradle and springboard' of the ducal dynasty. With its more than 200,000 inhabitants it is the largest Burgundian city, and capital of the Côte d'Or; readily accessible from north or south, since the fastest trains stop there, and a branch autoroute now links it with the autoroute du Sud. It is conveniently reached from Switzerland via the Jura; or from Italy by way of Chambéry or Grenoble. If Burgundy itself is something of a *pays de transition*, Dijon is an unmistakable cross-roads. This means that it is naturally busy, and inevitably noisy. The Cloche is an excellent, though expensive, hotel on the northern side of the Square Darcy, with service as good as you will find anywhere in the world; but the Chapeau Rouge has lost all its charm through striving for an international chic. You may prefer, however, to stay in one of the nearer villages along the Route des Grands Crus – Gevrey-Chambertin, Fixin, or Marsannay-la-Côte. Here I can only speak of Chez Jeannette at Fixin,[1] eleven and a half kilometres from the centre of the city, where you will be very comfortable, whether you occupy a room called 'Jonquil' or a room called 'Jacinthe'. In Dijon you may eat well at sharply escalating prices. The two famous restaurants in the Place Royale – Les Trois Faisans and Le Pré aux Clercs – have now been amalgamated, and I have no doubt that M. Raco-chot, who governed the former for so long, is turning in his grave.

It would be Utopian to expect a city which has never boasted of being behind the times to avoid the discordant appearances of industrialism, and ungracious to begrudge it the prosperity which industry deserves. But once you have passed through the huge, new agglomeration on the western

1. Pronounced 'Fissin'.

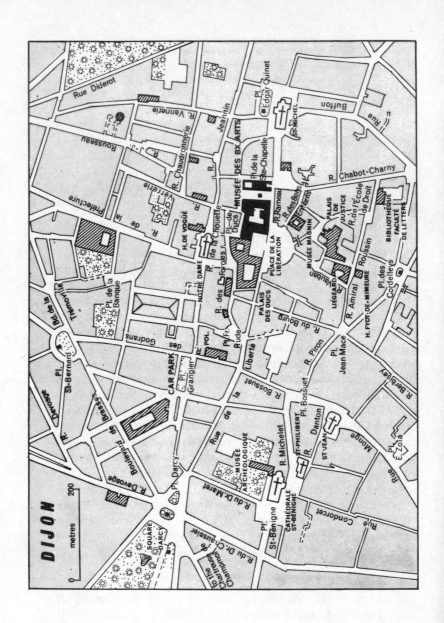

outskirts of the city, you may plunge securely into the past. The city was prosperous even in Roman times, as the bas-relief of a wine merchant and tradesman bears witness. Known as *castrum Divionense*, it was an important military and trading post. The walls stood 30 feet high and 15 thick, with 33 towers and 4 gates. Water from the Suzon and the Renne turned the mills, and Gregory of Tours reported them to be 'full of fish'. 'To the west', he wrote, 'the terraced slopes of the rich hills are covered with vineyards where they produce so noble a Falernian that the local inhabitants despise the wine of Askalon'. In the Middle Ages the stepped gables of the wooden houses, roofed with thatch, thin stone slabs (*laves*), or coloured varnished tiles, testified to Flemish influence. The curfew rang from the tower of St Jean, as the night watchman went his rounds, a steel bonnet under his hat, on the look out for the prowling *coquillards* François Villon not improbably among them.

There was some truth in a tourist's reply to a questionnaire that Dijon was 'not a place for tourists who are in a hurry'. If you choose your moment when the pavements are less crowded and the noise of the traffic has died down a little, it is a pleasant place to stroll in; but you will soon wish yourself back to a time when to do so was pleasanter still. Even in the nineteenth century Sainte-Beuve could put his observations into verse:

> *Nous allions admirer clochers, portails, et tours*
> *Et les vieilles maisons dans les arrière-cours.*

or as an old rhyme had it

> *Gothique donjon*
> *Et flèche Gothique*
> *Dans un ciel d'optique*
> *Là-bas c'est Dijon.*

## 2

You will need at least a couple of days to explore Dijon in depth, and for the most part you will prefer to do so on foot. The Cloche has a capacious garage, but if you are coming into

the city from the south there is convenient parking in the
Place Emile Zola, just off the rue Monge, with meters that
require periodic renewal. In any event this is a good starting
point, for a few yards farther up the street will bring you face
to face with Gasq's statue of Bossuet outside the *chevet* of
St Jean. The church has lost both its spires and apse, and is
now disaffected. On its wooden doors I saw the following
scrawled up in white chalk: '*Dieu anarchie; ni Dieu ni maître*'
– and wondered what Bossuet would have thought of such
sacrilege in the city where he was born, and in the church
where he was baptized.

Jacques-Bénigne Bossuet (1627–1704) was the son of a
magistrate in the Place St Jean. Educated by the Jesuits at the
Hôtel des Godran, he was ordained to the priesthood in Paris
in 1652, and became successively Bishop of Condom and
Meaux, tutor to the Dauphin, and chaplain to the Duchess of
Burgundy. He was the friend of the exiled Queen Henrietta
Maria, who gave him on her death-bed an emerald which he
subsequently wore as a ring on his little finger. He preached
her funeral oration – not the least of his titles to justify
Michelet's description of Burgundy as 'the country of orators,
of stately and solemn eloquence'. He successfully opposed
Fénelon and the Quietists, and here a parallel has been drawn
between Newman and Manning. For if Bossuet wrote with
Newman's grace and subtlety, he defended his theses with
Manning's intransigence, although the theses were diametric-
ally opposed. His statue does not belie the description inspired
by the tercentenary of his birth in 1927:

'In his clear and healthy face, the happy equilibrium of
his expression, his high intelligent forehead, his pleasant
mouth which seems to be speaking even when it says
nothing, in all this concentrated power, we recognize the
Burgundian of good blood.'

He belonged, wrote Brunetière,

'to that ancient *noblesse de robe*, where the taste for literature went rather generally hand in hand with a piety
sincere, but always reasonable and willingly argumentative.
He played the part of a conciliator . . . for he descended

from one of those families in which Gallicanism had become
like a second nature. He was well aware that no obstacle
stood any longer in the way of 'reunion' but the claims of
the Holy See to interfere in matters of temporal government.'

Turning left along the rue Danton, you come almost
immediately upon the **Cathedral of St Bénigne,** reputedly a
disciple of St Polycarp, Bishop of Smyrna, and sent in the
second century to evangelize Roman Gaul. He was believed to have preached and converted at Dijon and Autun
before being thrown into prison with three mad dogs and
executed by order of Marcus Aurelius. One of his catechumens,
Leonilla, helped to bury him; and it used to be the custom for
the sick to pour wine into the holes through which the rings
that fettered him in his cell were said to have been run. A
monastic community was formed around his tomb, richly
endowed by King Bontran; but it was only in 869 that
the abbey was placed under the rule of St Benedict. The
primitive church was rebuilt from top to bottom, and on a
much larger scale. Two buildings stood, the one above the
other, each with a wide transept and a rotunda at the east end.
Here, at the beginning of the tenth century, the body of St
Bénigne was enshrined with the remains of other saints
brought from a neighbouring cemetery.

This Carolingian basilica was considerably reshaped by
Abbot Guillaume de Volpiano, who was responsible for the
immense romanesque rotunda, three storeys high, a masterpiece of construction and design, described by Raoul Glaber
as '*le plus merveilleux de toute la Gaule*'. In 1110 the church
was badly damaged by fire, and its restoration was not complete until 1147. But the building lasted only a short time. In
1280 Abbot Hugues d'Arc, seized by the Gothic fashion,
razed it to the ground and work began on the church as it
stands today. The abbey was secularized at the Revolution,
and became the chathedral of Dijon in 1792. This promotion
was poor compensation for the vandalism which accompanied
it. The two upper storeys of the rotunda – for this was not
affected by the transformation which the rest of the building
had undergone – were totally destroyed, and the lower storey

was filled in with the rubble. It was not until 1843 that the construction of a new sacristy revealed it; and work upon its radical restoration proceeded over the next twelve years.

The cathedral of St Bénigne – with its sober Burgundian proportions, triforium gallery running all the way round a three-sided apse, its western towers two-storeyed, octagonal and uniform, its low spires roofed with red and green tiles, and the sculpted birds on the pinnacle above – is not without a certain grandeur. But the **Crypt** – whatever mistakes or conjectures may have impaired its restoration – is among the miracles of the romanesque. (Visits from 7 to 12.30h, and from 14 to 19h.) You reach it by a stone staircase at the east end of the south transept. Its proportions are exactly as Abbot Guillaume planned it, and much of its material is the same, however refashioned. It was not easy to decide, among the débris of walls and pillars, which stone should go in what place. But the rotunda is no temptation to pedantry. You will be content to admire the three circles of pillars – eight in the inner circle, sixteen in the outer, and twenty-two half pillars flush with the enclosing wall. There are annexes to the north and south of the small rectangular space at the west end, where the body of St Bénigne was venerated; and at the east end an oratory, also rectangular, thought to have served as a Lady Chapel. The vaulting can hardly be original, since it covers what was formerly open to a cupola; and the capitals – centaurs, ravens, and monsters – have given rise to some debate. They probably belong to the same period of late romanesque sculpture as the tympanum of Christ in majesty, also from the abbey of St Bénigne, which you may admire in the Musée archéologique. If you make the effort to reconstruct in your imagination what the crypt must once have looked like when, as the Chronicle tells us, ten windows illuminated the sanctuary; when stairways in two side turrets led to the second storey, which was supported by 68 columns; and when 36 of these adorned the third storey, dedicated to the Blessed Trinity and vaulted like a crown – you will hardly dispute the judgement that the rotunda of St Bénigne 'anticipated by a thousand years the most startling experiments of Le Corbusier'.[1]

1. *Bourgogne Romane*: p. 54.

The **Musée archéologique,** close alongside and occupying part of the former monastic buildings, is mainly devoted to Gallo-Roman antiquity. (Open on weekdays 9 to 12h, and 14 to 17h (or 16h in winter). Sundays and public holidays 10 to 12h, and 14 to 18h (or 16h in winter). Closed on Tuesday.) The exhibits have been collected from the site of the Bolards, near to Nuits-St-Georges, where Dr Planson, in 1964, discovered the outline of the streets from the exceptional dryness of the lucerne – a clover-like plant with spikes of blue and violet flowers; from Genlis, a little farther to the east, where the traces remain of ancient roads and Gallo-Roman villas; and from the thermal establishment south-west of Sens. All these places were on the main trade routes of the time. There are Dionysiac scenes on a vase from Alésia, the funerary stele of a man holding a vessel from St Romain, a seated mother – goddess from Noyers-sur-Serein, Epona on horseback from Censy, a hunting Hercules from Escolives, the head of Minerva with hollowed out eyes from Gissey-sous-Flavigny, the very finished statue of a boy holding a dog from Villiers-le-Duc, and wooden statues from the sources of the Seine discovered in 1963. The altar to the goddess Sequana, found at the same time, now stands in the church at Salmaise. Swords and arrows from the Bronze and Iron Age, and Merovingian axe-heads and door-handles are also to be seen.

In the lower room the immense head of a bull (eleventh century), and a bronze statue of Sequana on her boat, compel admiration. Here, too, are the ex-voto offerings that represent the limbs she was supposed to have healed; a wine merchant, a pilgrim, a horse-dealer, the head of a lion, and the tall statue of a young man reading a book. No object in the museum, however, is quite so remarkable as the immense **Dortoir des Benedictins** – a superb example of thirteenth-century monastic architecture, 70 metres in length, supported by its two rows of columns. Here we emerge into the Middle Ages with the tympanum – a Last Supper – from a side door of St Bénigne; the head of St Bénigne and the Christ in Glory from the central doorway; and a coloured, very realistic, fifteenth-century Nativity where the Child is feeding at its Mother's breast. A retable of the mid-sixteenth-century from Baigneux is particularly worth attention. St Veronica, the Crucifixion, and the Resurrection occupy its three parts. And do not overlook the bust of Christ, attributed to Claus Sluter, from the Calvary of Champmol.

## 3

Your next itinerary – easily to be made on foot – will take you from the ages of faith to the dawn of the age of reason. If you have refilled your motor in the Place Emile Zola, you have only to follow the rue Bossuet to its junction with the rue de la Liberté, turn to your right, and a few minutes' walk will being you to the **Place de la Libération,** formerly the Place Royale, which opens out in a graceful semi-circle in front of the Palais des Ducs, or, as it came later to be called, the Palais des Etats. An equestrian statue of Louis XIV once stood in the middle of it, but this was broken up by the Revolutionaries in 1792 and sent to the foundries at Le Creusot to serve as raw material for cannon. Such vandalism is now universally regretted, but it will require all the arts of municipal diplomacy to replace the statue of a crowned head in the centre of a republican city – quite apart from the fact that Jacques Gabriel's beautiful work is strictly irreplaceable. Nevertheless, the Place Royale is a reminder that the *Roi Soleil* was extremely fond of Dijon, where, as he said, 'the company is good, and where one lives with the greatest pleasure and in the greatest security under the protection of a careful and constantly active police'.

To describe the evolution of the **Palais des Etats**[1] into its present shape; the plans of competing architects and their dependence upon civic finance; the modification of original designs – would take us beyond the scope of this survey, and tax unduly the observation of the visitor. It will be enough to note its successive functions and distinctive features. The palais was built to accommodate the Three Estates, which

1. To visit the Cour de Flore, the salle des Etats, and the chapelle des Elus, you should apply to the custodian on the left of the courtyard, who will give you a ticket that will also cover a visit to the Musée des Beaux Arts. To visit the buildings of the Cour d'honneur, you should apply to the mayor's offices on the 1st floor between 8 and 10h, or between 14 and 16h.

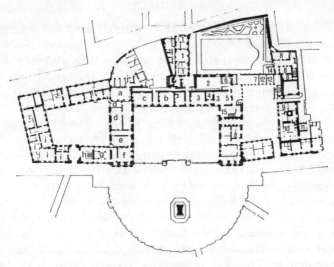

## PALAIS DES ETATS

PARTIE DES ETATS: *a* Chapel of the Etats. *b* Office of the Alcades. *c* Office of the Clergy. *d* Chamber of the nobility. *e* Chamber of the Third Estate. *f* Chamber of the Etats. *g* Archives. *h* Staircase of the Salle des Etats. *i* Apartment of the Elu from the Clergy. *j* stables and coach-house.

THE ROYAL QUARTERS: 1 Apartments. 2 Stables. 3 Offices. 4 Laundry. 5 Kitchens. 6 Butler's pantry. 7 Coach-house. 8 Piquerie and cook-shop. 9 Pastry kitchen. 10 The Prince's kitchens. 11 New poultry yards. 12 Butcher's quarters. 13 Charcoal-burner's quarters. 14 New ice-house. 15 The Prince's staircase.

assembled every three years from 1688, and their permanent executive, who discharged the duties of a civil service under the Governor, who was himself responsible to the King. The royal emblems that adorn the building were a compliment to the Princes de Condé, who governed the province for so many years. The Estates originally met in various Burgundian cities, and then from the beginning of the seventeenth century in the Couvent des Cordeliers at Dijon. They soon, however, felt the need of a permanent meeting place, and obtained permission from Louis XIV to install themselves in the Logis du Roi – formerly a part of the ducal palace, to which Louis XI and subsequent governors had added such auxiliary buildings as they required.

Of the ducal palace there remains the **Tour de Bar**, raised by Philippe le Hardi between 1360 and 1365, and so called after René de Bar, King of Sicily, who was imprisoned there. In front of it are the **Kitchens** built by Philippe le Bon in the

second quarter of the fifteenth century. Two great fireplaces
have their lintels supported by columns; eight ogival arches
converge upon the central vault; and a round stone indicates
the orifice through which the air could enter. The room is a
striking example of civic architecture in the Gothic style, and
one is not surprised at the Gargantuan feasts that were
served up from it. It adjoined the Tour de Bar by an interior
courtyard, of which the well can still be seen. There also
survives the vaulted passage leading from the Cour d'honneur
to the Place des Ducs, and a section of the first floor – the
original Guard Room – which now forms part of the museum.
Gone, alas, is the beautiful Sainte Chapelle, begun by Duke
Hugues III in 1172 and finished in the late fifteenth century.
Here the members of the Golden Fleece had their seats in
choir; and here the *Sainte Hostie* – consecrated Host –
presented to Philippe le Bon by Pope Eugenius IV, was
venerated until it was publicly burnt at the Revolution, and
the monstrance which enclosed it despatched to the Mint.
The chapel was replaced by a theatre.

The Palais des Etats as you see it today consists of a wide
rectangular courtyard, the Cour d'honneur, with two smaller,
interior courts, the Cour de Flore and the Cour de Bar, to the
left and right as you face the palace. The buildings on the east
side of the Cour de Flore, which separate it from the Cour
d'honneur, were erected under Louis XIV, those on the south
under Louis XV, and those on the north and west under
Louis XVI. The north front of the Cour de Bar dates from
Louis XIII, the north section of the west front under Louis
XIV, and the south section under Louis XVI, and the south
front from the same period. The court is bounded to the east
by the Tour de Bar, and a small section surviving from the
reign of Philippe le Bon. These are both enclosed by the new
wing, built under Napoleon III to house the Musée. Of the
two wings to the main building the western was built in
1709–1710 with the **Escalier du Prince,** which is now the
principal staircase of the Musée, but only completed in 1782.
Louis XVI – less attached to the city than Louis XIV – bowed
to the request of the *Elus* and bequeathed 'the land around his
Logis to Dijon'. The three large rooms on the first floor of the
western wing – the *'aile de Condé'* – which now serve as

offices for the Mayor and his assistants, were adorned with
mantelpieces sculpted by Jean Dubois (1626–1694). These
recorded the triumphs of Louis XIV, of which the Revocation
of the Edict of Nantes, where the King is seen, club in hand,
towering above the grovelling figure of heresy, was the least
worthy of celebration. The panelling was executed during the
first part of the eighteenth century. The main doorway of the
western wing, giving on to the rue Condé, lacks the original
tympanum – destroyed in 1785 in order that the doorways to
each of the two wings should be more perfectly symmetrical.
But it remains an impressive entrance with the figure of
Justice and a pair of gambolling Cupids surmounting it, and
a frontispiece where drums and helmets, draperies, grapes,
and palm leaves mingle in elegant profusion. In the opposite,
and eastern, wing of the Palace the salon Condé and the salle
des Statues are remarkable for the decorative work of a
Dijonnais sculptor, Jérome Marlet (1731–1810). Note
especially the medallions of the four seasons over the door of
the Salle des Statues.

If you are inclined to feel that the grandeur of Burgundy
was extinguished with its Dukes, you need only mount the
**Grand Staircase,** with its wrought iron balustrade, which
leads to the Salle des Etats. The landing projects on either
side and, with its balustrade, curves round to join the main
walls of the building. Looking back you see the statues of
Vigilance and Justice, and going forward you enter the hall
under a circular gallery supported by four pillars. From here
you can easily imagine the Three Estates in session, clergy on
one side, nobles on the other, commonalty in between, and
the Governor on a dais at the farther end. Just as impressive,
and aesthetically more interesting, is the **Chapelle des Elus.**
Certain architects of the eighteenth century found this dis-
proportionately high but the only way to give it sufficient
light was to place three windows under the groined vault.
By raising the decoration of Corinthian pilasters, supporting
a frieze and architrave, and a cornice in bold relief, the
architect of the chapel was able to compensate for a height
which some found excessive. The leaves of the door, and the
arcaded panels between the pilasters, are superbly sculptured;
and the alternation of white stone and marble with polished

woodwork is reinforced by the mottled pink marble of the
altar, the gilt candelabra on either side, and Jouvenet's
*Descent from the Cross*, also framed in gilt and brought from
the Sainte Chapelle to hang above the retable. It seems
reasonable to suppose that the general plan of the decoration
should be attributed to Jacques Gabriel, since it was he who
gave the designs for the marble ornaments to Spingola and
for the woodwork to Verberckt. The style of these is similar
to work executed under Gabriel's direction at Versailles.

The Palais des Etats brings you back to the eighteenth
century when Dijon had about 100 streets, 15 squares, 2266
houses, and was one of the best paved cities in France. Here
was concentrated the essence of what the Goncourt brothers
wrote of the province as a whole:

'You then found in that happy Burgundy a cordial good
humour; a healthy mindedness, strong and full; a warm
and generous gaiety; a bravura that spoke in a local idiom;
fraternity, youth, and the genius of good wine. The people
matured without growing old, and for nearly a century
they never lost the laughter of their Noëls. The Condés
encouraged this well-being and these songs . . . there,
between Horace and Rabelais, Burgundy gave birth to its
own wits.'

Stendhal did not regret the Dukes, for he saw what Dijon
owed to its Parliament:

'The artists of Dijon are fortunate if they happen to
please the Parliamentary society, for this is the class which
here forms the aristocracy, and it is generally allowed to
have a lively mind. The men that I meet in the streets of
Dijon are small, astringent, lively, and choleric; you can
see that their temperaments are all governed by good wine.
For you need more than a logical brain to make a superior
man; you need a certain temperamental fire.'

Exceptional even in this society was the most famous of the
presidents, Charles de Brosses (1709–77), born in Dijon, the
son of a councillor in the Parliament. He worked his way up
from the magistrature, and his epigram on the execution of a
certain criminal, like other of his sayings, passed into popular
currency: 'We hang him today: tomorrow he will sit in

judgement on us.' He was so small that when he spoke in public he was obliged to stand on a stool. Diderot wrote that 'it makes me die of laughter to see him in his official uniform, with his merry little head, mocking and ironical, lost in the immense forest of hair which comes near to obscuring the rest of his tiny face, unless the corners of his lips are turned up'. He was a *bon vivant* and a writer of some erudition. His *Letters from Italy* – passed eagerly from hand to hand – his *Histoire des Navigations aux Terres Australes*, and *Traité de la Formation des Langues* were noted by the Académie française; but his election was frustrated by Voltaire, who had rented one of his properties near Ferney, described it as 'a rendezvous for owls', and imagined that de Brosses had given him the use of the wood for nothing. De Brosses advised him 'never to write when you are out of your wits, lest you may blush in your right mind for what you have written when you were mad.' He wished to have no further dealings with a man, 'justly admired for his talents, but overbearing and dishonest in business'. De Brosses was the animating spirit of the Académie de Dijon, and his biographer wrote of him that 'his verve is spontaneous and fresh, and his muse a beautiful girl, sometimes a little disorderly, but buxom and forthcoming. We are not shocked by the liberties of his pen.' In the eighteenth century, according to Sainte-Beuve, de Brosses stood 'in the first rank of those independent, witty, and enlightened men whose careers were still provincial. At a time when the provinces were becoming increasingly effaced – when eminent persons were obliged to pay their respects to the life of Paris, and to the general and agreed code of behaviour in France, so to speak – he remained sturdily faithful to Burgundy . . . He is the last and the most considerable of the great provincial men of letters, who preserved even in their new ideas something of the charm inherited from former times.'

4

Installed in the east wing of the Palais des Etats is the **Musée des Beaux Arts**[1] – the largest and most important museum in

1. The Musée is open from 9 to 12h, and 14 to 17h from 1 February to 30 June; and to 18h from 1 July to 15 September. It closes at 17h

France outside Paris. A bequest of modern paintings has notably enriched it, and these will be on exhibition as soon as the necessary room has been found for them. When you enter the **Salle des Gardes** you feel yourself to be at the heart of the duchy – and a heart that has not ceased to beat. The room was built and sumptuously decorated by Philippe le Bon for the '*joyeuse entrée de Charles le Téméraire*' in 1474. But the Téméraire did not enter it a second time; of the great dukes only Philippe le Hardi and Jean sans Peur, with his wife, Marguerite de Bavière, came to rest there after their bodies had been transferred from the Chartreuse. Nevertheless, as you contemplate these superb effigies, it seems as if the dynasty has recovered in death everything it had gained, and lost, in life. Other tombs may move you more than these; few can equal them in magnificence.

Jean de Marville, Claus Sluter, and Claus de Werve worked at **Philippe le Hardi's Memorial** from 1385 to 1411. The recumbent figure, watched over by two angels, rests on a black marble sarcophagus, surrounded by an alabaster arcade in which 41 *pleurants* (mourners) – clergy, relatives, and officers of state, but all hooded – circulate in a doleful procession, each with a different gesture or in a different attitude of grief. Here a monk is cleaning his ear, and there wiping his nose. When I last visited the museum these had been temporarily displaced in order to show their exquisite workmanship more closely. I wished, however, that they had not been disturbed.

Genial and authoritarian, Philippe had fought against the English while he was still a boy, calling out to his father: 'Look after your right flank' – in the middle of a battle. On 26 November 1364 he entered Dijon as Duke of Burgundy and made the city his capital. It then had two monasteries and seven parishes, and above it rose eighteen towers. Although

from 16 September to 15 November, and at 16h from 16 November to 31 January. On Sundays it opens at 10h. It is closed on New Year's Day, Christmas Day, and in the morning of public holidays.

On Tuesdays you can visit only the salle des Gardes, the salon Condé, the salle des Primitifs flamands, and the salle des statues. (Enter by the central courtyard of the Hotel de Ville.) On Saturday evenings from 1 April to 15 November, certain rooms are illuminated and you can visit them to a musical accompaniment.

Philippe was inclined to neglect the duchy in favour of his other possessions, the circumstance of his funeral gives one a notion, not only of what the duchy thought of its Duke but of what it thought about itself. The expenses of the ceremony, set out on a parchment roll eight feet in length, are preserved in the archives at Dijon. The Duke's body (he had died in Flanders) was clothed in the habit of a Carthusian monk; the entrails were buried on the spot; and his heart consigned to the abbey of St Denis. The embalmed corpse was wrapped in 32 ells of waxed cloth and three cowhides, and placed in a leaden coffin weighing 700 lbs. Plate and jewellery worth 6000 gold crowns were pawned to pay the cost of these magnificent obsequies. The hearse was draped in cloth of gold embroidered with a crimson cross, and suitable draperies were sent to the twelve churches where the coffin was to rest on its way to Dijon, a blue banner at each of its four corners. It rested for nearly three weeks at St Seine-l'Abbaye, where the 60 mourners who had accompanied it from Brussels were joined by boys who now led the procession. This was met by the Mayor and Aldermen of Dijon, 100 burgesses, and 100 poor men dressed in black; and the body was interred at Champmol in the middle of the choir on 16 June – nearly three months after the life had left it.

The **Tomb of Jean sans Peur** and his wife was begun by Jean de la Huerta in 1443 and completed by Antoine Le Moiturier in 1470; it is similar in design to that of Philippe le Hardi. In 1412 Jean had made spectacular peace with his uncle, the Duc de Berri, on a big platform in the courtyard of the Abbey of St Germain at Auxerre. They both left astride the same horse after great feasting. This magnificence was characteristic of his reign, and contributed to his popularity in the province. He founded the Order of the Grands Ducs d'Occident to work 'for Burgundy, its art and its tradition'; the members were entitled to wear the ribbon of the order *en cravate* with the gold seal of the Duke himself attached to it. Before his own 'ordination' he took a bath, said a prayer, and then, arrayed in brown boots, white tunic, and red surcoat, leaped on to his horse without touching the stirrups, and unhooked an *écu* fixed to a post with the end of his lance as he rode off at the gallop. He would appear to have lived up to his motto – '*Valeur du corps et bonté d'âme*' – for he was a generous patron of the arts, and a superb host. We are told how, at a ducal banquet, the 'clinking of the knives and forks would replace the clash of arms'.

There is no reason to question the duc de Brabant's portrait of Jean sans Peur:

'Although there was something haughty and uncontrolled in his character, he was easy for those who worked for him. He listened to their advice, and once you had gained his confidence he trusted you completely. He liked to reward you for your services, and he knew the right way to do it. He had also the qualities appreciated by men of war; untiring, never sparing himself, and enduring patiently hunger and thirst, cold and rain. He was short but robust, with clear blue eyes and a firm expression in them; full in the face, giving you the impression of health and strength.'

Other descriptions emphasize his suspicious character – he always carried a weapon under his robe – and state that he was 'of a more amorous and wanton disposition' than his father.

The shades of the other great Dukes seem to hover over the tombs of their predecessors, as if in protest against their exclusion from so magnificent a mausoleum. Both the luxury and the humanism of the Burgundian court were seen at their height under the rule of Philippe le Bon. He had a vast library and employed 176 artists to adorn his palaces and châteaux; for it was not for nothing that he had watched Van Eyck at work on the *Adoration of the Lamb*, and called him into his service. He was at once pious and immoral; fond of music, but shocked by licentious plays. On the occasion of his marriage to Isabella of Portugal in 1430 he founded the Order of the Golden Fleece, in emulation of the English Order of the Garter, and inspired by the judge Gideon, who delivered Israel from the Midianites, deducing divine assistance from the dew on a piece of lamb's wool stretched out in the sun. The members of the order wore a woollen dress at the beginning of their investiture, and then assumed a red velvet tunic lined with white satin and embroidered with gold. At Vespers on St Andrew's Day they paraded on horseback, two by two, accompanied by 200 gentlemen, 12 trumpeters, heralds and clergy.

Dijon: Puits de Moise in the Chartreuse de Champmol.

Dijon: Tombs of the Dukes of Burgundy in the Musée des Beaux Arts. 'Other tombs may move you more than these; few can equal them in magnificence.'

Wine press of the
Dukes of Burgundy

Château de Clos Vougeot

From 6000 in 1436 the population of Dijon had doubled in 25 years. In 1443 there were 4000 employed in the cloth trade – weavers, cutters, dyers, and bleachers; and markets for meat, fish, wine, vegetables, eggs and fruit supplied the needs of the town. The Roman *thermae* became the ducal hot-rooms. Philippe le Bon built a cauldron for 6000 gallons, and four public baths – separately assigned to men and women – but in the late fifteenth century both the baths and the brothels were abolished.

The protocol at Philippe's court was exacting and precise; three genuflections were required when you approached the ducal presence. The feasts were described by Michelet as '*fougueuses kermesses*', and this was putting it mildly. At the '*Banquet du Faisan*' an immense pâté was wheeled into the hall, and 30 musicians emerged from it. Then a church appeared on the table, bells rang out, and a trio of choristers began to sing. The *pièce de resistance* was an elephant with a tower on its back, from which the chronicler, Oliver de la Marche, disguised as 'Our Mother the Church', addressed the guests inviting them to make the sign of the Cross. Philippe was a good mixer, and inclined to avoid troublesome situations – a useful aid to popularity. Ordered to shave his head after an illness, he requested his nobles to do the same, and out of regard for him 500 of them did so. Chastellan, a chronicler of the time, describes him 'of medium height and straight as a reed, bony rather than fleshy, with a broad and full forehead, thick and highly coloured lips, prominent veins and gray eyes. His mere appearance proclaimed him an emperor. His mouth was as a seal and his words were like a document. He was true as fine gold, and whole as an egg. The distant parts of the world and the Saracen voices saluted him as the Grand Duke of the Setting Sun because of the quantity of his lands, possessions, and domains all grouped together.' A fine portrait of Philippe le Bon by Roger van der Weyden hangs in the Salle des Gardes.

Charles le Téméraire had justified his soubriquet, but he was something more than the freebooting adventurer it suggests. He was muscular and bowlegged, with thick, dark, curly hair, olive complexion, round face, and slightly prominent lower lip. His shoulders sloped, and he walked with his head thrust forward and eyes on the ground. When he raised them Chastellan describes them as 'gray, laughing, and angelically clear'. He was faithful to his wife and concerned for the poor; noted for his cleanliness and austerity; fond of archery and chess; and although his own voice was unmusical, he had musical tastes. His piety was at once sombre and bellicose, for he believed that a sovereign was forced to make war to expiate his sins and those of his subjects. He hated France and Louis XI; or rather, as he put it, he 'loved her so well that he wished her to be governed by six kings instead of one'. Edward IV gave his opinion, rather condescendingly, that 'the establishment of Charles le Téméraire was for a Duke great and magnificent'. It was probably a good deal more magnificent than his own. Married at seven and widowed at twelve, he had suffered from a difficult childhood. He was distressed by the presence and importunity of his father's mistresses and bastards, and he sought consolation in books – the stories of Lancelot and Gawain, and the voyages of Marco Polo. These may well have fed the romantic miscalculations of his policy. He married, *en deuxième noce*, Margaret of York, but they had no male issue, and the doom of the great duchy was sealed. As Victor Hugo put it, 'Dynasties are founded by the bold, and brought to destruction by the rash.'

The charitable judgement of Philip de Commines on Charles le Téméraire may stand:

'I see no reason why he should have incurred the anger of God, except that he attributed all the honours and graces he received in this world to his own intelligence and virtue, rather than to God, as he should have done. For in truth there was much virtue and goodness in him . . . No prince gave audience more freely to his subjects and servants. He was not cruel at the time I knew him, but he became so before his death. He was magnificent in his dress, as in everything else – a little too much so – and very ambitious for glory. This was more responsible than anything else for leading him into war. He would have liked to resemble those princes of former days, who left a great name behind them, and he was as bold as any man of his time.'

Two retables in gilded wood, ordered by Philippe for the Chartreuse and now in the Salle des Gardes, are of astonishing richness. They were sculpted by Jacques de Baerze, and painted by Melchior Broederlam. The Crucifixion has kept its colours, but they have faded from the saints and martyrs on its pair. A third retable of the Antwerp school (fifteenth century) hangs between them. On the wall above, a Flemish tapestry dedicated to Notre-Dame de Bon Espoir, also came from the Chartreuse.

Of more local than general interest is the **Salle Rude.** François Rude (1784–1855) was born in Dijon, where his father was a saddler and blacksmith. He studied sculpture at the Ecole des Beaux Arts, and afterwards in Paris, and admitted that he had 'wasted seven years of my life in academic studies'. He also continued for some time to work at his father's forge; followed his master, Frémiet, into exile at the Restoration; and married his daughter in Brussels. Essentially a classicist, he was described as 'that Roman who smoked a pipe', and since his beard was 30 centimetres long a vivid picture of him is called up into the mind's eye. His work did not belie his favourite maxims that 'everything is in nature, everything comes from nature, and everything returns to nature'; 'to observe is virtually to create'; and 'I don't believe in genius; genius is hard work.' He executed *Le Départ des Volontaires* on the Arc de Triomphe, which has been compared to 'a great shout of enthusiasm going up from the entrails of France'. In the Dijon museum his statues of an old warrior, and a little Neapolitan fisher boy, and his maquette for *La Marseillaise*, are worth attention; and particularly his *Hebe and the Eagle*, justifiying Stephen Liégard's encomium – '*Que la vierge a du charme et que superbe est l'aigle.*' Rude rarely failed a proper sense of the superb, and we shall meet him again among the vineyards of the Côte d'Or.

Among the many other sculptures in the museum the following may be singled out. The funeral effigy of Jacques Germain (1424); a wooden Circumcision from Champmol; a Sainte Véronique of the French school (early fourteenth century); a saint reading, of the Burgundian school, typically unromanticized (late fifteenth century); the busts of Claude Jehannin by Jean Dubois (1626–94); of Antoinette de Fontette praying in profile; of President Joly de Blaisy by the same artist, half kneeling and seeming about to invite us 'to sit upon the ground' and 'tell sad stories of the death' of Presidents; of Louis XIV by Antoine Coysevox (1640–1720); and of Rameau, handsome and intelligent, by Jean-Jacques Caffieri (1723–1792). François Pompon's beautifully simplified *Crane*, like his *Polar Bear* in the Square Darcy, rather puts Rude in the academic shade; and more elegant in the classical tradition is Hubert Yencesse's *Diane*, slim and boyish with her cropped hair and huntress's bow.

Among the paintings you should notice an attractive portrait of Jean de Bourbon by Corneille de Lyon; a lovely Flemish Nativity by the Maître de Flemalle, with a Memlingesque Virgin, and a cow peering through the broken slats of the stable (*circa* 1425); and a Presentation in the Temple of the same school, where the two donors are kneeling, side by side, in the foreground, should not be missed. Notice Larguillière's portrait of President Bouhier; Alexis Piron roaring with laughter at his own epitaph – 'Here lies one who was not even an academician'; Nattier's portrait of Marie Leszczynska, and Manet's of Méry Laurent. A portrait of Diane de Poitiers at her toilette, naked to the waist and fingering her jewel box (Ecole de Fontainebleau: late sixteenth century) gives the impression of a woman who knew when she was on to a good thing, and that Chenonceaux was not too good for her. The contrast with Jean Tassel's Catherine de Montholon – the long hands clasped in prayer, as Dürer might have painted them, and the rugged face brooding over the white collar and below the black veil – is very striking. The Italian school is represented by the smooth Milanese serenity of Luini's *Virgin and Child* and Lorenzo Lotto's placid and thick-necked *Portrait of a Woman*; the Dutch by Frans Hals' *Gentleman*, a shade less jolly than usual; and the Flemish by Rubens's *Virgin and St Francis of Assisi*, where the features of Isabelle Brandt are plainly to be distinguished.

The original wooden doors of the Palais de Justice, carved by Hugues Sambin (*circa* 1583), are also to be seen, with the crozier of St Robert in silver gilt (late eleventh century), and a plaque of the Virgin and Child in Limoges enamel of the thirteenth century. A ciborium from Cîteaux and a Virgin and

Child, both of the fourteenth century in Parisian ivory, show the French influence in competition with the Flemish.

Outside the main entrance to the Musée stands the **Statue of Jean-Philippe Rameau** (1683–1764). This suggests (but no more) the man who was said 'to have flutes in place of legs' and to be 'more like a ghost than a man'. A fellow Dijonnais, meeting him in the gardens of the Tuileries, described him as 'nothing more than a long organ pipe without the bellows' – and indeed both his father and his brother were organists. Rameau was composing fugues at fourteen; was elected to the Académie de Dijon in 1781; and his music was sometimes compared to the architecture of Versailles. This is a little surprising since he was praised for 'introducing the voice of nature into music', and claimed himself to take 'nature in its beautiful simplicity' as his model. After travelling in Italy he won the competition for the post of organist at the Madeleine, but returned to Dijon in the wake of an unhappy love affair. The lady who had inspired *Castor et Pollux* chose to marry his brother instead. Rameau went back to Paris and married a singer, the daughter of one of the royal physicians. Diderot – whom an imperialist view of the duchy might claim as a Burgundian, since he was born at Langres – wrote of:

> 'this famous musician who delivered us from the plain-chant of Lulli that we had been psalm-singing for more than a hundred years; who gave us so many unintelligible visions and apocalyptic truths about the theory of music, which neither he nor anyone else understood; and who composed a certain number of operas, where the harmony, the snatches of song, the disconnected ideas, the clash of triumphs and victories, the flights and murmurs of sound – enough to leave you out of breath – and the dancing airs, will live for ever.'

Rameau, who could not bear the barking of a dog in the gardens of the Palais Royal, could hardly stand any better the voice of the priest he summoned to his death-bed because he sang out of tune.

5

A third itinerary will take you back into the same quarter, where the **Church of Notre-Dame** stands just north of the Palais des Etats off the rue de la Préfecture. This was built between 1220 and 1225, and finally consecrated in 1334. It is often quoted as the consummation of Burgundian Gothic, where the aim was to use a minimum of matter to achieve a maximum of effect, and to assure equilibrium and elegance by the employment of a narrow space. It was not, however, the fruit of a local tradition, but an importation from the north, related to a 'vast international family stretching from Canterbury to Switzerland'. It was finally overwhelmed by influences from the Ile de France, and it suffers as we see it today by comparison with the masterpieces of Burgundian romanesque. In Notre-Dame de Dijon a porch of two bays leads into a six-bay nave and polygonal apse. The church has three storeys and three passages – one over the dado, one in the triforium, and one at the base of the clerestory. The exterior seems to have been inspired by the collegiate church of St Yves at Braine, in the Aisne, with a small buttress atop a larger one; possibly by way of the ducal Sainte Chapelle at Dijon, which was a replica of the Braine ground plan. You will notice that the terminal walls of the transept have only two storeys with interior passages above the dado and at the level of the triforium. The upper storey is open with a large rose window, while the lower has five lancets of equal size in the window wall but only three openings in the inner screen. The lancets are framed by colonnettes rather than mullions, reminiscent of the transepts at Canterbury. Soufflot so admired the vaulting that he had a model of it constructed in wood, and the whole church fulfilled Viollet-le-Duc's ideal of Gothic as a 'permanent scaffolding' that unifies the interior.

The nave is 49 metres long and 17.50 metres in height, and the aisles are almost exactly half as tall as the nave. The western end of the nave is open to the three-aisled porch, and Viollet-le-Duc described the double western piers as 'a masterpiece of design'. Here you can observe the characteristic Burgundian use of the internal buttress. In the nave the

height of the bays is greater than that of the clerestory and
triforium combined; in the choir they are about equal. The
proportions of the church are rather tall, so that you can
easily imagine the two thin towers that were intended to
complete it. The architect suppressed the usual western arch,
prolonging the volume and structure of the nave right up to
the sensational façade where three rows of gargoyles in
sixteen arches – one of them a head with three faces anticipat-
ing Picasso by several hundred years, and inspired no doubt
by a similar instinct of *blague* – exhibit a fantastic fertility of
invention. The lamp brackets inside the church have much in
common with the choir stalls at Montréal; in both of them
the spirit of irony and mischief is suffused with faith.

Above the gargoyles you will observe the jacquemart –
a mechanical Flemish clock – brought from Courtrai as a
trophy of war by Philippe le Hardi in 1382. In the apsidal
chapel to the right of the high altar a black Virgin in wood
of the twelfth century was the object of special veneration
after the liberation of the city from the Swiss; she has Swiss
bullets in her apron. Its second liberation, from the Germans
in 1944, is commemorated by a modern Gobelins tapestry.
On the north wall of the exterior you should notice a sculptured owl which the young Dijonnaises used to touch in the
hope of getting themselves a husband. Among the daughters
of Notre-Dame de Dijon were the churches of Semur and
St Père-sous-Vezelay, which we have already visited.

You should not miss the **House of the Comtes de Vogüé**,[1]
on the north side of Notre-Dame, with its very fine classical
stonework. This was one of the first houses in Dijon normally
occupied by dignitaries of the Parliament, and dates from the
early seventeenth century. The caryatids over the mantelpiece
in the Salle des Gardes, and the Flemish tapestries, are worth
attention. In the same quarter, running parallel with the rue
de la Liberté, is the **Rue des Forges.** This has a number of old
houses of which the Hotel Chambellan (nos. 34 and 36) is
especially notable. It was built in the fifteenth century by a
rich family of drapers, and is now the offices of the Syndicat
d'Initiative. The Maison Milsand (no. 38) has a fine Renais-

1. A visit can be arranged by the office du Tourisme de Dijon in the
Place Darcy.

sance façade in the style of Hugues Sambin; and the Musée
Perrin de Puycousin, at no. 40, houses an interesting collection
of popular Burgundian art. Waxwork figures give an added
realism to the reconstruction of provincial life. This was the
birthplace of Hugues Aubriot, provost of Paris under Charles
V, who built the Bastille, and a number of bridges over the
Seine.

**Saint Michel,** which stands at the eastern end of the rue de
la Liberté beyond the Palais des Etats, was begun at the end
of the fifteenth century in a far flung gesture of flamboyant
Gothic. Work upon it was then held up for lack of money,
until a Renaissance façade was added. The two towers were
not built until the seventeenth century, and a third rises from
the transept crossing. The *Last Judgement* on the tympanum ·
over the west door is the work of a Flemish artist, Nicholas
de la Court. The *mésalliance* between Gothic and Renaissance
lies heavily on the façade, but the woodwork in the choir is
worth attention.

You should now retrace your steps to the Place Royale – as
I insist on calling it – and turn down the rue Vauban which
leads out of it at the southern end. The first street on your left
will bring you at once to the **Palais de Justice,** where the
Parliament of Burgundy used to meet (visits: 8 to 12h, and
14 to 18h. Closed on Saturday, on Sunday afternoon, and in
August). The door is a copy of the original by Sambin (now
in the museum) and you will notice the panelled vault in the
magnificent Salle des Pas Perdus, and the splendid ceiling of
the Salle des Assises, transported from the former Cour des
Comptes. Two houses of particular interest stand close by;
the Hotel Fyot de Mimeure in the rue Amiral Roussin, and
the Maison Liégeard, 21 rue Vauban. The second of these has
four watch towers on its Renaissance façade.

For another itinerary in Dijon a car will be useful. About
half a mile from the centre of the city, along the road to Paris
via Sens, stands a psychiatric hospital which shelters what
remains of Philippe le Hardi's **Chartreuse de Champmol,**
designed by Drouet de Dammartin (apply to the custodian
between 8 and 18h). The first stone was laid by Marguerite of
Flanders, and the second by Jean, Count of Nevers, in 1383,
and the building was consecrated five years later. Before its

destruction at the Revolution it was described as a 'Burgundian St Denis' and 'white as the habit worn by the disciples of St Bruno'. Today only the door of the church and the turret of the tower – 'light and slender, with a tuft of gilliflower on the edge, like a young lad leading a greyhound on the leash' – are left standing, and with them Claus Sluter's **Puits de Moise,** which took its name from the spring over which the base was built. Above the door Philippe and Marguerite of Flanders, sculpted from life, are shown kneeling with their guardian saints, St John the Baptist and St Catherine. The statues were all executed by Sluter, called to Dijon in 1385 to succeed Jean de Marville as official sculptor to the duke. The *Puits* – or well – was the base of a Calvary that originally stood in the middle of the cloister. Six of the Old Testament prophets surround the hexagonal pillar, and of these the statue of Moses is particularly impressive. All are pregnant with an inward vision; Jeremiah a little sour, Zachariah benevolent and bowed, Daniel a trifle bewildered, and Isaiah with the years heavy upon him. Sluter's nephew, Claus de Werve, carved the charming and coy little angels under the cornice. One has a hand to its chin, one to its cheek, a third to its nose. The well was formerly painted, and an attempt to reproduce the original colouring has been made on the reduced scale model now to be seen in the Musée des Beaux Arts.

The Emperor Charles V declared that, if the duchy had reverted to the House of Burgundy, he would like to be interred at Champmol; and when Eleanor of Austria had the remains of the Dukes of Burgundy shown to her, certain of them were so well preserved that she could recognize the shape of their mouths. 'I thought', she said, 'that we got our mouths from our Austrian ancestors, but I see now that we have them from our ancestress, Marie de Bourgogne, and other Dukes of Burgundy from whom we are descended. I shall tell this to my brother, the Emperor, when I see him.'

Turn to your left on leaving the Chartreuse along the Avenue Albert I, and then to your right up the Chemin de Chèvre Morte. This will bring you to the wide Boulevard Pascal, where you should turn right again and follow it to the roundabout where it is joined by the Boulevard Joffre. Here the first street to your right will take you to the **Sanctuary of the Sacré Cœur,** a skilful modern adaptation of Burgundian romanesque. The crypt and baptistry are particularly successful, and the windows are the work of contemporary religious artists.

The rue Marceau will now take you south to the Place de la République, and thence by the rue de la Préfecture to the back of the Palais des Etats, and so to the rue de la Liberté. Turn down the rue Chabot-Charny out of the square opposite the theatre, and follow it to the Place Wilson. Here you are on the threshold of the **Cours du Parc,** which Louis XIV described as '*la plus belle plantation de mon royaume*'. It was begun by the 'grand Condé' – never sparing of the *grande geste* – and finished by the duc d'Enghien and his son. Three lines of trees stretch for nearly a mile from the entrance of St Pierre to the park designed by Le Nôtre. Here in 1769 the English, with four competitors, won a horse-race in less than three minutes. Elsewhere in the 'green belt' of Dijon the trees were planted in star formation (1716), and the visitor will agree with the verdict that 'in few towns of France are the outer districts more smiling'.

The rue du Transvaal, leading west out of the Place Wilson, will bring you to the Place Suquet just to the north of which you will find the **Musée de l'Hôpital** (visits – advised only in summer – from 9 to 12h, and from 14 to 18h. Closed on Saturday and Sunday). This was the former hospice du Saint Esprit, founded in the thirteenth century, and rebuilt in the seventeenth by Martin de Noirville, a pupil of Mansart. The museum is installed in the fifteenth-century Jerusalem chapel, and contains a number of manuscripts and miniatures relating to the foundation of the hospital. From here you have an easy drive south, if you are staying outside the city, or north to the Square Darcy if you are settled at the Cloche.

You will not wish to leave Dijon without taking note of more than one native son who has left no tangible memorial. **Bernard de la Monnaye** (1641–1728) lived here for more than sixty years and worked as a Councillor in the Chambre des Comptes. Eventually his '*Noëls*' – popular songs which had little to do with Christmas – excited the indignation of the clergy, and he moved to Paris. Nevertheless, of his four children three entered religious orders. He was also a devoted husband:

*Nous fumes moins époux qu'amants*
*Dix lustres avec toi m'ont paru dix moments.*

and his word upon the death of his wife was not to be forgotten: '*Je hais la clarté du soleil.*' He won the prize for his verses, awarded by the Académie française, with such monotonous regularity that he was asked not to compete any more. These were written, as he boasted, in 'Latin, Greek, French and Burgundian'; and although Paris was his '*séjour*', his '*patrie*' was Dijon. The city has always been a happy hunting ground for the bibliophile, and I recommend a visit to the Libraire Le Meur in the rue Chabot-Charny on the right hand side as you go down from the municipal theatre. Browsing there I was reminded of de la Monnaye's own bookseller-publisher.

'The politeness and urbanity of this respectable old man delighted all those who paid him a visit. His conversation was both serious and amusing, and one hardly realized how old he was. He seemed to have kept his flowers to decorate his declining years.'

Other figures who deserve a place in the pantheon of Dijon's celebrities are Claude Bernard (1568–1641), who was converted by preaching a 'cod' sermon, in which he set out to satirize the preachers of his day, and earned his title of 'the St Vincent-de-Paul of the prison cells' – for experience had taught him that 'there is no certainty in earthly judgements'; and the physicist Edmé Mariotte (1620–84), who maintained that 'to be of any public use one must verify by a number of new experiments what the Ancients and the Moderns alike have said or written'. Nor should we forget Gustave Eiffel (1832–1923), who was born at Dijon, although Paris has some right to claim him. After working on the railway bridge at Bordeaux, the Douro viaduct and the Panama canal, he constructed the Eiffel Tower for the Exhibition of 1889, and was given the right to exploit it for twenty years. He installed a meteorological laboratory inside it, and at the age of 80 became interested in aviation. Few people will quarrel with the couplet:

> *Qu'on la trouve laide, qu'on la trouve belle*
> *Paris ne serait pas Paris sans elle.*

If you are offered a drink in Dijon, your host will probably propose a *Kir*. Elsewhere this is known as a Vin Blanc Cassis, but the Dijonnais have christened it after the popular Chanoine Kir, for many years Maire of Dijon and a member of the Chambre des Députés after the Second World War.

Many people who have never been to Dijon are familiar with its mustard. This has been made since the fourth century to a recipe of Palladius, son of Exuperantius, Prefect of Gaul. A single hogshead containing 300 quarts of mustard was consumed at a banquet given by the Duke of Burgundy to King Philip de Valois in 1336. It was favoured by Pope John XXII, who called his worthless nephew '*Premier Moutardier du Pape*'. The rhyme went:

> *De trois choses Dieu nous garde:*
> *De bœuf salé sans moutarde,*
> *D'un valet qui se regarde,*
> *D'une femme qui se farde.*[1]

1. May God keep us from three things
   Salt beef without mustard
   A servant who looks at himself in the mirror
   And a woman who makes herself up.

# CHAPTER ELEVEN

# The Pays-Bas and
# Valley of the Seine

❧

## 1

With the riches of the Côte to right and left, and the sudden splendour of the Montagne at your back, you may not immediately be drawn to the flat country that stretches away to the east, traversed by the inevitable Canal de Bourgoyne. Nevertheless, there is much hereabouts that should not be missed. If you are staying at Fixin the D.31 from Gevrey-Chambertin, very close by, will take you to the N.396 at Noiron and thence, due south, to all that remains of the **Abbey of Cîteaux** – a distance of eighteen and a half kilometres. Alternatively the N.396 will take you there direct from Dijon. Cîteaux is among the principal sites of Christendom, although there is little to see there. It is a place for reverie and retrospect. The Vouge, that gave its name to Clos Vougeot, runs between the deep woods, and on its banks, close to the Etang de Cîteaux, the monastery was founded in 1098 by St Robert, St Albéric, and St Stephen Harding – the last an Englishman. The Cistercians took their name from the Roman Cistercium, and their rule was an austere adaptation of the way of life and prayer laid down by St Benedict. The three founders were successively abbots of the new monastery, but it failed to prosper until St Bernard and his brethren arrived there in 1114. This was the beginning of the prodigious Cistercian expansion until, a hundred years later, more than a thousand abbeys had been founded in Europe and Palestine.

The great church at Cîteaux followed the simple plan of which we have seen examples at Pontigny and Fontenay, but it was not so fortunate in its preservation. The Dukes of the first Burgundian dynasty, and certain nobles, were buried there; yet this did not prevent the sacking and exploitation of the abbey in 1589, 1596 and 1636, and its suppression in

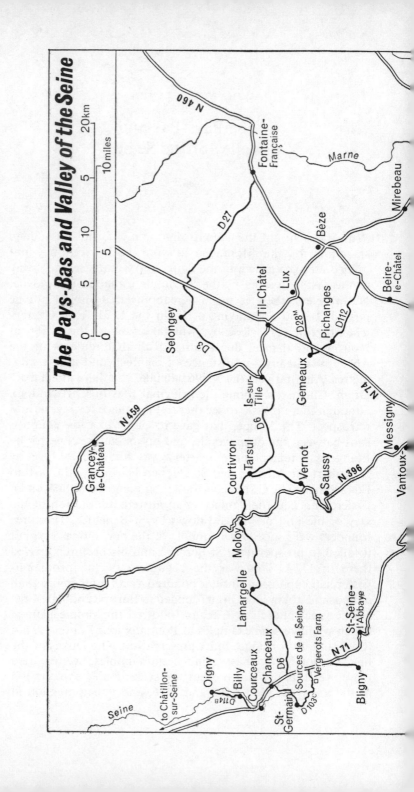

# The Pays-Bas and Valley of the Seine

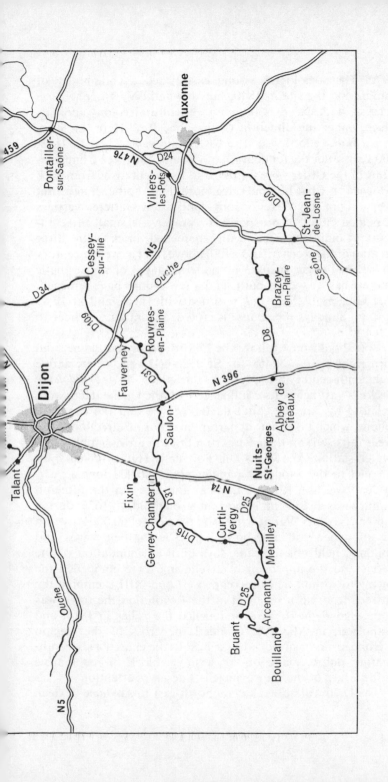

1970. The sociologist Young established a community of families on the site in 1840, but this had only an ephemeral success, and six years later an agricultural colony took its place, under the direction of the abbé Rey. Here, at least, was a faint reflection of the Cistercian way of life. In 1898, 800 years after the foundation of Cîteaux, the three Congregations of the Order were united, and representatives from each returned to what became once more their mother house. But they did not stay there for long. Only a few scattered vestiges remained either of prosperity or prayer – a small fifteenth-century building faced with enamelled brick with three arcades of the cloister, and a hall above; and a twelfth-century chapel no longer in use. A modern chapel of no aesthetic interest has now been built, and a few monks have returned. The Gregorian chant has returned with them, and at 10.45 a.m. on Sundays the chapel is crowded from far and near to listen to it.

You should now follow the D.8 to Brazey-en-Plaine, and turn right on the N.468 for **St Jean-de-Losne,** where a fine eighteenth-century bridge crosses the Saône – *'belle et indolente rivière'* – just below its confluence with the Ouche. Here, too, or close by, are the canal de Bourgoyne and the canal du Rhône, which take their departure in opposite directions. The great rafts sent on their way from St Jean are assembled in a 'water station' known as the Port-de-la-Hutte, linked by a channel to the Saône. It handles about 40,000 tons a year. St Jean was the Roman Latona, and early in the fifteenth century was already an important stronghold. In 1636, during the Thirty Years War, it withstood the siege of 60,000 Austrian troops, when 150 able-bodied men, with their wives and children, held out for nine days until an inundation of the Saône and the approach of a relieving force compelled the enemy to withdraw. In recompense Louis XIII exempted the citizens from all taxes, and at the Revolution the town was christened *Belle Défense*. It repelled the Allies in 1814, and Napoleon, in May 1815, added the cross of the Légion d'Honneur to its armorial bearings. In the church a sixteenth-century pulpit, made out of a single block of red marble with statues of the four evangelists deserves attention.

The D.20 will now take you north-east to **Auxonne** (sixteen

'The preparation—silent, skilful, and industrious—never stops until the end of September.'

The officers of the Confrérie du Tastevin in procession for the Feast of St Vincent.

Château de Sully: view of the west front.

and a half kilometres). This has earned – and merited – the title of the *Station Verte de Vacances*; and indeed if you have a taste for camping, swimming, and boating in pleasant surroundings, you will hardly find a better stopping place in the valley of the Saône. The Centre Nautique has cruising and water-skiing rights over 1300 metres of the river. Jouffroy's statue of a young and pensive Bonaparte stands in the principal square, for it was here that Napoleon, a young second-lieutenant of eighteen, served in the garrison from 1 May 1788 to 1 September 1789, when he left it for Corsica on compassionate leave because his widowed mother was in financial difficulties. He returned to Auxonne with his brother Louis on 1 June 1790, and left it again for good in April 1791, having earned his promotion to first lieutenant.

The gateway to the arsenal of the former garrison, built by Vauban, now gives entrance to the **Halles,** with its square wooden pillars supporting the flat, thickly beamed roof. The arsenal of Auxonne played an important part in furnishing the Revolutionary armies for their campaigns in Germany and Italy. The **Musée Bonaparte** in three rooms of the château contains Napoleon's legendary three-cornered hat, and the portable table and chair which he used on his campaigns. You will find the way to the museum clearly indicated to your right when you have crossed over the bridge. It is open from 1 May to 15 October from 10 to 12h and 15 to 17h, and from 14 to 18h on Sunday and public holidays. At other times you may apply to M. Louis Py, 21 rue Marin; or phone the museum itself: 36.30.20.

A tour of the **Ramparts** will give you some idea of the military importance of Auxonne. The château was begun in the reign of Louis XI, and completed under Louis XII and François I. It was one of the first to be adapted to the use, and the threat, of artillery; and the only one of its kind now to be seen in Burgundy. Then you will come, successively, to the Porte de Comte (1503), and on the same boulevard to the Tour Belvoir, a relic of the medieval fortifications. To the north of the town is the Porte Royal, built by the comte d'Aprémont, the engineer who planned the whole *enceinte*; and the immense Tour de Signe, close by, though it dates from the Middle Ages, was given a new coat of arms – and a

C.G.B.—O

salamander – by François I. The barracks, in the same quarter of the town, are an impressive building of pink stone, designed by Caristie (1763). The ramparts are seen at their most intact as they face the river. Two pepper-pot towers on the northern and southern bastions indicate the entrance and exit to the moat.

The mainly fifteenth-century **Church of Notre-Dame** has a twelfth-century romanesque tower over the transept, and in the third chapel of the right aisle a fine statue of the Virgin with a bunch of grapes, attributed to Claus Sluter. Over the Renaissance portal are 22 statues of the prophets, reconstructed in 1853 by the sculptor Buffet; six of them are evidently copied from the Puits de Moise at Dijon.

Proceeding north along the N.476 you come to Pontailler on an island in the river, and thence by the N.459 to **Mirebeau.** The thirteenth-century church has a stern exterior corresponding to the sombre history of the town. It was besieged in 1015 by King Robert, at war with Duke Otho Guillaume, and again in 1636 by the Imperial troops. After three days they captured and pillaged the town, destroying 118 houses. Certain parts of the fortifications are still to be seen. The church is a typical example of Burgundian Gothic with four bays in the nave; a sixteenth-century pulpit; and some good fourteenth-century statues.

The road leads on to **Bèze** and the source of the river from which it takes its name. The water gushes out from a spring among the plane trees at the rate of 1200 to 1500 litres a second, through what is known as the '*trou du Diable*'. We shall presently see how Chambertin was indebted to the monks of Bèze (q.v., p. 225), and two towers of their monastery, founded by Duke Amalgaire in the seventh century, remain. The interior of the church is remarkable for the elevation of the transept crossing, where a pair of tribunes are set above the side chapels with prominent arcading to each. The influence of Cluny can be seen in two of the capitals. The town has some attractive old houses, and a notable thirteenth-century façade in the square.

Turning right on the N.460 you will come to **Fontaine-Française** (eleven kilometres). Just outside the town, on 5 June 1595, at a place called 'le Pré Moreau', Henri IV gained his decisive victory over the forces of the Ligue, under the command of the duc de Mayenne and the Constable of Castille. This effectively put an end to the wars of religion. It was an astonishing feat of arms, for the King had only 510 cavalrymen facing an army of 15,000 men. The walls of the medieval fortress which gave him hospitality after the battle have been preserved, and form part of the elegant château built in 1750. It is well worth a visit, for you will be following in the footsteps of many famous guests, including Voltaire and Mme de Staël, who liked to frequent the literary salon of Mme de Saint-Julien. Regency furniture and Flemish tapestries decorate the *salon rose*, the *salon vert*, and the guard room (the château is open between 15 April and 30 September on Thursday and Saturday from 15 to 18h). In ducal times Fontaine-Française was an enclave directly dependent on the French crown – hence its name.

The D.27 will bring you to the long straight N.74, which runs from Langres to Dijon and, crossing it, to Selongey. Just outside the village to your right you will find a little chapel with a colonnaded porch, dedicated to St Gertrude. This was founded by a traveller from Brabant who was attacked by brigands and claimed to have been saved by the saint's protection. You are now among the forests of the plateau de Langres, which continue, almost without interruption, to Châtillon-sur-Seine. We shall not venture far in this direction, but it will be worth your while turning left out of Selongey on the D.3 and then right on the N.459 to **Grancey-le-Château** – an easy 21 kilometres. Here you can see the moat, drawbridge, and imposing chapel – formerly a collegiate church – of the medieval stronghold. The chapel has a thirteenth-century apse, some good statues and a painting attributed to van Dyck. Alongside it the elegant eighteenth-century château overlooks a park. The interior, which contained much fine furniture of its period, was occupied by the Germans during the Second World War, and found in a deplorable state when they left it.

From Grancey you can return by the same road, bearing left at Is-sur-Tille for **Tille-châtel** and one of the most interesting romanesque churches in the Côte d'Or. Notice the square tower with eight arched openings; the tympanum of Christ and the four evangelists; and the three levels of roof over the choir. The nave has five bays, with a wooden sixteenth-century Calvary where the hands and legs of Christ are mutilated. There is shell vaulting in the corners of the transept crossing and semi-circular vaulting in the nave. Lancet windows are set above the three chapels in the apse, and the capitals in the choir – birds with human heads – are exceptionally fine.

A strange story attaches to the 'tomb of St Honoré'. A stone coffin was unearthed outside the church by a grave-digger who was immediately struck dead as a punishment for his indecent jokes. When the coffin was carried into the church a child at its mother's breast exclaimed '*O sancte Honorate!*'; and it was supposed that the name of the saint whose tomb had been profaned was thus innocently revealed. More substantiated is the beheading of Florent, the son of a Roman governor, at Tille-Châtel – and more worthy, one would think, of veneration.

Your way home lies through **Lux** (N.459), the site of another curious happening. Here you will catch a glimpse of the late sixteenth-century château, and perhaps of the poly-gonal chapel in the park. In the early eighteenth century a Comtesse de Saulx-Tavannes shut herself up in a room in one of the towers, leaving her niece to sleep in the passage. One morning the door of the countess's room did not open, and the niece was found lying outside, unconscious and demented. When the door was forced, the room was found empty, except for a single slipper scattered on the floor. There was no way out except through the door, and the walls, ceiling, and floor were carefully searched. The mystery of the countess's disappearance and the niece's dementia has never been explained. Edgar Allan Poe could have tried to solve it in one way, Henry James in another.

By turning to the right at Lux, you can take the D.28M to **Gemeaux,** just on the farther side of the N.74. Here the church has a good romanesque doorway, and a fresco of St Vincent surrounded by branches of the vine. A vineyard nearby once had some importance, although this is not a wine-growing district. The local dialect at Gemeaux made people believe that the inhabitants were descended from a

Gallic tribe. You should now turn left on the D.112, noting the fortified church of **Pichanges,** and join the N.460, which will bring you, on the right, to the château of **Beire-le-Châtel.** This was built at various times between the seventeenth and nineteenth centuries, and the chapel was open every day to visitors in the summer of 1973. Another eighteenth-century château at **Arcelot,** a few kilometres farther south, can be admired from the road.

Here you should turn off on to the D.34, and then at Cessey-sur-Tille on the D.109 for **Fauverney,** where the romanesque church has been very thoroughly restored. The cupola over the sanctuary with its intricate vaulting in each corner gives one a feeling of the south There are two towers, one round and the other square. The church has a nave and two side aisles, and a statue of the Virgin outside, with hands folded on her breast, deserves attention. Close by, on the D.109, you will come to **Rouvres.** Here the bosses in the nave are lively examples of medieval caricature; notice also two statues of St John the Baptist – one in wood, the other (early fourteenth century) in stone, wearing a fur garment lined with woven material; the seventeenth-century candelabra; sixteenth-century choir stalls; and a fifteenth-century coloured Vierge de Pitié. From Rouvres the D.31 will bring you back to Gevrey-Chambertin (sixteen kilometres).

2

A second expedition takes you out of Dijon on the N.71 to **Talant** on the outskirts of the city. The magnificent early thirteenth-century church is built over a two-aisled crypt, and it contains some admirable bas-reliefs – the Apparition of the Stag to St Hubert is especially notable – and a Sepulchre which has kept its colour. On the hill to your right is **Fontaine-lès-Dijon,** the birthplace of St Bernard, and the sense of history – if of nothing else – demands that you should visit it. A group of buildings behind the church includes a tower of the château that belonged to Tecelin le Roux, the father of St Bernard, and the **Chapelle des Feuillants,** built by order of Louis XIII and Anne of Austria in 1614. This occupies the site of the room where St Bernard was born. Beside the church is a memorial to the soldiers who died during the Franco-Prussian War, and in the defence of Dijon.

The road now climbs past the deep rocky gorge of Val de Suzon on your right, to **St Seine-l'Abbaye.** The place takes its name from a Benedictine monastery founded in the sixth century by St Seine (Sequanus), son of the Comte de Mesmont. The river, to which we shall come presently, is called after the saint, not the other way about. He was buried in the abbey, which was destroyed more than once, but after its reconstruction in 981 it became prosperous and powerful. On two occasions, in 1688 and 1674, Louis XIV slept in the abbatial palace. The church, which reached its present form between 1375 and 1439, marks the transition from Burgundian romanesque to a Gothic inspired by the Ile-de-France. The nave has sexpartite vaulting, and the 22 paintings illustrating the life of St Seine on the reverse side of the fifteenth-century enclosure to the choir are of particular interest. The intercession of the saint used to be invoked against drought and – to make assurance doubly sure – water from the river named after him was sprinkled on the curé by the local inhabitants. On the south side of the enclosure a sequence of paintings show St Seine presenting a knight to the infant Jesus carried on the shoulders of St Bartholomew, and St Bartholomew presenting a child to the Blessed Virgin. These were executed by Brother Claude de Durestal in 1531. Some fine tombstones, dating from the fourteenth century, are set against the walls of the transept crossing. Notice the unusually high triforium and gallery; the flamboyant choir screen; and the faded photographs of those killed in the First World War, framed on the wall of the south transept. Only one of the two western towers was completed. The graceful *fontaine de la Samaritaine* stands outside.

Your approach to the **Sources of the Seine** will depend a little on your respect for this particular river. For reasons stated earlier in this guide I have a certain prejudice in the matter, and feel that the Seine has usurped a prestige which more properly attaches to the Yonne. Your easiest way is to follow the N.71 for a few kilometres and turn off to your left on the D.103. This will bring you to a farm called Les Vergerots, and notices put up by the city of Paris – to whom the site belongs – ensure that you cannot lose your way. However, if your mood is reverential and you feel like stretching your legs, take the D.103D, just after leaving St Seine, and follow the footpath to your right out of the village of Bligny. This will give you a pleasant walk through the forest where the Romans erected a temple to the goddess of the river that rises there. The principal spring trickles out in a little hollow planted with fir trees and disfigured (rather than embellished) by the statue of a nymph executed by Jouffroy in 1865. It bears all the marks of a period when Napoleon III was Emperor of the French, and Baron Haussmann the Préfet of a city that might have been content with the maturity of the Seine without appropriating its birth. The site has been reduced to absurdity by the inscription on the grotto: '*qui donne son nom au Département de la Seine*'. Bureaucratic self-importance could go no further. Vidal de la Blache, in his *Tableau de la Géographie de la France*, explains why this has become something of a hallowed spot, and also, implicitly, why, like so many other places of the kind, devotion has done so much to spoil it:

> 'The waters that people like to commemorate are either those which have led them in their wanderings, or those which have struck their imaginations by the mystery and beauty of their source.'

A little outside the artificial enclosure a second spring comes out of the ground among the débris of a Gallo-Roman temple. Traces of the peristyle were discovered, and evidence that Jupiter and Juno were worshipped here, as well as the goddess of the spring, Sequana. The river goes underground near the hamlet of Courceaux, reappears a little farther on at Billy, and at **Oigny** you may see the remains of the abbey which was the first to harness its waters for a mill. Thereafter it receives various tributary streams, and you can follow its rapid growth from the N.71 all the way to Châtillon-sur-Seine.

The nearest village to the sources of the Seine is St Germain, and from there the D.103C takes you back to the main road at **Chanceaux.** The house that once belonged to Captain Brigaudet, killed at the side of Jean sans Peur on the bridge at Montereau, can be seen, with a pretty seventeenth-century statue, and a garden still tended with the art brought to this country by Matius, the friend of Augustus. You now have an attractive route back to Dijon. Follow the D.6 across the wooded plateau through Lamargelle and Moloy to **Courtivron,** where the château, built at different times from the twelfth to the eighteenth century, may be examined closely from the outside. In 1973 this was permitted from 15 July until the end of August at any time of day. Then turn south at Tarsul and join the N.396 at Vernot, where the road winds through the Bois de Malte to Saussy and on to Messigny and Vantoux-les-Dijon. At **Messigny** you will find some fifteenth-century houses at the side of the road, and in the church a fifteenth-century pulpit, with painted panels taken from an early reredos, seventeenth-century statues by Dubois, and a number of fine tombstones. At **Vantoux** the eighteenth-century château stands in the middle of the fields on the right bank of the Suzon, from which you are never far away until it flows into the Ouche at Dijon.

You should not leave Fixin (or Dijon if that is where you are staying) without a further short exploration of the Montagne. Climb the Combe de Lavaux out of Gevrey-Chambertin and proceed to **Curtil-Vergy,** where a massive, ivy-covered tower stands among the limestone rocks on the hill. This is all that remains of the fortress from which the Sieurs de Vergy ruled the countryside. It was destroyed by the Huguenots under Henri IV. Above it, at the head of a steep road, stands the twelfth-century church of **Vergy** in a superb situation. The exterior has been well restored, and similar work was going on inside when I was last there. It is normally closed, except on Sunday afternoon and public holidays.

Continue along the D.109E and the D.25 to **Arcenant,** where the west end of the nave in the church is bridged by a life-size statue of St Martin of Tours on his horse with the beggar alongside him (*circa* 1500).

If you are in the mood for further exploration, and a good meal, with beautiful country all the way, follow the Combe Portuis to Bruant; turn sharp left on the D.8, right again on the D.25, and right on the D.18. The first turning on your left will then take you to **Bouilland,** and the Hostellerie du Vieux

Moulin. Here you may eat as well, if rather expensively, as anywhere on the Côte and in perfectly tranquil surroundings. You will do well, however, to book a table, and if you choose to stay the night there, fair warning is obviously advisable, since the place has only eight rooms. Bouilland is not more than ten kilometres from Arcenant, although the route is complicated. The D.25 will take you direct from Arcenant to the N.74 at Nuits-St-Georges, and thence to Dijon or Fixin as required.

# CHAPTER TWELVE

# The Côte[1]

❧

1

It is perilous to assert of Shakespeare that he did not know what he was talking about but when, in *King Lear*, he allows a character to contrast the 'vines of France' with 'the milk of Burgundy', and even to refer to the latter as 'waterish', one can only conclude that he was singularly ill-informed. Erasmus, it is true, had apostrophized *'Bourgoyne, heureuse mère d'hommes, que tes mamelles ont un bon lait'*; but then Erasmus came from the Low Countries, where burgundy has always been popular, particularly in the southern areas readily accessible by river and canal. Besides, Shakespeare may not have known his Erasmus; and there is, after all, a difference between milk and water. His ignorance was not altogether surprising. Burgundy was slow to find its way across the Channel to the tables of the common drinker or the connoisseur. Claudius in *Hamlet* drained 'his draughts of Rhenish down', and Falstaff sang the praises of 'sherris sack'; with Dr Johnson and Sir Walter Scott claret had an undisputed priority. No doubt the long connection with Bordeaux was partly responsible for this, for it was easy for the great casks to come by sea to London and Edinburgh, Cork and Limerick. George Meredith was the first great English writer to give burgundy its due. Harry Richmond described it as 'the wine of princes', and many of us will claim a share in the compassion extended to a character in the same novel: 'Poor Jorian – I know no man I pity so much. He has but six hundred a year and a passion for burgundy.' In these days of astronomic prices we feel the pinch if we have a passion for Beaujolais. It was only towards the end of the nineteenth

1. For much of the information in this chapter I am indebted to Stephen Gwynn's *Burgundy* (1934) and Mr H. W. Yoxall's excellent *The Wines of Burgundy* (1968).

century, as the habit of eating in restaurants grew, that people began knowingly to talk about 'a little place' where a good burgundy could be had for a moderate price. Chesterton wrote of drinking 'the blood of kings for half a crown a bottle'; and it was over a Moulin à Vent – strictly, of course, a Beaujolais – at the Moulin d'Or in Soho that he met Belloc for the first time. Nevertheless, of the serious connoisseurs that I have known I cannot recall one who specialized in burgundy rather than claret. I belong to a dining club called the Old Burgundians, but it is only rarely that a red burgundy finds its way on to our table; and I notice that the fifteen menus printed at the end of George Saintsbury's *Notes on a Cellar Book* include only five red burgundies and two white.

Neither the Burgundians themselves, nor those who visited or invaded their country, had any reservations about the excellence of their wine. The Dukes described themselves as '*Seigneurs des meilleurs vins de la Chrétienté*'; and Petrarch had a simple explanation for the prolonged sojourn of the Popes at Avignon. 'If the cardinals wish to stay on the other side of the mountains, it is because there is no Beaune wine in Italy, and they cannot imagine a happy life without their liquor. They regard it as a second element, and compare it to a nectar of the gods.' For a time, however, there was heavy competition from champagne, and it was Louis XIV who settled the matter, as he settled so much else. The King's digestion had suffered from overeating, and his physician, Fagon, was sent on a tour of the country to discover the wine best suited for his royal patient. He picked on Romanée: 'Tonic and generous, Sire, it will agree with a robust temperament such as yours.' This established the primacy of burgundy at Versailles, and the partisans of champagne were simply referred to M. Fagon, who well deserved that a street should be named after him at Nuits-St-Georges. But, as André Lachet testifies, the average, hard-working native of the Côte does not require a Romanée to challenge his appreciation.

'Watch this old Burgundian take a wide glass, warm it paternally in his two hands, pour into it a little wine, shake it, look at it closely, turn it round, place it in the light to make sure that it's clear, piously and lovingly inhale its

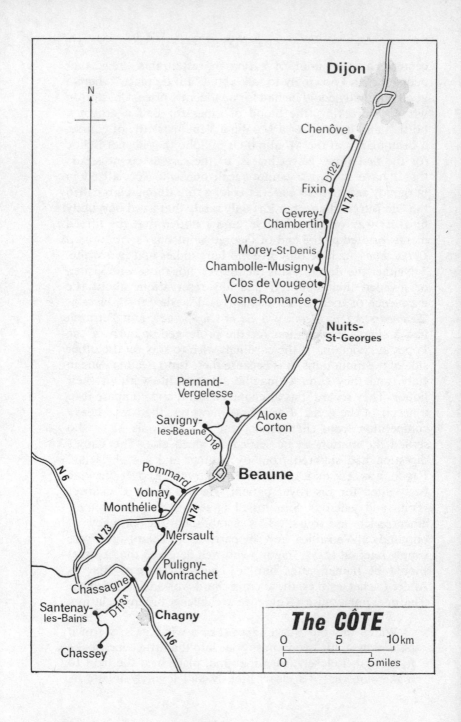

Dijon

Chenôve

D122

N 74

Fixin

Gevrey-
Chambertin

Morey-St-Denis

Chambolle-Musigny

Clos de Vougeot

Vosne-Romanée

Nuits-
St-Georges

Pernand-
Vergelesse

Savigny-
les-Beaune

D18

Aloxe
Corton

N 6

Pommard

Beaune

Volnay

Monthélie

N 74

N 73

Mersault

Puligny-
Montrachet

Chassagne

Santenay-
les-Bains

D 113ᴬ

Chagny

N 6

Chassey

The CÔTE

0        5        10km

0                5 miles

bouquet, and finally drink it very little at a time, sipping it in a series of repeated motions like a bird.'

The Côte has been compared to 'a long and talkative street warming itself in the light of the rising sun', for, of course, it faces almost due east. Yet, except in the villages and small towns – or larger ones like Beaune and Nuits-St-Georges – it is too busy to be talkative, and its aspect will vary according to the work that is going on there. The plateau above the Côte is composed of sandy limestone, and the effects of erosion, weather, and cultivation have broken this down into soil and rubble which fall down the slope to nourish and drain the vines. Good earth from elsewhere is also carted on to the better vineyards. Some little way up the slope of the Côte de Nuits there runs a narrow outcrop of marl-stone, which creates a limy clay soil perfectly suited to the produce of wines of the highest quality when it is blended with the silt and scree. The vines were planted in rows to facilitate the passage of horses, and latterly of the tall narrow tractors, although formerly you would have seen cherry and pear trees dotted about among them. In late autumn, before they have been pruned, the vines have the colour of dark pink or delicate violet. In winter they look skeletal and almost dead, brown as the soil which, as they say, would have been the poorest in France if it were not also the richest. In spring the vine growers are engaged in pruning the vines, weeding the ground, and waging a patient war against the insects and other enemies; the oidium, black-rot, and pyrale. The snails – a Burgundian speciality – like to feast on the rich leaves. Georges Lecomte gives the recipe for catching them.

'You ambush them in the morning, while they are parading nonchalantly on the humid leaf, and when their slow, fleshly promenade makes one think of the throat of a voluptuous woman shuddering under a gross and clumsy caress.'

The summer is an anxious vigil with eyes and mind upon the weather, for a sudden hailstorm, excessive rain, or a prolonged drought may ruin the vintage. Nature is mistress here whatever man may do to aid or combat her. A popular writer had reason to exclaim: 'Perhaps you imagine – you bourgeois – that the vintage consists of singing in chorus. Not at all – for us the vintage is a serious matter. We have to prepare for it.' The preparation – silent, skilful, and industrious – never stops until the end of September; and when the grapes have been gathered in, there is the first pruning, the dressing of the vines, and the light manuring of the soil. I have been told that in some cases chemicals are used, and that many people will drink wine only from naturally manured vineyards.

The **Côte** stretches for 56 kilometres from Dijon to Santenay – with an important gap in the hills at Beaune – and to drive along it is like running your eyes down the wine list of a great restaurant. Before turning south we shall do well to retrace our steps a few kilometres to **Chenôve,** just outside the city limits of Dijon. Here you may visit the **Pressoir des ducs,** set up by Alix de Vergy, widow of Duke Eudes III, in 1228. The great building, as Stephen Gwynn describes it, 'was filled with scaffolding of fourteen-inch beams clamped together and wooden screws of tne same diameter which raised and lowered a block of stone weighing twelve tons and a half, whose descent could crush out the solid residue from sixty casks of new wine. There it is still, a Gargantuan relic – still in perfect working order, and up to the end of last century still used.'[1] In the *cuverie* you will notice the stone carvings of a bird, a pair of dogs, and a bouquet of flowers. Notice on your left, as you leave Fixin, the attractive romanesque church of **Fixey,** with its black and yellow tiles on the tower, small lancets, and plain walls supported by strong timber work. The road runs alongside the vineyards of Marsannay-la-Côte, and at **Couchey** you will find the remains of a late sixteenth-century château, a late fourteenth-century church, and adjoining it an interesting crypt. The Renaissance château at **Brochon** was built by the poet, Stephen Liégeard, and the pavilion in the park was beloved of Crébillon. There is a charming inscription on a house in the village:

> *Qui a la paix chez soy*
> *Vit comme un petit roy*

and in the church a Eucharistic *oculus* on the right of the apse.

1. *Burgundy* (1934).

On the hillside above Fixin we meet once again the rhetorical statuary of François Rude. The **Parc Noisot** belonged to an officer of the first empire, who was a friend of Rude and commissioned from him the statue in bronze of Napoleon 'awakening to Immortality'. The custodian's house contains a little museum of Bonapartist souvenirs, including Noisot's uniform, a model of Napoleon's house at Longwood, and the standard of the 1st Grenadiers of the Imperial Guard, who were present at the Adieux de Fontainebleau. The statue bears the following inscription: '*A Napoléon, Noisot, grenadier de l'île d'Elbe, et Rude statuaire, 1846.*' The bronze bust of Rude by Cabet stands near by, and from it a path leads to the tomb of Noisot (also a bust by Cabet), where the old campaigner had wished to be buried 'upright and facing his Emperor'.

Most of the district north of Beaune is known as the Côte de Nuits, and everything south of it as the Côte de Beaune. The best wine is produced on the lower slopes, where the hills elbow gently out into the plain; that is to say, as you proceed along the route des Grands Crus, you will generally find the great names upon your right. All the wine entitled to these prestigious labels is made from the *pinot* grape; a more ordinary Passe-tout-Grains is produced in part from the *gamay* – locally despised as '*menteur et déloyal*' – on the left hand side of the road, as the land levels out towards the Saône. This contains two thirds of *gamay* to one of *pinot*, with sugar added if so desired. The *crus* reckoned as *hors ligne* – Romanée-Conti, La Tâche, Clos Vougeot, and Chambertin, with their near runners up, Richebourg and Musigny, all belong to the Côte de Nuits, and we shall not be long in coming to them. Indeed, Clos de la Perrière at Fixin itself, where 105 acres are under cultivation, will sometimes sell at the same price as Chambertin.

If you want to touch the very core of what Michelet called the '*aimable et vineuse Bourgoyne*', and that 'extra something essential for the flowering of a local genius', which another writer has defined as the secret of the Côte d'Or, you will find it in the château of **Gevrey-Chambertin,** and in the personality of its proprietor, Madame Masson – although she herself is not a native of Burgundy. She will receive you with a straight-

forward, unpretentious courtesy and lead you back, before
you know where you are going, to the days when the château
was built and to a communal, quasi-religious way of life
which still persists, however secularized, among the vine
growers of the Côte d'Or. She is one of them herself, and you
realize that she knows what she is talking about. She will
show you the instruments of her craft: the *bsou*, the Celtic
name for a triangular hoe; the *bigleu* for digging; the *hâche*
for pruning; the *beraton*, or deep basket for gathering the
grapes; the *tonneau*, or *pièce de vin*, into which the contents
of ten *beratons* are poured; the magnums, which preserve the
forms of the old demi-john. In the château, originally owned
by the powerful Sieurs de Vergy, you will be shown the *salle
des oubliettes*, later used as a lavatory; the *meurtrières*, which
afterwards changed their shape to give a wider range for the
flight of arrows; and the cellar, from which you will certainly
not wish to come away empty-handed.

Two-thirds of the produce at Gevrey-Chambertin comes
from the presses of a co-operative association of 139 small
proprietors holding about 150 acres. Where the economic
basis of Bordeaux is capitalist, in Burgundy it is co-operative,
and that much closer to the socialism of the medieval guilds.
Everything sold from the *commune* of Gevrey is legally
entitled to call itself Gevrey-Chambertin, and it is all made
from the *pinot* grape. But it must be distinguished from Le
Chambertin, which comes from a slope of 60 acres just to the
south of the village of Gevrey. This has been called '*le roi
des vins de Bourgoyne*', and notices clearly define the limits of
its kingdom. It was Napoleon's favourite wine; and it became
universally popular in 1813 when Boieldieu sang of its
beauties in his comic opera *Le Nouveau Seigneur du Village*.
Bonaparte preferred it at five or six years old, never drinking
more than half a bottle at a meal, and complained bitterly
that he was compelled to drink claret on St Helena, since
claret was more easily brought there by sea. Chambertin has
been compared, on the one hand, to 'the Good Lord gliding
down your gullet in a pair of velvet trousers', and on the other,
to the fifth, seventh, and ninth symphonies of Beethoven!
Curious that anything so strictly incomparable as wine should
evoke such far-fetched comparisons. Hilaire Belloc concluded

his speech before the Saintsbury Club at the Vintners Hall in London with the following peroration: 'When that this too too solid flesh shall melt and I am called before my Heavenly Father, I shall say to him: "Sir, I don't remember the name of the village, and I don't remember the name of the girl, but the wine was Chambertin".' Other *crus* from the same *commune* are Charmes-Chambertin and Mazis-Chambertin; they are splendid wines – Princes of the blood royal, if you like – but they stand below the throne. Gevrey-Chambertin, since it is not classified as the produce of a particular *clos*, may be described as a Gold Stick in Waiting, but still with its place at Court. The wines of Gevrey-Chambertin are as good as any for laying down; the lasting powers of red burgundy tend to diminish as you go farther south.

Gaston Roupnel, the author of *La Bourgoyne, types et coutumes*, is buried at **Gevrey**. He was rightly proud of his *commune*, and would have agreed with Alexandre Dumas that 'nothing makes you see the future in rosy colours like looking at it through a glass of Chambertin'. The seventeenth-century addition to a medieval stronghold in the village encloses the garden of the house where Jobert de Chambertin once lived. Gevrey has a fourteenth-century church with a notable baptismal font.

The culture of the vine, like so many other of the arts and crafts, owes much to monasticism. In 630 Amalgaire, Duke of Burgundy, granted to the Abbaye de Bèze a tract of land at Gevrey, part of which was already planted with vines. The monks quickly planted the rest of it and enclosed it with a dry wall, and this became known as the Clos de Bèze. Then, as the story goes, a certain Bertin, who owned the adjoining land, emulated the monks so that the Champ de Bertin came to rival the Clos de Bèze. The monks, not to be outdone, bought out the descendants of Bertin and joined the two properties together. In 1219 they sold it to the Chapter of Langres, who in turn made it over to a wine merchant called Jobert. He added Chambertin to his name and by his management of the vineyard established its reputation. Today the 60 acres of Chambertin and Clos de Bèze are the property of thirty owners. They produce a yearly average of three hundred barrels, or 70,000 bottles, of robust, aristocratic wine. To see it under the right light and in the right glass was compared by Stephen Gwynn to 'seeing the best of Titian'. To describe its taste or suggest its bouquet stretches the limits of analogy. In the following triolet Bernard de la Monnaye maliciously associated the Protestant reformer Théodore de Bèze with the *clos* of the same name:

> *Bèze qui produit ce bon vin*
> *Doit passer pour très catholique.*
> *J'estime plus que Chambertin*
> *Bèze qui produit ce bon vin*
> *Si le disciple de Calvin,*
> *Bèze, passe pour hérétique,*
> *Bèze qui produit ce bon vin*
> *Doit passer pour très catholique.*

The Cistercians from Cîteaux planted the greater part of **Morey-St Denis,** which lies next along our path, and here the most precious *clos* was bought by a convent of nuns, the Bernardines of Tart. It came to be known as the Clos des Dames de Tart (17½ acres), and subsequently Clos de Tart. Immediately adjoining it is the village of **Chambolle-Musigny,** and the vineyards called after it; but here again you must not confuse the excellent wines produced in the *commune* of Chambolle with Le Musigny, which is a prince of the blood, if not an heir to the throne. As in the case of Gevrey-Chambertin, the village has annexed the name of its most famous *cru*. The 24 acres of Musigny stretch right up to the scrub of the higher slopes, and the difference between the soil on either side of the dividing line is such that the vine growers are said to wipe it off their boots when they leave the vineyard, lest a particle of it should be wasted. As Gaston Roupnel has written:

'The great vintage dates from long before the year of its birth . . . its excellence derives from origins deep buried in the earth from which it came. Before it could begin to be born, it was necessary that the earth in which it was engendered should become a thing ancient in use. and that its cradle should be a tomb where the ashes of the years and the dust of the centuries had accumulated.'

George Saintsbury, in his *Notes on a Cellar Book* recalls with
delight a Musigny of 1877, and we need not go so far back –
if that were still possible or even desirable – to find an equal
pleasure in a wine whose beauties do not belie its name. A
Musigny Vieilles Vignes de Vogüé 1945 was served at Perse-
polis in 1971 to celebrate the 2500th anniversary of the
Persian Empire. Thirty-three out of the thirty-six acres of
Bonnes Mares – evidently a corruption of *Bonnes Mères*,
since it was also acquired by the Bernardines – lie in the same
*commune*. If you ever come across a little white Musigny do
not neglect it.

At Chambolle-Musigny the *route des grands crus* unfortunately comes to an end, and you are thrust on to the N.74,
a nightmare of commercial traffic hurtling south from Dijon.
To join or, worse, to cross it where there are no lights is an
exercise fraught with peril. But you have no choice. In a
moment, however, you will see the noble Renaissance château
of Clos Vougeot standing proudly among its vineyards away
to your right, and you will turn up with relief to visit it.
Roupnel maintained that 'in a world of revolution' the wine
of Clos Vougeot was 'the one remaining royalty of right
divine'. Then, compelled as a native of Gevrey-Chambertin
to recognize the royalty of Chambertin, he accorded Clos
Vougeot an imperial crown. Colonel Brisson would not have
disputed the title when he commanded his troops to present
arms before the château – a gesture which has become
canonical in the French army.

St Bernard and his monks, needing material for their new
abbey at Cîteaux, found a useful quarry in the *commune* of
Vougeot, and slopes nearby suitable for the cultivation of the
vine. By the middle of the twelfth century they had built a
cellar, and a hundred years later the *cuverie*, with four gigantic
presses, were in place. These were made of oak from the
forest of Cîteaux, and ten men on each arm were required to
manipulate them. You can see them for yourself, although
they are no longer in use. In 1162 Duke Eudes II renounced
his rights over the Cistercian vineyards, and in 1164 Pope
Alexander III – who was caught up so uncomfortably in the
quarrel between Henry II and Becket – placed the abbey of
Cîteaux and the Clos Vougeot under papal protection. He is

said to have been encouraged to do so by judicious gifts of its produce. Gregory XI rewarded a later abbot with a cardinal's hat soon – but not too soon – after receiving a present of 30 hogsheads. The château, or *manoir*, as we see it today was built by Dom Loisier, forty-eighth abbot of Cîteaux in 1551, and his successors ruled there until 1790. A new cellar was built above ground and in such a way that the sections of it where the wine was laid down were enclosed to admit the passage of cooler air. At the Revolution the property was bought by a timber merchant from Paris, who defaulted on his agreed instalments, and the last cellarer of Cîteaux, with the appropriate name of Dom Goblet, administered it for the nation. In 1791 he went into retirement with a private cellar so renowned that Bonaparte sent for some of its contents to celebrate the victory of Marengo. The monk's reply has passed into history: 'I have some Clos Vougeot forty years old: if he wants to drink it, let him come here. It is not for sale.' One cannot help wishing that in these days of easy laicisation a few similar ex-cellarers were scattered about the Côte d'Or. In 1818 the property passed into the hands of a man who had made a great deal of money out of Napoleon's victories; and in 1889 it was sold to a consortium of wine merchants.

There was a piquant contrast between the preaching of Cîteaux and the practice of Cluny. At Cluny, St Bernard recalled with indignation:

'In the course of one midday meal, three or four times, a goblet half full will be brought and offered; until after various wines have been smelt at rather than drunk, touched with the lips rather than drained, by expert testing and swift instinctive discernment one at last out of the many is chosen for its strength.'

As Stephen Gwynn, from whom I borrow the above translation, has observed, this is exactly the right way to approach a sequence of the best burgundies, except that the Cluniac connoisseurs laid a too exclusive emphasis on strength. The contrast is not only piquant but also ironical between the preaching of St Bernard and the practice of his workers at Clos de Vougeot. He was interested in another kind of vine-

yard, where no one would have disputed his competence.
The château, as distinct from the *clos*, belongs to the
Confrérie des Chevaliers du Tastevin, founded in 1934 after
three disappointing vintages to promote the appreciation, and
naturally the purchase, of burgundy. Fifteen *disnées* are held
annually in the cellar of the château, which easily accom-
modates four hundred people. Each *disnée*, or *chapitre*, is
preceded and accompanied by the *intronisation* of the new
members – *chevaliers*, *commandeurs*, or *grands officiers*. The
bizarre ritual for this ceremony was inspired by Molière's
*Divertissement du Malade Imaginaire*. A scarlet and orange
ribbon, with silver *soucoupe* attached, is suspended round the
neck of the new member, who is expected to wear it for the
rest of the evening and at any subsequent *chapitre*. The
officials of the *Confrérie*, in academic robes, also of scarlet
and gold, enter the cellar in procession, preceded by trumpeters and halberdiers, and the more important *intronisations*
take place on a stage from which the 'Cadets de Bourgoyne' –
a sun-tanned choir of vine growers – have enlivened the
evening with old Burgundian songs. Each *chapitre* has its
appropriate name, and a *tenue de soir* is prescribed for all of
them, except for the 'St Vincent Tournant' in January,
which is held at noon – and finishes when the evening is
already well advanced.

There is some excuse for describing the banquets of the
Tastevin as a gastronomic Glyndebourne; though they are
considerably more expensive, quality is the hall-mark of both.
The insignia of the *Confrérie* are bestowed not only on
politicians, ambassadors, men of letters, and amateurs of wine
from the four corners of the earth, but also on those who work
in the vineyards and could not afford, one supposes, to attend
many of the *disnées* at their own expense. *Haute couture* is
evident all around you, but *haute cuisine* is here no respecter
of persons, and the *milieux* mix agreeably. I have myself
attended four *chapitres* of the Tastevin since 1958. The first
was the 'St Vincent', where I was '*intronisé*' as a *chevalier*.
The ceremony took place at Aloxe-Corton – for while the
banquets are always held at Clos Vougeot, the 'St Vincent' is
preceded by '*intronisations*' at various villages along the Côte.
On this occasion the *cuvée* of Corton-Charlemagne was the

chosen site. The road up to the village was bordered with decorated Christmas trees; in the window of the school plasticine models of the vintage were on display; and one entered the church for the Mass under a triumphal arch of wine casks. The preacher, if I remember rightly, was the Canon Bourgeon, whose eloquence on the subject of the local industry has earned him several *cures* in the neighbourhood. If, *per impossible*, there had been a teetotaller in the congregation, he must have left the ceremony with a conviction of mortal sin. Very impressive was the procession with its banners coming down the road from Pernand-Vergelesses in the shelter of the valley, for St Vincent – a Spanish deacon martyred in the dawn of Christianity – was reported himself to have cultivated the vine, and has therefore become the patron saint of vine growers.

The *chapitres* of the Tastevin are never wanting in theatrical appeal, for there on the stage is M. Léon Rappeneau leading his 'Cadets de Bourgoyne'. M. Rappeneau would alone make a visit to the Tastevin worth while. His mobile, expressive features and alert physique belie his eighty years, and you very easily cast him for a role in Molière. In fact, he taught elocution for many years at the Conservatoire in Dijon, where Edwige Feuillère was a pupil. But he was never tempted on to the professional stage. The fifteen 'Cadets de Bourgoyne' entertain audiences at Deauville and elsewhere, and whatever they are singing reminds you of the Burgundian infantry on the march.

> *Joyeux enfants de la Bourgoyne*
> *Je n'ai jamais eu de guignon*
> *Et guand je vois rougir ma trogne,*
> *Je suis fier, je suis fier*
> *Je suis fier d'être Bourguignon.*[1]

My second *chapitre* was the 'St Hubert' early in December, when I was promoted to the rank of *Commandeur*. This was attended by the 'Piqu'Avant-Bourgoyne' from the Forest of Châtillon. The music of the Mass, celebrated in the church at

---

1. Happy children of Burgundy, I have never had bad luck,
 And when I see the red in my cheeks, I am proud, proud,
 proud to be a Burgundian.

Vougeot, was rendered on the instruments of the chase, the
blare of the brass greeting one from some distance as one
drove out from Dijon. You dropped your note for the
collection in the mouth of a hunting horn, carried round by a
lady in blue and scarlet uniform, wearing an eighteenth-
century tie wig; and an enormous hound stood quietly in
leash at the foot of the choir throughout the ceremony. I have
also twice attended the 'chapitre de l'Equinoxe' at the end of
September when the grapes are ripe for the vintage and glasses
are being raised for its success. At the last of them I had the
honour of presiding, and was made a Grand Officier. The
result of the vintage will not be known until the following
spring. Regularly, on the eve of Palm Sunday, about a
hundred and twenty people assemble in the cellar of the
château to hear the verdict of the *Tastevinage*. For the past
ten years a jury of competent persons have deliberated
throughout the morning to decide which wines of the previous
vintage deserve the Tastevin's approval. In 1972, for example,
230 out of 369 submitted received the coveted *étiquette*. Each
bottle must be judged on its total merits, future promise as
well as present performance, and the verdict is declared
during dessert at the luncheon that follows.

A little farther along the same disagreeable N.74 we come
to **Vosne-Romanée**. The village might just as well have called
itself Vosne-Richebourg or Vosne-La Tâche, for both these
prestigious vineyards are included in the *commune*. But
Romanée deserved the suffix by nature as well as by name.
In 650 a tract of land was granted by Clotaire to the clergy of
Bèze, who preceded the Cistercians in cultivating the vine on
the Côte d'Or; and in the thirteenth century Alix de Vergy
made over her vineyard at Romanée to the Abbey of St
Vivant in the adjacent *commune* of Nuits, where Alix had her
château. One portion of the Romanées belonged to the
Abbey of St Vivant, another – La Tâche – to the Chapter of
Nuits, and a third was in lay ownership. This was sold in the
eighteenth century to the Prince de Conti, against the bidding
of Madame de Pompadour, and thus acquired its name.
Romanée-Conti (4½ acres) is unique among French vineyards
in having preserved its original stock, in spite of the phylloxera, until 1946; and with La Tâche it is unusual in belonging

to a single proprietor. The tiny vineyard has been described as 'the central pearl of the Burgundian necklace'. Romanée Conti and La Tâche between them produce only about twenty-five thousand bottles in a good year; they are among the most expensive wines in the world. I have drunk only one bottle of Romanée-Conti, and do not expect to drink another this side of Elysium.

Also included in the same *commune* are Richebourg and Grands Echézeaux. Grands Echézeaux has been slow to make its way on to English wine lists because – or so it is said – people find it difficult to pronounce. It is not at all difficult to drink.

Practically adjoining Vosne-Romanée is the important town of **Nuits-St-Georges.** With the neighbouring *commune* of Prémeaux it marks the end of the Côte de Nuits, of which it is nevertheless the commercial centre. The vineyards of these *communes* cover about 950 acres, and the wines they produce anticipate already the gentler and shorter lived *crus* of the Côte de Beaune. You must distinguish between the forty officially classified premier *crus*, entitled to call themselves Les St-Georges, and the ordinary wines of the *commune*, which will be labelled Côtes-de-Nuits, or Côtes-de-Nuits-Villages. The *étiquette* Nuits-St-Georges has been much abused; if you see it on any but a most reputable wine list, you are never sure what you are buying. Yet here I can speak from experience. I bottled myself a hogshead of Nuits-St-Georges 1957, and the following year the same quantity of Côte-de-Nuits 1959, and there was nothing to choose between them. Both were delicious, and still show no evidence of decline. This confirmed the judgement of Stephen Gwynn that 'a wine sold as Nuits, or Nuits-St-Georges, by an honourable wine merchant' – and mine was very honourable indeed – 'should be not only a *vin fin*, but a wine having a special delicacy that distinguishes it from the slightly stronger growths of Gevrey and Vosne.' Louis XIV recommended Nuits as a cure; and others have recommended it as an aphrodisiac. The saying went:

> *Un verre de Nuits*
> *Prépare la votre.*

The **Church of St Symphorien** at Nuits-St-Georges is worth a visit for its sculptured figurines on the narrow lancet windows of the apse, an *Ecce Homo* where the eyes of Christ are blindfolded, and for the fifteenth-century tombs of Jehan d'Argilly and his four children.

2

We must now follow the N.74 for a few painful kilometres to Aloxe-Corton, and turn up right to **Pernand-Vergelesse**. This produces an excellent wine which suffers, like Echézeaux, from its rather complicated name and is sometimes dishonestly sold as Aloxe-Corton. If it dropped the 'Vergelesse', an unhappy confusion with Pernot might result. The village will always be associated with the name of Jacques Copeau (1879-1949). I had been interested to see an impressive portrait of Copeau – dark, lean, and somewhat prelatical – in the offices of the mayor at Dijon, and was glad to realize that he was so well remembered. Copeau was born in Paris and was closely associated with André Gide and Jacques Rivière in the foundation of the *Nouvelle Revue Française* before passing from dramatic criticism to active work in the theatre. His seasons at the Vieux Colombier, and particularly his production of *Twelfth Night*, which Granville-Barker declared to be the best he had ever seen, established him as a new and original master of *mise-en-scène*. Everything at the Vieux Colombier was 'promising' declared André Suarès, a sensitive poet of the time 'but the promise is great'. Copeau was too little a Parisian at heart completely to fulfil it; and in 1924 he left Paris for Pernand-Vergelesse, where he gathered round him a company of young actors – to whom the village postman gave the name of *Les Copiaux*. They rehearsed in a disused *cuverie* lower down the hill on the road to Aloxe-Corton – you can see it on your left as you approach the village – and gave performances in the surrounding countryside, travelling in a bus with their costumes and properties, and announcing by a drum when the play was about to begin – sometimes in a garden or a park, sometimes in a square or a dance hall. Copeau was longing for a fresh impulse, and he obtained it from a fresh audience.

I spent an afternoon with him in the garden of his house at Pernand in July 1945, four years before his death; he talked much of Granville-Barker, who had tried to do for the English theatre what he had done for the French, for Barker also could have said of himself: '*L'insatisfaction m'habitait*'. His house stands at a corner of the street that bears his name, and is now lived in by his son, M. Pascal Copeau, who will show to anyone who venerates the memory of his father the rooms where he worked and slept. These have been kept exactly as they were in his lifetime with the photographs, now faded, of Rivière and Claudel, Dostoievsky and Gide, Péguy, Baudelaire, and Verlaine; and some *maquettes* of his productions.

The whole area of Aloxe-Corton and Pernand-Vergelesse used to belong to Charlemagne, and the great white wine of the *commune* bears his name. When the Saracens ravaged Saulieu and sacked the church of St Andoche he gave these vineyards to the clergy in compensation for their losses. Both red Corton and Corton-Charlemagne (to be distinguished from Corton *blanc*) rank among the *grands crus*. The former was the favourite wine both of Voltaire and Maupassant, and such liking as one may have for Voltaire is not increased by the fact that he gave Beaujolais to his guests! Greuze – whose painting we shall meet at Tournus – was a visitor here and executed his fine portrait of Madame Lebrault while he was the guest of the Comte de Grancey. The château of **Corton-Grancey** has a *cuverie* where they still tread the grape. The Clos du Roi is so called after Henri II, who owned it in 1555; one likes to think of its juice moistening the lips of Diane de Poitiers.

The village and vineyards of **Savigny-les-Beaune** (945 acres) can be reached quickly from Pernand without incurring the discomforts of the N.74. Over a stone arch nearby an inscription proclaims, without exaggeration, that '*les vins de Savigny sont des vins nourissants, théologiques, et morbifuges*'.[1] One cannot ask more of any fermented liquor. The village has considerable charm, at the foot of the Bois Noel, with a stream, the Rhoin, running through it, which eventually finds its way into the Saône. The polygonal rotunda of the

1. Suitable to chase away depression.

sacristy (fifteenth century), and the château rebuilt under Louis XIII, with its semi-circular, eighteenth-century stables, flanked by pavilions, are well worth inspection. You may find it worth while to drive up the valley from Savigny to where the *roche percée* stands up on your left. The story goes that Marguerite de Vergy pursued by a demoniacal horseman owed her safety to the powers on high, who obligingly opened an arcade in the rock. The cavalier was obedient to the command of Yeats's epitaph: 'Horseman, pass by'. From Savigny you have an easy run along the D.18 into Beaune. Here parking is not easy; your best chance is in the rue de l'hôtel-Dieu beyond the couvent des Cordeliers.

**Beaune** takes its name from the god Belenus – thought by some to be a Gallic variant of Apollo, although the ambiance of the town is more Dionysiac than Apollonian. Beaune is the capital of the Côte. *Vinum Belense super omnia vina recense*[1] was a medieval boast, and Erasmus sighed to live in France 'not to have the command of armies, but to drink the wine of Beaune'. In 1328 Reims paid it the compliment of consuming 150 barrels to celebrate the Coronation of Philippe de Valois; in 1377 Du Guesclin received a pipe from the grateful citizens of Bayeux as a reward for his martial exploits against the English; in 1512 Louis XII sent 36 puncheons to James IV of Scotland as a reassurance that the 'auld alliance' still stood firm; and in 1701, we are informed, the wine of the Côte-de-Beaune was an annual item of some importance in the Pope's personal expenditure. In the *Grand Livre des Vins*, kept here since 1747, many celebrated persons have inscribed their names – the Duke of Alba, the Comte de Ségur, Marshal Leclerc, General de Larminat. Notable among them is Edmond Rostand, whose opinion of himself at least equalled that of his admirers. 'Your wines will become very famous at my table. I am Edmond Rostand, author of *Cyrano de Bergerac*, known all the world over. I'm telling you that in your own interest, as well as in my own.' Beaune itself has never been reluctant to endorse its modest share in this admiration. As one of its popular rhymers put it:

1. Let the wine of Beaune be known beyond all others.

*De Beaune, l'on médit en vain*
*Tout cela, pures calomnies!*
*Beaune produit d'excellent vin,*
*Ergo, Beaune est fertile en excellent genies.*[1]

The *commune* of Beaune has 1345 acres under the vine, but of these less than 200 produce a wine of outstanding quality. They include, among the *premiers crus*, Beaune-Grèves de l'Enfant Jésus – commonly ranked superior to the others. It is as suave to the palate as it is to the ear. But the name of Beaune, like that of Nuits-St-Georges, is too often taken in vain. All that glisters like a ruby is not worthy of the 'slopes of gold'; you need to be as sure of the name on the head of your invoice as of the name on the label of your bottle.

When you see Hospices de Beaune on a label you are rightly impressed; this was served to King George VI and Queen Elizabeth at the luncheon given in their honour at Versailles in 1937. Twenty-four red and eight white vineyards of the first importance have in the course of time been bequeathed to the Hospices, all of them in the Côte de Beaune but not all in its *commune*. For you must not forget that the Hospices – or Hôtel-Dieu – was founded as a hospital in 1443 by Nicolas Rolin, chancellor of Burgundy under Philippe le Bon. You may see his portrait in the Louvre, kneeling before the Virgin and Child. Louis XI observed – with or without good reason – that 'having made so many people poor and homeless, he could well afford to make his peace with the Almighty by providing for some of them.' The Hospices survived the anti-clerical legislation since the Dames Hospitalières from Flanders were not technically a religious order, however strongly their fifteenth-century costume might suggest the contrary. Fifty aged folk still live in the Hospices, 60 orphans are looked after and educated, and the poorer citizens of Beaune are entitled to be nursed there. You may visit the long ward with its curtained cubicles, and an altar at one end so that the bedridden can hear Mass – a superbly proportioned room where space creates serenity. Viollet-le-Duc thought this so beautiful that he longed to be ill there.

1. No use to speak ill of Beaune – all that is pure slander.
   Beaune produces excellent wine, and it follows that Beaune is
   fertile in genius of the first order.

You also see the original pharmacy with the blue and white vases for ancient remedies; and the kitchen where the food is cooked over log fires under Gothic chimney-pieces. Modern facilities are not lacking either; there is an operating theatre and up-to-date pharmacy; and the sisters pay this much respect to the climate that in summer they change their habits from blue to white. But none of this would have been possible if Rolin and his wife, Guigone de Salins, had not endowed the Hospices with some of the finest vineyards on the Côte. Two of them bear the names of its benefactors.

The glare of publicity falls upon the Hospices on the third Sunday in November when the wines of that year are auctioned. The tradition goes back to 1851, and for a long time the sale – which is also a ceremony – took place in the courtyard of the Hospices, decorated with tapestries hung out for the occasion. Now it has been transferred to the closed market of the town, where there is more room for happy spectators and hopeful buyers – and the tapestries still embellish the proceedings. Tasting takes place on the previous day, and tickets both for this and the auction itself are dear and not easily obtainable. The wines, sold in lots of 304 bottles, are auctioned *à la chandelle*; the last bidder before the candle goes out gets the lot, and the precise moment of its extinction sometimes leads to controversy. Candlelight is also *de rigueur* for the dinner held the same evening, close to the Hospices, in a bastion of the city walls. This is the second of what are called *Les Trois Glorieuses* – the first having been celebrated the evening before by the Tastevin at Clos-Vougeot. The menu imitates, on a reduced scale, the virtuosity of a ducal feast; hot pâté of thrush, fillets of pike cooked in grapes, guinea-fowl cooked in wine of the commune, roast ham *forestière*, and a triumphal procession of great vintages from the Côte.

The Hospices is a superb example of late Gothic architecture. The façade of four storeys is crowned by a sloping roof of polychrome Burgundian tiles, a thin spire 30 metres high, dormer windows, pinnacles, and weather vanes. The **Cour d'honneur** has been described as 'a lodging for a prince rather than a hospital for the poor'. On two of its sides turrets and a double row of dormers stand out from the patterned tiling of the roof. The vanes are emblazoned with armorial bearings. A wooden gallery, supported by slender stone columns, runs round the first storey, giving the effect of a cloister at the ground level. In the centre stands an elegant well-head on its stone base behind a wrought iron railing. Two rooms of the second floor are occupied by a museum. In the first of them you may see under a glass case the signatures of Louis XIV and the Princess Palatine, who inaugurated the hospital's Livre d'Or, and six Flemish tapestries of the early sixteenth century. In the second hangs Roger van der Weyden's master-piece of *The Last Judgement*, commissioned by Nicolas Rolin. It formerly stood behind the altar in the *chambre des pauvres*, and is the finest painting to be seen anywhere in Burgundy. In the centre panel Christ sits enthroned on a rainbow among the clouds. St Michael weighs the worth of souls while the angels sound their trumpets on either side of him, and the Virgin and St John the Baptist implore the divine compassion. The Apostles and various other personages add their supplica-tions; among them are the supposed likenesses of Pope Eugenius IV, Philippe le Bon and his wife, Isabella of Portugal, Nicolas Rolin and his son, the Cardinal. Below, the dead emerge from their tombs, and either make their way towards a Paradise of gold, or are seen already suffering the contor-tions of the damned. The reredos used originally to be open only on Sundays and greater feasts; and on the opposite wall you may see what it looked like when it was closed, with the portraits of Nicolas Rolin and his wife and the *grisaille* paintings of St Sebastian and St Anthony, patrons of the Hospices, and the Annunciation.

The collegial **Church of Notre-Dame** was a daughter of Cluny. Begun about 1120, the ambulatory and small apses are good examples of Burgundian romanesque, but the total effect of the building is spoilt by a mixture of styles. The façade is encumbered by a broad, three-aisled fourteenth-century porch; the choir and flying buttresses are of the same date; and the tower, with its bays resting on romanesque blind arcading, is crowned by a sixteenth-century dome. The original Cluniac inspiration is shown by the fluted *colonnettes* of the triforium, and the proportions both of choir and nave are admirable. Notice in the second chapel of the left aisle, as you approach it from the west end, the frescoes representing the raising of Lazarus – attributed to a Burgundian artist, Pierre Spicre. In a room adjoining the church, at the end of the impasse Notre-Dame, you should not miss the five superb tapestries illustrating the life of the Blessed Virgin. These were woven from designs by Spicre, and given to the church in 1500. In the same place there is a fine sixteenth-century Pietà. Much work has been done to reveal the cloister and chapter house.

Very close to Notre-Dame is the former Hôtel des Ducs de Bourgoyne, an attractive Renaissance building in wood and stone. Today it houses the **Musée du Vin,** the most comprehensive to be seen anywhere. You enter the fourteenth-century *cuverie* by an impressive doorway and find the whole story of burgundy set out before you. On the first floor an immense Aubusson tapestry, designed by Lurçat, adorns the wall and elsewhere every variety of receptacle from which wine may be drunk will excite your nostalgia for vanished vintages.

It is rewarding to stroll about the streets of Beaune, where you can admire a number of fine timbered houses within a very small radius; the **Hôtel de la Rochepot** in the rue des Tonneliers, with its Gothic façade and two interior courtyards; a fine group in the rue de Lorraine; the charming Maison du Colombier in the rue Fraisse, which you can see from the *parvis* of Notre Dame; the Hôtel de Saulx in the place Fleury with its pretty turret and inner court. The Hôtel de Ville, formerly the Ursuline convent, contains the **Musée des Beaux Arts** and the **Musée des Métiers bourguignons.** In the first there is some good furniture, and a collection of paintings by Ziem, a native of Beaune; in the second examples of Burgundian craftsmanship in cooperage, glass-work, and ceramic. The thirteenth-century **Church of St Nicolas** in the vine growers' quarter of the town has a romanesque tower, and twelfth-century door under a tiled fifteenth-century porch. The tympanum shows St Nicholas rescuing three young girls whom their father is evidently threatening with a fate worse than death. But to capture the enchantment of Beaune you should make the *Tour des Fossés* – in other words walk around the ramparts in the shade of the plane trees, noting the different names that meet you as you view the city from changing angles – *rempart des Lions, rempart des Dames, promenade des Buttes* – and the stout bastions that rise from the grass at their feet.

A word of caution is here in place. You have come from where the wine is grown and made to where it is bought and sold. If Beaune likes to think of itself as the temple of burgundy, it is a temple from which you will sometimes feel inclined to drive out the money-changers. Bidding from America and Japan is pushing the price of the finer *crus* beyond the average – or even the more than average – European purse. The continent, which was the cradle of wine, is in the way of losing its most cherished offspring. A great number of exporters have their houses in Beaune, and you are invited to visit their cellars and taste a wide variety of wines drawn off from the tempting rows of casks. But you will need to be very thick-skinned if you leave the premises without making a purchase that, may be, you can ill afford. Particularly attractive are the Caves des Cordeliers in the thirteenth-century **Couvent des Cordeliers** in the rue de l'Hôtel-Dieu, with its arcaded courtyard, pointed turret at the angle of the roof, and balustraded gallery at the level of the first floor. The church was destroyed in 1796; only the side chapels survived, but a polychrome reredos in stone of the Adoration of the Magi was saved and can now be seen in the *Cour d'honneur*. You will be encouraged to taste whatever you like, and you will be in no hurry to quit that hospitable cellar. But do not – unless you are quite shameless – confuse a *dégustation* with a free drink.

I have already directed you to the rue Monge in Dijon, but Gaspard Monge (1746–1818) more properly belongs to Beaune, where he was educated by the local Oratorians. At fifteen he was constructing a pump for extinguishing fires, and a year later his design for town planning so impressed an officer of the engineers that he was sent to study mathematics at Mézières. In due course this resulted in his *Traité de Géométrie Descriptive* and his *Traité Statique*. He rallied to the Revolution, founded the Ecole Polytechnique, and supported Bonaparte. When the pupils of the Polytechnique declined to congratulate Bonaparte on assuming the title of Emperor, Bonaparte not unreasonably complained to their principal. Monge replied: 'We had a great deal of trouble turning them into republicans; give them time to become imperialists. Besides you must let me tell you that you have been rather quick in changing yourself.' Monge had served under Bonaparte in Egypt, and could talk to him as man to man. He was an avid reader of the Bible, Plutarch, and Corneille, and a keen lover of wine.

Of the vineyards immediately south of Beaune the best known are **Pommard** and **Volnay**. Pommard was named after a temple dedicated to Pomona, goddess of fruits and gardens; it was a favourite wine of Victor Hugo. Volnay earned the Latin tag: '*Et sine Volneo nulla gaudia mero*', and history has paid it many compliments. Philippe de Valois found it much to his taste, and Duke Eudes IV sent six dozen casks of it to the French court. Louis XI ordered the entire vintage of 1477 to be sent to Plessis-les-Tours; Cardinal de Bonsi despatched a heavy consignment to Warsaw for the Coronation of John Sobieski; and the fame of the wine spread to northern Europe when a group of Protestants from Volnay left the country in 1687 after the Revocation of the Edict of Nantes. It has always been popular in England, although Pommard runs it close. Just a little farther along the road from Volnay you come to **Monthélie,** said to be the sunniest village on the Côte, with a church where the Cluniac influence is again predominant, and Auxey-Duresses – both reputable *communes*, but overshadowed by the great white burgundies, whose territory lies close at hand.

**Mersault** is a pleasant little town with a gaily roofed Hôtel de Ville, and its own Hospice, modelled on the Hospice de Beaune. Here, too, are the vast Cistercian cellars of the Comte de Moucheron, which can accommodate 400 hogsheads, and his collection of 300,000 different bottles. The *commune* can boast of nearly sixty *crus*, of which twenty are ranked of the highest class, and, like its neighbour Montrachet, made from the *chardonnay* grape. A Mersault-Charmes will appeal to you for obvious reasons, and a Mersault-Sous-le-Dos-d'Ane[1] may well excite your curiosity. The vineyards also produce an excellent red wine, Santenots, although you will rarely meet it on the English side of the Channel. The third of

1. Under a donkey's back.

the *Trois Glorieuses* is held at Mersault on the Monday following the auction at Beaune. The luncheon is known as the *Paulée* – a word that signifies the mid-day break, to which the vine growers, like everyone else, are naturally entitled. This is a popular festivity organized by the owners of the vineyard, who offer the wines from their private cellars in a spirit of hospitable emulation. The menu is simpler than at Beaune or Clos-Vougeot, but the robust fare is suited to robust appetities. I have never attended a *Paulée*, but I can believe that it brings you closer to the heart of Burgundy than either of the other *Glorieuses*. Mersault offers an annual prize of 100 bottles of its wine for the best book on the life, scenery, architecture – or wine – of the province. If this Guide were ever to be translated into French, I confess that I should be keeping my fingers crossed!

Just south again from Mersault we find the eighteen priceless acres of **Le Montrachet**. Courtépée, the historian of Burgundy, described it as 'the most excellent white wine in the whole of Europe', and although he might have met some contradiction from the banks of the Rhine, many have agreed with him. For Rabelais it was 'divine', and Alexandre Dumas declared that 'it should be drunk kneeling, with one's head bared.' Hilaire Belloc wrote to a correspondent that he proposed to drink a bottle of Montrachet 'to the confusion of my enemies'. I would prefer to drink one to the comfort of my friends. The vineyards of Le Montrachet and Bâtard-Montrachet – whose bar sinister is no occasion for shame – are shared between the *communes* of Puligny and Chassagne, who have each attached it to their names. Even Romanée-Conti, not content with its own pre-eminence, has bought a plot in Montrachet.

Nevertheless, red burgundy has the last word on the Côte, and one of the best. If you continue for about four kilometres down the D.113A from Chassagne, you will come to **Santenay-les-Bains.** Here the Roman baths have been converted into a modern spa, much recommended for digestive troubles, gout, and rheumatism. The springs are among the richest in the world for helium and lithium. The vineyards cover well over three hundred acres, and a hundred of these produce wines of exceptional quality. A bottle of Santenay – grown from the heart of the Roman amphitheatre in the hollow of the hill and close to the small twelfth-century Templar church – will not tempt you to challenge Saintsbury's distinction that, if claret is the queen of natural wines, burgundy is the king.

Turn to the left in Santenay; cross the canal on to the N.74; turn to your left again; and take the first road to your right. This will bring you very quickly to **Chassey** and the delightful, modern Auberge du Camp Romain. The hotel overlooks a wooded valley and not only provides excellent hospitality, but gives you a convenient stepping off place for future exploration.

CHAPTER THIRTEEN

# From Chalon to Autun

1

Although we have left the *grands crus* behind us, the *route des grands crus* reappears more modestly to the south of Beaune as the *route des vins* – for the vineyards continue all along this line of hills far beyond the limits of Burgundy. You may therefore admire the twelfth-century church at **Chassey,** noting the very fine Vierge de Pitié (late sixteenth century), and the font with its coloured inscription (1604). But if you enquire what there is to be seen of the Roman camp on the hill above the hotel you will get the answer: '*absolument rien*'. So proceed a little farther on the same road to **Chamilly** and take a look at the *château-ferme*, with its round tower in the valley below you to the left. The church has an *oculus eucharisticus* to the left of the altar, and a holy water stoup with four carved heads. The building itself, with its stone-roofed pointed tower, is very early romanesque, and pretty rough in texture.

Take a small road to the left out of the next village, Aluze, and this will bring you after three kilometres to **Rully** and the *route des vins*. Rully is distinguished both for its château and its white wine – smooth and a little oily. Of the latter you can read a good deal in the memoirs of Eve Francis, who liked to drink it in the company of Paul Claudel. She had memorably interpreted the role of Sygne de Coufontaine in his *L'Otage* and was still, in advanced age, reciting his verse with extraordinary sensibility and fervour. The interior of the château can be visited only by appointment but you may walk round the outside on Saturday and Sunday from 10 to 12h and 14 to 18h at any time between 1 April and 31 October. It stands on a rocky spur of ground beyond the village, and has been inhabited by the same family – the Comtes d'Aviau de Ternay – for five hundred years.

It was probably built in the thirteenth century and comprised a square keep and four towers linked by a round walk and watch towers. The whole building was crenellated and surrounded by a dry moat; and the only entrance was over a drawbridge, the siting of which is clearly marked on the south façade. On the round tower to the left of this you can see the opening which allowed the pigeons to reach their nests inside. There was room for 1200 of them. The present living quarters of the château seem to have been built at the end of the fifteenth century along three sides of the interior court; and the outbuildings at the end of the eighteenth. These are all roofed with *laves* – wide, flat stones that weigh heavily on the timbers underneath. The word apparently derives from the way the Burgundians used formerly to speak of '*lavant* (levant) *la piarre* (pierre)'. You will notice that the entrances to the stables and barns are all shaped like the handle to a basket. The château is surrounded by huge chestnuts; and even if you arrive there without making an appointment to see the inside, you may well find yourself engaged in friendly conversation with the châtelaine. From a distance of twenty yards or so on the terrace she will give you any information you require.

By the D.155 and the N.6 you may now conveniently reach **Chalon-sur-Saône** (the Roman Cabillonum), ten kilometres away on the other side of the Côte. The industrial outskirts of Chalon are forbidding, but the older quarters of the town by the river have considerable charm. Julius Caesar chose it as a depot for the storing of food during the Gallic wars, and King Bontran habitually lived here. Already, in the Middle Ages, it was famous for its annual *foire aux sauvagines* – wild water fowl. This has continued to the present day. Indeed, not all the furred and feathered booty brought from the Alps and the Jura, the Pyrenees and the Massif Central can be classified as water fowl. Foxes, badgers and polecats find their way into the market as well as otters, beech-martens and mink. Here, too, the French bowling championship is held every year. Under the *ancien régime* the inhabitants of Chalon had permission to fish in the Saône and to hunt around it; with or without permission they do so today. The construction of the canal du Centre at the end of the

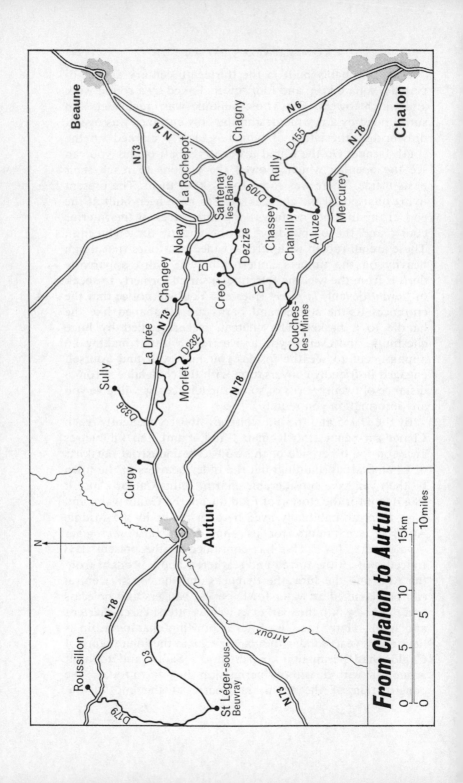

## From Chalon to Autun

Beaune

Chalon

N6

N74

N73

N73

D155

N78

La Rochepot

Chagny

Santenay-les-Bains

D109

Rully

Chassey

Chamilly

Aluze

Mercurey

Nolay

Dezize

Changey

D1

Creot

D1

Couches-les-Mines

N78

La Drée

D232

Morlet

Sully

D326

Curgy

Autun

Arroux

Roussillon

D179

D3

St Léger-sous-Beuvray

N78

N73

N

0        5        10        15km

0        5        10miles

eighteenth century, the canal du Bourgoyne, and the canal linking the Rhône to the Rhine, aided the commercial development of Chalon. And in 1839 the Schneider factories at Le Creusot founded the 'Petit Creusot' in the town. This now specializes in the production of copper-ware, and other metallurgical and pharmaceutical industries have followed in its wake.

Chalon's favourite son is Nicéphore Niepce (1765–1833). His statue stands in the small square opening out on to the Quai Gambetta, and a **Museum** devoted to his experiments in photography is clearly indicated on the left as you face the river. Niepce served as a sub-lieutenant with the armies of the Revolution, but was obliged to resign his commission for moral misconduct. He was the friend of Daguerre and discovered the principles of photography by using a simple box and the glass from a pair of spectacles. How this worked, with his diaphragm, fixed and folding cameras, and early photographs, you may see for yourself in the museum. He described his invention as follows:

'The discovery I have made and that I have called by the name of *heliography* consists in the *spontaneous* reproduction of the images received in the dark receptacle by the action of the light, with varying degrees of shading from black to white.'

In 1807 Niepce produced the design for an internal combustion engine, and this also can be seen.

If you turn up the rue Général Leclerc from Niepce's statue and take the first street to your left, you will find the **Musée Denon** on your right at the farther end of the Place de l'Hôtel de Ville. This handsome Renaissance building was the former Ursuline convent and is named after an eminent engraver of the *ancien régime*, who organized the museums of France under the Empire. The museum contains a number of interesting paintings and sculptures: Mirevelt's portrait of Elizabeth of Bohemia, and two by Larguillière; a Salvator Rosa; a fifteenth-century Last Supper; a sixteenth-century St Sebastian; and, once again, St Anne teaching the Virgin to read. Very remarkable is the collection of prehistoric flint instruments from the south-west corner of Burgundy, said to be the finest of its kind anywhere in the world; several Gallo-Roman bronzes; and a splendid Gallo-Roman group in stone; a gladiator at grips with a lion; and a number of Merovingian objects. The museum is open from 9.30 to 11.30h and from 14.30 to 17.30h. It is closed on Tuesday. The ticket will also admit you to the Musée Niepce.

Now return to the rue Général Leclerc, cross over it, and follow the rue du Châtelet to the **Eglise St Vincent,** noting the many charming old houses as you go along. This was a cathedral until 1700. The façade is nineteenth century, but parts of the interior – the pillars of the nave and choir, and the arcading – go back to the eleventh century. The Cluniac capitals include a person holding a piece of meat on a spike in front of two griffins, seated on their backs; the griffins carry the meat up to Heaven. Notice the low, fluted pilasters from which coupled columns rise straight to the sexpartite vaulting, and above the level of the clerestory. There is a high triforium, with passages above and below, and plain balustrade. A grilled balustrade runs round the choir and apse. There are five bays to the nave, and some good modern stained glass. But the principal treasure of the church is the **Tapestry of the Eucharist** in the south transept. Here you see the donor, Hugues Bouchet, with his wife and children, and the four panels illustrate Abraham, dressed as a knight, receiving the bread and wine from Melchisedech; Moses receiving the manna; the Passover; and the Last Supper. Here Christ is shown at the side of the table – not, as convention dictated, in the middle – and Judas has his back turned to the rest of the company.

The street to your left as you come out of the church will bring you back to the river, and turning right along the quays you may cross the first bridge to the island, which here divides the waters of the Saône. Immediately on your right is the **Hôpital,** a sixteenth-century foundation, with fine woodwork in the chapel, some sixteenth-century stained glass, a polychrome Pietà in stone, and a fifteenth-century Virgin with an inkstand. The refectory, with its pewter jugs and dishes, is particularly impressive. The Hôpital is open to visitors from 10 to 12h and 15 to 17h; if you apply to the concierge, one of the Sisters will take you round.

Adjoining the Hôpital is the fifteenth-century **Tour du Doyenne**. This originally stood near St Vincent, but it was demolished in 1907 and rebuilt on a point of the island. It is open from 1 April to 30 September, on Thursday and Saturday, between 14 and 18h; on Sundays and public holidays from 10 to 12h and 14 to 18h.

Crossing back into the town, you should follow the Quai Gambetta to your left, and then turn up the rue Michelet, opposite the next bridge. This will bring you straight on to the N.78, and after fourteen and a half kilometres to the charming village of **Mercurey**. Here you should pause for a few moments' *dégustation*, for Mercurey is a wine that, at its best, challenges many more famous *crus*. Then continue along the same road to **Couches-les-Mines**. Here the sombre and imposing château was captured by the partisans of Marie de Bourgoyne after its owner, Claude de Blaisy, had thrown in his lot with Louis XI. Considerably modernized in the last century, it has kept three of its thirteenth-century towers and its fifteenth-century chapel, with finely carved doors, built by Claude de Montaigne. You can visit it on Sundays and public holidays from 1 April to 30 June between 15 and 18h, and from 1 July to 1 September, every day between 10 and 12h and 14 to 18h.

Now branch off to your right on the D.1, and then on the D.38, to **Dezize**, and climb up the road on your left out of the village. Once clear of an adjacent hamlet, you will come upon a wide triangle of grass where a pair of dolmens lie among the bushes, not very easily distinguishable from the other rocks which litter the ground. It is worth while climbing to the top of the hill – for the road goes all the way – to where three crosses dominate the countryside. The view is magnificent. Down below lie the vineyards of Santenay and Chassagne-Montrachet; in the distance are the roofs of Chalon. You could not bid a more dramatic *au revoir* to the Côte d'Or.

2

It is the pride of Burgundy to have produced two of the greatest soldiers in the military annals of the French – Vauban and Lazare Carnot (1753–1823). Carnot was born at **Nolay,** which you will reach in a few minutes, driving north from Dezize. His genius was quick to declare itself. At the age of nine, watching a play in the theatre at Dijon, he called out to the actors: 'Get on the north side of that bastion; your own people are under cover, and you can capture the place.' Inspired by an admiration for Vauban, he joined the engineering corps in 1789, and won the '*éloge de Vauban*' for the Académie de Dijon. He was a friend of Condé, Governor of Burgundy and President of the Académie, but there is no reason to doubt that he gained the award on his own merits. When the brother of the King of Prussia offered him promotion, he refused and reluctantly accepted an appointment with the republican army.

Carnot had tasted the insolence of the *ancien régime*, for on sending a memorandum to the Secretary of State he had received no acknowledgement. He thereupon addressed a personal complaint to Louis XVI, but the reply – no doubt from an official – asked merely: 'Since when has a poor plebeian not been satisfied to be a captain and a cavalier?' As a member of the Convention he voted for the death of the King, but admitted that no duty had ever weighed more heavily upon him. The Brunswick manifesto tipped the scales in his divided mind. 'Louis XVI would have been saved if the Convention had not deliberated with daggers at their throats.' In his relations with Bonaparte he approved neither the consulate for life, nor the imperial régime, although Bonaparte offered him 'everything you want, when you want it, and how you want it.' Later he rallied to Napoleon; was appointed Governor of Antwerp; and acted as Minister of the Interior during the Hundred Days. He was then 60 years old. But Carnot had little taste for politics; and his recipe for those who practised them has not been generally followed:

'The true friend of the people is the man whom you have to spend a long time in persuading to assume a political responsibility; who retires from it as soon as he can, and is poorer than when he took it on; who gives himself to it from a sense of duty; acts more readily than he talks; returns with eagerness to his family; and resumes the exercise of the private virtues.'

Carnot returned whenever he could to his family at Nolay, teaching them Latin and mathematics and, when they were little, wheeling them about in a wicker pram. He was also a great walker. A man of warm humanity both in the council chamber and on the battlefield, he defended Danton and closed the curtains and windows of his house on the day when the great tribune was executed; just as he had obtained the reprieve of a young soldier comdemned to death for failing to rejoin his regiment. 'I thought you were a Brutus,' the lad remarked. 'Yes,' replied Carnot, 'when I have to be.' When Napoleon offered to make him a count, he objected that he neither wished to 'wrap up his name in a sobriquet, nor to bring fresh enemies against Napoleon by a noisy refusal.' He went into exile at the Restoration, and died at Magdeburg. He has been called 'the Cincinnatus of the Revolution'. His statue stands in front of the house where he was born, and which still belongs to his family.

Do not miss the fourteenth-century **Halles** at Nolay, with their superb timber work and heavy limestone roof.

You should now follow the N.73 to **La Rochepot**. This was the birthplace of Philippe Pot (1428–94), the principal chamberlain of Charles le Téméraire, ambassador to the English court, and a more adroit politician than his master. The château with its six pepper pot towers stands on a steep incline. The primitive structure was refashioned in the fifteenth century, but the keep was razed to the ground at the Revolution. The roof displays an attractive chequer-board pattern of red, black and yellow tiles. Inside you will admire the Chinese room with its Buddha, lacquer bed, and blue enamelled fireplace; the Gothic chapel; the guard room, where the whole village could gather in the lower part; the captain's room, with its walls three metres thick; the dining-room, with its high-backed tapestried chairs; and the enormous pitchforks in the kitchen. The château was bought by President Sadi Carnot in 1893, and you can see the vase presented to him by the Empress of China. Also a Louis XIII baby's chair, and a stone carving of the Trinity – one of only three examples in France.

La Rochepot has an interesting romanesque church with capitals of Balaam and the ass, and the Annunciation.

Now return to Nolay, continue west along the N.73, turn left at Changey, whence a short detour will bring you past the gatehouse of the château at **Morlet** – an interesting example of Renaissance military architecture (1584). One high gable of the château is visible from the road, and an isolated stone arch in the garden. If you follow the D.234 through the village you will quickly find yourself back on the N.73 at La Drée, and then turning to your left, where a signpost points to the **Prieuré du Val St-Bênoit,** en route for one of the most romantic sites in Burgundy. The little road winds through a thickly wooded valley until a path to the right indicates where you should leave your car. Walk down through the trees and you will come upon the ruins of the Priory. The dovecote, with its slate roof and wreathed in ivy, is still standing; also the west front, with a rose window. The interior is being slowly restored by voluntary workers, under expert direction. They sleep in the deserted farm buildings at the side – not, one imagines, very comfortably – and they will lucidly explain to you the work in progress. The *flamboyant* transept chapel has been pretty fully restored, and they are uncovering the choir and sanctuary, which has a flat *chevet* and thirteenth-century windows. There are also traces of a staircase to the monks' quarters; a romanesque credence in the transept; and the tomb of Marie de Couches has been discovered. The Priory was once a thriving community, but only two monks were found living there when it was suppressed at the Revolution. Its restoration is due to the generosity of the duc de Magenta, whose château at Sully we are now to visit.

The road through the Val St-Bênoit will bring you round to the N.73, which you should cross and immediately bear right for **Sully.** The original château was a stronghold of the Bishops of Autun, replaced in 1515 by Gaspard de Saulx-Tavannes. Nicolas Ribonnier is thought to have been the architect. You approach it along an avenue of large, flat-topped bushes, six on each side. On the left are the Renaissance stables. The château is surrounded by a wide moat, which is crossed by a five-arched bridge. Square towers are set at an angle of 45° to the main building, which is of lighter stone. You will observe a classical watch tower on the south front. The château has nineteen windows on the first storey as you face it from the west, and eight on the *mansarde*. From the north front an elaborate series of stone steps and terraces lead down to the moat – the most intricate and ostentatious that I have seen anywhere in the province. More appropriate and just as elegant are the four stone columns, each interspersed with a sunflower, four cannon balls and two pyramids, which ornament the balustrade along the moat on the western side. On the south front a thin spire indicates the chapel. The château can be visited from the outside, any day of the week, between 15 April and 30 September, from 10 to 12h and 14 to 18h. If you arrive there after 18h you will be told politely that this is the time when '*Madame la duchesse sort avec son chien.*' Madame de Sévigné described Sully as the '*Fontainebleau de la Bourgoyne*', and the interior court as '*la plus belle cour de château de France*'. You will be sorry not to have seen it.

In the seventeenth century the château had been acquired by Pierre de Morey, marquis de Vianges, and through the second husband of his daughter-in-law came into the possession of the MacMahons. The duc de Magenta inherits his title from Patrice-Maurice de MacMahon (1808–93), maréchal de France, who was born at Sully. After service in Algeria and the Crimea, where he captured the tower of Malakoff, MacMahon defeated the Austrians in a famous victory at Magenta. In 1858 he entered the Senate, and succeeded Thiers as President of the Third Republic. After a republican victory he dismissed his premier; brought in the duc de Broglie; and dissolved the chamber. After that he retired, observing that he had served many governments and missed them all, with the exception of his own.

Returning to the N.73 you should leave it a few kilometres farther on for the pure and early romanesque church at **Curgy**, close to the main road. This has a fine twelfth-century mural in the cupola of the apse, where Christ is seen with two angels and two horsemen of the Apocalypse. From Curgy you have an easy and quick drive into Autun.

3

**Autun** – the Roman Augustodonum (*dunum* was the Celtic word for a fortified hill) – took its name from Augustus, who founded the city after reducing the Gallic stronghold at Bibracte. It soon became a nursery of Gallo-Roman culture. The Emperor Constantius Clorus sent his secretary of state, Eumenus – 'the most intelligent of my companions' – to educate the conquered tribes.

> 'Our Gauls [he wrote] whose children are instructed in the liberal arts deserve that we should busy ourselves with cultivating their natural qualities. What better can we offer them than those treasures of the mind that money can neither give nor take away.'

Eumenus was the grandson of a Greek rhetorician, and knew well how to carry out his master's orders.

The main highway from Lyon to Boulogne passed through Autun and ensured its prosperity. Of the city's four gates and ramparts with 62 semi-circular towers, only the **Porte St-André** remains. It has two wide arches for the passage of vehicles, and two narrower ones for pedestrians. A military post at the side was converted into a church in the Middle Ages. Tradition held that St Symphorien, who came from a noble family of Autun, was beheaded alongside it in AD 179 during a festival in honour of Cybele, while his mother, from the other side of a wall, encouraged his fortitude. The Porte St André originally had an arcaded gallery above its four openings, and even without them it testifies to the importance of a city which was described as 'the sister and rival of Rome'.

You will not do better than stay at the Hotel St Louis et Poste, 6 rue Arbalète, which is centrally situated and reasonable in price. Its proprietor, a pupil of Escoffier and a veteran of two wars, long assured the excellence of its cuisine. Napoleon stopped here on 15 March 1815, and his room is piously preserved. The mayor had armed the royalists and forced the populace to hoist the *fleur-de-lys*, when the 13th regiment of dragoons from Lyon disarmed the *garde nationale* and would have sabred the mayor and the more compromised of the royalists but for the arrival of the general in command of the troops. Bonaparte cashiered the mayor and asked him by what right he threatened the citizens for carrying the national colours? To the crowd massed in front of the hotel he declared:

'My power is more legitimate than the power of the Bourbons, for I hold it from the people, and you can hear their acclamations.'

The scene was rather different when the motley army of Garibaldi passed through Autun in 1870. Here were 12,000 men in four brigades – Spaniards, Egyptians, Greeks, Poles, and the two sons of Garibaldi himself.

'One man was recruiting a battalion of children; another was aspiring to the command of convicts from the prison; prostitutes were parading about in staff officers' uniforms, with curving thighs and bulging bosoms; several of the women stretcher-bearers were dressed in provocative costumes. Not a day passed without complaints from the inhabitants; priests were molested; and shopkeepers robbed.'[1]

You will need to spend two nights in Autun. Here the great matters are the cathedral and the musée Rolin, and neither can be digested in a hurry. The **Cathedral of St Lazare** is perched up on a slope behind the ramparts at the extreme southern point of the city, close to the Tour des Ursulincs. We know from inscriptions preserved in the museum that by the end of the third century Christianity was firmly established at Autun, and in AD 314 the first bishop, Reticius, took part in the Council of Arles. Autun retained its title as the premier suffragan see of Lyon. At the end of the tenth century, in circumstances that remain mysterious, the body of St Lazarus was brought to the city by Bishop Gérard. The expulsion of the Saracens in 972 had by then opened the roads to a journey at once sacred and hazardous. But it was not until the first years of the twelfth century that Bishop Etienne de Bâgé, the friend and disciple of Cluny, undertook to enshrine the relic in a building worthy of the popular veneration it inspired. The ground for this was given to the chapter by Hugues II,

1. Paul et Victor Margueritte: *Les Tronçons du glaive.*

## THE CATHEDRAL OF ST LAZARE
## AT AUTUN

1 & 2 Simon Magus tries to ascend to heaven in the presence of St Peter, holding the key, and St Paul. Simon falls, head foremost. One can see the Devil, a rather picturesque figure, if you stand in the nave

3 The stoning of St Stephen

4 Samson pulls down the temple. A symbolic representation

5 Noah prepares to load the ark. Notice the axe in his belt

6 16th century door into the sacristy

7 Memorial statues to Pierre Jeannin, President of the Burgundian Parliament and minister of Henri IV, and his wife

8 The relics of St Lazare are preserved under the High Altar

9 Jesus appears to St Mary Magdalen

10 The second temptation of Jesus. Observe that the Devil alone is perched on the top of the temple

11 16th century window of the Tree of Jesse

12 Painting by Ingres representing the martyrdom of St Sympherien at the Porte St André

13 The Nativity

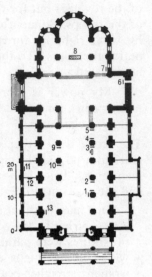

Duke of Burgundy, nephew of Pope Calixtus II, who had spent the Christmas of 1119 at Autun.

The new church was dedicated by Pope Innocent II on 28 December 1130. It could hardly have been completed in so short a time; when the records speak of the *ingressus* the reference is probably to the first bays of the nave and the sculptured portal. In 1195 the new church supplanted the old basilica of St Nazaire as the cathedral of Autun; and in 1469, when the romanesque tower of the transept crossing had been struck by lightning, Cardinal Jean Rolin, the son of Nicholas Rolin and a native of Autun, replaced it by a massive steeple. At the same time he raised the central apse, and substituted an ogival vault for the original cupola. Side chapels were added to the nave, but the eighteenth century brought ruinous alterations. The tomb of St Lazarus in the sanctuary was dismantled, and the tympanum of the Last Judgement sacrilegiously plastered over. This, however, saved it from worse

Autun: Eve, in the Musée Rolin. 'The expression of tremulous sensuality leaves one in no doubt as to which temptation she has succumbed.'

Autun:
Temple of Janus.

Paray-le-Monial: the Basilica. 'A total architectural rhythm mounting, like a Gregorian chant, from the apsidal chapels to the central octagonal tower.

sacrilege at the hands of the revolutionaries, who dedicated the cathedral to the goddess of Reason, and then to the Supreme Being. The nineteenth century (under the direction of Viollet-le-Duc) did much to redeem the damage. In 1939 the classical tower which had masked the ground storey of the apse was removed to the church of St Pantaléon; and in 1948 the magnificent head of Christ, relegated to the museum, was restored to its rightful place as the crowning glory of the tympanum. In 1934 the capitals which had been removed from the cathedral during the restorations were displayed in the Chapter House. Here you can study them more carefully than *in situ*; skilful copies now occupy their original positions inside.

The cathedral of Autun was planned in 1120 under the influence of Cluny, but whereas the abbatial church of Cluny had an ambulatory with chapels radiating out from it, the architect of Saint-Lazare was content with an apse and two smaller apses alongside it. The nave has seven bays spanned by slightly pointed arches; barrel vaulting; and pillars faced with fluted pilasters. Here the Roman antiquity of Autun makes itself felt; just as the blind triforium is obviously inspired by the arcading on the Roman gate. The pilasters go right up to the vaulting, their flight scarcely interrupted by the bands which encircle them. In contrast to the nave the side aisles have ribbed vaulting. The classical influence lends an undeniable grace to Saint-Lazare, but what will always bring you back to Autun are the capitals – unique and unexampled in the category of romanesque sculpture for their alliance of imagination and technique. Where nine artists are thought to have been at work at Vézelay, a single hand – Giselbertus – executed the finest, and the greater part, of the capitals in Saint-Lazare.

Let us first take a look at those in the **Chapter House.** These originally stood near the high altar, on the north side of the choir. Four of them describe the infancy of Christ. In *The Magi before Herod* the tetrarch is seated cross-legged in a richly embroidered robe, but his head, like that of one of the Magi, has been stolen. In *The Adoration of the Magi* both the Virgin and Child wear similar draperies falling in intricate folds to their ankles; the Child places his hand on the heavy

round container held out to him by the first of the Wise Men,
while the second respectfully raises his crown, and the third
uncovers his gift as much as to say: 'Look at this nice surprise!'
St Joseph, in the rear, with his pointed beard and knees
crossed, leans his cheek upon his right hand and seems to be
wondering what it is all about. The capital showing the *Magi
asleep and the Angel awakening them* with a dream is the best
known of the four. They share the same pillow and the same
rich counterpane. One of them has his eyes open and his arm
resting on the coverlet; the angel has touched his little finger
(not quite so little as anatomy would demand). The other two
– one of them bearded – are sleeping peacefully. The angel's
left hand is pointed upward in admonition. *The Flight into
Egypt* is not less remarkable. The Virgin, staring into space,
is contemplating a mystery greater even than this hurried
exodus, and the Child with his hand on an orb looks out over
the world He is presently to redeem. St Joseph trudges forward,
the bridle of the donkey in one hand, a stick over his shoulder
in the other. Notice how the movement of the donkey is
conveyed by its left leg sharply raised, and how the whole
group is supported by wheels which reinforce the general
effect of motion. This carving has been quoted as an example
of *'expressionisme intérieur'*; mysticism and mobility are
marvellously combined in it.

Also in the Chapter House are the *Presentation of the
Church* – probably by Duke Hugues II – to Etienne de Bâgé,
where the figure emerging from the clouds may be identified
as either Christ or Lazarus himself; and the highly dramatic
*Death of Cain*. Taking his cue from the text: 'And the Lord
set a mark upon Cain, lest any finding him should kill him' –
the sculptor has put horns upon the head of the first murderer.
Lamech, mistaking him for a wild animal, launches the
arrow while his son Tubalcain guides his left arm. Observe the
contrast between Lamech's benignant hunter's smile and the
anguish on the face of Cain.

Reliefs from the tympanum of the north portal include a
unique treatment of the Assumption, where the Virgin,
assisted by two angels, is rising from the tomb instead of,
as usually depicted, from the bed; a youth with cape and hood
who may have been a witness to the raising of Lazarus in the

central panel; and a figure, possibly of St Martin, who was especially venerated in Burgundy and the Nivernais.

Now stand in front of the west portal and study the **Tympanum**. This is composed of 29 pieces of hard, whitish limestone, not found in local quarries and similar to that found in the neighbourhood of Chalon and Tournus. A comparison with the Last Judgement at Vézelay, carved out of only nine blocks, will immediately strike you. It gains an added effect from the steep elevation of the narthex; and whereas at Vézelay you are caught up into the rhythm of the Christ figure, at Autun it is the still pose and the mingling of mercy and majesty in the head which rivet your attention. These are confirmed by the inscription:

> *Omnia dispono solus meritosque corono*
> *Quos scelus exercet me judice poena coercet.*[1]

The mandorla is supported by two standing and two flying angels. At the extremities of the upper and lower registers angels send out their summons through long horns. In the upper, Mary is in Heaven with two seated figures – perhaps Elijah and Enoch – who were caught up there while still alive. The inscription beneath the lower register

> *Quisque resurget ita quem non trahit impia vita*
> *Et lucebit et sine fine lucerna diei.*[2]

introduces the resurrection of the elect, with St Peter and the Apostles, below. An angel on the lintel divides them from the damned.

Among the elect three are cloaked and the others naked, except for a trio of ecclesiastics. There are two pilgrims with staff and scrip; one carries a cross en route for Jerusalem, the other a cockle-shell as he makes his way to Compostella. An angel escorts three children. The damned are all naked, and you will pick out the miser with his bag of money, the drunkard with his barrel of wine, the adulteress with a pair of snakes biting her breasts, and a head gripped by a large pair of diabolic claws. Here again the inscription below is pertinent:

1. I am alone the lord of all things; I punish the wicked and give a crown to those who have deserved it.
2. All who have not been betrayed into an evil life will rise thus, and the light of eternal day shall shine upon them.

*Terreat hic terror quos terreus alligat error*
*Nam fore sic verum notat hic horror specierum.*[1]

On the right of the immense Christ – the only static point
in the whole composition – St Michael weighs a soul in the
balance, while another in mid-air is on its way to Heaven.
The Devil faces the Archangel, and on the extreme right a
larger devil is carrying a toad, and the head of Leviathan
looms behind Hell's gate with a flaming cauldron above.
Notice how the figures of the Apostles nearest to Christ are
also the closest to Him in size. This deliberate elongation was
justified by what Focillon called the *loi du cadre*. Indeed the
mark of the tympanum is the equilibrium of drama and style.
Observe the emotion of the figure emerging from the sarcophagus on the left of the upper arch; the compassion on the
face of St Peter; and the Devil's intensity of malice.

The calendar is illustrated all around the outer arch. The
seasons are indicated by a man in a short tunic, with flowers,
for spring; a nude figure with a cloak and his face covered, for
summer; while a tunic and cloak, and a thick coat and hood,
symbolize respectively autumn and winter. The months are
shown as follows. January: a man feasting; February: a
man warming himself; March: pruning; April: the feeding of
animals; May: a knight on horseback; June: a man eating
fruit; July: a reaper; August: threshing of the corn; September: the vintage; October: feeding of the hogs; November:
getting in the firewood; December: killing the hogs for
Christmas. Some of these are similar to the carvings of the
same subjects at Vézelay, where it has been conjectured that
Giselbertus got his training.

The tympanum of Saint-Lazare is not only a masterpiece of
sculpture. It will tell you a great deal of how the men of the
Middle Ages behaved in this world, and of what they believed
about the next.

You should now study the capitals on either side of the
central doorway. These include an illustration of the *Fox
and the Crane* from Aesop's fable – a warning against trickery;
*Abraham dismissing Hagar and Ishmael*; and the *Six Elders*

1. May this terror frighten those in prey to a terrifying error, for their
fate is shown by the horror of these figures.

*of the Apocalypse*. On the south side *Gratitude* is shown by
St Jerome removing a thorn from the lion's paw; and alongside is the *Presentation in the Temple*, where you will observe
the disproportionate size of the chalice on the altar, and the
*Conversion of St Eustace*, complete with horse, dog, spear
and horn.

In the left hand chapel as you enter the church you will
find a key to the **Capitals** in the apse, choir, and nave. There
were originally fourteen in the apse, but two are missing. In
those that remain you should note two distinct traditions: the
simple upright acanthus leaf with a pair of figures, typical of
the Brionnais, and the crisp leaves deeply undercut, characteristic of Cluny before 1095. The Roman influence is clear in
both, for antique capitals with the crisp acanthus were found
at Autun. The beardless figure on a throne – third from the
north on the second storey – is certainly by Giselbertus;
indeed, many of the capitals on this storey are thought to
have been among the first examples of his work after his
arrival in Autun. Of those in the choir note particularly the
restored *Journey to Emmaus*, probably by a pupil, where
Christ has a staff and the innkeeper is opening the door to
Him; the allegory of *Lust* where Cupid is an innocent youth
mistaking a knife for an arrow, and where the Devil's axe
and the woman's wreath are borrowed from a medieval
representation of the pagan gods; and a figure, perhaps of
Constantine, who visited Autun in 311, or in imitation of the
equestrian statue of Marcus Aurelius, which once stood in
front of St John Lateran at Rome, and was believed to
represent the first Christian emperor. Alternatively it may
symbolize the triumph of Christianity over paganism. The
stylistic resemblance between the capitals in the choir suggests
that they were carved in quick succession.

In the nave I draw your attention to *God speaking to Cain*,
where the body of Abel can be seen in the foliage (south-west
pier of transept crossing, facing south); the *Tree of Jesse* (on
the west face of second pier); the *Dream of Nebuchadnezzar*
(on west face of sixth pier on south side), where a pilgrim
with a scrip and staff is shown above a spreading fruit tree,
and a figure with an axe stands below; the intensely dramatic
*Suicide of Judas*, similar to the treatment of the same subject

that we have admired at Saulieu; the *Building of the Ark*, where two animals and a woman's head are seen in the windows of a two-storeyed wooden house, and two men are loading a sack; and the *Appearance* of *Christ to Mary Magdalene* (on the west side of the third pier of the north arcade), which will again remind you of Saulieu. On the right face the women find the tomb empty, with an angel sitting on it, and run away in fear; and on the face opposite two of them discuss their experience. You should also notice *Samson bringing down the Temple* (one pillar only), betrayed by Delilah and blinded by the Philistines; the *Stoning of St Stephen* (on the west face of the third pier on the south side), where St Paul is seated behind three persecutors; *Daniel in the Lions' Den*, where Habbakuk carrying food to his reapers is held by an angel in mid-air; the *Three Hebrews in the Fiery Furnace* (on the east face of the sixth pier), covered with a cloak by a flying angel, and behind them regular tongues of flame; *Samson breaking the lion's jaw*, with the head of a victim under its left paw; *Moses and the Golden Calf* (on the south wall of the south aisle facing the fourth pier); the *Conversion of St Paul*, his knees bent to suggest prostration, and his baptism in a barrel (on the north face of the fifth pier of the north arcade); *St Peter in Chains* on the west side of the same pier, and his subsequent liberation by an angel; the *Sacrifice of Isaac* (on the north face of the seventh and last pier of the north arcade), where the angel, by a happy inspiration of Giselbertus, already has hold of the ram; and the *Nativity* (on the westernmost capital of the north wall of the north aisle), with the Child in a tub, a sloping bed occupying the whole space, and St Joseph seated on the left. The large flower on the back wall is an echo of St Bernard's fourfold application of *flos* to the Virgin, the Infant Jesus, the town of Nazareth, and the Annunciation.

On the doorway to the north transept four capitals remain *in situ*; they illustrate the parables of Dives and Lazarus, and the Prodigal Son, and the raising of the widow's child at Nain.

It is calculated that six or seven days would have been required to carve one historiated capital. On this reckoning Giselbertus might have spent a year over the capitals in the nave, and perhaps four or five years over the west doorway. It will take you several hours, and not a little physical effort, to study his work with the attention it deserves; and an electric torch will be useful. Or, if you are exhausted by your first visit, you will come back for a second or a third. And when you have digested the detail you will agree with Henri Focillon that here is 'sculpture which is in close harmony with architecture or rather which is dictated by it, conforms in its proportions and modelling to the very shapes of the architectural members to which it is applied or for which it is a substitute.'

The **Musée Rolin,** just to the right of St Lazare, occupies a wing of the house built for the chancellor Nicolas Rolin in the fifteenth century, and the nineteenth-century hôtel Lacomme, which replaced the principal quarters of the hôtel Rolin. A courtyard encloses the two parts of the museum. On the ground floor of the hôtel Lacomme are seven rooms given up to Gallo-Roman antiquities; notably a little three-horned bull on a stone altar; a Roman helmet, with a human face, decorated with bay leaves; a third-century sarcophagus with the very free carving of a boar hunt; the seated figures of husbands and wives; wrestlers, gladiators and acrobats; various brooches, jewels, and statuettes illustrating the fashions of high society; and in the last room the stele of a man pouring out wine into a jar. In the salle Fduennc there is a model of the temple at Bibracte, which it will be useful to carry in your head (or on paper) when you visit the site.

On the ground floor of the hôtel Rolin you will find the crowning masterpiece of Giselbertus – the recumbent nude of *Eve* yielding to temptation. This was discovered in 1856 during the demolition of a house built in 1769. It is 72 centimetres high and 32 centimetres thick. Eve is whispering to Adam, who may have been touching the foliage to the left of her head. The head, arms, and legs are virtually carved in the round, and the statue is unique in medieval sculpture. The expression of tremulous sensuality leaves one in no doubt of the temptation to which she has succumbed.

Other rooms contain superb examples of romanesque sculpture, especially the statues saved from the tomb of St

Lazarus with St Andrew, Martha and Mary; and the inscription *'Lazare veni foras'*; a Resurrection where Christ is supported out of the tomb by two angels; the head of a miraculous crucifix venerated by St Othon in the ninth century; and the black marble tomb of Queen Brunéhaut. On the first floor is the famous *Nativity* by the Maître de Moulins, where Cardinal Rolin figures as donor; the equally fine polychrome statue known as the Vierge d'Autun; and a lovely painting on wood of the Resurrection (1505). The Risen Christ is with Mary Magdalene in the centre; the empty tomb is on the left; Christ with the other women is in the background on the left, and on the right with the disciples on the way to Emmaus. The museum is open from 15 March to 30 September between 9.30 and 12h and 14.30 and 19h; from 1 October to 14 March between 10 and 12h and 14 to 16h (17h on Sunday). It is closed on public holidays, and on Tuesday in winter.

The remains of the **Roman Amphitheatre** stands just off the Promenade des Marbres inside the ramparts and south of the Porte St André. It was the largest in Gaul, and as many as fifteen thousand spectators came to watch its wild beast and gladiatorial contests. You will find a number of Gallo-Roman sculptures and bas-reliefs set into the drinking fountain of the arena.

Other Roman and medieval antiquities can be seen in the twelfth-century chapel of St Nicolas, now the **Musée Lapidaire,** in the Boulevard Larrcau. This is open from 9.30 to 12h and from 14.30 to 18h in summer, and from 10 to 12h and 14 to 16h in winter. For tickets apply to the Musée Rolin.

At Autun you are once again on the fringe of the Morvan. Take the N.78 out of the town and follow it as far as Roussillon (22½ kilometres). Then turn left down the D.179 through the Forêt de Glaine and the Gorges de la Canche, and right on the D.18 for St Léger-sous-Beuvray. From here you climb steeply to the summit of **Mont-Beuvray,** the Celtic Bibracte. It was an archaeologist of Autun, Bulliot, who first suspected in 1859 that remains of the *oppidum* might be discovered there; and subsequent excavations revealed the traces of several houses, temples, shops, and a forum. Some of the objects found are now in the Musée Rolin; others at the prehistoric museum of Saint-Germain near Paris. Five kilometres of fortifications surrounded the place. The inhabitants worked in iron, copper, tin, gold, and silver; specialized in enamel and jewellery; and dyed their hair in chalky water to make it blonde. Very little is now to be seen *in situ*, but you should note the little chapel of St Martin, who came here in AD 376. It was raised in 1876 on the actual *cella* of the temple to Dea Bibracte. An immense panorama stretches out before you from the plateau, but if you want to be alone with nature do not go there on a Sunday afternoon.

You can return to Autun on the D.3 from St Léger by way of **Monthelon**. Here the fifteenth-century château, where St Jeanne-de-Chantal lived with her gross and debauched father-in-law from 1602 to 1609, and often received St François-de-Sales, has been well restored and may be visited from the outside from 15 April to 31 October between 8 and 18h. The eleventh-century church is in good condition and beautifully appointed. It contains the pulpit from which St François-de-Sales used to preach, and the relics of St Jeanne are preserved in the altar of a small apsidal chapel with its three lancets and three low arches supported by thick pillars. Her youngest child, Charlotte, is buried under a mosaic.

Away to your left, and isolated in the middle of the fields, as you approach Autun, is the **Temple of Janus** – two sides of a square tower, 24 metres high, where the traces of vermilion can be seen on the inside walls. Nothing is known of the divinity to whom it was consecrated, for it acquired the name of Janus only in the sixteenth century.

Charles-Maurice de Talleyrand-Périgord (1754–1838) was promoted to the see of Autun in 1788. He had hoped for Bourges, where the bishop was subject to fits of apoplexy. Only thirty people attended his consecration, and they included neither his mother nor his uncle. Although he charmed the Burgundian clergy and represented them at the meeting of the States-General, he showed little interest in his diocese, and left it on 4 April 1789. He was one of only four prelates to support the Civil Constitution of the Clergy; and when he was excommunicated he sent the following invitation to the duc de Biron: 'Come and console me by having supper with me. Everyone must refuse me fire and water, so this evening we will have cold meat and iced wine.'

# CHAPTER FOURTEEN

# From Autun to Charlieu

❧

## 1

Take the N.78 out of Autun, going east, to **St Emiland** (seventeen kilometres). Here there is an interesting church with an exceptionally tall choir, and star-shaped vaulting in the chapel to the right of the apse. Notice the fluted pilasters to the arches under the tower, and the open-air pulpit in the churchyard. Then strike south along the D.131 for **Epiry,** where Bussy-Rabutin was born and baptized in the château. In a country renowned for the pleasures of the chase one is never surprised to come upon the traces of that insatiable *coureur*. The fifteenth-century château stands on a slope, approached down a long avenue, and is built on three sides of a courtyard with four round machicolated towers of pinkish stone. It can be visited from the outside at any time except on Saturday and Sunday.

The D.131, and then the D.1, will now take you quickly to **Le Creusot.** This is hardly a tourist attraction, but its importance in the history of industry demands at least that you shall drive through it and, if you are interested, give it an hour or two of your time. Coal was discovered here in the early sixteenth century – enough, we are told, to demand 'six horses or four oxen' for its transportation, and worth 'as much wine as a man could drink'. In the course of time this attracted the raw materials necessary for the production of steel, bricks, cement, pottery and ceramics. As late as 1774 France imported all its steel from Britain, but at the end of that decade a start was made to steel production, and in 1782 a 'royal foundry' was established at Montcenis. This was the first time that coal had been used in France to feed the furnaces for which wood had never been lacking. The foundries were written off as a dead loss after the fall of Bonaparte, but in 1836 Joseph-Eugène Schneider, and his brother Antoine, bought them for two million francs. A year later they began to build steam locomotives, notably 'La Gironde', which ran between Paris and Versailles, and steam engines for ships. In 1841 one of their engineers invented the steam-hammer, which stands in the carrefour du 8 Mai at Le Creusot as a symbol of the city's prosperity – for this had enabled the foundry to expand its production in a great variety of ways. In 1942 the Allies dropped 1200 bombs and incendiaries on the Schneider factories at Le Creusot and Montchanin, and the Germans retaliated in 1944, when the works were once again in French possession. Today they employ 10,000 people and make of this district something exceptional in the rich Burgundian landscape. Much, if not most, of what you will have seen hitherto was the work of those who had rendered unto God the things that are God's; that is no reason why you should not render unto Schneider the things that are Schneider's. You would not get very far without them.

In the eastern sector of the town is the **Château de la Verrerie,** so called because here were manufactured the *cristaux de la Reine,* brought to Le Creusot from Sèvres in 1787. They were not to bear her name for very long. In 1833 the kilns ceased to function altogether and the place was bought by a commercial group as a monument to former craftsmanship. The kilns are still preserved, however, in two buildings which flank the château. They can be visited on Thursday and Saturday between Ascension Day and All Saints from 14 to 18h. You can also be shown the factories at Le Creusot by applying to the Direction, Service de Réception, 60 rue Clemenceau, on Thursday from 14 to 16.30h. A visit to both factories lasts two and a half hours. They are closed during August.

Now follow the D.1 to Montcenis and the D.228 to the **Massif d'Uchon** – seventeen kilometres. This has been described as a 'Breton landscape'. Among its features are rock formations known as *'la griffe du Diable'* (the Devil's claw) and *'la pierre qui croule'.* The latter is an enormous stone of porphyroid granite, 8 metres in circumference and 2.30 metres in height. It has ceased to *'crouler'* since 1872, but until then it was the object of much popular superstition. The village of

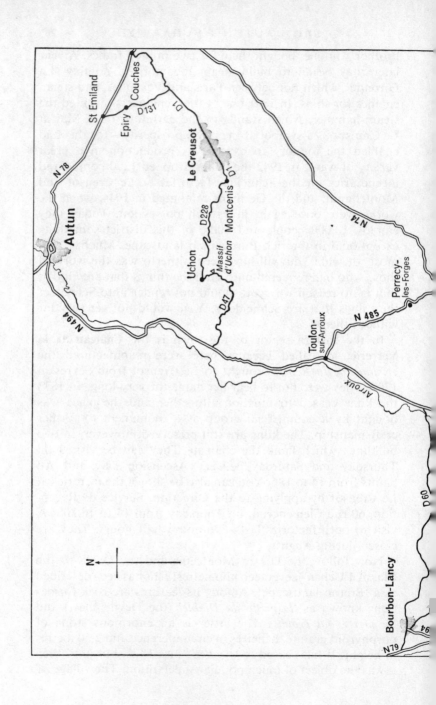

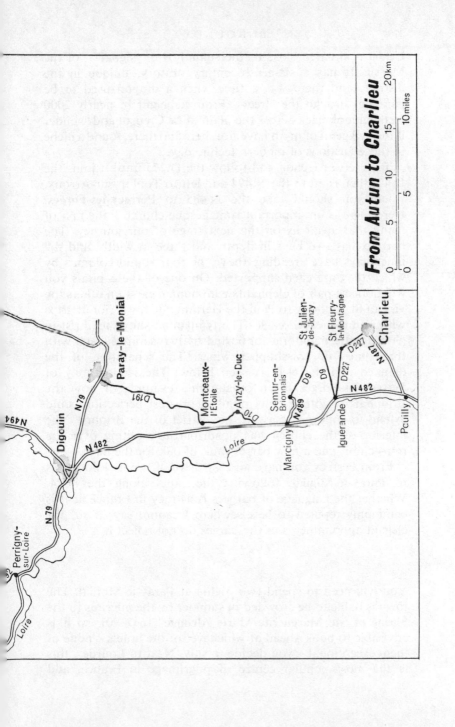

## From Autun to Charlieu

20km

10miles

Perrigny-sur-Loire

N 79

Digouin

N 482

N 494

N 79

Paray-le-Monial

D191

Loire

Montceaux-l'Etoile

Anzy-le-Duc

D10

Marcigny

N489

Semur-en-Brionnais

D9

D9

St Julien-de-Jonzy

St Fleury-la-Montagne

Iguerande

N 482

D227

D227

N 482

Charlieu

Pouilly

**Uchon** is situated close to the summit – or 'signal' – of the Massif. It has a sixteenth-century oratory, unique in the district; and there was a time when a dragon used to be paraded through the streets. From a height of nearly 2000 feet you look back across the plain to Le Creusot and wonder if the evil genii of myth have not, here and there, found a niche in those bastions of modern technology.

Turn left at Uchon and follow the D.275 until it joins the D.47; then right to the N.494 and left to Toulon-sur-Arroux, where you should take the N.485 to **Perrecy-les-Forges.** Here there is an important romanesque church – the first of many that await us on the next stage of our journey. The narthex has two bays in depth and three in width, and the inner bays have arcading above the four round columns by which they are each supported. On one of the capitals you will notice a pair of elephants with human ears; on others the visit of St Anthony to Paul the Hermit, and a warrior at grips with a three-headed eagle. The tympanum shows a Christ in glory, and a mandorla supported by two seraphs, each with three pairs of grasshopper wings. The separation of the damned and the elect is seen below. The iconography of Perrecy-les-Forges is an outstanding example of how the Brionnais sculpture at its point of greatest perfection could extend its influence beyond the district of the Brionne. The interior of the church has quadripartite vaulting over the retro-choir, and a new barrel vault of oak for the nave.

From Perrecy you have an easy drive of twenty kilometres to **Paray-le-Monial,** following the canal along the N.74. Whether the language of bargees is as racy in France as it is commonly reputed to be elsewhere I cannot say; if so, the elegant appointments of the barges do not reflect it.


2


You will need to spend two nights at Paray-le-Monial. The town is liable to be crowded in summer by the pilgrims to the **Shrine of Ste Marguerite-Marie Alcoque** (1647–90); so it is advisable to book ahead at whichever of the hotels – none of them exceptional – you decide to stay. Next to Lourdes, this is the most popular centre of pilgrimage in France, and

international accents – some of them very strange – resound
on every side. Marguerite-Marie was born at Lhautecour in
the diocese of Autun, and was educated in a convent at
Charolles. Paralysed at ten, and unable to walk for four
years, she returned home, and at fifteen went to live with her
uncle. In 1671 she entered the Visitation convent at Paray-le-
Monial, prepared to follow the rule – '*se rendre extraordinaire
à force d'être ordinaire*' – for the inhabitants of her village
were prompt to remark that she did not look in the least like
a prospective novice. Nevertheless, her vocation was the
reverse of ordinary, however much she may have tried to
make it so. Expressing a wish to be 'a candle burning itself
out before God', she was at once energetic and visionary. As
a result of her revelations she begged Louis XIV to establish
the cult of the Sacred Heart, and although this was little to
the taste of the *Roi Soleil* the devotion spread, becoming a
touchstone of orthodoxy at the time of the Jansenist dispute.
Its aesthetic manifestations have not been happy, but Teilhard
de Chardin was among those who have seen beyond the
unattractive image to the reality it represents. The Visitation
convent was confiscated at the Revolution, and the sisters
planned to settle at La Charité-sur-Loire. They refused,
however, to give up the body of Marguerite-Marie; the
coffin was sealed on orders from the mayor of Paray-le-
Monial; and the sisters were allowed to return. Marguerite-
Marie was beatified in 1864 and canonized in 1920. You may
visit the *Sanctuaire des Apparitions*, where she received her
principal revelations, and where her body is preserved in a
gilt and silver shrine; also the former lodging of the pages to
Cardinal Bouillon, where many souvenirs have been preserved,
and her cell faithfully reconstituted. Both are close to the
Basilique du Sacré Cœur. The gardens of the **Convent** are open
to the public on the Feast of the Sacred Heart – the second
Friday following the feast of Corpus Christi – and on 17
October, the anniversary of St Marguerite-Marie's death. In
the Parc des Chapelains, also close by, where the ceremonies
in connection with the pilgrimage take place, a diorama
illustrates the story of her life. This is open from 1 May to 17
October.

At Paray-le-Monial you stand at one end of what is widely,

and justly, publicized as the *Circuit des Eglises romanes*, but
even if you are more interested in architecture than in hagio-
graphy the relation of one to the other is strikingly evident in
the great **Basilica** at Paray. The domain on which it stands
was offered to the abbot of Cluny, St Mayeul, by Lambert,
Comte de Chalon, towards the close of the tenth century, on
the advice of his son, Hugues, Bishop of Auxerre. Hugues
was the great-uncle of Hugues de Semur, the future abbot of
Cluny; so it was natural that the planning of the church,
consecrated in 1004, should follow the Cluniac model. Its
design and elevation are exactly similar. The chief difference
is the shortness of the nave – only three bays – at Paray, but
this happily enhances its height – 22 metres as far as the
vaulting. The church was, in fact, a good deal too big for a
community of 25 monks – but St Hugues would always build
for size as well as for splendour. Some thought that at Cluny
he confused the two.

He might, however, have felt himself justified by the words
of his own testament: 'All my effort was to love You'; and
St Marguerite-Marie might have justified him by the words
of the Apparition: 'I am your beginning and your end'. For
the cult of St Marguerite-Marie and the Sacred Heart has
more than filled the void left by the dispersion of 25 monks.
One feels that the church was built for a purpose of which
neither its founder nor its architect had the least idea, and
that only with the centuries has it come into its own. The
Revolution spared it; the recomposition of the narthex and
the restoration of the upper storey of the tower were undertaken in 1856; the church was raised to the status of a minor
basilica in 1858; and in 1935 the medieval fresco of Christ in
majesty was uncovered over the apse. The installation of a
new organ has only recently completed the renovation of the
interior; and the regular pilgrimages give to the church a life
which is lacking at Fontenay and Pontigny. If you have ever
been to Lourdes or Lisieux, you will heave a large sigh of
relief that there was no need for a new basilica at Paray-le-
Monial.

The narthex, probably built between 1050 and 1080 and
rather clumsily restored, has two bays and two storeys. The
upper is used for exhibitions and has an opening on to the

Paray-le-Monial: the Basilica, interior view of the apse.

Abbaye de Charlieu: Christ in glory from the north door.

'The Paschal Lamb broods in the centre of the outer arch, while on the tympanum Christ is seated in a mandorla between two angels.'

Abbaye de Charlieu: Tympanum from the inner door of the narthex.

nave. A staircase in the thickness of the wall backing on to
the nave leads from one storey to another. Two square
towers frame the narthex, and of these the northern is more
complex in design. It belongs to the same family as others we
shall presently be examining in the Brionnais. Two things will
strike you as you enter the church. First the elevation –
pointed arches; the columns faced, as at Autun, with fluted
pilasters; blind triforium; clerestory; and barrel vaulting.
Here a Gothic elegance is combined with a romanesque
sobriety, and the effect is enhanced by the tall delicate
columns round the apse. But what lends mystery and magic
to the church is the lighting, achieved not by stained glass
but by extremely skilful fenestration. The upper windows in
the nave, transept crossings, and choir form an unbroken
chain, while from the apse and ambulatory a double row of
lancets  the upper ones much smaller than the lower – flood
the sanctuary with light. In the wall dividing the cupola of the
apse from the bay of the choir a tiny lancet and an *oculus* on
either side cunningly aid the perspective. You can study the
fenestration just as well from the outside, where it forms part
of a total architectural rhythm mounting, like a Gregorian
chant, from the apsidal chapels to the central octagonal tower.
The medieval symbolism of light that we paused to examine
at Sens is illustrated just as strikingly at Paray-le-Monial –
and none the less so for the absence of colour.

The oriental motifs in the sculpture on the north and
south doors are a reminder that Hugues of Cluny paid two
visits to Spain, in 1072 and 1090, at the very time that he was
planning the church at Paray. He was evidently impressed by
the Moslem virtuosity in the elaboration of pure form, as you
can see from the lintels on both these doorways. Except in the
case of two reversed heads, any representation of the human
form is avoided altogether. Form and light – each attained by
a masterly technique – combine to give a singular perfection,
a tender *gravitas*, to the basilica at Paray-le-Monial.

The **Musée du Hiéron,** devoted to the theme of the Eucharist,
is well worth a visit. You will find it on the northern outskirts
of the town at the junction of the rue Pasteur and the rue de la
Paix. Here are paintings by Tiepolo, Guido Reni, Mignard and
Lebrun; and an exceptionally fine tympanum of the twelfth

century from the priory of Anzy-le-Duc. The Christ is seated in a mandorla, supported by two angels; and on the lintel the Virgin has the Child on her knees, with the four evangelists and four holy women respectively to her right and left. The museum is open from 1 May to 31 October between 9 and 12h, and 14 to 18h. From 15 June to 15 September exhibitions of contemporary religious art are held here.

At the western end of the rue de la Paix stands the square sixteenth-century tower of **St Nicolas.** The church to which it formerly belonged is now disaffected.

If time permits you may find it worth your while to take the N.79 east to Perrigny – regretting that the château at **Digouin** with its eighteenth-century theatre is not open to the public – and the D.192 to **Bourbon-Lancy** – a distance of 26½ kilometres. From here you look down on to the valley of the Loire, and the Bourbonnais beyond. The town is a thermal spa of some repute. It was originally the home of a Gallic tribe who worshipped the divinity of the waters, and Julius Caesar was said to have bathed in them after the capture of Alésia. His example has been followed by Louise de Lorraine and Henri III, Richelieu, the 'grand Condé', Guy de Maupassant, and Paul Bourget. Five springs, radio-active and very rich in helium, feed the baths which still have their clients. The artisans and shopkeepers were given their charter in 1259, and Bourbon-Lancy is now a centre for the manufacture of agricultural machinery, employing 1500 workers. In the chapel of the **Hospice d'Aligre** on the southern edge of the town you will admire the pulpit, given by Louis XIV to Mme Elisabeth d'Aligre, abbess of St Cyr. To the left of the chapel, on the landing of the great staircase, is the silver statue of the marquise d'Aligre, a generous benefactress of the hospital.

The **Museum** at Bourbon is installed in the former church of St Nazaire (eleventh and twelfth centuries). You will find it on the northern outskirts of the town in the rue du Musée. It contains a number of local antiquities, including Merovingian sarcophagi; and is open on Tuesday, Thursday and Saturday from 15 April to 15 September between 15 and 17.30h.

At the end of the narrow rue du Commerce, which leads south from the avenue de la République, you will come to the even narrower **rue de l'Horloge,** where the Tour de l'Horloge, the Fontaine Sévigné, and and an attractive sixteenth-century wooden house are worth inspection. You may find it convenient to visit these on your way to or from the Hospice, for they are not far apart on either side of the thermal station and the casino.

Do not return to Paray-le-Monial without driving six kilometres south on the N.79A and the N.79 to the eighteenth-century château of **St-Aubin-sur-Loire.** Its proportions and furnishings alike exhibit the discreet elegance of the *dix-huitième*. The château is open to visitors every afternoon from 15 April to 31 October. From St Aubin you may follow the N.79 direct to Paray-le-Monial,

3

Assuming that you have arrived at Paray in the evening, you will have spent two days, and three nights, in exploring Paray itself and in undertaking the expedition outlined above. You may now set out to follow the **Circuit des Eglises romanes** with such diversions as the itinerary suggests. Your first halt is at **Montceaux-l'Etoile,** twelve kilometres to the south on the D.191. Here you need look no farther than the tympanum over the west doorway – the first of many similar masterpieces that await you in the Brionnais. For generally speaking, as you follow the circuit, what arrests you at first is the sculpture rather than the building. At Montceaux-l'Etoile the Ascension of Christ, brandishing the Cross of Victory on a mandorla supported by angels with their backs to it, is watched by a gesticulating group of Apostles and the Blessed Virgin. You will notice that the Keys of St Peter are almost exactly the same size as himself. On the capital to the right an armed angel is slaying a dragon; and on the left is a saint apparently suffering from a stomach ache. This may be St John after consuming, in a dream, the book proffered to him in Chapter 10 of the Apocalypse.

The D.174 will bring you after three kilometres to **Anzy-le-Duc.** In 876 the Chevalier Letbald and his wife Altasie made a gift of their villa at Anzy for a Benedictine priory. This was never dependent on Cluny, but on the abbey of St Martin at

Autun. One of its monks, Bernon, became, however, the first abbot of Cluny, and Hugues – its first prior, though he is not to be confused with St Hugues of Cluny – enjoyed a similar reputation for sanctity. He died in 930, and his tomb attracted such large numbers of pilgrims that it was decided to build a church worthy of so popular a cult. The present building, which is a small masterpiece of the romanesque, was erected in two stages; first, the choir, constructed over the very fine crypt which had served as the priory church up to that time, and the transept; then the nave and side aisles. A stone set in the high altar tells us that the completed work was dedicated to 'The Most High and Indivisible Trinity, to the Venerable Cross, and to the Holy Mother of God and Virgin Mary.' One can only say that the church is worthy of its dedication.

The priory suffered from the English under the Black Prince, and the Huguenots under Prince Casimir; in 1562 a thunderbolt destroyed the spire on the church tower; on 8 August 1594 it was severely burnt by the forces of the Ligue; and in 1791 it was sold to the highest bidder. Fortunately, however, the church was not included in the sale. Abandoned to any and every use – principally for a distillery – it was bought in 1808 by four inhabitants of the village, and ten years later the commune acquired it as their parish church. Cluny and Anzy-le-Duc have each been described as a 'metropolis of the romanesque', illustrating between them the architectural history of Burgundy. Cluny we can do little more than reconstruct on paper; Anzy-le-Duc we can still admire. Here, according to the best authority, was the model for Vézelay: 'the same two-storeyed elevation, the same profile of the rounded arches, the same composition of pillars and half-columns. Only the proportions are different.'

The three-storeyed, octagonal, Lombard tower is perhaps the finest in the Brionnais. The judicious distribution of the bays on each storey delicately counteracts the massive diameter of six metres, so that the effect is one of elegance combined with strength. The west portal was badly damaged at the Revolution, when the author of the sacrilege received three sols for each angelic or saintly head struck off. Nevertheless, the tympanum is of great beauty and betrays a strong Byzantine influence. The Christ of the Ascension is seated with a book in His hand, and in a mandorla supported by two angels, standing with their faces to it. On the lintel the Virgin and the Apostles appear with their tunics lightly ruffled by the breeze – an exceptionally realistic touch. The twenty-four elders of the Apocalypse on the first archivolt, each with his cithern and golden cup, are of a slightly later date. Observe the straight pointed nose typical of Cluniac iconography. Notice also the ornamental consoles below the cornice on the exterior walls. These are sculptured with a kind of truculent fantasy – masques and grimaces, and moustachios galore – the full gamut of medieval caricature. It seems likely that the two small apses at the end of the *chevet* were added after the completion of the church, since the crypt does not extend underneath them.

As you pass inside, you will notice that the barrel vaulting of the nave has been slightly modified to permit a clearer lighting. The cupola over the transept crossing is divided into eight sections to support the octagonal tower above. No trace of the Gothic or the neo-classical disturbs the uniformity of a pure and primitive romanesque. The **Capitals** in the choir probably date from 1050 or even earlier; those in the nave from a little later. Notice in particular on the pillar nearest to the choir on the north side of the aisle two men pulling each other's beards in anger, while two more embrace in amity. A young man shrugging his shoulders seems to imply that the quirks of humanity are beyond his understanding. On the pillar opposite, the vegetation of virtue springs from the waters of life; and on the two next to it a pair of lions have their paws on a man's head. Is this perhaps an image of damnation? A similar idea appears to be expressed on the second pillar to your left as you go down the nave, where the sinner, naked and on his back, is on the point of being devoured by demons. On the other face of the same pillar Samson is mastering the lion; and on the next pillar to the east St Michael is at grips with the devil. The second pillar to your right illustrates 'the marriage of true minds' and 'the expense of spirit in a waste of shame'. In the centre are a couple united in holy wedlock, while on either side the flute-player incites to lust, and the sinner – with his partner on the ground – is left to the solitude of his indifference or remorse.

On the east face of the first pillar to your left, where beasts are gently licking at a naked figure, a similar complacency in the toils of temptation is subtly indicated. The person in question is lending himself to it with half an ear, and presumably with half a mind. Unfortunately the fresco in the apse, which figures the Ascension, and those in the two smaller apses, have been clumsily restored. The latter are barely decipherable.

A remarkable **Tympanum** is set into the wall of what was formerly the Priory enclosure. On the left, the Virgin is seated in profile, the Child on her lap and her feet resting on a foot-stool, as she receives the gifts of the Magi. On the right is the fall of Adam and Eve; and underneath we see the elect emerging from their graves, while the damned are chained to a serpent's tail.

Take the D.10 out of Anzy-le-Duc and, joining the N.482, continue south to **Marcigny,** where the interest lies in the museum, housed in the Tour du Moulin. A Flemish *Portement de Croix* is of great beauty: and among a wide variety of exhibits you will admire the pottery of the sixteenth, seventeenth and eighteenth centuries, the Delft porcelain, the paper tapestries (eighteenth century), the hand-painted playing cards, statues of St Sebastian (sixteenth century), St Stephen (fifteenth century), St George and the Dragon (sixteenth century), an Italian Christ in wood (thirteenth century), and a Negro's head in ebony. The timber work on the third storey is particularly fine; 50 beams and a central pillar support the conical roof in three stages of intricate construction. To appreciate this you should turn on the light switch 10 feet to the left of the door. Do not miss the original millstone in the basement, and the fifteenth-century St Anthony from St Bonnet de Cray. The essence of the Burgundian character is distilled in an inscription:

> *Bourguignon salé*
> *L'épee au côté*
> *Barbe au menton*
> *Saute Bourguignon*[1]

1. The racy Burgundian
   Sword at his side

By way of the N.489 you now come to **Semur-en-Brionnais,** an attractive village set on high ground among vines and fruit trees. A former priory and eighteenth-century law court (now the town hall) adjoin the romanesque church. Again you notice the octagonal tower, with two stages of windows – the lower ones blind – and for the upper ones three-columned arches. The *chevet* has three apses, and any impression of squatness is relieved by the high gables of the choir and transept. The west portal is elaborately sculptured with a bearded Christ in majesty, a pair of angels, and four beasts to symbolize the four evangelists. The wide lintel below may well puzzle you. Who are these 'grave and reverend signors' seated in conclave, and why is one of them sitting on the floor, and why is an angel helping him to get up? The scene represents an episode in the life of St Hilary, to whom the church is dedicated. Refused admittance to the council of Seleucia, divine intervention was required for him to take his place among the prelates. The interior of the church has a triforium passage round the nave, fluted pilasters – as at Autun and Paray-le-Monial – rising to the triforium level, and a single column reaching to the base of the barrel vault. Laughing figures support the bays of the apsidal chapels. Most remarkable is the round projecting tribune at the west end, resting on the keystone of the portal arch. This was probably built in imitation of a similar tribune in the chapel of St Michel in the abbey church at Cluny. Indeed, the Cluniac influence is particularly evident at Semur-en-Brionnais.

You should certainly visit the **Château** where St Hugues of Cluny was born; a rectangular keep of the ninth century with two small round towers which in the eighteenth century served as a prison. It stands close beside the church, and is open from 9 to 12h and 15 to 18h on Sundays between Easter and 30 June; every day, except Tuesday, from 1 July to 15 September; and on Sundays from 16 September to 1 November. A guide will take you round. The château is the setting for a *Son et Lumière* on Thursday, Saturday and Sunday throughout the summer.

If you arrive at Semur about midday – which you should do

And beard on his chin
Jumps to it – like a true Burgundian.

on the assumption that you have left Paray-le-Monial in good time after breakfast – you may eat very pleasantly and cheaply at a little hotel on your right in the main street as you leave the village in the direction of Charlieu.

At **St Julien-de-Jonzy** it is once again the west portal that arrests us. The tympanum and lintel are carved out of a single block of sandstone. On the former Christ, with two angels in support of the mandorla, has His feet on an eight-pillared building, and the lintel shows an extremely animated scene of the Last Supper. A single figure is kneeling in front, and at either end of the table you see the Washing of the Feet. The tablecloth falls in regular folds of a remarkable delicacy and realism with the feet of the Apostles visible underneath. Most of the heads are missing. Notice the capital on the left of the closed porch, where a horse is biting the arm of a man holding a cow.

Your next stop is at **Iguerande,** following the circuit, which is everywhere clearly signposted. Here there is no tympanum over the portal, but much interesting sculpture inside. On the first pillar to your left a man is blowing through a horn while another man is listening. A cyclops with an eye in his forehead is blowing through a pipe of Pan. Mythical beasts appear on the capitals in the west end of the choir, and you will notice the owls at the base of the left pillar of the choir arch, and an ear and a face on the first pillar to your right as you enter the church.

Not all the tympanums of the Brionnais are of equal aesthetic value. By the time you get to **Fleury-la-Montagne** anecdote is beginning to take over – albeit amusingly – for here the Christ in majesty seems perfunctory beside the ascended Christ of Montceau-l'Etoile; and all your attention is drawn to the Magi on the lintel. They approach the Virgin on the right in a lively cavalcade. The first is kneeling with his gift; the second and third are still on horseback; while the horse belonging to the first is being guarded at the rear. The wide interior of the church with its three naves has been inconsiderately modernized.

Your way is now clear to **Charlieu,** the southernmost point of your journey. This was a busy trading post in Gallo-Roman times on the road between the valley of the Saône

and the valley of the Loire. Today it is a centre of the silk
industry, both in factories and in private workshops. The
**Abbey** was founded in 871 and attached to Cluny sixty years
later. In 1050 it became a priory, and was subsequently
fortified by Philippe Auguste, under whose protection it
remained. The church was rebuilt in the eleventh century,
and the narthex added in the twelfth. In all this work the
inspiration of Cluny is plain to see. Only two monks were
living there when the abbey was secularized in 1789. Once
described as 'the most embellished of all the daughters of
Cluny', very little of it was left standing.

Nevertheless what remains is of the first importance.
Excavation has uncovered the foundations of the primitive
sanctuary and of the churches built on the same site. Different
colours on the stones indicate to which original building they
belonged. The eleventh-century church had three aisles, the
collaterals forming an ambulatory round the choir with five
chapels opening out from it. The plan of the church was
similar to that of Anzy-le-Duc. But of all this only the first
bay of the nave, and the narthex are intact. The latter is two-
storeyed, and the upper part served as the muniment room.
The capitals below – a head with horns and hands over its
eyes, illustrating maybe the shame of cuckoldry; a head with
cow's ears and fanged teeth – are similar in their robust
fantasy to others we have seen in the Brionnais. Notice also
on the left, as you enter what remains of the church, two men
tempted by lions and evidently wondering if they shall yield
to a temptation which is rather difficult to understand. But
the marvel of Charlieu is the sculpture on the north face of
the **Narthex**. For a description of this I refer you to the
authors of *Bourgoyne Romane*:

'A solitary genius, impossible to place in any established
category of time or school, seems to have been abruptly
projected from the darkness into the blinding light of his
own creation, for he has devoted to the sacrament of the
Altar the most prodigious association of themes. He may
have formerly sculpted the highly expressive diabolic
figures which support the pilasters of the choir at Semur-
en-Brionnais. His chisel, which miraculously relieves the

stone of all its heaviness, his ardent visual imagination
nourished on the Bible, and the religious frenzy of an epic
temperament, all triumph at Charlieu.'

The sculptures are set above two doorways of unequal size.
Both of them prefigure the Eucharist and the Ascension. On
the lintel of the smaller one we see vividly represented a scene
of ancient sacrifice; and on the tympanum the miracle at
Cana. In the recessed order above are the *dramatis personae*
of the Transfiguration: St Peter, St James, St John, Moses,
Elijah; and Christ transfigured at the crown of the arch.
These figures have an almost baroque mobility; and the
iconography owed much, no doubt, to Peter the Venerable,
who introduced the Feast of the Transfiguration into the
Cluniac calendar in 1132. This enables one to date the work
with reasonable accuracy.

A similar exuberance is seen in the carvings over the larger
doorway. The Pascal Lamb broods in the centre of the outer
arch, while on the tympanum Christ is seated in a mandorla
between two angels and the four symbols of the evangelists.
His feet rest on a portico, and the segment of a pillared
building to His right suggests that this is in fact His throne,
thus emphasizing His domination over all earthly powers.
The Virgin, the Apostles, and a pair of angels are all seated
below; and the scene lacks in consequence the animation
that we admired at Montceaux l'Etoile. The Ascension is here
an established fact rather than an astonishing event. Notice
the figure of Lust on the left of the doorway, conceived as a
nude woman in the coils of a serpent and gnawed at by an
enormous toad. Notice also inside the narthex a Gallo-Roman
sarcophagus of the second century retrieved from the crypt
of the Carolingian church.

The **Private Chapel** of the Prior (fifteenth century) is
immediately on your left as you enter the abbey grounds. It
contains a charming statue of the Virgin with a bird. Adjoining
it is the cloister, which also survives from the same period.
The six arcades, supported by twin columns, on the eastern
side appear to have come from the ambulatory of the second
church (eleventh century). A well-head of some antiquity
stands against the west wall. The abbey can be visited on

application to the caretaker in the house opposite, in summer, from 9 to 12h and 14 to 17h; and in winter from 9 to 12h and 14 to 17h. It is closed on Monday. Note that the north face of the narthex can be seen at any time since it looks on to the street, so placed no doubt to attract the pilgrims. It will attract anyone with eyes to see, and alone warrants a visit to Charlieu. Next door to the caretaker's house is the **Tour Philippe Auguste,** an imposing keep that Philippe considered 'very useful to the Crown'.

Just as you are leaving the town by the D.2 on the road to Pouilly and Roanne – although this will not be your present direction – you will pass on your right the **Couvent des Cordeliers.** The Gothic cloister (late fourteenth century) was sold to the United States, but was bought back by the State in 1913. The virtues and vices of monasticism are illustrated by the capitals on the north side. The church of the same period has a single nave with three lateral chapels to the south, built a century later. Until recently it was in process of restoration. The convent can be visited from 9 to 12h and 14 to 18h (or 17h in winter), except on Monday. Apply to the caretaker in the second house to your right beyond the gate.

Now retrace your steps into the town, and the second turning to your right off the Boulevard Thiers will bring you to the **Hôtel de Ville,** formerly the hôtel de la Ronzière, a handsome eighteenth-century building. Some fine Aubusson tapestries embellish the salle du Conseil. It is open to the public from 9 to 12h and 14 to 18h, except on Saturday afternoon, Sunday, and Monday morning. There is no entrance fee, but the caretaker will expect a modest remuneration.

In the seventeenth-century **chapel of the Hospital,** just opposite, an eighteenth-century gilt wood reredos, and altar frontal of Cordoba leather, are worth inspection.

Now turn to your right and a few steps will bring you to the Place St Philibert. The thirteenth-century **Church** is of interest only for its furnishings. A monolithic stone pulpit (fifteenth century); choir stalls with painted panels (fifteenth and sixteenth centuries); the statue of Notre-Dame-de-Charlieu in a side chapel (sixteenth century); a fifteenth-century reredos of painted stone in the chapel of St Anne to the right of the choir illustrating the Annunciation and the Nativity; and in the chapel of the Cordonniers to the left of the choir a seventeenth-century Pietà, and a statue of St Crépin (Crispin), the patron saint of shoemakers. There are several couvents des Cordonniers in France, but Crépin is the rarest of Christian names – perhaps because it is too painfully associated with the Battle of Agincourt. I know two or three people called Crispin, but I have never yet met a Crépin, nor even heard of one.

You can stay modestly in Charlieu at the Lion d'Or, but note that the restaurant is closed on Friday evening. There is more varied, and probably better, accommodation at La Clayette, twenty kilometres farther north, which lies on the next lap of your itinerary; and although you will have had a pretty full day behind you, it may be worth your while to push on.

# CHAPTER FIFTEEN

# From Charlieu to Cluny

✤

## 1

Shortly after leaving Charlieu on the N.470 you come to **Châteauneuf**; not to be confused with the Châteauneuf we have already visited in the Côte d'Or. The church is unusually tall with three bays to the nave, pointed arches, flat sculptured columns in the apse, and an arcade with four openings round the crossing. Observe the stone statue of the Good Shepherd. The tympanum is blank above the west portal, but there are carvings of the twelve Apostles on the lintel. You will notice a monstrance in stone outside. The sixteenth-century château can be viewed from the exterior at any time, and if you happen to pass it after dusk on a summer evening you will find it floodlit.

Your way is now clear to **La Clayette** (pronounced 'Claite'), perched above the valley of the Genette, and a renowned centre for horse-racing. There are two decent hotels: the Poste et Dauphin in the main street on your right, and the Bourgoyne, next door to the château, on the road to Charolles. The lake, with the water power it provided for manufacturing, assured the prosperity of La Clayette long before the château was built in 1380. Situated on the frontier between the *comté* of Mâcon, which depended on the King of France, and the Charollais, which was a fief of the Dukes of Burgundy, La Clayette was directly involved in the quarrels of the Hundred Years War. The local *seigneur*, who had been page to the Duchess of Burgundy, was faithful to his Burgundian allegiance, and by the Treaty of Arras (1435) La Clayette, with the rest of the Maconnais, remained a Burgundian possession. Its fidelity was rewarded with the permission to hold three annual fairs. During the wars of religion the lake protected the château from the depredations of either party; it owed much, no doubt, to the volatility with which the châtelain, Claude

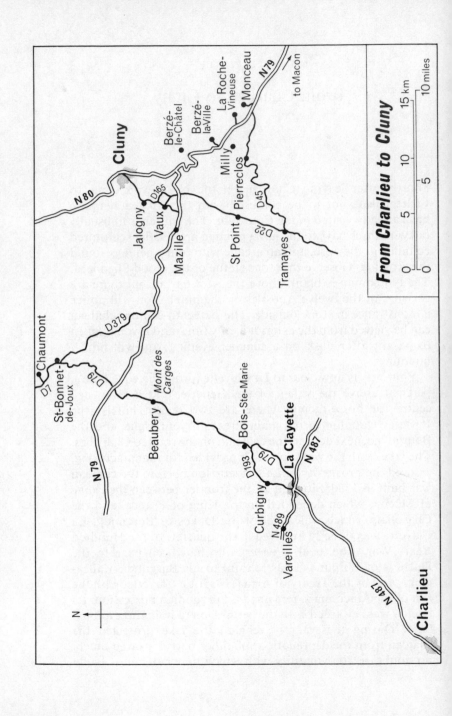

From *Charlieu to Cluny*

de Chantemerle, changed sides in the conflict. The Revolution also spared it material damage, although it was naturally requisitioned and the Feast of the Supreme Being was celebrated in the park. In the nineteenth century it was altered a good deal, and a wing was added in the style of the Renaissance. It is not open to the public, but you may admire the large round tower, with its onion-shaped lantern, rising out of the wide moat where the carp proliferate, and the west façade looking on to the road with its much thinner machicolated towers on either side of the entrance.

It will be worth your while taking the N.489 out of La Clayette to admire the remarkably fine church tower at **Vareilles**; and then, returning by the same road, follow the D.193 to **Curbigny,** where you will observe four very primitive capitals in the church. On the left of the nave, six men locked in struggle, and three others apparently linked in amity; on the right a man on horseback with some figs, and another grasping indefinable objects in each hand.

Then continue along the D.193 and turn off to your right for **Bois Ste-Marie,** where the church demands close attention. A double stairway leads up to the west portal. The tympanum shows the Flight into Egypt and St Joseph looking nervously behind him. The façade has romanesque arcading, and on the left is a carving of the Virgin and Child, much defaced. There are three bays to the nave with round pillars reaching up to the imposts of the barrel roof. The ambulatory with its six bays, two large pillars and two smaller ones in the rear to support them, is unique in France. Blind arcades run north and south of the transept crossing. There are three lancets over the ambulatory, two over the crossing, eight – upper and lower inclusive – on each side of the nave, and one over the west façade. But the most interesting feature of the church are the **Capitals.** Notice in the left aisle, as you go down it towards the choir: a mermaid; dogs' heads; warriors fighting with shields and swords; four birds; four lions or possibly dogs; and human heads. In the right aisle: a man fighting; a man being attacked by a wild boar, while another on his right with uplifted sword or club seems to be defending him; eagles; a man seated with folded hands being bitten by lions (or dogs), while another standing behind the animal on its right clasps

its head and a third holds out a loaf; a man tortured by a pair
of devils, one of them clawing his head, and the other stuffing
a red-hot poker in his mouth; and two men clasping their
foreheads, deep in thought or anxiety.

We must now leave the romanesque, although we shall
soon be returning to it. This is the district of the **Charollais,**
which has changed hands like a head of its famous cattle. In
1237 it belonged to the Duke of Burgundy, who gave it to his
grand-daughter Beatrice in 1272. Beatrice married Robert de
Clermont, the son of St Louis, and their grand-daughter of
the same name brought the province as her dowry to Jean,
the first Comte d'Armagnac. In 1390 it was sold back to the
Duke of Burgundy, who made it over to his eldest son. After
the death of Charles le Téméraire it was taken by Louis XI,
and given to Philip, archduke of Austria, by Charles VIII. In
1529 it passed to the Emperor Charles V, and in 1556 to
Philip II of Spain. Confiscated by Louis XIV in 1674, and by
the Prince de Condé in 1684, it returned to the Crown under
Louis XV. There must, one concludes, have been 'something'
about the Charollais!

That 'something' is today its two million heads of white
cattle bred on 400,000 hectares of the rich pastures of the
Arconce. In size the breed is second only to that of Normandy,
and in quality second to none. At the market of St Christophe-
en-Brionnais 1000 animals are sold every Thursday from
May to December; and at Charolles on the fourth Thursday
in October 1200 to 1500 young bulls. In December an international competition is held there for an *élite* of reproductive
cattle. Artificial insemination is practised on the milking
cows. These extremely picturesque events fall outside the
holiday season, but an *entrecôte grillé Charollais Marchand de
Vin* may be enjoyed at any time of the year; and you have
only to look out of the window to see where it comes from.
At Charolles itself there is nothing particular to see. You
will, however, eat as well at M. Dussably's Grand Hotel
Moderne as anywhere in the district. If the insistent piety
of Paray-le-Monial – or, more precisely, of its *clientèle* – has
got on your nerves, M. Dussably will come to your rescue,
for Charolles is an easy drive of thirteen kilometres from
Paray on the N.79. You will do better, therefore, to run out

Cluny: Professor Kenneth Conant's model of the abbey church as it originally stood.

Cluny: another model showing the part standing today.

Taizé: window in
the Church of
the Reconciliation.

Bourg-en-Bresse: The Eglise de Brou. 'This exuberance of sculpture and
stone is inspired by conjugal fidelity.'

there for dinner while you are staying at Paray, rather than give yourself an unnecessary détour from Bois-Ste-Marie.

Follow therefore the D.79 to Beaubery and turn up to your right for the summit of the **Mont des Carges**. This was a centre of resistance during the German occupation; a monument to the maquis of Beaubery and the battalion of the Charollais stands on the top. The view from here is magnificent on every side. The road circles the hill and rejoins the D.79, which will take you across the N.79 to St Bonnet-de-Joux (22 kilometres from Bois-Ste-Marie). Follow the D.7 out of the village to your left, and you will come to the **Château de Chaumont** about three kilometres farther on. This has remained in the same family – La Guiche – since 1416, but it was not until 1502 that Pierre de La Guiche – who had negotiated the marriage between Henri II and Catherine de Medici, and served as ambassador in England, Germany, Italy and Spain – undertook the building of the present château, and obtained permission at the same time to establish a weekly market at Chaumont. This still survives at St Bonnet-de-Joux. The greater part of the château was demolished in 1801, and rebuilt during the nineteenth century in the neo-Gothic style. This is what you see as you enter from the road. But the eastern façade, dating from 1510, has survived, although it now stands on a terrace above the slope, and robbed of its large pointed tower. More remarkable by far than the château are the stables, 65 metres in length, built between 1648 and 1652 by Henriette de La Guiche, Duchess of Angoulême. The equestrian statue of Philibert de La Guiche, Grand Master of Artillery under Henry III and Henri IV, dominates the central doorway. Philibert had accompanied Mary Stuart when she returned to Scotland as queen, and as Governor of Mâcon had prevented the Massacre of St Bartholomew in the town. There was room on the vast ground floor of the stables for 99 horses, and doubtless an extra one could have been squeezed in. But only the king had the right to 100 horses; hence the equestrian statue, which avoided any risk of *lèse majesté*. Four superb stone staircases with handsome balustrades and 34 steps lead up to the first storey, where the men-at-arms were lodged. An entire forest is said to have been felled to provide the roof. The vaulting inside is supported by its original 28 columns, and there is now stabling for eighteen horses with double troughs. Various horse-drawn vehicles are on show; phaeton, tilbury, hunting-brake, coupé, victoria, waggonette, pony trap, and stage coach. The four great chimney-pieces at either end of the main hall are embossed with a crown, and the monogram of Henriette de La Guiche. Below it are the armorial bearings of the duc and duchesse d'Angoulême. These combine the arms of the Royal House of France, crossed with the bar sinister, and those of the La Guiche, surmounted by the crown of a Prince of the Blood Royal, and encircled by the collars of the Order of the Holy Spirit and the Order of St Michael. You will find them elsewhere in the building. The stables record many prizes won at the Concours Hippique de Paris before the Second World War. They can be visited every day from 15 April to 31 October between 10 and 18h, and are floodlit in July and August.

Now return through St Bonnet, follow the D.379 until it joins the N.79, and bear left for Cluny. At **Mazille** you will find a romanesque church, of which the exterior is in perfect condition. The tower has two storeys of double lancet windows, with the west door and gabled façade to one side. The interior was shut, however, when I was last there. On the hill above, a hideous new monastery for Carmelite nuns stares across the valley. I was told that the sisters, officially enclosed but considerably enfranchized, can be seen tilling the soil in all weathers.

You should now turn left on the D.165, and then left again on a small road signposted to **Vaux.** It winds up the hill and brings you through a tunnel of young beech in front of a little romanesque church which has been lovingly restored by the scouts of Cluny and the villagers of Vaux, working during their week-ends from November 1971 to October 1972 under expert supervision. The result is as perfect as we found it at Alise-Ste-Reine. Six steps lead up to the narthex, and into the church, which dates from the eleventh century, with apse, tower and capitals of the twelfth. The stained glass in the lancet windows was also designed and made by the scouts, and the seventeenth-century wooden altar came from the neighbouring priory of Mazille. The whitewashed walls of the

single nave are inscribed with texts from St Paul and St John
in a red, blue, and green cursive script; and a folio of modern
coloured photographs is set up on a reading desk fixed to the
north side of the choir arch, illustrating the texts alongside
them. Where so many churches in Burgundy confirm the
present dechristianization of the countryside, this one is a
shining exception.

Returning to the D.165, you should turn to your left and
join the D.465 at Jalogny. This will bring you into Cluny
after a few minutes' drive.

## 2

The influence of **Cluny** has been so pervasive throughout the
latter part of our journey that the place, when you come to it,
is liable to disappoint. What it stood for, in the building of
churches, the carving of stone, or the cultivation of vines, can
more easily be studied elsewhere. Nevertheless, it would be
impious to pass it by. There is still a good deal to see, and
even more to remember; and here we may quote from words
spoken at the millenary celebrations in 1919.

> 'Between the two great intellectual cultures, the classical
> and the Christian, which divided the world, its desire was
> to create an understanding. Like the great minds of the
> fourth century, its doctors reconciled "wisdom" with the
> Gospel; and when they affirmed the Faith, it was neither to
> curse nor to condemn the imperishable works bequeathed
> to us by the reason and the imagination of pagan antiquity.
> A man like Peter the Venerable could be the chief theologian
> and chief man of letters of his time; combat the heretics
> and stretch out the hand of friendship to Abelard; comment
> on the scriptures, and talk like Plato. This great monk is
> something more than a name; he is the symbol both of his
> Order and of his country.'

The abbey was founded by Guillaume le Pieux, Duke of
Aquitaine, on 11 September 910; and the gift included a great
deal of fertile land. It was soon exempt from episcopal jurisdiction, and independent of any temporal power. Popes came
to the abbots for advice, and kings bowed to their arbitration.

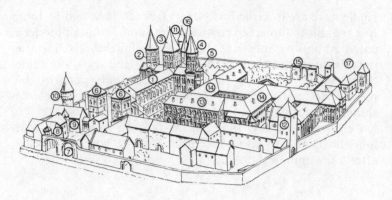

### THE ABBEY CHURCH OF CLUNY
### AT THE END OF THE 18TH CENTURY

1 The abbey church of St Peter and Paul
2 The Tower des Bisans
3 The Tower of the Choir
4 The Tower de l'Eau Bénite
5 The Belfry
6 The Barabans
7 Principal entrance
8 Palace of Jean de Bourbon
9 Palace of Jacques d'Amboise
10 Fairy Tower
11 Round Tower
12 Tower des Fromages
13 Façade of Pope Gelasius
14 Claustral buildings
15 Gate into the gardens
16 Lamp tower
17 Granary

It counted 1450 foundations in different parts of Europe from Poland to Spain, and more than ten thousand monks lived by its Benedictine rule. Addressing St Hugues in 1098 Pope Urban II described them as '*la lumière du monde*', and the saying ran in Burgundy:

> *Partout où le vent vente*
> *L'abbay de Cluny a rente.*[1]

St Bernard, however, had his sarcastic reply to the Pope: 'Does the light only shine from a candelabra of silver or gold?'; and he denounced abbots vowed to poverty who could not go twelve miles without a train of 60 horses or more. Later they acquired the habit of commuting as they chose between Cluny and Paris. The decadence had set in; and by the sixteenth century the abbey was an easy prey to the

1. Wherever the wind blows,
   The abbey of Cluny has property.

Huguenots, who pillaged the library and robbed the church of much treasure. The Revolution consummated its decline. Closed in 1790, it was subsequently put up for sale, on the pretext that the labour required for its upkeep could be more usefully employed elsewhere; and it was bought by a merchant from Mâcon, who demolished the nave. Further mutilation followed, and by 1823 nothing remained of the greatest church in Christendom but the fragment that you see today. The mind reels at the thought of such iconoclasm.

There had, in fact, been three churches at Cluny. The foundation stone of the third and largest, dedicated to SS Peter and Paul, was laid in 1088; Urban II consecrated the High Altar on 25 October 1095; and exactly 35 years later Innocent II set his seal on the completed church. It was conceived by Hugues of Semur, who reigned for 60 years, and brought to fruition by his successors. Of the seven great abbots who gave Cluny its prestige only St Hugues was a Burgundian by birth. The interior of his church was 177 metres long, only 9 metres short of St Peter's at Rome. It comprised a narthex, five aisles, two transepts, four large towers over the choir and apse, and two much smaller ones at the west end. This concentration on the choir and sanctuary was no doubt inspired by the 'Holy of Holies' in Solomon's temple, from which so much in early Christian church architecture was derived. There were 301 windows, and 225 stalls. The vault over the apse was entirely painted, and supported by a marble colonnade. The nave of ten bays was 100 feet high. The pointed arches were faced with fluted columns and Corinthian capitals, rising to a barrel vault. There were five bays to the narthex, and a tympanum surmounted the west portal. The hierarchy of forms and levels, as you saw the *chevet* from the outside, and the triple windows within, were imitated a little later at Paray-le-Monial. Throughout this immense building the classical note predominated both in proportion and in detail; St Hugues would have seen to that. It is easy to appreciate what Albert Thibaudet meant in describing Cluny as 'a Benedictine Versailles'.

Your best approach to it is by the rue d'Avril, where a number of early medieval houses with balconies above their arcaded lower storeys are almost contemporary with the abbey itself. This brings you to the monumental romanesque gateway to the vast monastic enclosure. Through it you see the octagonal **Tour de l'Eau Bénite,** flanked by its square turreted staircase – known as the **Tour de l'Horloge.** To your left are the two abbatial palaces. The first, built by Abbot Jean de Bourbon in the fifteenth century, is now the Musée Ochier; the second, built by his successors (1485–1518), is the **Hôtel de Ville.** A pleasant public garden surrounds it. The rue Kenneth Conant beside the terrace of the museum will bring you to what remains of the façade of the narthex – the toothing on the north side of the flamboyant portal and the base of the square towers. From here you can judge the colossal dimensions of the church which once stood in that tragically empty space. The southern crossing of the great transept, alone left standing, marks approximately two thirds of its total length, and the tall trees to the east of it the site of the *chevet*. The ensemble of the Tour de l'Eau Bénite and the Tour de l'Horloge is a little reminiscent of the Rhineland churches and cathedrals. Cluny had close relations with the empire, and St Hugues was the godfather of the Emperor, Henry IV. Did he encourage, perhaps, that famous journey to Canossa? He would certainly have approved of it.

The abbey is now maintained by the Ecole Nationale des Arts et Métiers, and a competent guide will show you round. But a little preliminary homework is recommended. You enter by a small door in the place de l'Abbaye, from which a staircase leads down into the north arm of the eighteenth-century cloister, and from the end of this, on your right, a second staircase with an elegant wrought-iron balustrade takes you into the crossing of the romanesque transept. This is all we possess of the great church of Cluny. Two bays with semi-circular vaulting frame the octagonal cupola which supports the **Tour de l'Eau Bénite,** rising to a height of 32 20 metres – a unique example of how the architects of the romanesque could prefigure in audacity the builders of Amiens and Beauvais. Only in the second bay, beyond the cupola, do we find the usual Cluniac elevation with the pilasters separated by triple, round arcading, and three bays also framed by circular archivolts. The decoration shows a

certain Moslem influence, but it has been justly observed that
'the details of the ornamentation, whatever their merit, dis-
appear in the majesty of the ensemble.' Two chapels open
from the transept to the east. The second, dedicated to St
Martial, has a little turreted staircase on the right leading to
the romanesque chapel of St Michel. An inscription which
records its consecration by Bishop Pierre of Pamplona
(d. 1115) enables one to date the construction of the transept,
and to show how far the building of the church had pro-
gressed during the early years of the twelfth century.

Of the smaller transept to the east of the larger one very
little remains except the flamboyant **Chapelle de Bourbon** – a
lovely example of late Gothic – and the romanesque apse.
You may trace here within very narrow limits the evolution
of Cluniac architecture from the period of the abbey's
greatest prosperity and prestige to that of its decline.

Leaving behind you the monastic buildings reconstructed
in the eighteenth century, you now cross the formal gardens –
noting a lime tree of great antiquity which has been given the
name of 'Abelard'. For Abelard took refuge at Cluny towards
the end of his life; and Peter the Venerable, who welcomed
him there, absolved him on his death-bed at St Marcel-lès-
Chalon. On your right stands the monks' granary, built by
Abbot Yves I between 1257 and 1275. The ground floor, with
its double nave and ribbed vaulting, was originally the cellar
and contains a number of sculptures from the abbey and the
town. The upper storey has fine timber work of chestnut wood,
and here you can see not only a model of the abbey church
as Professor Conant has reconstructed it, but also the reproduction on a reduced scale of the former sanctuary with the
capitals from the choir. There are ten of them arranged in a
semi-circle surrounding the altar of Pyrenean marble, and
they tell us beyond a doubt where the sculptors of Saulieu,
Vézelay, and Autun acquired their technique and found their
inspiration. More clearly, I think, than anything else, they
illustrate the genius and the ethos of Cluny.

Moving from left to right, we admire them in the following
order: three athletes; a bee-keeper apparently cleaning out his
hive; three silhouettes symbolizing the theological virtues; a
second version of Justice armed with a whip; allegories of

spring and summer; the 'garden of Cluny' watered by the
rivers of the four Gospels; and the five tones of plainchant.
It has been suggested that these capitals illustrate a letter
written in the eleventh century by St Peter Damian in praise
of Cluny; that the athletes and the beekeeper stand for
manual labour, and the others for the practice of virtue and
the celebration of the Divine Office. There is no certainty,
however, that they stood in the order in which we now see
them; and those extraneous to the series mentioned above –
the Fall of Adam and Eve, the sacrifice of Abraham, and the
promise of the Redemption – were not only favourite subjects
in the iconography of the time, but illustrated the historical
sanction for the monastic life, and indeed for Christianity
itself.

The abbey can be visited from Easter to 30 June at hourly
intervals from 10 to 11h and 14 to 16h during the week, and
from 9 to 11h and 14 to 17h on Sunday and public holidays.
From 1 July to 30 September it is open from 9 to 11.30h and
14 to 16.30h, with half-hourly visits; and from 1 October to
Easter there are hourly visits from 10 to 11h, and 14 to 16h.
It is closed on Tuesday.

A *Son et Lumière* entitled *Cluny, énergie de Dieu* is given
from 1 July to 30 September, starting at 21.30h and finishing
at 22.15h.

Other capitals are to be seen in the **Musée Ochier**; also the
keystone of the fifth bay in the narthex, a carved head that
might have been the work of a Greek sculptor long before
Praxiteles, and the twelfth-century carving of the Paschal
Lamb with the charming inscription

> *Hic parvus sculptor Agnus*
> *In celo magnus.*

surrounding it like a halo. Your understanding of Cluny will
be greatly enhanced by the splendid series of water-colours
made by Professor Conant and his pupils. These show you the
abbey as it was in the twelfth century, and you may compare
them with models of St Bénigne at Dijon, the second church

1. Here I am sculpted like a little lamb
   In Heaven I am great.

at Cluny, and La Charité-sur-Loire. The museum is a centre for romanesque studies, and can be visited between 1 April and 31 October from 9 to 12h, and 14 to 18h; and between 1 November and 31 March from 10 to 12h and 14 to 16h. It is closed on Tuesday. A film, with commentary, is shown at stated times, and gives a clear introduction to the complicated story of Cluny.

Still within the *enceinte* of the abbey is the **Tour des Fromages** (eleventh century), from which you get a splendid view of the town if you can face a climb of 120 wooden stairs. Entrance can be arranged through the local Syndicat d'Initiative. The lower storey is a good example of military architecture, and you should notice the pre-Roman motif on the lintel of the window, a design found in several country churches of the Autunois.

Immediately opposite the Tour des Fromages is the **Church of Notre-Dame,** one of the first Cluniac churches to be enlarged and transformed when the Gothic came into fashion. Of the narthex only the pavement remains. The nave with seven bays has a triforium gallery and clerestory immediately above. There are some good modern windows in the apse and in the shallow transepts. Observe the large male heads supporting the pillars of the choir, and the smaller ones below the columns of the crossing, and at the inner corners of the arches in the nave. If you have a mind (or feel an obligation) to attend Mass at Notre-Dame, nerve yourself for a liturgical charade which might well bring Peter the Venerable out of his grave with bell, book, and candle.

The body of that great man lies under a thick block of concrete in the **Haras,** or stables, built out of the stones from the abbey and its dependencies, immediately to the north of them. They now accommodate 91 stallions in winter – cobs, saddle-horses, and trotters from Normandy and the Charollais – and in the summer are put out to grass. You may inspect them (when they are at home) by applying to the caretaker, who will expect a small remuneration.

Cluny lies between two hills: La Cras with its dry and rocky soil, and the rich pastures of Le Fouettin. The Roman tiles and ochre-coloured walls lend to the town a southern look, and from the Promenade du Fouettin, replacing the

former ramparts, you get an enchanting view of Cluny itself
and the valley of the Grosne.

The best hotel is not the most outwardly inviting, but the
Moderne, close to the station and on your left as you come in
from the N.80, will reward you with reasonable comfort and
an excellent cuisine. Just to the north of it the **Church of St
Marcel** has a fine octagonal, three-storeyed, romanesque
tower, with a rather cheeky polygonal brick spire, 42 metres
in height. This will be your first impression of Cluny, as you
enter the town; and a night or two spent at the Moderne will
confirm its welcome. But note that the restaurant is closed on
Monday.

### 3

A single expedition from Cluny will bring you face to face,
and almost simultaneously, with the eleventh and the nineteenth centuries, each at a point of its ripest self-expression.
Follow the N.80 to the south and observe, away to your left,
the feudal château of **Berzé-le-Chatel.** This protected the
southern approaches to Cluny, and belonged to the oldest
barony in the Mâconnais, raised to a *comté* by Henri IV. It
stands on a high slope among vineyards, whose Mâcon Viré
is among the specialities of the district and well deserves its
reputation. You can visit the outside from the terraces between
22 April and 15 October any day of the week from 9 to 12h,
and 14 to 18h. The château is equally impressive seen from
the road, and it is only incidental to your immediate purposes.
For just below it stands the *chapelle des moines* at **Berzé-la-
Ville,** where the *primavera* of the twelfth century renaissance
flowers in fresco on the walls; a masterpiece which, in its kind,
has no equal in Burgundy and no superior anywhere in
France.

At the end of the eleventh century the little 'obedience' of
Berzé – for it hardly claimed the rank of a priory – was
definitely attached to the abbey of Cluny, largely, it seems,
because it was a convenient bolt-hole for St Hugues when his
abbatial cares weighed heavily upon him. Berzé was one of
the three foundations mentioned by name in his last will and
testament. He had a particular reason to remember it, for on

one of his visits the place was struck by a thunderbolt and a
great part of it went up in flames. The terrified monks were
astonished to see their abbot emerging from the ruins, safe
and sound, and attributed his escape – naturally enough – to
divine protection. He entrusted the restoration of the chapel
to a brother monk, Séguin, but the magnificent frescoes that
bring us there today are probably of a slightly later date.
Berzé was sold, with other property of the Church, at the
Revolution and passed through various hands. Then, in 1887,
the local curé discovered the head of Christ beneath the
whitewash which had providentially preserved it, and gradually the whole painting was uncovered. Shortly after the
Second World War, the chapel was bought by Miss Joan
Evans, the distinguished archaeologist, and in 1947 presented
by her to the Académie de Mâcon. It can be visited at any
time by applying to the caretaker, who lives in the adjoining
courtyard.

The eighteenth-century priory stands on a triangular spur
of rock, and commands a splendid view. Like many others,
it was more adapted to the life of the soil than the life of the
cloister, and it has taken on the colour of the surrounding
hills. The lower storey of the chapel may well have served as a
crypt, for traces of wall paintings were discovered there, but
it was soon reduced to the status of a cellar for the new wine.
Today it would pass unnoticed were it not for the emphasis it
gives to the chapel above. This has a single nave with a barrel
vault, slightly inflected, and a central arch resting on foliated
capitals. Three windows in the apse, one south of the main
arch, two south and three north of the nave, light the frescoes
to advantage. Patches of colour, impossible to decipher,
prove that the walls of the nave were also painted, but whatever subjects may have been treated on them can only have
served to introduce the Christ in majesty which presides over
the apse, with the other figures and scenes alongside it. These
utilize at every point their structural framework, so that the
rush of colour overflows the triumphal arch and spreads on
to the surface of the wall between the choir and the apse,
where the Paschal Lamb appears in the *oculus* with angels in
almost horizontal support.

The Christ, seated on a cushion, gives a blessing with his

right hand, and with his left proffers a phylactery to St Peter. You will notice the deep blue of the mandorla, studded with three round holes which must originally have held pieces of metal and glass to represent the stars. Groups of apostles and saints are shown on either side; and in the scuncheons of the arcading round the apse are the busts of the seven wise virgins, holding up their vases of oil. Several of these seem directly inspired by the mosaic of the Empress Theodora in the church of San Vitale at Ravenna. The blind arches at each extremity of the apse are occupied, on the left, by two scenes which illustrate the imprisonment and beheading of St Blaise; and on the right by the martyrdom of St Vincent of Saragossa, who, like St Laurence but not here to be confused with him, was roasted to death on a gridiron. The legend records that St Blaise had forced a wolf to bring a piglet to a poor woman, who turned it into brawn and brought it to him in prison. The Prefect Dacien, sceptre in hand, looks on at the martyrdom of St Vincent while a pair of executioners feed the flames with pitchforks. The diagonal pattern of this fresco – emphasized by the downward thrust of the pitchforks – considerably taller than the figures who manipulate them; by the folds of the draperies; and by the attitude, equally free, of the Prefect seated on the right, occupying half the space above the gridiron, and larger than the two executioners put together – is as daring in its disproportion as it is sure in its accomplishment. On the wall below the arches appear the figures of seven saints, among whom St Sebastian is twice commemorated.

So much for the iconography of Berzé-le-Ville. No description, however, can convey the delicacy and brilliance of colour – purple and green, ochre and azure – nor the virtuosity of design. Here is the Byzantine serenity, but little of the Byzantine stiffness. The martyrs are at peace even in the throes of their sufferings, already participating, as it seems, in the tumultuous adoration to which the concavity of the apse lends a technical support. Here is the transcendent Christ of St Irenaeus – 'God has no need of anybody' – but drawing everybody to Him in a convergent act of worship.

Another circuit is recommended by the Syndicat d'Initiative

de Mâcon, for Mâcon was the birthplace of Alphonse de
Lamartine (1790–1869). He belongs less to Mâcon, however,
than to the Mâconnais. The son of a small landowner of the
*petite noblesse*, ruined by his fidelity to the *ancien régime*,
Lamartine spent his childhood at **Milly,** barely a kilometre
from Berzé-le-Ville on the N.79. Here you may see the modest,
square, double-fronted house around which he wrote *La
Vigne et la Maison* – not without considerable transpositions
– and *Isolement*, the first of the *Méditations* which secured
him an instant popularity. At Milly, he wrote, 'everything
remembers me, everything knows me, and everything loves
me.' He was to recall 'the sweet and melancholy voices of the
little frogs that sing on summer evenings, as they do on the
marshes'. Here was the wide, light, corridor with its spacious
cupboards, the kitchen on the right and the dining room on
the left, with the buffet and pinewood table; the ten bedrooms
and the roughly hewn stone staircase. Lamartine's mother
used to call Milly 'her Jerusalem', and he himself liked to go
back there to sleep from time to time, imagining that he heard
'the voice of my mother when I wake up, the footsteps of
my father, and my sisters' happy cries, and all those sounds
of youth, of life, and of love which, for me alone, echo
beneath the old beams. They no longer have anyone but me
to hear them, and to prolong them for a little while.'

If you follow the N.79 to a point just beyond La Roche-
Vineuse and turn up to your left, you will find the **Château
de Monceau,** now an old people's home, which you may visit
from the outside. (From 15 March to 15 September, between
15 and 18h. Closed on Monday, Wednesday, and Friday.)
This belonged to the family of Lamartine, and here the poet
liked to live in great style. Among the vines you can see the
kiosk – appropriately christened 'Solitude' – where he wrote
his *Histoire des Girondins*. Then retrace your steps, and turn
off on the D.45 to **Pierreclos** and the château, visible from the
road, where Mlle de Milly – the 'Laurence' of *Jocelyn* –
inspired the affection of the abbé Dumont, the Voltairian
curé of Bussières. The curé left the priesthood, but eventually
returned to it. He confided his troubles to Lamartine, who
revered him both as a friend and a master, and composed the
epitaph on his tomb. This stands against the *chevet* of the

church at Bussières, and there is also a memorial plaque on the wall of the former presbytery.

Now follow the same road, as it winds among the hills of the Mâconnais, to its junction with the D.22 at Tramayes. Then turn north to **Saint-Point**. In the little church, typically Cluniac in style, under its deadening plaster, there is a fresco of Christ in majesty with the four evangelists in the apse, and also two paintings by Madame de Lamartine – an English-woman, *née* Marianne Birch. She is buried with her husband in an adjoining chapel. To the left of the church a road leads up to the **Château** behind its four horse-chestnuts, massed pansies, Japanese cherries and prunes, oranges in their tubs, and box hedge. (Open every day from 10 to 12h, and 14 to 19h in summer, 18h in winter.) A very old magnolia climbs up the tower, and you may see the stone bench and table under the immense lime-tree where Lamartine composed the *Méditations*. He was, as we have seen, a great man for châteaux, and he preferred Saint-Point even to Montceau and Montculot. Here he could indulge his semi-pantheistic reveries and his humanitarian dreams.

> *Il est sur la colline*
> *Une blanche maison*
> *Une tour la domine:*
> *Un buisson d'aubépine*
> *Est tout son horizon*
> *Là jamais ne se lève*
> *Bruit qui fasse songer.*
> *On peut finir son rêve*
> *Et le recommencer.*[1]

'It seems to me', Lamartine had written, 'that I am only a part of all other men, that they are a part of my own flesh, and that I am a part of theirs. I think that this is what they call love.' He had other notions about love, as you can see for yourself in the rooms now reconstituted in a special wing of the château as they might have appeared in his life-time, with the furniture and appointments proper to his bedroom,

---

1. A white house stands on the hill, with a tower above it. A bush of hawthorn occupies the whole horizon. No noise disturbs you there. You can finish your dream, and start it all over again.

study, and salon. Here is the bust of 'Graziella', whom he had
planned to meet on the Lac de Bourget but who died in Paris
before she could keep the appointment. Here is the bust of
'Elvira', the daughter of a Neapolitan fisherman, with whom
he had a passionate liaison. In an engraving by Aymon de
Virieu she appears with her fishing basket. There is the bronze
of the poet's favourite greyhound, Fido, buried on a snowy
day in February 1869; and Mme de Lamartine's rocking-
chair, and the holy water stoup which she had sculpted.
Among other souvenirs are the poet's *dot de mariage* (1851);
his top hat; his travelling writing desk; the bed on which he
died; letters from Balzac, Joseph de Maistre, Victor Hugo,
Chateaubriand, and Alfred de Vigny; the walls of his study –
padded to prevent interruption from the world of which he
felt himself to be so intimately a part – and the portrait of his
daughter, who died when she was only ten years old. This
was painted by his wife, and you can also see the mantelpiece
which she decorated in ceramic, with copies of her favourite
authors – Homer, Dante, Racine, and Corneille. Lamartine –
so handsome and so humourless – remains a *locus classicus*
of nineteenth-century romanticism in France, and about a
kilometre away in the adjacent woods the oak still flourishes
under which he wrote *Jocelyn* – for he was always careful to
find the right tree. You would never describe him as a typical
Burgundian; yet his feeling for the landscape of the Mâconnais, more especially in its autumnal moods, transpires again
and again in his verse.

> *Montagnes que voilait le brouillard de l'automne,*
> *Vallons que tapissait le givre du matin.*[1]

We shall meet him again at Mâcon; but here at Saint-Point
we can feel the force of his apostrophe:

> *Objets inanimés, avez-vous donc une âme*
> *Qui s'attache à notre âme et la force d'aimer?*[2]

1. Mountains veiled by the mist of autumn,
   Valleys carpeted by the winter hoar-frost.
2. Inanimate objects, have you then a soul
   Which attaches itself to ours, and forces it to love?

# CHAPTER SIXTEEN

# Taizé and Tournus

✣

1

If I were asked to state a preference for one part of Burgundy over another, I should have to choose the Mâconnais – all that hilly and wooded district stretching north and slightly east of Cluny. There are no towns of any size until you get to Tournus, and no hotels or restaurants of repute. Indeed, if you wish to savour the country at leisure – and you will certainly have no desire to hurry through it – you will do well to invite the hospitality of Taizé, which, for its own special reasons, must, of course, detain you. Nor must you expect to follow a straight itinerary. The roads wind among wide or narrow valleys and fields of rose-coloured campion, with here a church and there a menhir, and an occasional château which you may or may not be able to visit. And always to the east the high ridge of the Monts du Mâconnais shuts you off from the valley of the Saône. For Lamartine this was an autumnal landscape because he had an autumnal temperament; but I have found it just as beautiful in spring.

Assuming that your immediate destination is Taizé, you will be wise to take a roundabout route to get there. Leave Cluny by the N.80, passing a little distance to your right the ruins of the *château-fort* at **Lournand,** where the monks stored their treasure in time of war, and turn off on the D.7 for **Donzy-le-National.** Here the romanesque tower has a clock on its south face – which is unusual. Then take the D.41 to **St Vincent-des-Prés** – a pure romanesque structure with a square, flat-topped tower and a shallow arcading on the west front. You will find the same feature on the much more celebrated church at Chapaize. The interior has unusually thick pillars, but the whole church is unfortunately under plaster. Join the D.14 and follow it through Salornay and Cortevaix to the N.481 just south of **Cormatin.** This beautiful

Tournus: Church of St Philibert, the nave, facing west. 'The grandeur of
St Philibert owes not a little to its nudity.'

Tournus: Church of St Philibert, the crypt.

château was the birthplace of the distinguished novelist, Jacques de Lacretelle. A Parisian to his finger tips, Lacretelle does not forget his Burgundian origins:

'I owe it to Burgundy to have known the last representatives of a peasantry innocent of the least servility, but so naturally devoted that they wept to recall the face of their dead masters. This was a personal misfortune that they never forgot, and they showed a gentle obstinacy in talking to me about it. Their names – Philibert, Mariette – were the names of another time; their faces were sunburnt with toil, but wrinkled with goodness of heart.'

They do not look any different today

The **Château** has two wings enclosing a *cour d'honneur*; the third was demolished in 1830. The furnishing is exceptionally rich with good paintings by Nattier and others. The rooms – salle Ste Cécile, salon des Gobelins, cabinet du Maréchal, salon des Princesses – do not belie their names. You may visit them under a guide from Easter to 31 May, and from 1 to 15 October between 9.30 and 11h, and 14 and 17h; from 1 June to 30 September between 9 and 11h, and 14 and 17h. The château is closed on Monday, except for public holidays when it is closed on Tuesday instead. The visit lasts for half an hour.

The **Church** at Cormatin contains a remarkable *Vierge de Pitié* on wood (fifteenth century) of the Burgundian school. The figures of Louis XI and Cardinal La Balue – both hereditary enemies of the Dukes – appear respectively as Herod and Caiaphas.

Turning south you should strike off immediately to your right on the D.14, and then to your left for **Ameugny**. The twelfth-century church of pink limestone from the local quarries, with its squat tower and blind arcading on the façade, is massive for its size. Five steps lead up to the raised choir.

The ecumenical community of **Taizé** was founded in 1940 at a time when the Christian civilization of the West was threatened with a destruction all the more certain and insidious because many Christians were unable, or unwilling, to realize the danger besetting them. The comparison is striking with

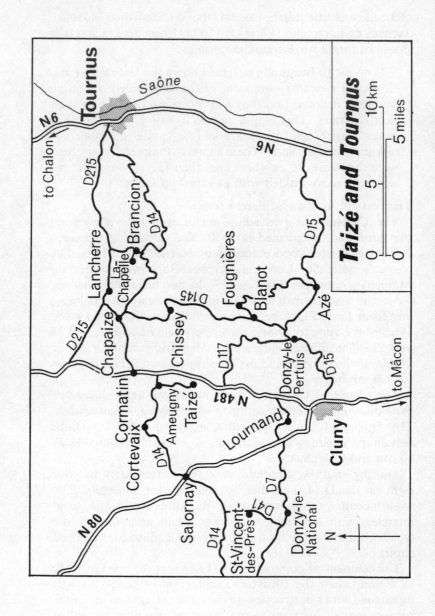

the exodus of the desert fathers, and the first establishments of St Benedict. The proximity of Taizé to Cluny is profoundly illustrative, although monasticism was well into its stride before the great design of St Hugues was conceived and realized. Frère Roger, the founder and prior of Taizé, came there as a newly ordained pastor from his native Switzerland in 1940. The village was just south of the demarcation line between occupied and unoccupied territory, and for two years Frère Roger's house was a refuge for members of the Resistance and for those fleeing from Nazi persecution – many of them Jews. A visit from the Gestapo luckily found him in Geneva, and it was here that he was joined by his first companions. After the Liberation they returned to Taizé, and made contact with a camp for German prisoners of war near by. The prisoners were allowed to visit them and share in their community prayer; and when the Church of the Reconciliation was built in 1962 it was so called as a reminder that those who had once been enemies had in fact been reconciled in that place. The seventy or so brothers who form the Community commit themselves for their entire lives by a form of the traditional monastic vows. The brothers, from all the main Christian traditions, both Reformed and Catholic, share in a common life, but none renounces his respective allegiance. The centre of all this are the moments of common prayer, and if you are present at one of the daily offices you will have no means of telling which brothers are Lutheran, Reformed, Anglican, or Roman Catholic. The origins of the Community were in the Reformed tradition, but a vital moment in its history was the invitation from Pope John XXIII for Brother Roger and others to be present at every session of the Vatican Council as official observers. Later, Pope Paul VI invited Brother Roger to accompany him on his visit to Colombia. The Prior of Taizé has a representative at the Vatican. Recently, the Community was visited by the Archbishop of Canterbury, and the list could be continued indefinitely.

The Community in Taizé has no intention of founding other communities, unlike the vast network which spread out from Cluny across Europe. But you will never find all the brothers in Taizé at the same moment. Small groups go and live for a provisional period in other continents: in Brazil, in

Calcutta, in Africa, for example. The brothers themselves are not all European in origin; besides those of almost every European nationality, you will find brothers from America, Africa and Asia.

Since 1966, Taizé has been a gathering point for young people between 18 and 29 years old. If you are between those ages, you would be well advised to do like them in order to assimilate what Taizé is about. That involves coming for several days, and during that time, besides the common prayer, you will find meetings of various kinds organized. They generally begin on each Monday evening throughout the year. The best plan is to bring your tents, sleeping-bags, blankets, because conditions at Taizé are Spartan. But there are also dormitory tents available for those who have none of their own, and each person's needs are taken into account. All who come are fed from a central kitchen. The meal may not be elaborate, but it will generally be hot and sufficient. Taizé has captured the imagination of the modern world, and particularly the modern youth. It gives an answer to anxiety, and the pilgrims come away from it, as they come away from Lourdes, not perhaps cured in the way they had hoped, but immensely fortified none the less. To share their expectations you have to live with them, however briefly. Otherwise you have no alternative but to visit the place from Cluny.

You must at least attend the midday or evening office in the Church of the Reconciliation, but you should first visit the little romanesque church in the village which has been placed at the disposal of the community. Do not be deterred by the notice outside: 'cette église ne se visite pas'. This means that you are not encouraged to wander about in quest of architectural detail. You will not, in fact, have any desire to do so, for the church is very dark, and it may well recommend you to contemplation. You will notice, however, the warm amber stone of which the building is made, and the modern sculpture outside figuring the Nativity and the visit of the Magi. The Bible is open on a lectern in the middle of the nave. It is impossible to imagine a place more dense with prayer, and when you step inside you will be unlikely to find yourself alone.

The **Church of the Reconciliation** stands back from the road on your left as you approach the village from Ameugny. It was built of concrete in 1962, and is well adapted to its purpose. The west front can open to include in the congregation the crowds assembled outside. Four concrete pillars support the roof on the south side, and the windows on the south wall, designed by a brother and made in the community workshop, illustrate the Annunciation, the Epiphany, Palm Sunday, the Transfiguration, the Resurrection, the Ascension, and Pentecost. The floor slopes steeply towards the west, and the plain altar has twelve candles suspended above it. On the left is an icon of the Blessed Virgin, and in the crypt are chapels set aside for the celebration of Mass according to the Latin or the Orthodox rite. The daily rhythm of hymns, psalms, Gregorian chants, prayers and readings is punctuated by long intervals of silence; and the brethren enter for them individually, so that one has the impression of a slow, spontaneous gathering of the faithful rather than a disciplined assembly – although there is no informality or tiresome improvisation in the Office itself.

From Easter 1970, Taizé was preparing with young people all over the world, many of whom will never be able to come to Europe, to hold a worldwide Council of Youth. During the four and a half years of this preparation, the numbers coming to Taizé increased dramatically; and when the Council of Youth opened on 30 August 1974 there were something like 40,000 young people on the hill. From every continent, and over 100 countries, these young people spent hours together in prayer, and in a celebration of the Risen Christ.

Adjoining the Church of the Reconciliation is a booth where the pottery made by members of the community is for sale. It is of excellent quality, and the brethren run their own press, which has produced a finely illustrated edition of the Jerusalem Bible. Nowhere is the visitor disconcerted by the commercialized *bondieuserie* which disfigures other places of piety or pilgrimage. For although there are no miracles recorded at Taizé – and nobody expects them – and no tomb of a martyr or saint to be venerated, the place satisfies just as fully the instinct to go on pilgrimage to a particular spot for a particular purpose. And the pilgrims, young and old, come to Taizé from farther afield than they ever came to Canterbury or Compostella; not, perhaps, in the same security of faith, but in quest of what Taizé is prepared to offer them – *'une audacieuse aventure'*.

## 2

A sequence of romanesque churches – one or two of the first importance – awaits you in the lower foothills of the Mâconnais. Take the D.117, off the N.481 just south of Taizé, to **Donzy-le-Pertuis,** with its fine tower, and then on the D.15 to **Azé,** where the grotto, with a subterranean river running through it, is well worth exploration. This was a prehistoric site, and a museum in the village houses a collection of prehistoric and Gallo-Roman remains. The grotto can be visited from Palm Sunday to 30 September between 9 and 12h and 14 and 19h. In winter Azé has facilities for skiing when enough snow has fallen.

You must now turn north for **Blanot.** Here the priory church has a curious tall tower with squat, overhanging roof and outside steps leading up to the belfry. A number of Merovingian tombs may be seen close by. There is a good pottery in the village from which I obtained a sturdy but graceful milk jug now in daily use. Taking the D.446 out of Blanot you come to the hamlet of Fougnières, and about half a kilometre farther on a road to your left will take you to the extensive series of **Grottoes** on the eastern flank of Mont Romain. Twenty-one of these can be visited, and by the time you have been through them you will have walked for more than a kilometre. They penetrate the hillside to a depth of nearly a hundred yards, and are open to the public from Palm Sunday to 30 September between 9 and 12h, and 14 and 18h. From 1 October to All Saints Day only on Sunday and public holidays. Returning to Blanot, follow the D.145 to **Chissey,** where the church has a square tower, single nave, four bays, and five arches round the apse. Notice the capitals: the Angel warning St Joseph, and the Nativity with attendant angels and shepherds on the last pillar against the north wall; and on the last pillar but one David and Saul, David and Goliath, and David playing on the harp. Continue along the

D.145 until it joins the D.14, and turn left for **Chapaize.** Here the Benedictines of Chalon formerly had their novitiate, but of the priory nothing remains but the superb Lombard tower of St Martin – 35 metres high – dominating the valley. The apse is a little later than the rest of the church, which dates from the early eleventh century, and the deplastering of the interior had not been completed when I was last there. Its proportions, however, with three aisles and unusually thick pillars, are extremely impressive.

Just to the north of Chapaize, on the D.215, are the ruins of the priory at **Lancharre.** This convent of canonesses, all of noble birth, was founded in the eleventh century. Each of them lived in her own little house with her personal servant. In the twelfth century they embraced the rule of St Benedict and were dependent on Cluny, protected by the Sieurs de Brancion. The church was built in 1300, and parts of the nave and the apse are still standing. Knights were buried there by permission, and you may see their tombs. The status of the priory was raised to an abbey in 1636, when it moved to Chalon, and thereafter the abbesses were appointed by the kings of France. The Revolution put an end to what must have been a highly aristocratic way of contemplation.

Going east on the D.215, and then south on the D.159, you will come to **Brancion,** unmistakable on its hill. The château dates back to the tenth century, and for the next three hundred years it was the bastion of the family which bore its name. Their nickname was 'Gros', and they certainly lived up to their motto: '*Au plus fort de la mêlée*'.[1] Joinville tells us that Jocerand de Brancion met his death by the side of St Louis in the battle of Mansourah (1250), but his son was ruined by equipping an army for the Crusade, and sold his estate to the Duke of Burgundy in 1259. It passed to the French Crown in 1477.

The **Château** has been well preserved by its present owners, and sign-posts will tell you how to visit it. After passing through the gate at the entrance to the village – with grooves for letting down the portcullis – you should note the following. The sanctuary stone which guaranteed asylum for 24 hours; the house and tower of Beaufort, built by Eudes IV, 19th

1. In the thick of the fight.

Duke of Burgundy (d. 1350); the Assize Hall of the Dukes with the fireplace emblazoned with the arms of the Valois dynasty; the Chaul side-tower with openings from which the archers could shoot in three directions; the original foundations of the castle; the keep, where Joinville's narration of Jocerand de Brancion's death is inscribed above the fireplace in the big hall; the guard room, the Tour de Longchamp, and the Tour des Archives, where all the records of the castle are said to have been burnt during the wars of religion; the watchtower; and on the edge of the *enceinte* the site of the former gibbet. Nowhere else in Burgundy is it easier to reconstruct the feudal way of life and justice. The château can be visited every day from Easter to 11 November from 8 to 19h. During the rest of the year on Sunday from 8.30 to sunset. At other times by arrangement in advance with M. Bernadotte, 71 Bresse-sur-Grosne.

You should notice the fifteenth-century **Halles** in front of the château, the communal bakehouse – still in use up to 1930 – and a number of fifteenth-century houses.

The romanesque **Church of St Pierre** – late twelfth century – has been beautifully restored. The fourteenth-century frescoes are remarkable. In the chapel to the right of the choir, Pilgrims arriving in Jerusalem; on the choir arch, Christ in Majesty; on the south wall of the choir, the Resurrection of the Dead at the Last Judgement; in the chapel on the left, the Nativity; on the wall of the north side-aisle, God weighing souls in a sheet; and above the apse a romanesque angel with six wings. Notice also the *gisant* of Jocerand de Brancion, presented by the Académie de Mâcon in 1959.

At **La Chapelle,** at the foot of the hill, there is a workshop for the restoration of frescoes; and if – which is fairly unlikely – you should find yourself at Brancion on Christmas night, you can attend a *soirée folklorique*, arranged by the Matisconia Society, with château and church floodlit.

There is also the '*Noël des Vins*', organized by the Vignerons de Saint-Vincent. Various legends have become attached to Brancion; the monk who was tied to the tail of a mad bull, and the Devil who was tricked by a little shepherd boy into enumerating all the drunkards in Burgundy – for all eternity. I must add that I have never myself set eyes on a drunkard in

Burgundy. It goes without saying that they know *what* to drink; and they also know the when, and the how, and the how much.

The D.14 winds over the last ridges of the Mâconnais and brings you down into **Tournus**. The plain widens out before sloping gently through the town to what Julius Caesar called the *lentissima* Saône. You have seen it already in its upper reaches, but this is a different world. The autoroute cuts through it slightly to the east, draining off a good deal of the traffic that once turned the N.6 into a motorist's nightmare. The latter skirts the edges of Tournus, but do not let that deter you from eating at the Greuze, just outside the gateway of the former abbatial *enceinte*. It was here that I once saw Pope John XXIII – when he was still Monsignor Roncalli – enjoying his *écrévisses*. Only two or three years ago one could stay at the Greuze – and very comfortably but I see that the latest edition of Michelin makes no mention of rooms. If this is the case, you will probably do well enough at Le Sauvage in the Place Champ de Mars.

Both its situation at an important crossing of the river, and its aspect – ochre walls and Roman tiles heralding the Midi – emphasize at Tournus the character of transition particular to Burgundy as a whole. Whether you are headed for Provence, or for Italy by way of the Mont Cénis, or for Switzerland by way of the Jura, you are bound to pass through it. Yet it stretches so quietly on its banks that for one reason or another you will want to linger. The Romans certainly did so as they followed the 'way of Agrippa' from the *oppidum* of Mâcon to the port of Chalon-sur Saône. Here St Valerian was martyred at the end of the second century, and the pilgrimage to his tomb inspired the foundation of a monastery by Charles le Chauve in 875. This was destroyed by the Hungarian invasion of 937, and when the church was rebuilt it sheltered not only the remains of St Valerian but also those of St Philibert – a Gascon who founded two important abbeys in the seventh century – which the monks had brought from their primitive foundation at St-Philibert-de-Grand-Lieu. This explains the dedication of the church, whose 'majestic simplicity' Victor Hugo so admired. Part of it, at least, was consecrated in 1019, and a fresh dedication of the sanctuary, by then almost finished, took place in 1120. Apart from minor Gothic additions, **St-Philibert-de-Tournus** stands today as a transcendent, but hardly typical, example of the romanesque. For there is nothing remotely comparable to it in France or elsewhere.

The narthex faces you like a fortress, and its three bays with their round pillars of pinkish stone from the local quarries at Préty confirm the impression of simplicity and power. The roof is supported by a ribbed vaulting in the centre and transversal barrel vaulting at the sides. Observe the fresco of an angel supporting a Christ in glory – now effaced like most of the other wall paintings in the church. One cannot, however, regret their disappearance, for the grandeur of St Philibert owes not a little to its nudity. You reach the upper storey of the narthex by a tower at the corner of its south aisle. Here the modified barrel vault is divided by round arches, and a great double arcade, known as the '*arc de Gerlannus*', opens on to the interior of the church. The name is taken from a mysterious inscription that you will observe halfway up the archivolt on your right. This dates the arch at about AD 1000. Notice the two capitals on the columns which support the archivolt; on the left an extraordinary human mask, and on the right a person, seen in profile, who has one hand raised in blessing and the other grasping a hammer. With the capitals in St Bénigne at Dijon, these are the earliest examples of romanesque sculpture to be found in Burgundy.

The structural symphony of the nave is best appreciated from the tribune of St Michael's chapel on the upper level of the narthex. Five bays divide it, and the immense columns – not so thick as those in the narthex – rise to the roof without interruption by triforium or clerestory; indeed the absence of these gives to the church its originality and contributes to its *élan*. Half-columns of the same type are attached to the walls of the side-aisles, and support the ribbed vaulting. The round arches which divide the barrel roof of the central aisle rest on short half-columns springing from the top of the pillars, and the whole interior is lit by small windows set high up above the bays – sixteen in the nave and three in the north aisle, and no less than thirty-three in St Michael's chapel. The delicate colour of the stone saves the church from too stark an austerity without impairing its strength. The lack of decorative detail and structural complication leaves one all the freer to admire its breath-taking technical accomplishment.

St Philibert is one of the rare churches – Gloucester and Durham are other examples – where the splendour of the nave tends to outshine the choir and sanctuary. At Tournus there is an evident distinction, though it hardly amounts to a disproportion, between the two; and this is emphasized by the whiteness of the stone in the choir, as well as in the crypt. It has been suggested that while the choir was reserved to the monks, the nave was used by the pilgrims who had access to the crypt, and the twin shrines of St Philibert and St Valerian, by a staircase leading down to it from the north transept. The crypt follows exactly the plan of the *chevet*, with a semi-circular ambulatory, three chapels opening out of it, and two more to the north and south of the lateral bays. The central space is divided by five thin columns – two of them from the primitive church and perhaps originally from a Roman temple – with capitals that suggest a nineteenth-century restoration. Here is the sarcophagus of St Valerian, despoiled of its relics, and you should notice the twelfth-century fresco in the chapel on your right. The transept crossing and the choir seem to indicate a double stage in their construction, as the technique of building became more sophisticated. The central apsidal chapel now contains the relics of St Philibert. The transept crossing is surmounted by an octagonal cupola, where the pendentives are carried by six little columns, while two others support the archivolt framing the bays of the main surfaces. It remains to note the capital of bizarre masks and human heads, precisely sculptured, in the south transept; and to be grateful for the Gregorian chant which more than probably will greet your entrance into what may justly be described as the mother church of the romanesque.

A number of the **Abbatial Buildings** survive. To the right of the narthex a door leads into the north arm of the eleventh century cloister of St Ardain, with its four bays and ten blind arcades along the south wall of the church. At the end of it you will find an entrance to the south transept. The chapter house was rebuilt after a fire in 1237 with an ogival vault.

The library of the abbey, which is also the library of the town, is open on Tuesday, Thursday, and Saturday from 14 to 18h. Leaving the cloister by the Place des Arts you have an admirable view of the *chevet* of the church, the twelfth-century Cluniac tower, and the late fifteenth-century abbot's lodging. Then, returning to the Place de l'Abbaye, you should on no account miss the refectory, a superb twelfth-century hall, with steps leading up to the reader's tribune; the dormitory, 120 feet long, with brick rib vaulting; nor the still-room, now used for exhibitions. Vast cellars stretch underneath.

Tournus has two interesting museums. The **Musée Perrin-de-Puycousin,** facing St Philibert on the north side of the church, is installed in the seventeenth-century house which formerly belonged to the municipal treasurer, and was bequeathed to the town by the eminent literary critic, Albert Thibaudet (1874–1936). It is devoted to folk-lore with wax models in regional costume – forty of them in nine rooms populating a farm in the Bresse or a kitchen in Tournus, busy at their looms or setting their still-room in order. The museum is open between Palm Sunday and 1 November from 9 to 12h and 14 to 18h. It is closed on Tuesday.

The **Musée Greuze** in the rue du Collège does honour to a native of Tournus. Jean-Baptiste Greuze (1725–1805) was born here of an artisan family, and studied first under Grandin at Lyon and then in Paris. He was much admired by Diderot – '*C'est vraiment mon homme que ce Greuze*' – and the Goncourts wrote of '*Ces têtes blondes qu'un rayon éveille, que le soleil caresse et frise.*'[1] Greuze went to Italy and fell in love with the daughter of a duke; it may be her likeness that we meet in '*L'Accordée du Village*' and '*La Laitière*'. He was a friend of the Encyclopaedists, but lost his pension after the Revolution. With his tendency to sugar the portrait, he was much sought after, although he refused to paint the Dauphine because she was too made up. He was later eclipsed by the fashionable neo-classicism of David. Greuze married unhappily and separated from his wife. 'I hope you'll come to my funeral', he remarked to a friend. 'You'll be there all alone, like a poor man's dog.'

1. These blonde heads of hair wakened by a ray of sunlight, and curled and caressed by it.

In the Tournus museum you may admire his engravings of *La Mère Bien-aimée* – with six children, a grandmother, and her husband with a gun: *Le Père expliquant la Bible*, with a grandmother and seven children; and *L'Heureuse Union*, dedicated to any father of any family. There are portrait engravings of Rameau, Gluck, Diderot, and Robespierre; and pastels of himself in youth and old age. Another, of Madame Greuze, is enigmatically entitled *Philosophie endormie*. Greuze's vision of married life triumphantly survived his own experience of it.

The pharmacy of the **Hôtel de Ville** contains a fine collection of earthenware, each piece housed in its separate niche. It can be visited from 9.30 to 11h and 15.30 to 17h. You will also admire the old houses in the rue du Dr-Privey, rue de la République, and rue du Midi. The *Eglise de la Madeleine*, on the banks of the Saône, has nothing to compare with St Philibert, except the twelfth-century porch with the birds standing beak to beak on the foliated capitals.

# CHAPTER SEVENTEEN

# La Bresse and Mâcon

❧

1

Leave Tournus by the N.6 going south, and take note of
**Le Villars** on your left, where the twelfth-century church is
twinned with another, now put to agricultural use. Readers
of Anatole France will find themselves here in the last chapter
of *La rôtisserie de la reine Pédauque*, where the Burgundian
curé is divided between his vocation and his vines. Then turn
off to the right on the D.210 for **Farges-lès-Mâcon,** and its
eleventh-century church with pillars not unlike those of St
Philibert. At **Uchizy,** a little farther on, you will not only
admire the tall church tower, with its five stages, built towards
the end of the eleventh century by the monks of Tournus, but
you should take a close look at the inhabitants. These are
thought to be the descendants of a Saracen colony, established
here after the victory of Charles Martel. Others maintain,
more probably, that they are of Illyrian or Hungarian descent.
Former generations were reputed to have dark eyes, brown
hair, thick eyebrows, burnished skin, and white teeth. The
girls wore their hair short, and went about in knee-length
skirts; the women wore turbans. At a wedding the bride and
bridegroom approached the church by different roads, the
fathers wearing red cloaks. Pyrrhic dances and the *farandole*
struck an exotic note in the Mâconnais.

When the resources of pharmacy were exhausted hereabouts – as they quickly were – resort was had to pilgrimage.
The arthritic went to St Jean-des-Eaux, near Tournus; the
deaf to St Humé; others to St Cultaté at Uchizy, and St Criat
at Verzé, whose shrine is now a stable. Faith was built on
superstitition, sometimes of the darkest kind. Lost in the
woods near Igé was the Pierre de l'Ecorcherie, used for human
sacrifice. But these abandoned sites are hardly worth a detour,
unless you have a mind for wandering in a lovely landscape

and your time is unlimited. Following the D.210 to Vire, turn left on the D.15, and beyond the fortified gate at Vérizet you will cross the Saône, and join the N.433A for Pont-de-Vaux. You have now left the Saône-et-Loire for the Ain, and trespassed beyond the limits generally set down for your journey. But this is a case where trespassers need not be prosecuted.

The N.433A, D.6, D.1, and N.75 will bring you to **Bourg-en-Bresse** – the sole reason for suggesting a detour of nearly fifty kilometres. There is little to detain you on the way, although you will observe the same difference between the landscape on the east and west banks of the Saône as we noted farther north. The Bresse is in fact an extension of the Pays-Bas, and the passage from one department to another is immaterial. Nevertheless, beneath its placid and fertile exterior, the Bresse secretes a definite character of its own. The clayey subsoil is carpeted with lime and produces a rich harvest of maize. Buckwheat and rye mix with it to form a special flour. The isolated farms are built of red bricks and tiles round a large yard with a lofty shed for the machines, a smaller yard opposite, and a big hall in the house. Bunches of maize hang over the doors, and the ears of corn are kept in grilled hutches suspended above the ground, separate from the farms. Each farm has its pool; there are a great number of small ponds and lakes; and hedges divide the fields. Maize was introduced here in the sixteenth century, and it has become the regional dish, served up in a variety of ways. On festal occasions men still wear thick boots, a large black felt hat, and blue blouse; the women are in black with a little round white bonnet with frilled edges. Old customs persist – the fire of junipers on New Year's Day when all the rooms are filled with smoke to bring good luck; and the Feast of the Rats on 29 December, which threatens retribution for those who work that day and fail to go to Mass.

But what has brought fame to Bresse is its poultry. The breed was started 350 years ago. The chickens are left at liberty until they are rounded up for the Monday market at Louhans, and the great Foire de la Baume, near St Germain-du-Bois, on 26 August. For her *poularde demi-deuil* the celebrated Mère Fillioux from Lyon ordered 20,000 fattened

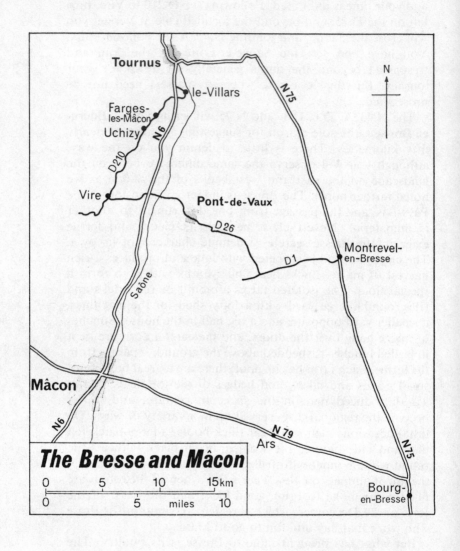

**The Bresse and Mâcon**

0    5    10    15km

0         5         miles         10

pullets a year from Louhans, all of them plucked at seven or eight months old. A metal band in three colours was strapped to the leg of each authentic Bressan bird; black if it came from Louhans, grey from Bony, and white from Besy. It is not without significance that Fernand Point, the fabulous virtuoso of La Pyramide at Vienne, spent his youth at Louhans – an easy drive east from Tournus on the N.471, and very attractive with its arcaded streets, market gardens, and pharmaceutical museum. The Bresse produces some decent local wines. Among the white, the Roussette de Virieu and the Roussette de Seyssel; among the red, Mondeuse and Château Laman; and the Cerdon *rosé*. Nor need you confine yourself to chicken. Barbey d'Aurevilly wrote that a *gigot* from the Bresse was 'tender as a woman's buttocks'.

The Paix et Terminus at Bourg-en-Bresse is one of the most attractive hotels in Burgundy (19 rue Baudin, close by the station). It combines space and comfort with a nineteenth-century, slightly faded elegance. Do not be deterred by the absence of a restaurant. You will eat as well as you can wish, or can afford, at any one of three restaurants opposite the flamboyant Gothic church. The lesser, or the least, expensive will satisfy any reasonable appetite, and in these you may well find the company more to your taste. In the tenth century Bourg was nothing more than a collection of huts surrounding a *châteaufort*, but the line of feudal overlords died out, and in the thirteenth century the place passed to the Dukes of Savoy, under whom it grew and prospered as the capital of a province. In 1536 the Duke refused passage to the troops of François I en route for Italy, and the King seized the province; but Henri II restored it twenty-three years later. In 1600 the Bresse was invaded by Henri IV, who attached it permanently to the French Crown. Today it is a flourishing market town, and a centre for the making of furniture, in the style known as *rustique Bressan*, from the wood of ash, wild cherry, and pear-trees. If you happen to pass through the town on the third Saturday in December, you will see in the covered market an astonishing display of poultry, their skin moistened to the colour of pearl by a lavish bath of milk. And if you are dreaming of a turkey for Christmas, you may well change your ideas.

The celebrated **Eglise de Brou** stands on the N.75 about a mile from the centre of the town. In 1480 Philippe, comte de Bresse, was seriously injured in a hunting accident, and his wife Marguerite de Bourbon vowed that, if he recovered, she would transform the modest priory of Brou into an abbey. Philippe did recover, but his wife died before she could keep her vow. Its fulfilment was entrusted to her son, Philibert le Beau, who had other matters on his mind – including an exceptionally happy marriage; and it was not until his sudden death from cold after hunting in the Jura, twenty years later, that his widow, Marguerite d'Autriche, the grand-daughter of Charles le Téméraire, recognized in her bereavement a sign of divine displeasure. To ensure the repose of her husband's soul she set about, in 1506, the construction of the great church where they both are buried. The building was in the hands of a Flemish master-mason, Van Boghem, who completed the work in nineteen years (1513–32), after the new monastic quarters and three sides of the cloister had already been erected. Marguerite died two years before the church was consecrated. By a miracle it escaped the ravages of the wars of religion and the Revolution, but the monastery became successively a stable for pigs, a prison, a barracks, a home for beggars, and a lunatic asylum. In 1823 it was turned into a seminary, and today it houses the Musée de l'Ain. The church, though scrupulously preserved, is no longer used for worship.

Coming to it so closely after St Philibert-de-Tournus, Paray-le-Monial, and Autun, you must try to preserve an objectivity if you cannot forswear a preference. The Renaissance has supplanted the romanesque, but do not forget – indeed you will not be allowed to forget – that this exuberance of sculpture and stone is inspired by conjugal fidelity. Of all the great churches in France, that at Brou is the most passionately personal. On the tympanum of the west portal Philibert and Marguerite, with their patron saints, are shown at the feet of Christ. The church is dedicated to St Nicholas of Tolentino, because it was on the feast of St Nicholas that Philibert had died, and the statue of St Nicholas stands on the dividing pillar. The initials of Philibert and Marguerite, linked by an embroidered cord, appear again and again as a dart of the interior decoration. The church of Brou is contemporary with the château of Chenonceaux, and is equally typical of the French Renaissance; the one a monument to an historic marriage, the other to an historic liaison. Notice, as you enter, the luminous whiteness of the stone, quarried from Révermont. Time has not touched it. The pillars, made up of several thin columns and framing four bays, rise without interruption by capitals or imposts to the star-shaped vaulting. The triforium gallery with its highly wrought balustrade runs at a lower level in the transepts and towards the west end. Notice in the south transept the sixteenth-century window of Susannah accused by the Elders (above), and acquitted by Daniel (below). An elaborate rood screen separates the nave and transept from the choir.

Onwards from here you visit the church with a guide. The 74 **Stalls,** designed by Jean de Bruxelles, and made within two years, are a *tour de force* of intricate realism. The Middle Ages peep through the Renaissance in the person of a wife spanking her husband with a broomstick. On the north side are scenes from the New Testament, and on the south from the Old, with alternating satirical motifs – a gourmet with his hand in his mouth, and a miser with his hand in a money jar. Among the statuary of the choir is a figure of St Catherine, which Hilaire Belloc described 'of a beauty beyond this world and smiling like an early spring morning in Paradise; dumb with beatitude.'[1] He thought the sculptures of Brou 'the finest in Europe'. They are very far from being that, but their virtuosity is still astonishing.

A number of artists collaborated over the three **Tombs** of Marie de Bourgoyne, Philibert, and Marguerite. The ornamentation and smaller statuary were executed, for the most part, in a Flemish workshop set up at Brou with French, German, and Italian assistants. A German, Conrad Meyt, trained in Flanders, was responsible for the three princely effigies, sculpted in Carrara marble. They lie on a black marble slab, their heads resting on a finely embroidered cushion. A dog, symbol of fidelity, is shown at the feet of the two princesses, and a lion – emblem of strength – at the feet of the prince. Cherubs and sibyls escort them, all three, to Paradise. Marguerite and Philippe are represented twice over; first as

1. To Mrs Raymond Asquith: Letters from Hilaire Belloc, 1958.

living people, and then as corpses in their shrouds. On the foot of Marguerite you can see traces of the gangrene which was popularly believed to have caused her death. On the canopy above you can read her motto: '*Fortune infortune fort une*'. This is not easy to translate, but it conveys the sense of a woman implacably pursued by misfortune. She had certainly lived up to it.

The **Windows** in the choir were also the work of a local studio. They represent the appearance of Christ to Mary Magdalen, and His visit to her, taken from engravings by Dürer; and to the left and right Philibert and Marguerite with their patron saints. Above them are the armorial bearings of their families; Savoy and Bourbon for the Duke, and Empire and Burgundy for the Duchess. On the left of the choir the chapel named after Marguerite d'Autriche, contains a magnificent reredos of white marble, which illustrates the seven Joyful Mysteries of the Virgin. Three statues surmount it; the Virgin and Child with St Mary Magdalen and St Marguerite. A superb window, again inspired by a Dürer engraving, celebrates the Assumption with Philibert and Marguerite again kneeling beside their patron saints. The frieze illustrates the Triumph of the Faith. Christ in a chariot is drawn by the Four Evangelists and characters from the Old Testament, while the Doctors of the Church and the Saints of the New Testament hurry in the rear. This is the reproduction of a drawing made by Titian for his bedroom. Titian and Dürer – how strongly the Renaissance makes itself felt in this church, which is among its first fruits!

The pavement of the chapel and choir was originally of blue ceramic and Italian design, 'so beautiful', says the chronicle, 'that one is almost sorry to walk on it.' It has unfortunately disappeared. Adjoining the chapel are Marguerite's two oratories, built one above the other with a connecting staircase. They are, in fact, a private suite of rooms with a fireplace, and an opening through which she could have assisted at Mass. The chapel beside them is named after her favourite counsellor, Laurent de Gorrevod. It has a fine window illustrating the incredulity of St Thomas. On the other side of the choir is the parallel chapel of the abbé de Montécuto, with the **Pilgrims of Emmaus** in richly coloured glass.

Such then is the Eglise de Brou – a phenomenon and, in its own genre, a masterpiece. It inspired Matthew Arnold to verses too mediocre for reproduction here. Indeed the references to 'mountain meadows' and 'mountain pines' suggest a very slight acquaintance with the fat pastures of the Bresse; and the neo-Gothic romanticism of the poem – a kind of Pre-Raphaelite Puginesque – seems so remote from any impression the church makes on one today that it is difficult to put oneself in the shoes of an earnest Victorian man of letters whose belief went no further than 'a power not ourselves making for righteousness', as he stood

> where fair
> On the carved Western Front a flood of light
> Streams from the setting sun, and colours bright
> Prophets, transfigured saints, and Martyrs brave
> In the vast western window of the nave.

The Eglise de Brou is a purple passage of architecture; it is not an architectural *cliché*.

It is open from 1 July to 30 September between 8 and 12h, and 13.30 and 18.30h. From 1 to 31 October between 9 and 12h, and 14 and 17h. From 1 November to 14 March between 10 and 12h, and 14 and 16.30h. From 15 March to 30 June between 8.30 and 12h, and 14 and 18h.

An impressive *Son et Lumière* is given at Easter, Pentecost, and on Thursdays, Sundays, and public holidays from the end of May to the end of September. The musical accompaniment, mainly vocal, is extraordinarily apt.

You pass from the door on the right of the choir to the small **Cloister**, and the last of the three to be built. One of the galleries on the upper level led to the apartment which Marguerite had reserved for her own use, the other enabled her to reach her chapel by way of the choir screen. The monastic quarters led out of the great cloister, built in 1506. These rooms – refectory, dormitory, and chapter house – now contain the **Musée de l'Ain.** The third cloister – known as the *cloître des cuisines* – shows an Italian influence, and is all that remains of the former Benedictine priory. In the building at the end you can see the reconstruction of a typical *bressane* house, and in the adjoining rooms furniture and costumes of the district. Here is the kitchen with its fire in the middle, spinning wheel, dresser, grandfather clock, and loaves and spoons on a rack above the refectory table. Here, too, are the four-poster bed; peasants with clogs and tasselled caps, straw toppers, and bagpipes; the plough and threshing machine; an instrument for removing heavy logs and removing them with chains; and a gigantic wheel eight feet in diameter.

Elsewhere in the Musée you will find a portrait of Marguerite d'Autriche by van Orley (*circa* 1518); a beautiful Flemish triptych illustrating scenes from the life of St Jerome; a bust of the Emperor Charles V by Leo Leoni (1509–90); Millet's *La Gardeuse des Vaches* (1858); a number of drawings by Puvis de Chavannes; and an inferior Utrillo. Three rooms are given up to the theme of poultry in art from Gallo-Roman times to the twentieth century. Works by Pompon and Lurçat figure among the exhibits. The same ticket entitles you to visit both the church and the museum; but note that the museum opens and shuts a quarter of an hour later.

Do not overlook the **Church of Notre-Dame** in Bourg-en-Bresse. If you hear its chimes at 7h, 11.50h, or 18.50h, you may fancy you have heard them before. And you will be right, for they are modelled on those of Westminster Abbey. The church, built over a hundred years from 1505, is less interesting for itself than for what it contains – choir stalls (sixteenth century) of exceptional beauty, pulpit (eighteenth century), and organ buffet (seventeenth century). There is some good modern stained glass by Le Chevalier on your left, as you enter the building, and by Auclair on your right. In the sacristy you can see an exquisite Christ in ivory, a painting on wood of the Virgin and Child, and two leaves of a sixteenth-century triptych. But these are only visible before 9h.

2

We now enter upon the last lap. The N.79 heads straight for Mâcon – 34 kilometres. On the way you pass through the village of **Ars,** where a humble curé has been honoured with a huge basilica. Jean-Marie Vianney (1786–1859) was of peasant origin and born near Lyon. Inspired by an imperative

vocation, he was so unlettered that he failed the examination
to enter the Grand Seminaire, but was accepted after a private
interview with the Superior and Vicar-General. He arrived
with his mattress and the clothes he stood up in. He came to
Ars in 1818, and quickly impressed the parish by his sermons
– *'tellement simples qu'ils paraissent osés, tellement quotidiens
qu'ils sont eternels'*[1] – and his penitents by his gift for the
reading of souls. He would spend twelve hours in the confessional for days on end, judging a man's soul from the tone
of his voice or even before he had opened his mouth. 'Everything I hear', he said, 'breaks my heart . . . if I had known
what it meant to be a priest, instead of going to the seminary,
I should have escaped to a Trappist monastery.' He suffered
physically a good deal in spite of his tall, robust stature. The
sparse congregation of Ars grew until crowds came from far
and wide to hear him and seek his advice. He was canonized
in 1925, and a year later was recognized in the protagonist of
Georges Bernanos' great novel, *Sous le soleil de Satan*. The
basilica, designed by Bossan, the architect of Notre-Dame de
Fourvière at Lyon, is a very inflated reflection of his humility;
but various souvenirs in the presbytery bring him movingly
back to life.

In **Mâcon** you have the choice of several hotels, and you
should certainly eat at M. Duret's Auberge Bressane in the
rue 28 Juin 1944. It is here that the Académie Rabelais
appropriately hold their annual feast. The *poularde 'Marguerite
de Bourgoyne'* is the perfect *envoi* to a Burgundian odyssey,
preceded by the *quenelles de brochet*, which always seem to
taste better in Burgundy than elsewhere. To accompany one,
or both, you will need to look no further than the delicious
wines of the district – a Mâcon Viré (particularly a Clos de
Chapitre), beloved of the Curé d'Ars, or a Pouilly Fuissé.
With few exceptions these will not compare with the great
burgundies to the north or the best of the beaujolais to the
south, but, carefully chosen, they are a cut above a *vin
ordinaire*. We owe a debt to Charles Brosse, that immensely
tall vine grower from Charnay-lès-Mâcon, who introduced the
wines of the Mâconnais to Louis XIV. With two barrels of

1. So simple that they seem audacious, and so everyday that they are
out of time altogether.

his *meilleurs crus* on a cart, drawn by a pair of oxen, he arrived at Versailles after a journey of 33 days in time to assist at the King's Mass. The *Roi Soleil* was struck by his unusual stature, and asked that he should be presented to him. Without more ado, Brosse explained the nature of his errand, hoping to sell his wine to some noble of the Court. The King tasted it on the spot, and found it superior to the vintages from the Loire currently served at Court. Charles Brosse became quite a rich man, and spent much of his time travelling backwards and forwards from Charnay-lès-Mâcon to Versailles. It is not easy to imagine an enterprising wine-grower of today arriving at Buckingham Palace and being thus received. The *ancien régime* had its own notions of democracy, not always inferior to ours.

The Mâconnais vineyards extend from Tournus in the north to Romanèche-Thorins in the south. They cover 200,000 hectares, of which two-thirds produce a white wine from the Chardonnay grape. Until the nineteenth century the red predominated, but it never achieved the quality of the white. The five villages of the Pouilly district nestle among the limestone hills – so favourable to the Chardonnay – under the escarpment of the great **Solutré Rock**. Here the prehistoric hunters would drive their quarry over the edge, so that the bones of slaughtered deer and horses form a subsoil in the ground below. The place has lent its name to a period of the Stone Age (15,000–12,000 BC) when flint and the bones of reindeer were used to give eyes to needles and a sharp edge to tools and weapons. Excavation began here in 1866; 100,000 skeletons of animals were discovered; and in 1922 three human skeletons were found of an even earlier period, with others more recent (neolithic), and pottery and ceramics from the Bronze Age, more recent still. Examples may be seen in the Musée Municipal at Mâcon (see p. 330). Solutré is an easy drive of eight kilometres to the west of Mâcon along the D.354. Among other wines of the Pouilly district, Chaintré, less often seen on a wine list, can be warmly recommended.

The *Centre nautique national* at Mâcon organized the European rowing championship in 1951. This drew 50,000 spectators during the week, and every alternate year the

French rowing championship is held here, with competitions for wrestling, swimming, fencing, and gymnastics.

**Mâcon** itself is not an immediately attractive town if you merely pass through it along the wide quay; a place to pause in for a moment as you sip a café or a glass of wine. But this was the birthplace of Lamartine and here (as so often) he takes us into his confidence:

'The upper town is abandoned to silence and repose. You would think you were in a Spanish city. The grass grows in summer between the paving stones. The high walls of the former convents darken the narrow streets. A school, a hospital, churches – some restored, others dilapidated and now used as shops for the coopers of the district; a large square planted with lime trees at either end, where children play or old men sit in the sunshine on a fine day; in the outskirts long streets of low houses winding up to the top of the hill with openings on to the main roads; a number of pretty houses looking one way on to the town while on the other they already face the country and the green fields; and not far from the square, five or six mansions or large houses, nearly always shut, where the old families of the province come in winter: so much, then, for a glimpse of the upper town.'

Lamartine was born at 18 rue des Ursulines, and until his marriage he lived at the hôtel d'Ozenay, 15 rue Lamartine. In the Hôtel Senecé, just off the rue de la Barre as you go up from the quay, three rooms constitute the **Musée Lamartine,** with souvenirs of his literary and political activity. It should not be forgotten that in 1833 he was elected as deputy for Bergues (in the Nord) and shortly afterwards for Mâcon. He sat in the Assembly until 1851. His ideas had developed in a liberal direction, and in 1848 these carried him to the head of the Provisional Government, the proclamation of the Second Republic, and the maintenance of the tricolour as the national flag. He was triumphantly elected to the Constituent Assembly, and only his liberal principles prevented him from accepting the post of *ministre executif.* Preferring an executive commission of several members, he was abandoned by his supporters; and when, eight months later, he put forward his

name as a candidate for the Presidency, he received only
eighteen thousand votes against five and a half million for
Prince Louis-Napoleon. For all practical purposes this was
the end of his political career and, indeed, he was too much a
poet ever to be an effective politician. Burdened by debt, he was
obliged to sell the beloved house at Milly (see p. 175) and –
more painful still – to solicit help from the empire of which
he disapproved. He accepted the gift of a chalet at Passy from
the city of Paris, where a severe stroke in 1867 left him
virtually unconscious until his death two years later. A
national funeral was offered to his family, but they declined
it. The man who had proclaimed the brief dawn of the Second
Republic did not need the brash sunshine of the Second
Empire to shine upon his obsequies. The Hôtel Senecé, a
handsome Regency building and the headquarters of the
Académie de Mâcon, is open from 10 to 12h and 14 to 18h,
except on Sunday and on Monday morning.

You can appropriately say good-bye to Lamartine in the
**Musée Municipal,** formerly the Ursuline convent – a seventeenth-century building in the rue de la Préfecture. (Open
from 10 to 12h, and 14 to 18h. Closed on Tuesday, and on the
morning of Sunday and public holidays.) Here among the
relics and erudite reconstruction of Solutré, elegant furniture
and ceramics, paintings by Titian and Greuze, Courbet,
Monet and Braque, chalk drawings by Maillot, and water-
colours by Rodin, you will find the superb portrait of Lamartine by Decaisne. It is a *locus classicus* both of the poet and
his period. Slim and serious, romantic and a little irresolute,
seated on a leafy bank against an autumnal landscape, with
one hand caressing a whippet, obviously as well bred as its
master, while another gambols at his feet, a book bound in
red cloth or Morocco leather just visible to one side of the
canvas, Lamartine looks out upon the Mâconnais. We, too,
may look out upon it, and other landscapes we have seen,
here for the last time:

'the delicate and lively greens – delicate with a colour pale,
distant, and diluted; the resigned and pensive air of the
poplars in their serried rows; and above all, the thick and
humid woods. This land has drunk its fill; it will always be

green. But its beauty is the beauty of a face which has just wiped away its tears.'[1]

It remains to add that if Burgundy has drunk its fill of water, Burgundians have turned the water into wine.

1. Hyppolite Taine . . .

# Appendices

# Food

❧

This does not pretend to be a gastronomic guide, but here are a few delicacies to look out for. A wide variety of terrines and galantines, where game is mixed with pork, veal, or rabbit; the highly and justly reputed *jambon du Morvan*, and the *andouillettes*, which are a speciality at Mâcon and Tournus. In Chalon you should ask for the '*rosette*' sausage – flavoured with pimento and moist with fine mountain butter – and in Chagny for the '*judru*', another member of the same family.

For fish you will find trout plentiful at Autun; and along the Saône pike, tench, bream, roach, carp. They all lend themselves to a diversity of treatment at the hands of an experienced chef. *Bouillabaisse d'eau doux* (made with wine instead of oil); *meurette au vin rouge*; *pocheuse au vin blanc*, a speciality of Verdun-sur-la-Doubs; and *goujon* (gudgeon), lightly fried with yolk of egg – are all rewarding to the palate.

The valley of the Saône is particularly favourable to asparagus. Cauliflowers at Chalon, and turnips from Beaubery in the Charollais, served with duck, are to be recommended.

For poultry you need look no further than *volaille de Bresse*; and game is abundant. Wild boar and roebuck at Autun, La Clayette, and Paray-le-Monial; partridge and snipe at Tramayes or Matour; and plenty of wild water fowl. It has been suggested that jugged hare may have originated in lower Burgundy. Beef from the Charollais has its competitors from Normandy and the Limousin, but it is not defeated by them.

I have mentioned a number of local cheeses – Soumaintrain and Epoisses. You should also look out for Chevroton, a goat's cheese embalmed with mountain herbs, and sold in jars with vine or chestnut leaves; and '*le pourri*', where the milk of the cow and the she-goat are mixed with olive oil and white wine, and moistened with the *marc* of the district.

Snails – *escargots de Bourgoyne* – are nourished by the vineyards, and find their way on to the table all over the world. Only in Burgundy, however, can you be quite sure that they are Burgundian. *Grenouilles* (frogs) from Thoissey have a special flavour.

For dessert the tiny *pêches de vigne*, swallowed whole, are delicious, with the *gaufrettes mâconnaises* – sugar wafers curved like Roman tiles and tasting of vanilla.

## FISHING

There are 3500 kilometres of navigable rivers in Burgundy, and the fisherman should take particular note of the following:

The Saône: bleaks, roach, carp, perch and pike.

The Doubs: large trout.

The Grosne: chub, dace, and gudgeon; bream and carp at Malay, perch at Sercy.

The Arconce: bream in summer, chub in winter.

Other streams, all good for trout: the Ternin (from Autun), the Canche and the Selle, the Sornin (in the Brionnais), the Cousin, the Cure, the Mauvaise, the Mouge, the Telenchant, the Bourbonne (in the Mâconnais), the Cozanne, the Thalie (in the Chalonnais), and the Haute Grosne.

There is professional fishing on the Saône, the Doubs, and the Seille. For further information apply to the Syndicat d'Initiative at Chalon-sur-Saône.

# Communications

❧

Although I have assumed that you will be travelling by car, most of the important places in Burgundy are accessible, or nearly accessible, by train. From the Gare de Lyon in Paris you may get to **Sens** and, changing at **Laroche**, to **Auxerre, Toucy, St Sauveur,** and **St Fargeau.** The main line will take you on to **St Florentin, Tonnerre, Montbard, Semur-en-Auxois,** and **Dijon.** From here it is an easy run south to **Nuits-St-Georges, Beaune, Chalons, Tournus** and **Mâcon.** A line goes from Dijon through **Louhans** to **Bourg-en-Bresse,** and connects with the main line at **Mâcon.** From Dijon you may also get to **Autun,** and thence to **Paray-le-Monial, La Clayette, Cluny,** and again to **Mâcon.** For times consult the current Chaix. It should not be difficult from any of these centres to reach other places you may wish to visit by bus. Time-tables will be available at the local Syndicats d'Initiative.

### RESTAURANTS AND HOTELS

Many of these are referred to in the text, but I append them here, with others, for your better convenience. For size, style, and prices consult the current Michelin Guide.

| | |
|---|---|
| **Autun** | Hotel St Louis et Poste |
| | Hostellerie Vieux Moulin |
| | (quieter) |
| **Avallon** | Hotel de la Poste |
| | Hotel du Morvan |
| | Hotel du Moulin des Ruats |
| | Hotel du Moulin des Templiers |
| | (in the valley of the Cousin) |

| | |
|---|---|
| **Bouilland** (Côte d'Or) | Hostellerie du Vieux Moulin |
| **Beaune** (Côte d'Or) | Hotel du Marché |
| **Bourg-en-Bresse** (Ain) | Hotel Paix et Terminus |
| | Auberge Bressane |
| | Chalet de Brou |
| **Chablis** (Yonne) | Hotel de l'Etoile |
| **Chalon** (Saône et Loire) | Hotel St Georges et Terminus |
| **Charolles** (Saône et Loire) | Hotel Moderne |
| **Châtillon-sur-Seine** | |
| (Côte d'Or) | Hotel Côte d'Or |
| **Cluny** (Saône et Loire) | Hotel Moderne |
| **Dijon** (Côte d'Or) | Hotel Cloche |
| | Pré aux Clercs et Trois Faisans |
| **Fixin** (Côte d'Or) | Chez Jeannette |
| **Mâcon** (Saône et Loire) | Auberge Bressane |
| **Montbard** (Côte d'Or) | Hotel de la Gare |
| **Semur-en-Auxois** | Hotel du Lac (au lac de Pont) |
| **Sens** (L'Yonne) | Hotel de Paris et Poste |
| **Tonnerre** (L'Yonne) | Hostellerie Abbaye St Michel |
| **Tournus** (Saône et Loire) | Hotel Le Sauvage |
| | Hotel Greuze |
| **Villeneuve-sur-Yonne** | Hotel du Dauphin |
| (Yonne) | |

# Festivals and Fairs

❧

These dates do not hold exactly from year to year and it would always be wise to check them in advance from the French Tourist office.

| | |
|---|---|
| FOIRE DE DIJON | |
| Spring meeting | April 20–28 |
| FOIRE DE SENS | April 27–May 2 |
| SALON REGIONAL DE LA NAVIGATION INTERIEURE DE PLAISANCE, AUXERRE | May 12–19 |
| FOIRE DE MÂCON | May 18–27 |
| FOIRE D'AUXERRE | May 19–26 |
| FOIRE DE CHALON-SUR-SAÔNE | June 8–17 |
| FOIRE DE TONNERRE | August 30–September 2 |
| FOIRE DE MONTBARD | September 6–9 |
| FOIRE DE DIJON | |
| Foire gastronomique | October 30–November 11 |

# Short Bibliography

*Bourgogne romane*, with certain passages translated into English, 1968

R. Branner, *Burgundian Gothic Architecture*, 1960

Bussy-Rabutin, *Histoire amoureuse des gaules*, 1967 (New paperback edition)

J. Calmette and H. Drouot, *La Bourgoyne*: choix de textes, 1928

J. Calmette, *The Golden Age of Burgundy*, 1962

J. Carcopino, *Alésia et les ruses de César*, 1959

Yves Cazaux, *Marie de Bourgoyne*, 1968

G. Chabot, *La Bourgoyne*, 1925

M. Clément, *Les Grands Hommes de la Bourgoyne*, 1966

Albert Colombet, *Bourgoyne et Morvan*, 1969

K. J. Conant, *Cluny: les églises et la maison du chef d'ordre*

H. Drouot and J. Calmette, *Histoire de Bourgoyne*, 1928

Arthur Gardner, *Medieval Sculpture in France*, 1931

D. Grurot and G. Zarnecki, *Giselbertus, Sculptor of Autun*, 1961

Stephen Gwynn, *Burgundy*, Constables' Wine Library, 1934

P. Huguenin, *La Bourgoyne, Le Morvan, et La Bresse*, 1930

A. Kleinclausz, *Histoire de Bourgoyne*, 1924

A. Kleinclausz and J. Bonnerot, *La Bourgoyne et ses villes d'art*, 1953

A. Kleinclausz and J. Bonnerot, *Dijon et Beaune, Autun et le Morvan*, 1933

E. Mâle, *La fin du paganisme en Gaule et les plus anciennes basiliques Chrétiennes*, 1950

F. Mercer, *Les primitifs français: la peinture Clunysienne en Bourgoyne à l'époque romane*. Préface de Henri Focillon, 1931

Charles Oursel, *L'Art de Bourgoyne*, 1953

Réalités, *Merveilles des châteaux de Bourgoyne et de Franche-Comté*, 1969

Jean Richard, *Histoire de la Bourgoyne*, Presses Universitaires, 1957

V. Sackville-West, *Daughter of France*, 1959

Otto von Simson, *The Gothic Cathedral*, 1956

Emile Thevenet, *Le Beaunois gallo-romain*, 1971

Emile Thevenet, *Les voies romaines de la Cité des Eduens*, 1969

William R. Tyler, *Dijon and the Valois Dukes of Burgundy*, 1971

Richard Vaughan, *Philip the Bold*, the formation of the Burgundian state, 1962

Richard Vaughan, *John the Fearless*, the growth of Burgundian power, 1966

Richard Vaughan, *Charles the Bold*, last Valois Duke of Burgundy, 1973

Richard Vaughan, *The Valois Dukes of Burgundy*, inaugural lecture, University of Hull, 1965

Jean Virey, *L'Abbaye de Cluny*, 1950

*Visages de la Bourgoyne*, M. Bullien, P. de S. Jacob, P. Quarré, C. Oursel.

H. W. Yoxall, *The Wines of Burgundy*, 1968

# Index

❧

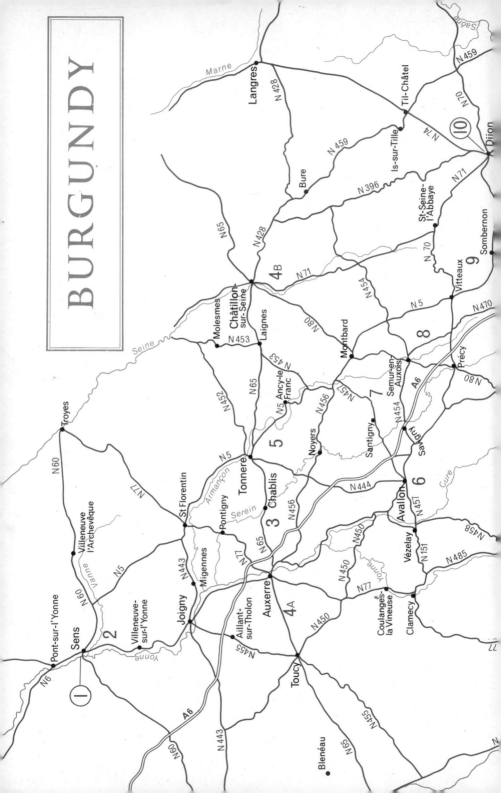